Library of Congress Cataloging-in-Publication Data

Gallacher, William R.
The options edge : winning the volatility game with options on futures / William R. Gallacher.
p. cm.
ISBN 0-07-038296-4
1. Commodity options. I. Title.
HG6046.G278 1998
332.63'28—dc21 98-11804
CIP

Irwin/McGraw-Hill

A Division of The **McGraw-Hill** *Companies*

1 2 3 4 5 6 7 8 9 0 DOC/DOC 9 0 3 2 1 0 9 8

ISBN 0-07-038296-4

The sponsoring editor for this book was *Stephen Isaacs,* the editing supervisor was *John M. Morriss,* and the production supervisor was *Suzanne W. B. Rapcavage.* It was set by The Publishing Services Group.

Printed and bound by R.R. Donnelley & Sons Company.

This book is printed on recycled, acid-free paper containing a minimum of 50% recycled de-inked fiber.

What can be done with fewer
is done in vain with more.

—William of Ockham

CONTENTS

PREFACE

The Options Edge will most likely appeal to readers with some practical experience in the trading of options. It has been written, however, to be accessible to inexperienced traders who have a strong desire to understand the workings of the options market. Compared with other technical books on the subject, *The Options Edge* is rather sparing in the use of algebra and complex statistical formulae. However, the book does delve deeply into the principles of statistical inference. It also analyzes a great deal of data, but data structured in a way that anyone with an affinity for numbers should find easily digestible. The author takes it for granted that anyone interested in options is interested in numbers.

Whereas much of what I have to say applies to options in general, including stock options, the findings of *The Options Edge* derive from, and are specifically relevant to, options on commodity futures. Before writing this book, I had to spend much time and effort constructing a data base from which to draw conclusions. This data base is included in full at the end of the book and may prove useful to other researchers who wish to check out, statistically, for themselves, questions they may have about different option trading strategies.

I would like to thank my fellow trader, Stephen Clerk, for his review of my manuscript in development, and Jürgens Bauer for his hands-on lesson at the option pit of the New York Cotton Exchange.

Bill Gallacher
SEPTEMBER, 1998

PART ONE

OPTION BASICS

CHAPTER ONE

ROADS LESS TRAVELED

Anyone who read the book I wrote on commodity futures trading can testify that I came down rather emphatically in favor of fundamental as opposed to technical trading. It is somewhat contradictory, I suppose, that 4 years after writing the futures book I should come out with *The Options Edge,* a study of option trading that is almost purely technical in nature. I have a defense, however, for there *is* a certain ideological consistency.

At the time I wrote the first book, I had never come across a convincing demonstration that trading commodities in a purely technical way could generate returns commensurate with the risks involved. Faced with a dearth of information, I decided to research the topic for myself, and that research formed the nucleus of *Winner Take All* (New York: McGraw-Hill, 1993). When I began to explore the subject of options, I found a similar situation; a lot of intellectual theorizing and fancy terminology but few hard data from which to draw any general or meaningful conclusions. As with commodity futures, I found myself compelled to research the subject of options from square one.

Certainly, much had been written on how to buy or write options and on how to structure combinations of derivatives and futures depending on one's objectives, but no studies had been directed at determining the writer's or the buyer's expectation in a general sense. There was little in the way of *empirical evidence* to suggest who wins and who loses or whether option trading results follow any patterns—whether there are any pointers to success, if you will. What's more, I could not relate all the complex formulae I saw in books to the option data that were reported in the financial press or to the option prices that appeared on quotation monitors in brokerage offices or on the Internet.

The concept of *fair value* was discussed theoretically but never checked out using actual market data. Authors talked about different measures of market volatility as predictors of future volatility without taking the trouble to compare these predictors in action. I didn't want theoretical conjectures. I wanted to know what would work and what wouldn't work and to understand if option theory correlated with option reality. T*he Options Edge* is the distillation of the results of a major empirical investigation into option pricing carried out over a 2-year period from 1996 to 1998—an investigation that evolved into a much larger project than I could ever have imagined, and an investigation that took on special relevance with the emergence of an extraordinarily volatile stock market in the latter half of 1997.

There are powerful reasons that observational research in the field of option pricing—empirical research as statisticians would say—has been so limited. First, it is difficult to *collect* historical data. And second, it is difficult to *structure* a data bank that may be tested for statistically valid conclusions. Yet, the much-neglected empirical approach to option pricing promises to yield the kind of pragmatic insight that no amount of theorizing is ever likely to uncover.

When I began this book, some very basic questions I had about options remained unanswered. I avoid casinos and never place bets on horses because the basic questions about casino gambling and horse betting have already been answered for me: The punter cannot win—certainly not in the long run. I had no such information about the potential profitability of trading options.

*

In October of 1997, in the days following the record one-day decline in the stock market, a friend of mine was seduced into *writing* options on the S&P500 stock index futures contract; option premiums were huge because of the enormous daily price swings in the futures. Unfortunately, these apparently huge option premiums were inadequate to balance the price volatility, and my friend got burned several times. He was no neophyte to trading and knew how difficult it was to make money as an option *buyer*. He was chagrined and somewhat puzzled at his lack of success as a writer. He asked me if I thought it was possible to make money as an option writer on a purely technical basis. I was in the middle of writing this book and gave him the best answer I could at the time: I don't know, but I'm also pretty sure that nobody else knows either. I did tell him, however, that I expected to have an answer in 6 months. Well, the 6 months are up and it's time to deliver.

While the focus of *The Options Edge* is most definitely empirical, I devote approximately half of the book to theoretical option pricing. I considered this necessary for the simple reason that almost all the existing books on options are exclusively theoretical in nature and that my readers would naturally want to correlate what I was writing with what had already been written elsewhere. Option theorizing is a terrain I share with many others in the field. Induction from empirical observation is a much less-traveled road.

Many, many theoretical works have been written on the topic of option pricing. Mathematicians—especially mathematicians anxious to display an encyclopedic knowledge of the Greek alphabet—are drawn to the subject as flies are drawn to a light bulb. The typical theoretical work on options covers a great deal of territory—mostly the same territory covered by all the others to be sure, with stock options getting most of the attention. Even the most celebrated of these books are not always accurate. Therefore, at the risk of offending certain sensibilities, I have directed the reader's attention to egregious instances of misleading information in the literature, especially where this information has been widely disseminated and even accepted as gospel.

Virtually all theoretical works on options are needlessly complex and of limited practical use in the real world of options valuation and options trading. Much of this complexity stems from the option trading community's uncritical allegiance to the *million dollar formula*—a wierd and unwieldy equation that has dominated the literature on options for the last 25 years. There is much less to this equation than meets the eye, and I have quite a lot to say about it in Chapter 4.

For all that, *The Options Edge* is concerned more with pragmatic issues than with theoretical arguments. I would rather search for something of practical value than come up with another set of abstruse mathematical equations of limited applicability in the real world. There is but one Greek letter (unavoidable) in this entire manuscript.

*

I approached the subject of options with certain preconceived notions that I expected, naturally, would be confirmed rather than refuted. For example, I expected to find a significant *writer's edge* in the overall market. In other words, I expected to be able to verify that the writer of an option enjoys a positive expectation and that the buyer of an option labors under the burden of a negative expectation, even though the outcome of any one option transaction is bound to be wildly unpredictable. I also expected to find that tracking market volatility would prove to be the key to identifying specific cases of option overvaluation or undervaluation and, conversely, that comparing option prices with their long-term historical norms would *not* be an effective key to valuation.

As a strong believer in the hypothesis that markets are becoming progressively more unstable due to information overload, I had a hunch that short-term volatility is on the rise while long-term volatility isn't, and that exploiting such a trend might prove possible. In a wider sense, I suspected—hoped, perhaps—that I could demonstrate it was possible to trade options, profitably, on a purely technical basis. Some of my preconceived notions were confirmed. A surprising number were refuted. Since human nature prefers confirmation over refutation, the process of hypothesis testing required that I continually review whether I was adhering to or straying from the scientific method.

Not all scientific research is useful or even honest; many published results suffer from "confirmation bias," a malaise which can contaminate the best-intentioned authorship. No one would accuse the Beardstown Ladies—a group of mid-western grannie gurus of the stock market—of deliberately spreading false news. Yet, the record shows that over a twelve-year period they became media darlings and published several books on the strength of an alleged trading acumen that later turned out to be little more than creative bookkeeping.

To my mind, two principles guide good research. The first is the principle of common sense. The formulation of a hypothesis *has to be considered suspect* if it is based purely on *observation* and cannot be reconciled with *common sense.* If you look long enough and look hard enough, you can always uncover correlations—seemingly beyond the bounds of probability—where pure chance is *still* the preferred explanation.

In a recently published book called *The Education of a Speculator* by Victor Niederhoffer (New York: Wiley, 1997), the erstwhile confidant of and advisor to the celebrated market guru George Soros makes the following observation:

> In a typical trading day, 3,100 issues are traded on the New York Stock Exchange and about 725, or 25 per cent show no change for the day. About 10 days a year, the percentage of unchanged issues falls to a low of 15 per cent or less. From 1928 to the present, these have been highly bearish events. On the other hand, when the percentage of unchanged stocks is 30 per cent or more, the market is bullish over the next twelve months (p. 119).

Let's grant that Victor Niederhoffer is correct in his observation that 25 percent of the issues *are* unchanged on the typical trading day, and let's further grant that there *is* an apparent correlation between the number of unchanged issues and the future direction of the stock market. Was Neiderhoffer prudent to deduce that this seeming correlation truly had *predictive* power, even while the premise on which it is based violates all principles of common sense? The scientist would say no, the dreamer, yes. It's hard to imagine how someone who has been around the markets—and around George Soros—could postulate *ten* major bullish and *ten* major bearish events *occurring* in one year, let alone suggest that these events could be tipped off by counting the number of unchanged issues on the New York Stock Exchange. I did notice that Neiderhoffer must have received at least *one* bad signal in 1997. The day after the record one-day point decline in the stock market in October, the financial press reported that he had been completely wiped out—selling puts on stock index futures!

*

Confirmation-bias syndrome can afflict amateurs and professionals alike, and it is usually—if the product of naivety—at least unintentional. There is another side to bad research that is more pernicious, and perhaps more pervasive, because it is always well-hidden. This is the violation of the principle of full disclosure.

If one of *my* hypotheses or pet notions turns out to be incorrect, or statistically meaningless, which is really the same thing, I could easily just fail to mention it and pretend that the study never took place. No one would be any the wiser. But this would be intellectually dishonest, and a severe disservice to other researchers. *Failure to report on an unwanted result is just as bad science as "fudging the numbers" to back up a desired result.*

The danger of committing such an error was brought home to me one evening while I was watching *Larry King Live*. Larry's guest was the editor of the major tabloid newspaper which had just broken the story that Frank Gifford, the television commentator, had been secretly photographed in the company of a woman of dubious repute in a motel room. The truth was that Gifford had been entrapped by the tabloid; he had been set up for the express purpose of tarnishing his squeaky-clean image. The tabloid editor was sanctimoniously defending his newspaper's tactics: "Well, he did it, didn't he? Nobody made him do it." Someone called in: "My question to the editor is this. If Frank Gifford had rebuffed the prostitute's overtures, would the paper have published *that*?"

CHAPTER TWO

FAST FORWARD

How's this for a dream investment? You can't lose more than your initial stake, but you can multiply this stake many times over. And should you change your mind at any time, you can always find a third party willing to buy you out at a fair price.

These are the tantalizing prospects offered to buyers of commodity futures options. They are also the prospects offered in a lottery, where the great majority of players are prepared to sacrifice their entire investment for an outside shot at coming up a big winner. The buyer of a lottery ticket enters the game with a substantial *negative expectation,* since there is a large "house take" to be subsidized before winnings are distributed. The size of this take is usually specified in advance, making the calculation of the negative expectation of a lottery ticket-holder fairly straightforward.

A widely held perception of option trading is that option buyers face a similar negative expectation, though until now no comprehensive studies have either supported or contradicted this perception. A primary objective of this book is to investigate the long-run expectations of options traders, both buyers and writers. A further objective is to investigate how traders may modify their basic expectations by employing selective strategies under different market conditions.

An option buyer must purchase an option from an option *writer,* the universal term used to describe a seller of an option, whether it be a put or a call. Option trading is a *zero-sum game;* the prospects faced by option writers are, by definition, exactly the reverse of those faced by option buyers. Neglecting transaction costs, option traders' net expectations have to balance out at zero.

*

An option writer is making an investment where he may lose much more than he can possibly gain. If he wins at all, it will be at an agonizingly slow pace; if he loses, he may lose in a very big way, and the loss may be incurred suddenly. What would induce anyone to enter into a deal with such apparently unattractive terms? The answer is one word—premium.

In exchange for offering the buyer the possibility of unlimited profits along with limited loss liability, the writer wants to be paid a fee up front, and paid rather well. If he asks a hefty price and finds buyers willing to pay the premium, the option writer may neutralize the transaction odds or even turn them in his favor. It is generally thought that the option writer receives an option premium which not only equalizes the odds on the bet, but additionally compensates him for the open-ended nature of the obligation he has assumed.

It might be helpful to review the *function* of an option on a commodity futures contract and to understand why options are traded in the first place. People who have yet to trade a commodity futures contract—some of my audience, perhaps—are unlikely ever to have come across a commodity option. Most people, however, will already be familiar with the concept of an option in other fields of economic activity. For example, the option is a common device in the film industry, where a film company offers the author of a novel a sum of money in exchange for the exclusive rights to develop the novel into a screenplay.

Such rights are typically granted by an author to a producer for a *limited time period* only and for a *flat fee*. The option has an *expiry date,* and, if the producer optioning the material fails to act upon the rights he has purchased, the option agreement expires. If that should happen, the author is then entitled to keep the proceeds received up front and is also free to option or sell the material elsewhere. The buyer of a screenplay option is essentially buying time in which to test the product. If the screenplay development turns out to be positive, the producer wants to be certain of having secured the production rights. If the screenplay development proves negative, the option fee is simply written off as a cost of doing business.

The essence of all option contracts is the *right* without the *obligation.* There are, however, significant differences between an option on a piece of property like a novel and an option on a commodity futures contract. In the case of a novel, the big unknown is its marketability in another medium, and this question will not be answered without a considerable investment of time and money. In the case of a futures contract, the price of the contract is known at all times during the life of the option; the big unknown is *the value the contract will have on the date the option expires.* If, at option expiry, the price of the futures contract that has been optioned has moved favorably for the buyer—up *or* down as the case may be—the option buyer will exercise the option. However, if the price of the futures contract has not moved favorably, or not favorably enough to give the option residual value, the buyer will let the option expire and forfeit the premium paid to the writer.

When a buyer purchases an option on a futures contract, he or she pays a *premium* to the writer in exchange for the right to buy or sell that futures contract at a fixed price—called the *strike price*—at any time during the life of the option. Options to buy are known as *calls;* options to sell are known as *puts.* The buyer of a call option hopes that the underlying futures contract moves or remains *above* the strike price of the option at option expiry, thereby giving the option real value. The buyer of a put option hopes that the price of the underlying futures contract falls *below* the strike price, allowing the commodity to be delivered to the writer at a higher price than its current value. Needless to say, the hopes of all option buyers are diametrically opposed to those of their writers.

*

Although a commodity futures contract is symmetrical in the sense that both the long and the short have the same exposure in the market and are therefore subject to *the same margin requirements*, there is a distinct asymmetry in the terms of the options contract. The buyer has limited risk exposure—albeit the entire investment—and need only deposit the option premium with his or her broker. No matter what happens, the worst outcome for the buyer is for the option to expire worthless, in which case the buyer loses the premium—but no more. The option writer, however, is faced with the same level of risk as a futures trader and has full contract liability and must post margin, just as in trading an outright futures contract.

Because of the skewed terms of the option contract—limited risk with unlimited potential for the buyer—options are attractive to futures traders who don't like using *stop-loss orders* to protect their positions. An option is a seductive instrument in many ways. For the buyer, an option position as opposed to a futures position has *built-in stop-loss protection.* Set against this advantage is the disadvantage of premium erosion, the inevitable decay of the time value component of the premium as the option expiry date approaches. Not everyone can bear watching an option premium erode to zero; for some traders, this experience is little better than a variation on the infamous Chinese water torture. So, for the buyer, the option contract has its negative as well as its positive aspects.

For the most part, option buyers and option writers approach the market with substantively different objectives. An option buyer is most likely concerned with making *one specific bet*. An option writer, however, is usually striving to *cover many markets simultaneously.* Since option-writing profits accrue slowly, and since option writers can suffer large losses when they are wrong, continuous and diversified writing can mitigate the pain for writers when they are very wrong on any one trade. Though continuously exposed to the risk of a large loss, an option writer can employ a number of defensive strategies. A troublesome option, for example, can be laid off by passing the risk on to someone else, albeit after the writer has sustained a substantial loss.

Option writing, in fact, is remarkably akin to bookmaking, casino management, or insurance broking, where "the house" accepts the inevitable hazard of having to make occasional large payouts because the house is taking in sufficient funds to cover these payouts and still generate a tidy profit. Statistics on the *long-run profitability* of option writing on commodity futures do not exist; it as a fundamental question that I probe at length in the second half of the book. Conventional beliefs notwithstanding, the hypothesis that option writers as a group are able to function as successfully as a casino, say, has simply never been put to the test.

*

The price of an option that is freely traded on a commodity exchange fluctuates *in response to price changes in the underlying commodity futures contract*. The same anonymity exists between an option buyer and an option writer as exists between the buyer and the seller of a commodity futures contract. Like a futures position, an option position may be closed out at any time through simple transference to a third party, via an offsetting transaction made in the options trading pit on the floor of the futures exchange. There are *fixed* strike prices at which options on futures may be contracted, and each option has a *fixed* expiry date, preceding the expiry date of the underlying future by up to five weeks. Some actively traded commodities, such as gold, currencies, and the S&P500 stock market index have options expiring *every* month.

The life of an option is always less than the life of its associated futures contract, with 6 months being about the maximum term. Since an option is traded right up to its moment of expiry, the *term to expiry* of an option continuously diminishes with the passage of time. It is possible to buy or sell an option with a term to expiry as short as 1 minute.

An option is defined by its strike price and by its date of expiry. For example, the buyer of an *August 360* gold call is buying the right to purchase a contract of August gold at $360 per ounce at any time up to and including the moment the option expires (expiry of August gold options is on the second Friday of July). Each listed option is traded independently of all others; for example, an August 360 gold call, and a September 370 gold call are separate and independent options contracts.

The price at which an option trades in the free market will depend upon the *strike price* of the option, the *prevailing price of the futures contract* to which the option is attached, the *anticipated price variability* in that futures contract, and the *time remaining until expiry* of the option. In the very short term, any increase in the price of a futures contract will result in higher call option values and lower put option values for options on that future. Likewise, any decrease in the price of a futures contract will result in higher put option values and lower call option values. Price variability in a futures contract will be the main determinant of the values that the market will place on its associated options. For this reason, and because there are so many options on each futures contract, price charts are not normally kept for options.

A call option is said to be *in-the-money* when its underlying future is trading at a price higher than the strike price of the option. An option which is in-the-money has real value even if exercised immediately; in practice, this is rarely done unless the option is so deep in the money that the buyer is willing to sacrifice a small residual option premium in favor of cash. When a call option has no immediate exercise value, it is said to be out-of-the-money, its market value deriving entirely from its potential, that is, the potential for the future to rise above the strike price during the remaining life of the option. Reverse arguments hold for put options. A put option is in-the-money when the futures price is under the strike price. An option with a strike price exactly equal to the futures price is said to be at-the-money and is the option in which trading is likely to be most active. Options are available at strike prices so far out of the money, and with such short times to expiry, that only a massive economic dislocation or a mammoth natural disaster could give them any terminal value. These options can be purchased for as little as $25, and very occasionally, like a lottery ticket, one of them will pay off.

*

Option statistics are published daily in the pages of the financial press. Figure 2-1 lists option prices prevailing on June 30, 1993 for gold futures. Working *down* the columns of Figure 2-1, note how the values of call options *decrease* as one moves from in-the-money strikes to out-of-the-money strikes and how the values of put options vary in the reverse direction. Working across Figure 2-1 from left to right, note how the values of options increase as the amount of time to expiry increases. On June 30, for example, the August 380 calls with less than 2 weeks until expiry closed at $3.90; the September 380s with 6 weeks until expiry closed at $10.20, while the October 380s with 11 weeks to expiry closed at $12.80.

Note particularly the row entry starting with the strike price of *380*. Since the August future has closed at 379.1, the *August 380* option is trading very close to the money. Put and call options trading close to the money will command very similar prices. Indeed, when a future trades exactly at a strike price, the puts and calls at that strike must trade at exactly equal prices. Precisely why this equality has to prevail will be illustrated in the next chapter.

Option values also increase with increasing market volatility. As of June 30, 1993, the gold market was the most volatile it had

Strike Price	CALLS Aug	CALLS Sep	CALLS Oct	PUTS Aug	PUTS Sep	PUTS Oct
350	29.40	31.70	33.20	0.20	0.90	2.50
360	19.50	23.00	24.30	0.30	2.20	3.30
370	10.00	15.50	17.50	1.00	4.60	6.40
380	3.90	10.20	12.80	4.70	8.80	11.60
390	1.50	6.50	8.30	12.30	15.00	16.60
400	0.60	4.20	6.10	21.10	22.70	24.10
410	0.30	2.80	4.20	30.90	31.00	33.50

FIGURE 2-1. Price quotations for gold options as they typically appear in the financial press. Quoted prices are in dollars per ounce and taken as of the close of trading on Wednesday, June 30, 1993. (August gold futures closed at 379.10 that same day.)

been in a year, the futures having risen $60.00 in less than 3 months. At that time, the 5-week at-the-money option was trading at $10.00. In early 1993, with gold in the doldrums, a similar 5-week option was trading at less than half this amount.

Option values are ultimately determined by the free interplay of supply and demand in the marketplace. A number of advisory services claim to be able to identify overvalued and undervalued option prices. If an option were *obviously* undervalued, it would obviously be worth buying, and buyers would quickly force the price up into some kind of equilibrium with other options having similar risk-reward characteristics. Similarly, if an option were *obviously* overvalued, it would clearly attract a lot of option writers on purely technical grounds. In practice, things are never that clear.

*

An option on a commodity future is a remarkably sophisticated instrument—the *ultimate derivative,* perhaps. Consider the levels of abstraction implicit, for example, in a put option on a treasury bond futures contract. The buyer of a Treasury bond put option is betting with an unknown opponent that the value of the government's obligation to an unknown lender, 30 years hence, will, within the short life of the option, decline by an amount sufficient to cover the price of the bet and still yield a profit!

PART TWO

OPTION THEORY

CHAPTER THREE

OCKHAM'S EQUATION

In the very short term, no one knows what the price of a commodity future will do. Everyone knows what it has done in the past, of course, but market tacticians disagree on how much useful information—as far as predicting upcoming price action—is encoded in recent price patterns. Some observers, myself included, believe there is little or no information on future price direction to be found in historical prices. Others swear by technical analysis, to the extent of ignoring market fundamentals altogether.

Regardless of trading philosophy, few serious players would dispute that in the very short term at least the price of a freely traded entity like a commodity future will fluctuate in a virtually random manner, even as it is responding to supply and demand considerations such as weather forecasts, farmers production intentions, the whims of consumers and economic policymakers, and the occasional mass-hysterical phenomenon sometimes called "the madness of crowds."

Commodity prices may change abruptly, as when instantaneous and substantial news must suddenly be absorbed into the marketplace. Jolts of this type arrive, by definition, in a random manner but create seemingly nonrandom commodity price patterns, especially when these patterns are viewed in retrospect on price charts and divorced from the news that gave rise to them in the first place. *Regardless of how nonrandom a trading market may appear in retrospect, at each instant of time that it was open and trading freely a temporary balance existed between the forces of supply and demand, as did a state of very temporary price equilibrium.*

Since the price of an option is a function of the price action in its underlying instrument, be it a commodity future or a stock, the price of an option is a derivative variable rather than an independent variable. Some pundits will argue that price action in an option presages upcoming action in the underlying instrument. Whereas this may be true in the case of stock options, where a sudden huge increase in options volume might be the result of insider trading, it is certainly not true of commodity futures where inside information does not really exist. I intend to treat options as pure derivatives, which means that I am going to be much more interested in the variability of futures prices than in the variability of options prices.

The relationship of paramount interest to option strategists is the relationship between an *option price* and the *variability of its underlying future* isolated from all other variables. The variability of the option price itself is of secondary importance, for that is affected by factors other than the variability of the underlying future: The price of an option, for example, will vary with the time remaining to expiry and also with the differential between the current futures price and the strike price of the option. All these numbers are continuously changing, making interpretation of an option price profile over time a rather pointless exercise. Needless to say, option price charts of the high/low/close variety are rarely seen.

*

There is considerable debate among market theoreticians on whether futures prices are random long-term. Fortunately, this debate is not relevant to the analysis of option prices. An option reacts as if the price of its underlying commodity future were a random variable and is not concerned with the direction of the futures market. Recent price direction in a commodity future, then, is irrelevant to the pricing of its options. The *size of recent daily price fluctuations* in a commodity future, however, is *the* single most important variable in the pricing of its options. The point is illustrated in Figure 3-1, a schematic representation of the familiar high/low/close daily bar chart for a

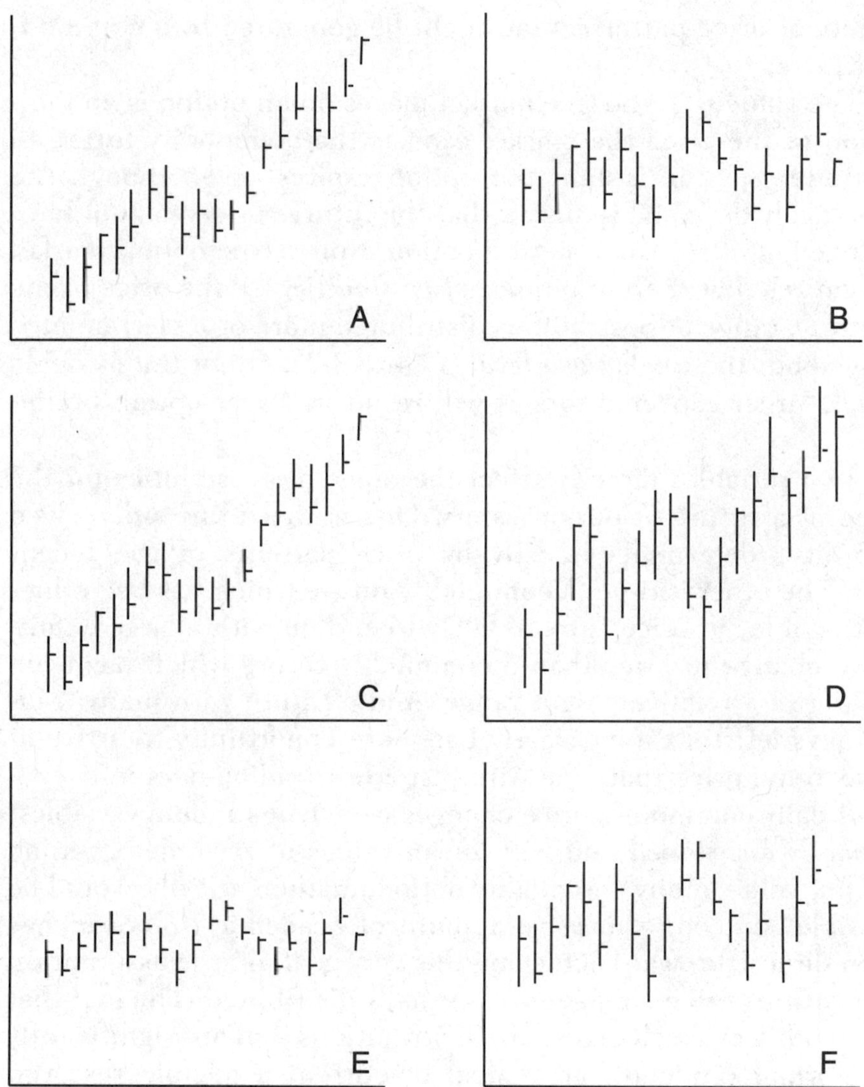

FIGURE 3-1. Daily price variability, *not* price direction of a futures market, is what governs the price of its options. Although market A has been trending steadily upward, while market B is stuck in a trading range, from an options valuation standpoint they are equivalent, and options at comparable strike prices would be priced approximately the same in both markets.

Markets C and D have risen by the same amount over the same time interval (about 20 days). Options on market D would be priced substantially higher than options on market C, because market D exhibits greater daily price variability. Markets E and F are both stuck in trading ranges, but again, options in market F would be priced higher than options in market E, because of the greater daily price variability.

variety of price patterns that might be generated by a commodity future.

The value that the free market places on an option is an indication of the price the market expects the commodity future to be trading at the instant the option expires. Even though the most likely outcome is always that the futures price will not have changed *at all* by the time the option expires, the option market recognizes that there is a *range of possibilities* for the price of the future, a range of possibilities distributed more or less symmetrically about the *unchanged level* (Figure 3-2). Other things being equal, larger expected ranges will result in larger option premiums.

Two variables directly affect the range of possibilities for the price of a future at option expiry. One is the future's perceived volatility—determined mostly by price patterns of the recent past. The other is time. A commodity future which has been fluctuating a lot in price is more likely to end up with a large cumulative change in price than a commodity future which has been trading in a relatively tight range. And a future with many trading days left till expiry clearly has more opportunity to arrive at an extreme price than one with just a few trading days left.

If daily commodity price changes were true random variables, *normally distributed* and with mean values of zero, determining the fair value of any commodity option, mathematically, would be possible. Indeed, a massive amount of academic firepower has been directed toward achieving this very goal, on the assumption that futures price changes *are* normally distributed. The fact that commodity price changes form distributions that are significantly nonnormal renders a great deal of current academic research into option pricing essentially useless, Nobel prizes in economics notwithstanding.

*

Although all commodity prices go through their own particular bull and bear phases, over the long term prices do not change dramatically. Periods of high prices in a commodity induce greater supplies along with a contraction in demand, and periods

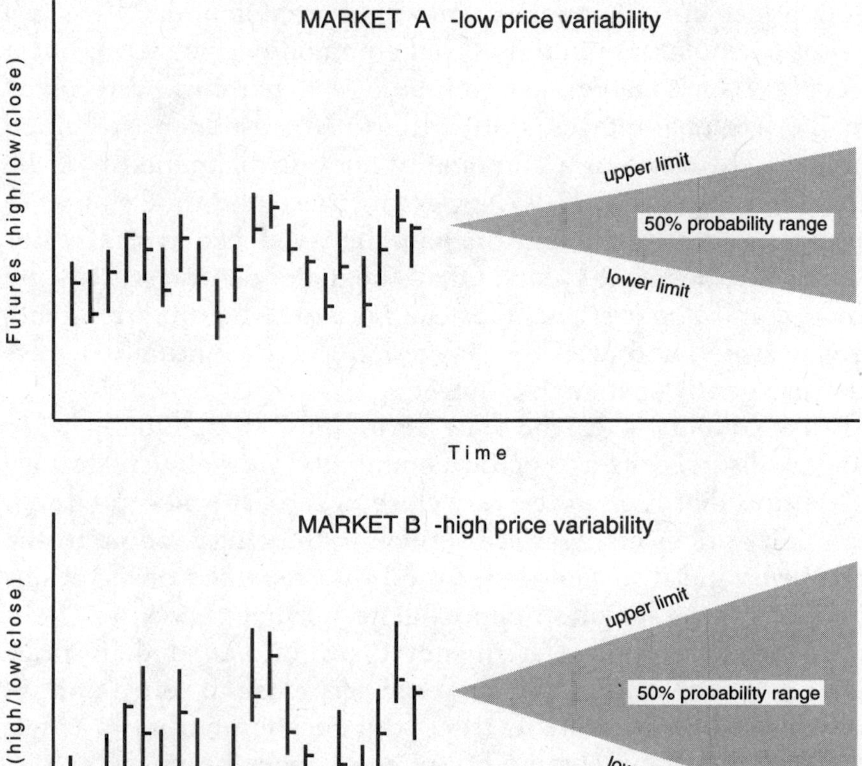

FIGURE 3-2. A high-variability futures market will project a greater range of likely *final values* than a low-variability futures market. Time is also a factor; the longer the trading horizon, the greater the opportunity for large accumulated price changes to develop.

In the two charts above, showing recent price history in both a low-variability and a high-variability futures market, probability envelopes have been projected forward in time. The limits of the envelopes define the 50 percent (arbitrarily chosen) probability limits within which the final futures price is expected to fall at any time in the future. The true relationship between probability and time is not a *linear* one as suggested in the schematic above. This is a refinement that will be explored in later chapters.

of low prices curtail supplies and stimulate demand. There is a long-term secular rise in the overall commodity price level, but it is small—1 or 2 percentage points a year, perhaps. Very occasionally, a global power shift will cause a sudden sustained change in the price of a commodity, such as happened with oil and gold in the early 1970s. Neglecting these one-time shocks to the system, even gold and oil have behaved like typical commodities for the last 20 years. Of all the major contracts, only the Standard and Poor's stock index can be said to be something of a one-way street, and even that juggernaut may eventually regress to a more gently sustainable uptrend.

Price stability over the long term implies that daily price changes observed in a specific commodity are going to form a distribution that is centered very close to zero. It is accepted that commodity prices changes are very close to being random in the short-term, and it is well-understood that repeated observations of random variables often approximate normal curves, or "bell" curves, when plotted as frequency distributions. If daily price change is a random variable centered very close to zero—and we know this to be substantially true—the question naturally arises: Why shouldn't daily commodity price changes be normally distributed?

Before attempting to answer this question, it's worth reviewing the properties of a *normal distribution*—in reality, a technical term for a rather fancy equation which in many cases accurately describes the distribution of a random variable.

The normal distribution is known to accurately describe such random variables as the heights or weights of people within clearly defined populations. For example, the average height for males in the United States is around 5'9" with above-average and below-average heights reasonably symmetrically distributed around this average value. The most widely accepted statistic defining a normal distribution is the *standard deviation,* a statistic whose value can be estimated from a large sample drawn from the population in question.

Once the standard deviation of a distribution is estimated, it is possible to predict, on the assumption of normality, the probability of occurrence of extreme values within that distribution. If the *observed extreme values* follow the expected probabilities, one can confidently assume that the original premise of normality is sound—at least, there will be no reason to suspect that the premise is unsound. But what if extreme observed values fail to conform in a big way with values projected from a normal distribution based on the sample data? What would be a reasonable and logical conclusion in the light of this finding?

One might conclude that the sample is nonrepresentative of the population it is drawn from and that the true distribution really *is* normal. Or one might infer that the population distribution is not normal at all. This second choice is not popular, because, if the normal assumption is suspect, it renders invalid much of the mathematical analysis that fills option textbooks.

Overwhelming evidence favors the hypothesis that price change populations are *significantly nonnormal*. There are simply too many occurrences of wildly improbable price changes—improbable, that is, on the normal assumption—to ascribe these aberrations to sampling error (see Figure 3-3, compiled from a year of coffee price data).

Why do price changes refuse to respect the normal distribution when so many naturally occurring random variables do so? Well, for one thing there is nothing natural about a commodity future; it is an abstraction by definition, and the pattern of prices it generates is the result of a highly complex set of human interactions. Is it possible then for commodity prices to be random, but random in some *abnormal* way?

When we talk about prices following a random walk, we are really talking about market players' reactions in a freely trading market being random. If we could isolate that part of futures price variability represented by players' reactions *after* news is "in the market" from that part of price variability arising from external market shocks, then indeed we might have a normal distribution of price variability.

But the reality is that *all* commodity markets are subjected to sudden and unpredictable infusions of information which result

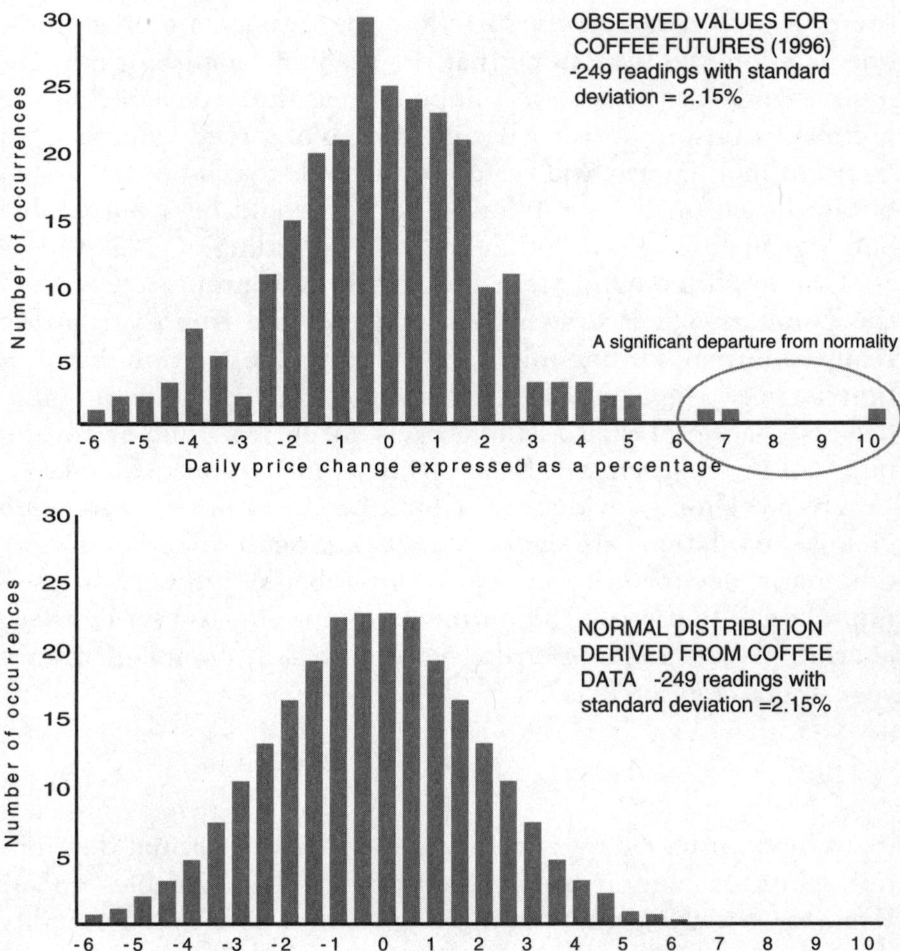

FIGURE 3-3. The upper chart is a frequency distribution of daily price changes for coffee for the whole of 1996 (249 trading days), with price change expressed as a percentage of absolute price level. The standard deviation was calculated to be 2.15 percent. The lower chart is a *theoretical* normal distribution with the same standard deviation and reconstructed, for comparison purposes, to correspond to a representative sample of 249 readings.

Even if the observations of the upper chart constituted a sample drawn from a *true* normal distribution, it could hardly be expected to show absolute conformance with normality, since it is just a sample. However, this chart exhibits a *very significant departure* from normality at its extreme values. Such a departure from normality can introduce serious errors into any option pricing calculation based on the assumption that daily price changes *do* come from a normal distribution.

in sudden instantaneous price adjustments: I'm talking about things like crop forecast surprises, unexpected political developments, weather scares, and so on. The price change distributions resulting from "external shocks" are by definition massively unquantifiable. However, there is no denying their existence.

When we look at a frequency distribution of daily commodity price changes, we are really looking at two distributions, one very normal, one highly abnormal. A failure to recognize this reality—an almost universal failure in conventional theory—can lead to many erroneous conclusions about how options are really priced in the marketplace.

Now that I have pointed out the shortcomings of the normal distribution assumption in quantifying price change distributions, I intend to develop an option pricing model based *on this very assumption.* There *is* method in such an apparently contradictory approach. Knowing the limitations of a theoretical model in advance may allow us to correct its deficiencies *after the fact* using empirical information extracted from real price data. This pragmatic approach, I submit, is quite different from the conventional theoretical approach to option pricing which revolves around a mathematically perfect formula not applicable in the real world.

There are other benefits from proceeding initially on the normal assumption. Perhaps most important, the reader will be able to directly compare the simplified option pricing model I'm going to develop from first principles with the "million dollar formula" that dominates options literature. Before attemping to construct this model, I would like to make a few observations on price distributions in general and discuss ways of expressing these distributions as succinctly as possible.

Commodity prices are expressed in such diverse units as cents per pound, dollars per bushel, and yen per dollar. Since we will be interested in price changes rather than in absolute prices, and since we will be wanting to compare price change distributions across a number of different commodities, it will be immensely useful to express all price changes as percentages of their absolute price levels.

If every daily price change—whether the commodity be soybeans, live cattle, sugar, or Japanese yen—is made dimensionless by dividing that price change by the absolute price of its future and then multiplying by one hundred, then all resulting measures of "spread" will be expressed as dimensionless percentages and will thereby be directly comparable. (If every option price is also expressed as a percentage of its futures price, then every option price will also be expressed in the same units as the daily price changes in its future.) Figure 3-4 shows daily price changes for coffee and silver, expressed as percentages of their absolute values of around $1.20 per pound and $5.00 per ounce, respectively, over the course of calendar year 1996. One thing is immediately clear from the "spread" of each of these distributions about its mean value: During 1996, coffee prices were much more variable than silver prices.

The degree of "spread" of a set of numbers about the average value (mean) of that set of numbers is most commonly specified by its standard deviation, a statistic which can be calculated for any set of numbers or for any continuously variable distribution. The calculation of the standard deviation of a set of numbers involves taking the square root of squares of differences from the mean. Another measure of spread of a distribution is its *mean absolute deviation*, which, in the case of daily price changes, is the average value of these price changes taking all readings as positive. In classical statistical analysis, the mean absolute deviation is much less used than the standard deviation. This is unfortunate, since the mean absolute deviation as a measure of variability has many advantages, not least of which is its ease of visualization and its simplicity of calculation.

Be that as it may, there is no denying that the standard deviation is the statistic conventionally used in developing option price models. Realistically, therefore, and for comparison purposes if for nothing else, the standard deviation has to be incorporated into any independently derived option pricing formula that I or anyone else dares to come up with!

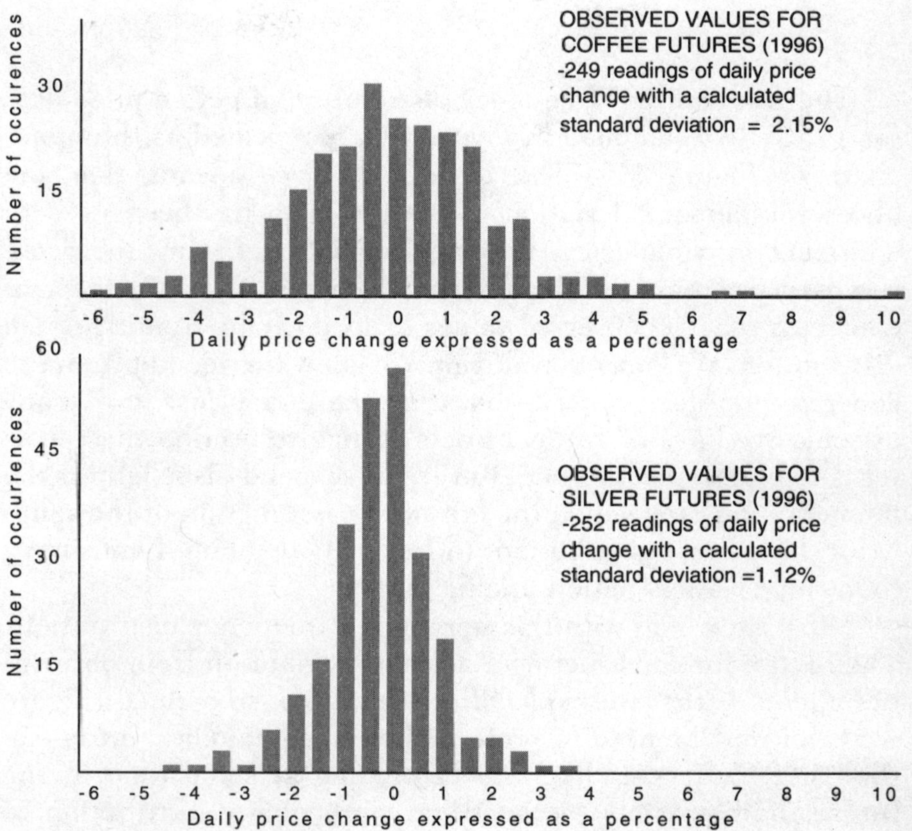

FIGURE 3-4. Frequency distributions of daily price changes for coffee futures and silver futures plotted to the same scale for direct visual comparison. The amount of dispersion about the mean value is most commonly measured by the *standard deviation*, a nonintuitive statistic whose calculation involves taking the square root of a sum of the squares. The standard deviation is the commonly accepted measure of the variability of a set of observations about its mean value, although the *mean absolute deviation* can also serve this purpose. The standard deviation of a frequency distribution is expressed in the same units as the variable on the x axis.

In the two charts above, daily price changes have been expressed as percentages of absolute price to make the standard deviations directly comparable. From the distributions it is clear that during 1996 coffee was much more volatile than silver, almost twice as volatile: the standard deviation of daily price changes for coffee was 2.15 percent, the standard deviation for silver 1.12 percent. Price variability can change dramatically with the passage of time. Traders who were active in the 1970s will recall when the situation was reversed; silver was much more volatile than coffee.

*

The "normalized" frequency distribution of coffee price data for 1996, first compiled in Figure 3-3, is repeated as the upper chart of Figure 3-5. The term *normalized* means that the observed standard deviation of the raw data has been used to construct a symmetrical normal distribution having the same standard deviation as the observed data set. The inference, of course, is that the observed values really do come from a normal distribution. We know they do not. We know they do not from the general empirical observation that there are just too many extreme readings of futures price change to ascribe these patterns to chance occurrence. But let us suspend disbelief, for the moment, and proceed on the erroneous assumption of the validity of the normal distribution. In following this line, I am simply following classical option pricing theory.

What do we do with this normalized frequency distribution? The reason for constructing a normal distribution from observational data is that the *probability distribution* so created (Figure 3-5) can now be used to project where a commodity future—in this case, coffee—is likely to be trading at some time in the future. It is possible to construct a probability distribution of daily price changes from data gathered over any time period one chooses. In the coffee distribution of Figure 3-5, a full year's worth of data was used in its compilation.

The more data one uses in constructing a probability distribution, the more representative and statistically sound that distribution will be. However, the farther back one searches in time, the more likely it is that distant data will no longer be representative of current daily price action. Commodity volatilities do change over time, and this changing volatility is definitely reflected in changing options prices. As far as arriving at the most representative probability distribution, there is really no way to decide which time period represents the best compromise between the benefits of increasing sample size and the benefits of using more recent data. If the price variability of a commodity were to remain constant, the problem of pricing its options would be much simpler, for then the observational data would be

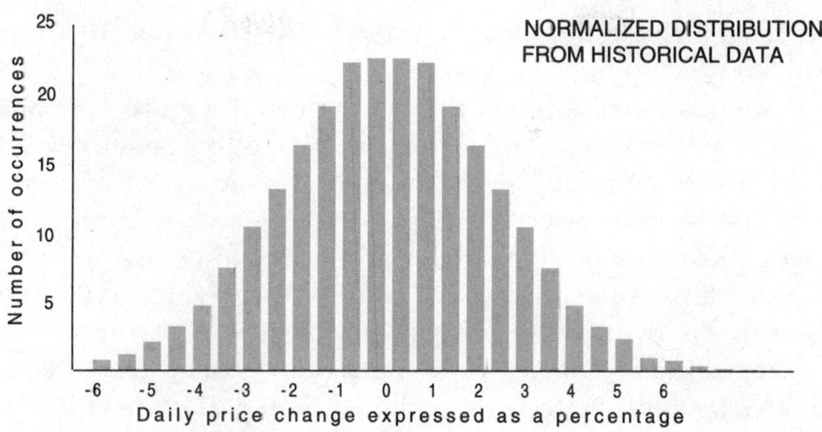

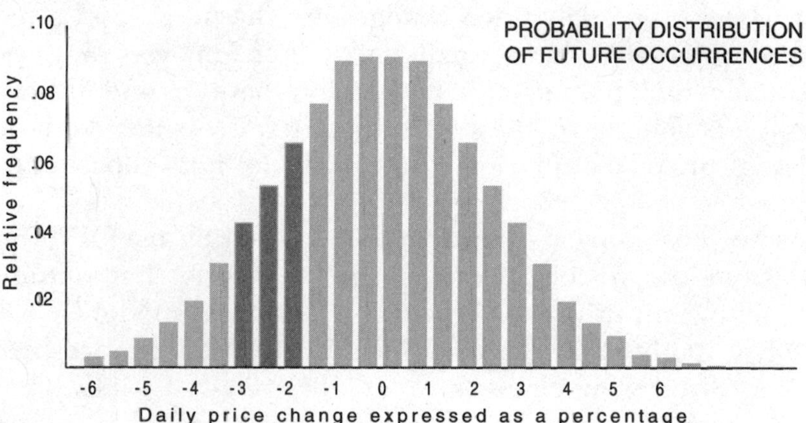

FIGURE 3-5. The upper chart shows the *normalized* absolute frequency distribution of daily price changes for coffee during 1996, with price changes expressed as a percentage of absolute price level as the x axis (repeated from Figure 3-3). The y axis of this chart can be rescaled as *relative frequency* by dividing number of occurrences at any given *x-bar* by the total number of occurrences.

From the relative frequency distribution of the lower chart, it is possible to project, on the normal distribution assumption, the probability that an *upcoming* daily price change will lie between any two limits of x. For example, the probability that a price change will lie in the range –1.5 to –3.0 percent is the sum of the three darker-shaded bars above. This probability turns out to be 0.042 plus 0.052 plus 0.065 which equals 0.159. Note that in a relative frequency distribution plotted as discrete vertical bars, as in the example above, the sum of the heights of the bars must necessarily add up to one—a certainty.

coming from a single time-invariant distribution. Again, we know this isn't so.

A frequency distribution of the type shown in Figure 3-5 does not provide any information on the *sequence* of observations. To get an idea of how price variability does change over time, one needs to look at daily price charts showing highs, lows, and closing prices. Scan any price chart for any commodity and you will find days of large price swings interspersed with days when the price hardly changes at all. You will notice strings of successive price changes in the same direction, mixed in with strings of days where advances alternate with declines. Some charts will retrospectively exhibit strong trends, others wide trading ranges. Most important, a commodity price chart will show *prolonged intervals of time* where large daily price changes are the norm, and other prolonged intervals where small daily price changes are the norm. All of which points to the conclusion that the random variable which is generating these price patterns is coming from an underlying price distribution that itself is not consistently volatile.

Despite these obvious limitations to extracting useful information from the historical record, the reality is that options traders, acting intuitively or employing statistical methods, will be closely watching the pattern of recent daily price changes in a commodity future for clues as to its upcoming volatility. They have little else to go on. Therefore, it seems reasonable to proceed on the basis that a probability distribution of price variability derived from recent price history—albeit over an arbitrary time interval—will prove useful in constructing an options pricing model, provided the limitations of that model are understood.

And where do we go from here? The answer is that for the moment we continue along the same well-traveled road other theorists have taken, working with an idealized model, but ever mindful of its limitations and of the ultimate need for stringent reality checks before any theoretically derived or empirically modified options pricing formula can be introduced into the real world of options trading.

*

Before the task of fair pricing an option from first principles can be undertaken, the concept of *mathematical expectation* has to be clearly understood. A commodity option is in essence a straightforward wager. When two parties make a wager on the outcome of a game of chance, both *hope* to win rather than *expect* to win. The truth is that in a fair wager the mathematical expectations of both parties are zero. One party may be more likely to win than the other, but expectations will be the same, because the underdog will be receiving odds from the favorite.

For example, a racehorse quoted at odds of 8 to 1 against is priced this way because the market, collectively, rightly or wrongly, believes that the horse has one chance out of nine of winning and eight chances out of nine of not winning. In other words, the market believes that the bookmaker has eight chances out of nine of winning, while the bettor has only one chance out of nine of winning. If a horse is fairly priced, expectations of bookmaker and bettor will be equal (neglecting the bookmaker's built-in edge), because the bookmaker will get only \$1 upon winning whereas the bettor will collect \$8.

The *expected value* of a random variable is the sum of each of its possible values, or intervals of values, multiplied by the probability of that value's occurrence. In the case of a bettor wagering on a horse at odds of 8 to 1 against, the random variable is the *bettor's payoff*. In a straight win bet there are only two possible values for this random variable; a positive value of 8 units if the horse wins, and a negative value of 1 unit if the horse loses.

$$
\begin{aligned}
\begin{matrix}\text{Bettor's}\\ \text{payoff}\end{matrix} &= \left[\begin{matrix}\text{(probability}\\ \text{of winning)}\end{matrix} \times \begin{matrix}\text{(winning}\\ \text{payoff)}\end{matrix}\right] \\
&+ \left[\begin{matrix}\text{(probability}\\ \text{of losing)}\end{matrix} \times \begin{matrix}\text{(losing}\\ \text{payoff)}\end{matrix}\right] \\
&= \frac{1}{9} \times (8) + \frac{8}{9} \times (-1) \\
&= 0
\end{aligned}
$$

The buyer and the writer of an option are essentially cast in the same roles as the bettor and the bookmaker, respectively. The option buyer has a low probability of winning a large amount, while the option writer has a high probability of winning a small amount. In an efficient market, the same equivalence of expectations that governs a racetrack wager holds true in an options transaction. Expectations in an options transaction balance at zero through the pricing of the option premium, because, unlike a racetrack wager, the amount to be won or lost in an options transaction cannot be specified at the time the transaction is made. The calculation of expectation, however, is basically the same, and *the fair price of an option is that premium paid by the buyer to the writer that makes both their expectations balance at zero.*

*

In attemping to derive an option formula from first principles, and for reasons that will become clear later, I am only going to consider at-the-money options. (Recall that an at-the-money option is one whose strike price is exactly equal to the current price of its future).

From Figure 3-6, a symmetrical frequency distribution of daily price changes in an idealized commodity future, it can be seen, graphically, how an at-the-money option premium must be priced so that expectations of the buyer and the writer are both zero. The frequency distribution covers *all possible outcomes* of daily price change, which means that numerically the sum of the vertical bars must add up to 1. And the probability that a price change will lie between any two values on the x axis is got by summing the heights of all the bars enclosed by these two values of x.

Consider first the purchase and sale of a 1-day at-the-money call option for which the writer receives the amount CP, the call premium. From a practical standpoint, option traders are interested primarily in options with weeks, even months, till expiry. The 1-day option is not commonly discussed in the literature, but all options eventually pass through the stage of being 1-day

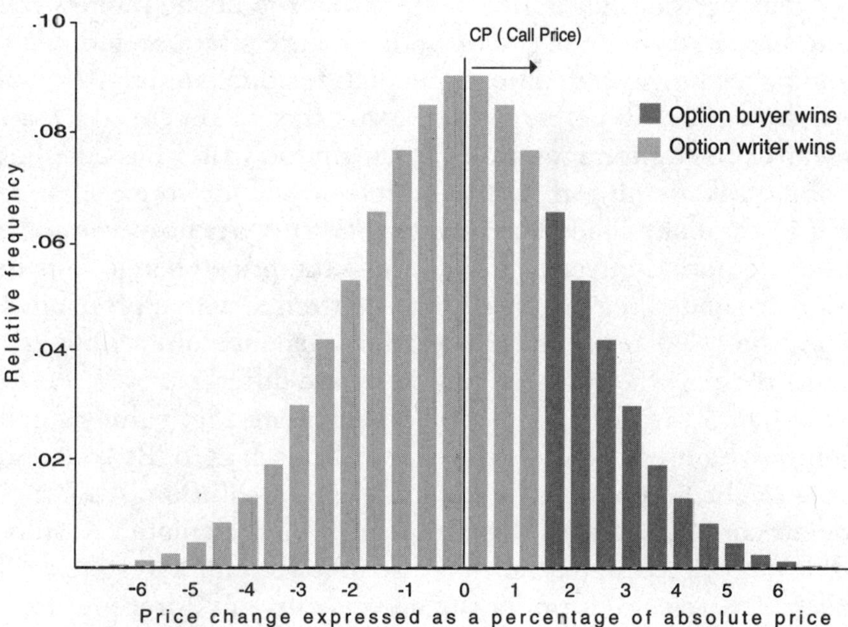

FIGURE 3-6. In order for the buyer of an at-the-money call option to win, the underlying futures price must change by a positive amount greater than the premium *CP* paid to the writer. Clearly, the option writer has a greater *probability* of winning than the option buyer.

If the futures price change is *negative,* the writer will profit by a fixed amount—the option premium, *CP.* If the futures price change is *positive but still less* than the call premium, the writer will also win, but by a progressively smaller amount as the size of the price change increases. If the futures price change *exceeds* the call premium, the option buyer wins.

The option writer's greater probability of winning is balanced by a correspondingly smaller payoff when that occurs. The buyer, of course, is hoping for a big payoff if the futures price change should happen to fall in the low probability, but high payoff, positive tail of the distribution.

For the moment, transaction costs, which are incurred by both buyer and writer, are not being considered.

options, and understanding how to fairly value a 1-day option is a major step in understanding how to value an option of *any* term to expiry. There are also compelling practical reasons for choosing 1 day as ground zero time; newspapers and quotation services report closing prices on a *daily* basis!

When a commodity future closes exactly at an option strike price (making that call option temporarily the at-the-money call option), *any positive price change* in the future after one more day of trading will give the call option some residual value at expiry. There is clearly a 50 percent chance that this will occur. Because he receives the option premium *CP*, the option writer has a higher probability of winning than the option buyer; any price change falling in the light-shaded area (Figure 3-6) is net positive to the writer. The option buyer can only win if the price change falls in the darker-shaded region, clearly an occurrence with a probability of less than 50 percent. Expectations balance out, however, because the payoffs to writer and buyer are different.

It is by no means obvious how to calculate that value of call premium which will balance the expectations at zero. By trial and error it might be possible to come up with a solution. A mathematician confronted with this problem would calculate the standard deviation, assume a normal distribution, and use statistical tables which give areas under the normal curve at different intervals along the x axis, but this would hardly be a straightforward procedure. It would also limit the scope of the solution by introducing the normal distribution assumption. The statistical table solution (or the polynomial expansion solution which is really the same thing) is the route followed by classical option theorists. And this is the fork in the road where we part company, because there is a much simpler solution to this problem unencumbered by the normal distribution assumption, a solution involving hardly any mathematics at all!

In Figure 3-7, we see the distribution of Figure 3-6 repeated but highlighted to illustrate the *buyer's expectation before the premium is paid*. The buyer's expectation before the premium is paid is net positive, because there is no price change of the commodity future which can cause him to lose. Remember, the terms of the option contract give the buyer the right to buy but not the obligation to buy. If the futures price change turns out to be negative, the buyer of the call option will simply let the option expire unexercised, at no cost. Before the premium is paid then, the option buyer's *expectation* can be expressed as follows:

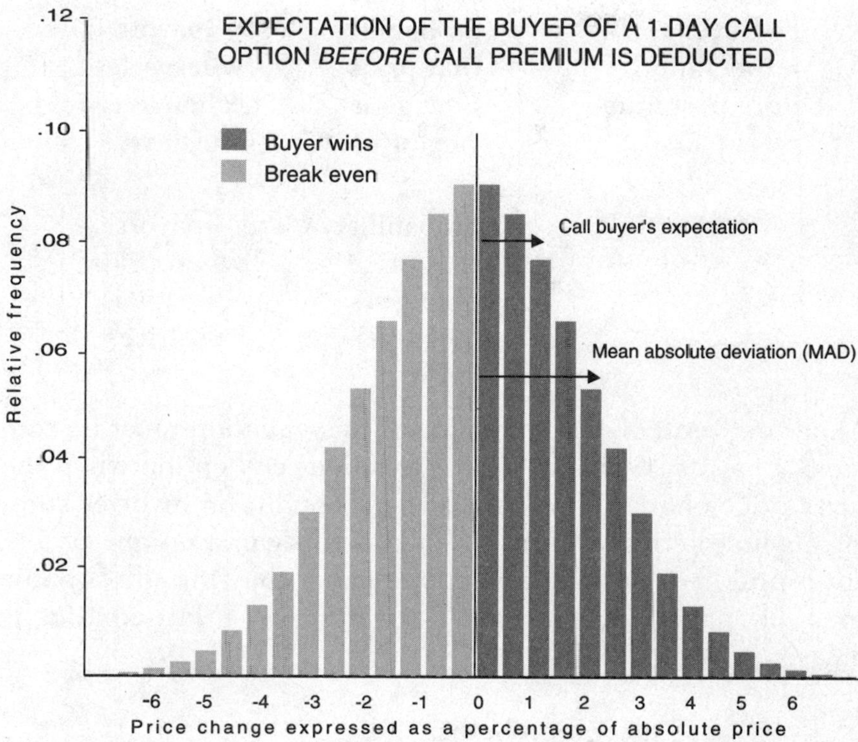

FIGURE 3-7. The call buyer's expectation *before the call premium is deducted* can be determined by summing each possible payoff multiplied by its probability of occurrence.

A 1-day at-the-money call option, by definition, pays off to the buyer with any positive price change and by the amount of that positive price change. With any negative price change, the payoff is zero. In terms of the frequency distribution above, the buyer's expectation is determined by summing the products of the height of each of the darker-shaded bars (expressed as a probability) multiplied by the price change associated with that bar.

The mean absolute deviation *MAD* of the price change distribution is defined to be the sum of the products of the height of each of the shaded bars multiplied by the price change associated with that bar, taking *all values as positive.* Defined in this way, the call buyer's expectation is exactly *half* of the mean absolute deviation. This relationship holds true regardless of the shape of the distribution, provided it is symmetrical about the y axis.

$$\begin{matrix}\text{Buyer's} \\ \text{expectation} \\ \text{before premium} \\ \text{is paid}\end{matrix} = \left[\begin{matrix}\text{(probability} \\ \text{that price} \\ \text{change is} \\ \text{negative)}\end{matrix} \times \begin{matrix}\text{(payoff} \\ \text{when price} \\ \text{change is} \\ \text{negative)}\end{matrix}\right] + \left[\begin{matrix}\text{(probability} \\ \text{that price} \\ \text{change is} \\ \text{positive)}\end{matrix} \times \begin{matrix}\text{(payoff} \\ \text{when price} \\ \text{change is} \\ \text{positive)}\end{matrix}\right]$$

The first term on the right side of this equation must be zero since the payoff is zero for an at-the-money call option when the futures price change is negative. The second term involves summing a whole series of terms, each consisting of a unique probability multiplied by a unique payoff, and covering all possible values of payoff when payoff is positive. Mathematically expressed:

$$\begin{matrix}\text{Expectation before} \\ \text{premium is paid}\end{matrix} = \Sigma(p_i \times X_i)$$

where p_i is the probability associated with interval X_i and all X_i's are positive. The *mean absolute deviation MAD* of the price change distribution is *defined* as its expected value taking all values of price change as positive, regardless of sign. Mathematically expressed:

$$\text{Mean absolute deviation} = \Sigma(p_j \times |X_j|)$$

where p_j is the probability associated with interval X_j where X_j may be either negative or positive. From symmetry considerations:

$$\Sigma(p_j \times |X_j|) = 2 \times \Sigma(p_i \times X_i)$$

Therefore,

$$\text{Expectation before premium is paid} = 0.5 \times \text{MAD}$$

Since we know that the *true* buyer's expectation *after* the premium is paid is zero, the call premium must be that quantity which reduces the buyer's true expectation to zero. In other words, the fair value call premium must be exactly one half of the near absolute deviation:

$$\text{Fair value call premium} = 0.5 \times \text{MAD} \qquad \text{(Eq. 3-1)}$$

Note that the call premium in the above equation will be expressed in the same units as the mean absolute deviation; if deviation is expressed as a percentage of futures price, so too is fair value call premium. Note also that the *mean absolute deviation* of a distribution is not the same as the mean deviation of signed values, which would be zero for a perfectly symmetrical distribution like a normal distribution. Both mean absolute deviation and standard deviation are measures of the dispersion or "spread" of a set of numbers around its average value, and are expressed in the same units.

Equation 3-1 relates the fair value of an option to the "spread" of its futures price change distribution in as simple and concise way as possible, using mean absolute deviation as the measure of spread. In traditional option pricing theory, however, the accepted statistical measure of spread is the standard deviation. Indeed, as we shall see in the next chapter, volatility is *defined* as the standard deviation—a rather unfortunate choice of definition, and a definition that has befuddled a generation of option traders and made books on option trading twice as thick as they ought to be.

What can be done with fewer is done in vain with more. (*William of Ockham,* thirteenth-century philosopher and iconoclast.)

*

Had mean absolute deviation become synonymous with volatility, life would have been much simpler. But it did not, and, like it or not, we are stuck with the standard deviation. If anything I have to say is going to be reconciled with what others in the field have already said, I am therefore compelled to expand Eq. 3-1 to include this term.

Frankly, I would not know how to develop, via the standard deviation, an option pricing formula for a normal distribution of price changes. Fortunately, I don't have to. In the particular case of a normal distribution centred on zero, there exists a *direct linear relationship between the mean absolute deviation and the standard deviation.*

$$\text{MAD} = \sqrt{(2/\pi)} \times \text{SD}$$

The quantity $\sqrt{(2/\pi)}$ simplifies to 0.7979, which is a number very close to 0.8000. Since any option pricing model is going to depend ultimately on sampled data, the degree of error in using 0.8000 instead of 0.7979 will be of a lower order of magnitude than any sampling error and therefore insignificant. I aim to keep this book as practical as possible. Therefore, henceforth, for ease of calculation, it will be convenient to use the slightly simplified relationship:

$$\text{MAD} = 0.8 \times \text{SD} \qquad \text{(Eq. 3-2)}$$

Combining Eq. 3-1 and Eq. 3-2 yields:

$$\begin{aligned} \text{Fair value call premium} &= 0.5 \times 0.8 \times \text{SD} \\ &= 0.4 \times \text{SD} \qquad \text{(Eq. 3-3)} \end{aligned}$$

It is worth noting that Eq. 3-1 is not limited by the shape of the distribution of price changes—provided the distribution is symmetrical. Equation 3-3 incorporates the normal distribution assumption and is more restrictive for that reason.

*

The distribution considered in Figure 3-7 is a distribution of 1-day price changes, and the standard deviation of Eq. 3-3, therefore, is the standard deviation of 1-day price changes. Let's see what happens when the trading time interval is expanded from 1 day to 2 days. The longer a random walk continues, the further the random variable may travel, so that the probability distribution of *accumulated* futures price change after 2 days of trading will not be the same as the probability distribution after 1 day of trading. After 2 days, there is opportunity for price changes *in the same direction* to accumulate into larger net changes than the changes possible after just 1 day's trading. The distribution of 2-day price changes will still be centred on zero since there is no directional bias, and it will still be symmetrical about zero, but the distribution will have longer tails and be "stretched" horizontally if plotted on the same scale as the 1-day distribution. Its standard deviation will have increased. The question is by how much.

It is a statistical fact that the distribution formed by summing two independent drawings from the same normal distribution will also be a normal distribution and that the standard deviation of this second distribution will increase by the square root of 2. It is similarly true that the distribution formed by summing t independent drawings will also be normal and that the standard deviation of this distribution will increase by the square root of t. That is:

$$SD_2 = \sqrt{2} \times SD_1$$

$$SD_t = \sqrt{t} \times SD_1 \qquad \text{(Eq. 3-4)}$$

where the subscripts $_{1,2}$ and $_t$ refer to 1, 2, and t days, respectively. There are approximately 254 trading days in a calendar year, and the statistic SD_{254}, the standard deviation of daily price changes *annualized,* has a special significance in the lexicon of options, where it is synonymous with the term *volatility* under that word's technical definition. Volatility as a descriptive term has entered the popular vocabulary due to the extremely large price swings witnessed in the stock market in 1997 and 1998. In the field of options valuation, volatility has a restricted and definite meaning, namely the *annualized standard deviation* of daily price changes. It is usually given the symbol v (by definition, therefore, $v = SD_{254} = \sqrt{254} \times SD_1$).

Equation 3-4 can now be expanded as follows:

$$SD_t = \frac{v \times \sqrt{t}}{\sqrt{254}}$$

Equation 3-3 established a relationship between the fair value of a 1-day at-the-money call option and the standard deviation of daily price change in its underlying future. It has now been established that if daily price changes are normally distributed, so too are accumulated price changes covering any period of time. By analogy, then Eq. 3-3 can be generalized for t, the time to expiry of the option, as follows:

$$(\text{Fair value call premium})_t = 0.4 \times SD_t \qquad \text{(Eq. 3-6)}$$

Combining Eq. 3-5 and Eq. 3-6,

$$(\text{Fair value call premium})_t = \frac{0.4 \times v \times \sqrt{t}}{\sqrt{254}}$$

The number of trading days in a year is an approximation; it is not the same for all commodities and varies slightly from year to year. If 16 is taken as an approximation to $\sqrt{254}$ (true value of 15.93), no significant error will be introduced into the equation. With this simplification incorporated, it is now possible to write:

$$(\text{Fair value call premium})_t = \frac{v \times \sqrt{t}}{40} \qquad \text{(Eq. 3-7)}$$

The fundamental option equation above was derived for a call option. By exactly the same reasoning an *identical formula* could

Suppose a gold future is trading at \$350 per ounce, its *350 call* at \$6 and its *350 put* at \$4. A trader who sells the *350 call,* buys the *350 put,* and buys the futures contract is guaranteed a profit regardless of the price of the futures contract at expiry.

If the contract expires at	\$360	\$340
Profit on *350* call	–\$4	\$6
Profit on *350* put	–\$4	\$6
Profit on future	\$10	–\$10
NET PROFIT	\$2	\$2

FIGURE 3-8. If an at-the-money call were to trade at a different price from the at-the-money put, a trader would be guaranteed a profit by selling the call, buying the put, and buying the futures contract. The numerical example above illustrates the necessary equivalence of the price of the put and the call.

A guaranteed profit is an impossibility—certainly on a commodity exchange.

be derived for a put option. The equivalence in price of the at-the-money call and the at-the-money put—even in hugely trending markets—may strike the reader as curious, but it is borne out by direct observation. It may also be demonstrated as necessarily true from arbitrage arguments (Figure 3-8). The reader should note, however, that put and call options that are out of the money by the *same amount* do not, in general, trade at the same price. The fundamental option equation may therefore be slightly generalized to include both calls *and* puts:

$$\text{ATMO}_t = \frac{v \times \sqrt{t}}{40} \qquad \text{(Eq. 3-8)}$$

where ATMO_t = the at-the-money fair value option price (put or call) expressed as a percentage of the futures price

v = the option volatility also expressed as a percentage of the futures price

t = the number of days until the option expires

*

Equation 3-8, which will henceforth be referred to as *Ockham's equation* (in tribute to its minimalist roots), links the theoretical fair value price of the two most actively traded options on a future with the *volatility* of the future and with the *time till expiry* of the options. Ockham's equation is theoretically sound and based on a number of simplifying assumptions already described, particularly (with the inclusion of the standard deviation term) the assumption that daily price changes come from a normal distribution. There is no requirement, of course, for *actual* option prices in the marketplace to conform to the values indicated by Ockham's equation, or any other equation for that matter.

If an option formula based on normal distribution assumptions cannot be expected to accurately forecast real options prices in the marketplace, what is the purpose of deriving it in the first place? The answer is that I have to confront the status quo. Furthermore, in the next chapter, it will become apparent that Ockham's equation is a special case of the famous Black-Scholes formula, which is used extensively in decisionmaking by a very large segment of the options trading public.

CHAPTER FOUR

THE WORD OF GOD

In 1997, the Royal Swedish Academy of Sciences awarded the Nobel prize in economics, plus a cash prize of $1 million, to two theoretical economists (and to another posthumously) for their research into option pricing models. From the press release:

> Robert C Merton and Myron Scholes have, in collaboration with the late Fischer Black, developed a pioneering formula for the valuation of stock options. Their methodology has paved the way for economic valuations in many areas. It has also generated new types of financial instruments and facilitated more efficient risk management in society.

This announcement was greeted with universal acclaim. Well, almost universal. It would scarcely be an exaggeration to say that since its appearance 25 years ago, the million dollar formula—the culmination of the above-mentioned research—has dominated option thinking with an authority of biblical proportions. Like the Word of God, everyone is expected to revere it, and no one is expected to understand it. The million dollar formula has been reproduced in virtually every serious book on options published since 1973, usually accompanied by a disclaimer of the *derivation of this formula is beyond the scope of this book* variety.

The original papers describing the development of the formula were written in a high academic tone, strictly for the consumption of Ph.Ds in advanced mathematics. Not only is the nomenclature clumsy and bizarrely complex, there are discontinuities in the logical presentation, where the authors, as part of their proof, cite other authors' proofs of such-and-such without bothering to verify or explain what such-and-such is or was. A typical rehash of the million dollar formula appears in Figure 4-1: This is the *simplified* version for use with options on commodity futures.

As a result of the formula's impenetrable logic, options authors by and large have been content to accept it at face value and simply regurgitate it when necessary. Comprehension of the formula has not been helped by explanations like this (intended for a general audience):

> Holding constant all the inputs to the options formula except the interest rate always increases the value of an option. To get a rough idea of why this is so, note that an increase in the interest rate reduces the present value of the exercise price. Since the exercise price is a potential liability to the holder of an option, this increases the value of the option. Fischer Black ("Fact and Fantasy in the Use of Options," *The Financial Analyst's Journal*, July–August 1975).

What's it all supposed to mean? And, this is just to get a *rough* idea, remember! Imagine what an in-depth explanation would be like! Now, I am not saying that the million dollar formula is incorrect. As a matter of fact, I know it to *be* correct, within the limits of its assumptions. What I do question, however, is its scope—in particular, its attempt to cover all the bases, when it should have been clear to the authors, *a posteriori,* that not all the bases could possibly be covered.

*

Consider, for a moment, the million dollar formula in its most general version as applied to commodity futures (Figure 4-1). Notice, first of all, that the formula contains a constant multiplying term e^{-rt} where r is the prevailing short-term interest rate expressed as a fraction, and t is the term to expiry of the option, expressed as a fraction of a year. The product of r and t is bound to be a *very small negative number,* so that the exponential multiplier will be a number very close to e^0 which itself is a number

THE MILLION DOLLAR FORMULA

$$\text{Theoretical call option price} = e^{-rt} \times [pN(d_1 - sN(d_2)]$$
$$\text{Theoretical put option price} = e^{-rt} \times [pN(d_1 - sN(d_2)]$$

$$\text{where } d_1 \equiv \frac{\log_e (p/s) + \left(\frac{v^2}{2}\right) \times t}{v \times \sqrt{t}} \quad \text{and } d_2 = d_1 - v \times \sqrt{t}$$

The variables are:

p	=	price of the futures contract
s	=	strike price of the option
t	=	time remaining to expiry expressed as a fraction of a year
r	=	current risk-free interest rate
v	=	volatility measured by the standard deviation
$\log_e$	=	natural logarithm
N	=	the cumulative normal density function

The cumulative distribution N can be read from tables or approximated from the formula:

$$x = 1 - z\,(.43618y - .12016y^2 + .93729y^3)$$

$$\text{where } y = \frac{1}{1 + .33261 \times |d|} \quad \text{and } z = .3989423\, e^{\frac{-d^2}{2}}$$

Then, $N(d) = x$ if $d > 0$, or $N(d) = 1 - x$ if $d < 0$

In the particular case of the at-the-money options with the interest rate taken as zero, that is, with $p = s$, and $r = 0$, the formula simplifies to:

$$\text{Theoretical call option price} = p \times [N(d_1) - N(d_2)]$$
$$\text{Theoretical put option price} = p \times [N(-d_1) - N(-d_2)]$$

$$\text{where } d_1 = \frac{v}{2} \times \sqrt{t} \text{ and } d_2 = -d_1$$

FIGURE 4-1. This is the million dollar formula in its *simplified* form for use with options on futures. The formula is advertised as being applicable to all options, that is, its scope extends to pricing *out-of-the-money options* as well as *at-the-money options*. In theory, the million dollar formula is correct. In practice, it doesn't work—unless the option is at-the-money, in which case a much simpler formula can be used.

very close to 1. For example, assuming an interest rate of 5 percent and a term to expiry of 6 calendar weeks,

$$r = 0.05$$

$$t = \frac{30}{254}$$

and

$$e^{-0.05 \times 0.118} = 0.9941$$

Using this exponential multiplier in the formula, and taking interest at 5 percent, the value of a 6-week option would be discounted by about one-half of 1 percent. I have no argument here, for a discounted premium makes sense given the way debits and credits are assigned in an exchange-traded options contract. An option buyer must pay the option premium to the option writer at the moment the transaction is made, and the writer may then invest the proceeds of the premium and collect interest. Common sense, therefore, suggests that in any option pricing formula the option price *should* be discounted by some interest rate component.

In practical terms, however, one has to question whether this discounting term, particularly an exponential term involving the variable t, is worth incorporating into the formula. In a low interest rate environment, we are looking at a discount of one-half of 1 percent on a 6-week option, with the size of this discount rising or falling more or less in a linear fashion as r and t vary. As will presently be shown, the *volatility component* in an options pricing formula contains an intrinsic inaccuracy of such a magnitude as to make any interest rate discount inconsequential.

In addition, as I shall also presently argue, the principal and perhaps only legitimate use of an options pricing formula is for comparison purposes (comparing options on *different commodities* and comparing options with different periods to expiry on the *same commodity*). For these reasons, and for ease of calculation, there is little harm in leaving the theoretical interest rate multiplier term out of any options pricing formula. If rigor be demanded, the interest rate discount may be applied as a straightforward percentage reduction to a formula-derived price after all other calculations have been completed.

In the development of Ockham's equation in the previous chapter, the interest rate factor was explicitly omitted. Therefore, in comparing Ockham's equation with the million dollar formula—an essential test of my credibility, to be sure—it will be appropriate to set *r* equal to zero in the latter.

The question of whether to include or exclude the interest rate term in an options formula is of minor significance compared with the more fundamental question of whether the million dollar formula in its general form has validity in the first place. The general formula attempts to price *all* options, that is, its scope extends to pricing both out-of-the-money options and in-the-money options, as well as to pricing at-the-money options. The inherent error in using a normal distribution in lieu of the true distribution of futures price changes has been demonstrated in the previous chapter. As a result of this error, *any* options pricing formula based on a normal distribution, using a standard deviation calculated from observed data, will most likely generate option prices that do not truly reflect fair value. The parameter *v*, a measure of the variability of the futures price and a necessary input to any options pricing formula, can only be estimated from empirical data. Any option price calculated from a formula can only be as accurate of the estimate of *v* used in the calculation, and if *v* is estimated from empirical data, there is no guarantee that it will be truly representative of the variability of futures prices.

One might have expected that mathematically focused researchers would think to question the validity of the normal assumption, or the validity of *some* assumption at least, since even a rough comparison of actual option closing prices published in the financial press against theoretically calculated values reveals tremendous discrepancies.

First, *actual* option prices do not diminish in value at strike prices progressively further out of the money at the rate predicted by the million dollar formula. This can easily be shown to be true by holding v and t and p constant in the formula, and solving for option price at different values of strike price s (Figure 4-2). The formula *progressively underprices* out-of-the-money options relative to the at-the-money option.

The reason for this underpricing of out-of-the money options is embedded in the erroneous normal distribution assumption. Since the true distribution of commodity price changes shows many more extreme values than the normal distribution would indicate, the preponderance of outcomes that will cause an at-the-money option to expire with a positive value will lie in the central part of the true probability distribution of daily price changes. With an at-the-money option, the effects of unexpectedly large price changes in the tails of the distribution are *minimized,* because of their infrequency relative to middle of the distribution outcomes. In contrast, the outcomes that cause an out-of-the-money option to expire with a positive value are those that lie in one of the extreme tails of the distribution, the area in which outcomes most exceed normal distribution predictions. With a far out-of-the-money option then, the error introduced by the ragged tails of the distribution will be *maximized.* The market understands "abnormality" from experience and consequently slaps a big surcharge on low-probability options. The million dollar formula, blind to this reality, has no means of accommodating it.

If the degree of relative underpricing at different strikes could be corrected, after the fact, by some *consistent* correction factor, it might still be possible to come up with a generalized options pricing formula that would work equally well for all strike prices. For example, in the comparison chart of Figure 4-2, the ratio of *actual* to *theoretical* option price clearly increases as a function of the amount by which the option strike price is out of the money, possibly in some quantifiable way. If deriving an empirical correction factor were possible via this ratio, as was establishing that this factor applied to both puts and calls, and applied in all commodity markets, then yes, it might be possible to

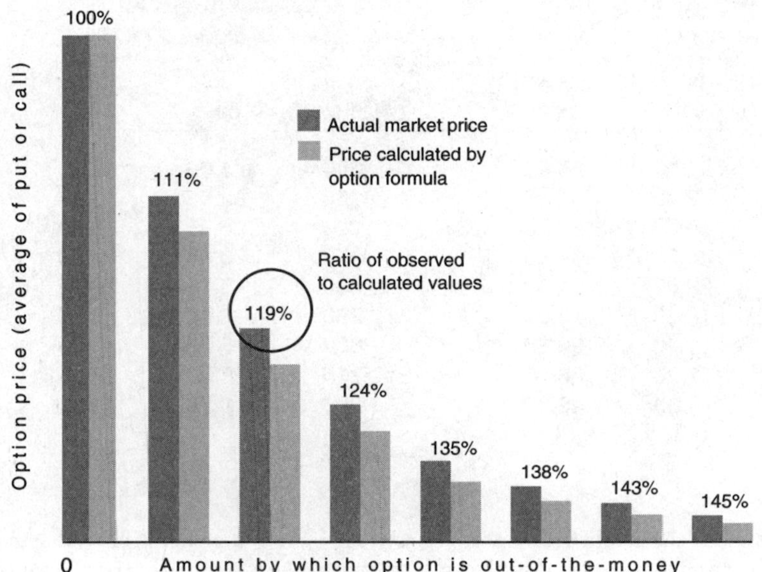

FIGURE 4-2. Option prices observed in the market-place and option prices calculated from the million dollar formula do not, in general, correspond with each other, as demonstrated in the chart above compiled from crude oil option data. To construct this chart, it was first necessary to determine *that value of v* which made the price of the at-the-money option calculated from the million dollar formula equal to the market price of that option. Then, by holding *v, t,* and *p* constant in the formula, out-of-the-money option prices could be calculated for different values of *s*, the strike price.

The discrepancy in options pricing between theory and reality results from the million dollar formula's assumption of a normal probability distribution of futures prices at option expiry, when the market knows from experience that this is not the case. Following the protocol above, formula-calculated option prices are *always low in relation to observed option prices,* the error increasing on a percentage basis as the option strike price moves out of the money.

modify the million dollar formula and make it *generally* valid. Unfortunately, nothing could be further from the truth. Relative option prices prevailing within different commodity markets exhibit *no mathematically quantifiable relationships.*

And there is a further problem associated with the general formula: It is clearly symmetrical with respect to the pricing of pricing of puts and calls with strike prices equidistant from the at-the-money strike (Figure 4-3). Simple inspection of option

S&P COMPOSITE (close as ot Nov 3,1997)			SOYBEAN MEAL (close as of Mar 27,1997)		
Strike	Nov calls	Nov puts	Strike	Jul calls	Jul puts
905	51.00	10.40	240	41.00	2.10
915	42.90	12.30	250	32.50	3.50
925	35.30	14.70	260	25.75	6.50
935	25.30	17.60	270	20.00	10.50
* *945*	22.00	21.30	280	15.75	16.25
955	16.30	25.60	290	12.50	23.00
965	11.40	30.60	300	10.25	30.75
975	7.50	36.70	310	8.00	38.50
985	4.60	43.80	320	6.25	46.75

* the at-the-money strike price

FIGURE 4-3. As the published option prices clearly show, a generalized and symmetrical option formula cannot possibly work for out-of-the-money options. The million dollar formula yields identical theoretical prices for puts and calls which are out-of-the-money by the same amount. Yet, on a day where December S&P futures closed at 945.70—making 945 the closest at-the-money strike, the *November 905 S&P put* closed at 10.40, while the *November 985 S&P call* closed at 4.60.

In some markets, calls are more expensive than puts. On March 27, with July soybean meal closing at 279.50, the *July 320 soybean meal call* closed at 6.25, almost three times as much as the equidistant *July 240 put.*

tables in the financial press reveals that no such symmetry exists in the actual market.

For example, during the growing season, out-of-the-money calls on a crop future command higher prices than equidistant out-of-the-money puts. The collective wisdom of the market, which is based on pocketbook experience, is smarter than any formula and recognizes that upside price surprises in something that is growing have the potential to be much larger than downside surprises. With stock index futures, the opposite situation prevails: Out-of-the-money *puts* are valued more highly than equidistant out-of-the-money *calls*—trading at more than double the price in many cases. To understand why stock index puts are much more expensive than stock index calls, the reader need only recall, in pain or in joy, the astonishing events of October 1987 (Figure 4-4).

THE NOVEMBER 1987 S&P PUT OPTION

Strike Price	Value of put option October 9	Value of put option October 19
260	0.25	61.00
265	0.45	66.00
270	0.65	71.00
275	1.00	76.00
280	1.65	81.00
285	2.25	86.00
290	3.35	91.00
295	4.50	96.00

FIGURE 4-4. For once, the doomsday scenarists were right. Buyers of wildly out-of-the-money puts who bought on October 9, 1987, must have felt like lottery winners just 10 days later. During this period, the S&P Stock Index future fell from 320.0 to under 200.0, a decline of unprecedented proportions. A *November 260 put* option, for example, bought for $125 on October 9, was worth $30,000 on October 19. This windfall for the option buyers was a disaster for the option writers. Just as maritime insurance rates rose sharply after the Titanic went down, so too did S&P option premiums after the stock market crash of 1987. They have remained high ever since, and moved even higher during 1997 and 1998 as a result of the tremendous daily price swings that are now commonplace.

Am I suggesting, then, that an option pricing model is of no value? Not at all. But only if its limitations are understood. We have to appreciate that option pricing is not nuclear physics, that there are no sublime relationships to be uncovered, and that bending the problem to suit the mathematics is counterproductive. It does seem to me that there are too many players in the option trading community who are ready to pay lip service to theoretical economists whose objectives are quite different from those of the average trader. A coterie of academics who seem never to have studied the financial columns of a newspaper—much less traded an option—have been allowed to dominate option pricing thinking, to press advanced mathematics onto the solution of problems which can be treated with simple mathematics, and in general to make the whole options business seem a great deal more complicated than it really is!

*

The subject of volatility in all its guises will be explored more fully in the next chapter. Suffice it to say at present, that because the parameter v cannot be objectively determined to everyone's satisfaction, there can be no objective test which will conclude whether an option is overvalued or undervalued—even when historical futures prices are representative of what is coming up.

We *can* nevertheless speculate on how instances of exploitable overvaluation or undervaluation are *likely* to arise. My suspicion is that situations of overvaluation or undervaluation—assuming these occur—will be consistent across strike prices, that is to say, *all* options on the futures of a given commodity will be overvalued or undervalued together. I would not expect to identify significant overvaluation or undervaluation by comparing options on the same commodity. Why? For one thing, with so many professional traders in the trading pit looking for arbitrage opportunities, it seems likely that options with different strikes and different terms till expiry will be forced into some kind of price balance with *each other*, based on pit experience alone. If I want to question the value of an *out-of-the-money* option, I will look to the historical relationship, seasonal or secular, that has prevailed between *that* option and the corresponding at-the-money option.

I *am* prepared to argue with the market's assessment of absolute value as reflected in the at-the-money option prices. In the empirical studies which follow in "Option Reality" (Chapters 6 through 9), I shall be concerned exclusively with at-the-money options—puts, calls, and straddles, where the strike price equals the futures price.

In Chapter 3, working from first principles, I deduced Ockham's equation for calculating volatility v, time to expiry t, or the at-the-money option price $ATMO_t$, when any *two* of these are known. The million dollar formula, of course, does exactly the same thing but in a more general way. If, in the million dollar formula, the strike price s is set equal to the futures price p, and the interest rate r is set to zero, we have exactly the conditions under

THE MILLION DOLLAR FORMULA — a calculation

Following the nomenclature of Figure 4-1,

$$t = \frac{50}{254} = 0.1968$$

$$d_1 = \frac{v \times \sqrt{t}}{2} = \frac{0.3\sqrt{0.1968}}{2} = 0.0666$$

$$\text{and } d_2 = -d_1 = -0.0666$$

And, since $|d_1| = |d_2|$, the calculated values of *x*, *y*, and *z* will be the same for both d_1 and d_2

$$y = \frac{1}{1 + .33261 \times |d|} = 0.9783$$

$$z = 0.3989423\, e^{\frac{-d^2}{2}} = 0.3981$$

$$\text{and } x = 1 - z \times (.43618y - .12016y^2 + .93729y^3) = 0.5265$$

leading to $N(d_1) = x = 0.5265$ (since $d_1 > 0$)

and $N(d_2) = (1 - x) = 0.4735$ (since $d_2 < 0$)

For an at-the-money call, with interest rate at zero, $p = s$, and $r = 0$.

So, theoretical call price $= p \times [N(d_1) - N(d_2)] = 0.0531 \times p$

which, expressed as a percentage of futures = 5.31%

FIGURE 4-5. A typical calculation for pricing the *at-the-money* call option on a commodity future using the million dollar formula. The term till expiry is 50 trading days and the volatility 0.3, or 30 percent. The interest rate is taken to be zero.

The million dollar formula is substantially more complex when pricing *out-of-the-money* options. Even this simplified version for the at-the-money option is awkward to calculate.

which Ockham's equation was deduced, so that the two formulae ought to agree in this restrictive case. And indeed they do (Figures 4-5 and 4-6). There is a big difference, however, in the

OCKHAM'S EQUATION — a calculation

Here is an alternative solution to the problem posed in Figure 4-5. As before, $p = s$, (since we are dealing with an at-the-money call), and r is taken to be zero. Term till expiry t is again 50 days and volatility v again 30%

If $ATMO_t$ is the theoretical price of a call option expressed as a percentage of the futures price, then, by Ockham's Equation,

$$\text{ATMO}_t = \frac{v \times \sqrt{t}}{40}$$

$$= \frac{30\sqrt{50}}{40}$$

$$= 5.30\% \text{ (as before)}$$

FIGURE 4-6. Ockham's equation solves the problem posed in Figure 4-5 much more economically than the million dollar formula, yielding an identical answer. Ockham's equation has the added feature that it can be solved for either v, t, or p, when any of these variables are specified. This is not possible with the million dollar formula which involves a polynomial function.

complexity of the calculations. What's more, in contrast to Ockham's equation, the million dollar formula may *not* be solved directly for volatility v, knowing time to expiry t, and the at-the-money option price $ATMO_t$.

I have tried to make the point, using empirical evidence, that it is only for at-the-money options that the million dollar formula or Ockham's equation can possibly have any legitimacy. Working back from an actual option price, both equations calculate a volatility based on the flawed normal distribution assumption, and this (implied) volatility will not necessarily correlate with a market volatility computed from the standard deviation of futures price changes. If (implied) volatilities are restricted to the at-the-money option, however, these volatilities may still prove valuable as comparative yardsticks. Notwithstanding the equations' inherent limitations, on no imaginable occasion can the million dollar formula provide any information not more easily obtained from Ockham's equation, repeated here, from Chapter 3:

$$\text{ATMO}_t = \frac{v \times \sqrt{t}}{40}$$

where

ATMO_t = the at-the-money option price expressed as a percentage of the futures price

v = the option volatility also expressed as a percentage of the futures price

t = the number of days till option expiry

Ockham's equation can be solved immediately for volatility or for option price. Alternatively, these same quantities can be obtained directly from the tables of Figure 4-7, generated from this same equation. So beware Black-Scholes, there's a leaner, meaner options pricing machine about to give you a run for your money.

Whenever the option equation is solved for v, that is, when the option price is known up front and the expiry time is specified, the quantity v so obtained is known universally as the *implied volatility* of the option. The following examples illustrate how the tables of Figure 4-7 may be used to derive and compare implied volatilities.

Example 4-1. On January 16, 1996, the March wheat future closed at $4.80 per bushel. The *March 480* call option which had 24 trading days till expiry closed at 11.5 cents. What is the implied volatility of this option?

Option price(p) ↓	Number of trading days till expiry (t) →																		
	2	3	4	5	6	7	8	9	10	11	12	13	14	15	16	17	18	20	22	24
0.25	7.1	5.8	5.0	4.5	4.1	3.8	3.5	3.3	3.2	3.0	2.9	2.8	2.7	2.6	2.5	2.4	2.4	2.2	2.1	2.0
0.30	8.5	6.9	6.0	5.4	4.9	4.5	4.2	4.0	3.8	3.6	3.5	3.3	3.2	3.1	3.0	2.9	2.8	2.7	2.6	2.4
0.35	9.9	8.1	7.0	6.3	5.7	5.3	4.9	4.7	4.4	4.2	4.0	3.9	3.7	3.6	3.5	3.4	3.3	3.1	3.0	2.9
0.40	11.3	9.2	8.0	7.2	6.5	6.0	5.7	5.3	5.1	4.8	4.6	4.4	4.3	4.1	4.0	3.9	3.8	3.6	3.4	3.3
0.45	12.7	10.4	9.0	8.0	7.3	6.8	6.4	6.0	5.7	5.4	5.2	5.0	4.8	4.6	4.5	4.4	4.2	4.0	3.8	3.7
0.50	14.1	11.5	10.0	8.9	8.2	7.6	7.1	6.7	6.3	6.0	5.8	5.5	5.3	5.2	5.0	4.9	4.7	4.5	4.3	4.1
0.55	15.6	12.7	11.0	9.8	9.0	8.3	7.8	7.3	7.0	6.6	6.4	6.1	5.9	5.7	5.5	5.3	5.2	4.9	4.7	4.5
0.60	17.0	13.9	12.0	10.7	9.8	9.1	8.5	8.0	7.6	7.2	6.9	6.7	6.4	6.2	6.0	5.8	5.7	5.4	5.1	4.9
0.65	18.4	15.0	13.0	11.6	10.6	9.8	9.2	8.7	8.2	7.8	7.5	7.2	6.9	6.7	6.5	6.3	6.1	5.8	5.5	5.3
0.70	19.8	16.2	14.0	12.5	11.4	10.6	9.9	9.3	8.9	8.4	8.1	7.8	7.5	7.2	7.0	6.8	6.6	6.3	6.0	5.7
0.75	21.2	17.3	15.0	13.4	12.2	11.3	10.6	10.0	9.5	9.0	8.7	8.3	8.0	7.7	7.5	7.3	7.1	6.7	6.4	6.1
0.80	22.6	18.5	16.0	14.3	13.1	12.1	11.3	10.7	10.1	9.6	9.2	8.9	8.6	8.3	8.0	7.8	7.5	7.2	6.8	6.5
0.85	24.0	19.6	17.0	15.2	13.9	12.9	12.0	11.3	10.8	10.3	9.8	9.4	9.1	8.8	8.5	8.2	8.0	7.6	7.2	6.9
0.90	25.5	20.8	18.0	16.1	14.7	13.6	12.7	12.0	11.4	10.9	10.4	10.0	9.6	9.3	9.0	8.7	8.5	8.0	7.7	7.3
0.95	26.9	21.9	19.0	17.0	15.5	14.4	13.4	12.7	12.0	11.5	11.0	10.5	10.2	9.8	9.5	9.2	9.0	8.5	8.1	7.8
1.00	28.3	23.1	20.0	17.9	16.3	15.1	14.1	13.3	12.6	12.1	11.5	11.1	10.7	10.3	10.0	9.7	9.4	8.9	8.5	8.2
1.05	29.7	24.2	21.0	18.8	17.1	15.9	14.8	14.0	13.3	12.7	12.1	11.6	11.2	10.8	10.5	10.2	9.9	9.4	9.0	8.6
1.10	31.1	25.4	22.0	19.7	18.0	16.6	15.6	14.7	13.9	13.3	12.7	12.2	11.8	11.4	11.0	10.7	10.4	9.8	9.4	9.0
1.15	32.5	26.6	23.0	20.6	18.8	17.4	16.3	15.3	14.5	13.9	13.3	12.8	12.3	11.9	11.5	11.2	10.8	10.3	9.8	9.4
1.20	33.9	27.7	24.0	21.5	19.6	18.1	17.0	16.0	15.2	14.5	13.9	13.3	12.8	12.4	12.0	11.6	11.3	10.7	10.2	9.8
1.25	35.4	28.9	25.0	22.4	20.4	18.9	17.7	16.7	15.8	15.1	14.4	13.9	13.4	12.9	12.5	12.1	11.8	11.2	10.7	10.2
1.30	36.8	30.0	26.0	23.3	21.2	19.7	18.4	17.3	16.4	15.7	15.0	14.4	13.9	13.4	13.0	12.6	12.3	11.6	11.1	10.6
1.35	38.2	31.2	27.0	24.1	22.0	20.4	19.1	18.0	17.1	16.3	15.6	15.0	14.4	13.9	13.5	13.1	12.7	12.1	11.5	11.0
1.40	39.6	32.3	28.0	25.0	22.9	21.2	19.8	18.7	17.7	16.9	16.2	15.5	15.0	14.5	14.0	13.6	13.2	12.5	11.9	11.4
1.45	41.0	33.5	29.0	25.9	23.7	21.9	20.5	19.3	18.3	17.5	16.7	16.1	15.5	15.0	14.5	14.1	13.7	13.0	12.4	11.8
1.50	42.4	34.6	30.0	26.8	24.5	22.7	21.2	20.0	19.0	18.1	17.3	16.6	16.0	15.5	15.0	14.6	14.1	13.4	12.8	12.2
1.60	45.3	37.0	32.0	28.6	26.1	24.2	22.6	21.3	20.2	19.3	18.5	17.8	17.1	16.5	16.0	15.5	15.1	14.3	13.6	13.1
1.70	48.1	39.3	34.0	30.4	27.8	25.7	24.0	22.7	21.5	20.5	19.6	18.9	18.2	17.6	17.0	16.5	16.0	15.2	14.5	13.9
1.80	50.9	41.6	36.0	32.2	29.4	27.2	25.5	24.0	22.8	21.7	20.8	20.0	19.2	18.6	18.0	17.5	17.0	16.1	15.4	14.7
1.90	53.7	43.9	38.0	34.0	31.0	28.7	26.9	25.3	24.0	22.9	21.9	21.1	20.3	19.6	19.0	18.4	17.9	17.0	16.2	15.5
2.00	56.6	46.2	40.0	35.8	32.7	30.2	28.3	26.7	25.3	24.1	23.1	22.2	21.4	20.7	20.0	19.4	18.9	17.9	17.1	16.3
2.10	59.4	48.5	42.0	37.6	34.3	31.7	29.7	28.0	26.6	25.3	24.2	23.3	22.4	21.7	21.0	20.4	19.8	18.8	17.9	17.1
2.20		50.8	44.0	39.4	35.9	33.3	31.1	29.3	27.8	26.5	25.4	24.4	23.5	22.7	22.0	21.3	20.7	19.7	18.8	18.0
2.30		53.1	46.0	41.1	37.6	34.8	32.5	30.7	29.1	27.7	26.6	25.5	24.6	23.8	23.0	22.3	21.7	20.6	19.6	18.8
2.40		55.4	48.0	42.9	39.2	36.3	33.9	32.0	30.4	28.9	27.7	26.6	25.7	24.8	24.0	23.3	22.6	21.5	20.5	19.6
2.50		57.7	50.0	44.7	40.8	37.8	35.4	33.3	31.6	30.2	28.9	27.7	26.7	25.8	25.0	24.3	23.6	22.4	21.3	20.4
2.60		60.0	52.0	46.5	42.5	39.3	36.8	34.7	32.9	31.4	30.0	28.8	27.8	26.9	26.0	25.2	24.5	23.3	22.2	21.2
2.70			54.0	48.3	44.1	40.8	38.2	36.0	34.2	32.6	31.2	30.0	28.9	27.9	27.0	26.2	25.5	24.1	23.0	22.0
2.80			56.0	50.1	45.7	42.3	39.6	37.3	35.4	33.8	32.3	31.1	29.9	28.9	28.0	27.2	26.4	25.0	23.9	22.9
2.90			58.0	51.9	47.4	43.8	41.0	38.7	36.7	35.0	33.5	32.2	31.0	30.0	29.0	28.1	27.3	25.9	24.7	23.7
3.00			60.0	53.7	49.0	45.4	42.4	40.0	37.9	36.2	34.6	33.3	32.1	31.0	30.0	29.1	28.3	26.8	25.6	24.5
3.20				57.2	52.3	48.4	45.3	42.7	40.5	38.6	37.0	35.5	34.2	33.0	32.0	31.0	30.2	28.6	27.3	26.1
3.40				60.8	55.5	51.4	48.1	45.3	43.0	41.0	39.3	37.7	36.3	35.1	34.0	33.0	32.1	30.4	29.0	27.8
3.60					58.8	54.4	50.9	48.0	45.5	43.4	41.6	39.9	38.5	37.2	36.0	34.9	33.9	32.2	30.7	29.4
3.80					62.1	57.5	53.7	50.7	48.1	45.8	43.9	42.2	40.6	39.2	38.0	36.9	35.8	34.0	32.4	31.0
4.00						60.5	56.6	53.3	50.6	48.2	46.2	44.4	42.8	41.3	40.0	38.8	37.7	35.8	34.1	32.7
4.20							59.4	56.0	53.1	50.7	48.5	46.6	44.9	43.4	42.0	40.7	39.6	37.6	35.8	34.3
4.40							62.2	58.7	55.7	53.1	50.8	48.8	47.0	45.4	44.0	42.7	41.5	39.4	37.5	35.9
4.60								61.3	58.2	55.5	53.1	51.0	49.2	47.5	46.0	44.6	43.4	41.1	39.2	37.6
4.80									60.7	57.9	55.4	53.3	51.3	49.6	48.0	46.6	45.3	42.9	40.9	39.2
5.00										60.3	57.7	55.5	53.5	51.6	50.0	48.5	47.1	44.7	42.6	40.8
5.20											60.0	57.7	55.6	53.7	52.0	50.4	49.0	46.5	44.3	42.5
5.40												59.9	57.7	55.8	54.0	52.4	50.9	48.3	46.1	44.1
5.60													59.9	57.8	56.0	54.3	52.8	50.1	47.8	45.7
5.80														59.9	58.0	56.3	54.7	51.9	49.5	47.4
6.00															60.0	58.2	56.6	53.7	51.2	49.0
6.50																	61.3	58.1	55.4	53.1
7.00																		62.6	59.7	57.2

FIGURE 4-7. Options on different commodities and options with different terms to expiry may be directly compared via a quantity called the implied volatility. From the table above, derived from Ockham's equation, and applicable only to *at-the-money* puts

Option price (p) ↓ — Number of trading days till expiry (t) →

p	24	26	28	30	32	34	36	38	40	42	44	46	48	50	55	60	65	70	75	80
0.60	4.9	4.7	4.5	4.4	4.2	4.1	4.0													
0.65	5.3	5.1	4.9	4.7	4.6	4.5	4.3	4.2	4.1	4.0										
0.70	5.7	5.5	5.3	5.1	4.9	4.8	4.7	4.5	4.4	4.3	4.2	4.1	4.0	4.0						
0.75	6.1	5.9	5.7	5.5	5.3	5.1	5.0	4.9	4.7	4.6	4.5	4.4	4.3	4.2	4.0					
0.80	6.5	6.3	6.0	5.8	5.7	5.5	5.3	5.2	5.1	4.9	4.8	4.7	4.6	4.5	4.3	4.1	4.0			
0.85	6.9	6.7	6.4	6.2	6.0	5.8	5.7	5.5	5.4	5.2	5.1	5.0	4.9	4.8	4.6	4.4	4.2	4.1		
0.90	7.3	7.1	6.8	6.6	6.4	6.2	6.0	5.8	5.7	5.6	5.4	5.3	5.2	5.1	4.9	4.6	4.5	4.3	4.2	4.0
0.95	7.8	7.5	7.2	6.9	6.7	6.5	6.3	6.2	6.0	5.9	5.7	5.6	5.5	5.4	5.1	4.9	4.7	4.5	4.4	4.2
1.00	8.2	7.8	7.6	7.3	7.1	6.9	6.7	6.5	6.3	6.2	6.0	5.9	5.8	5.7	5.4	5.2	5.0	4.8	4.6	4.5
1.05	8.6	8.2	7.9	7.7	7.4	7.2	7.0	6.8	6.6	6.5	6.3	6.2	6.1	5.9	5.7	5.4	5.2	5.0	4.8	4.7
1.10	9.0	8.6	8.3	8.0	7.8	7.5	7.3	7.1	7.0	6.8	6.6	6.5	6.4	6.2	5.9	5.7	5.5	5.3	5.1	4.9
1.15	9.4	9.0	8.7	8.4	8.1	7.9	7.7	7.5	7.3	7.1	6.9	6.8	6.6	6.5	6.2	5.9	5.7	5.5	5.3	5.1
1.20	9.8	9.4	9.1	8.8	8.5	8.2	8.0	7.8	7.6	7.4	7.2	7.1	6.9	6.8	6.5	6.2	6.0	5.7	5.5	5.4
1.25	10.2	9.8	9.4	9.1	8.8	8.6	8.3	8.1	7.9	7.7	7.5	7.4	7.2	7.1	6.7	6.5	6.2	6.0	5.8	5.6
1.30	10.6	10.2	9.8	9.5	9.2	8.9	8.7	8.4	8.2	8.0	7.8	7.7	7.5	7.4	7.0	6.7	6.4	6.2	6.0	5.8
1.35	11.0	10.6	10.2	9.9	9.5	9.3	9.0	8.8	8.5	8.3	8.1	8.0	7.8	7.6	7.3	7.0	6.7	6.5	6.2	6.0
1.40	11.4	11.0	10.6	10.2	9.9	9.6	9.3	9.1	8.9	8.6	8.4	8.3	8.1	7.9	7.6	7.2	6.9	6.7	6.5	6.3
1.45	11.8	11.4	11.0	10.6	10.3	9.9	9.7	9.4	9.2	8.9	8.7	8.6	8.4	8.2	7.8	7.5	7.2	6.9	6.7	6.5
1.50	12.2	11.8	11.3	11.0	10.6	10.3	10.0	9.7	9.5	9.3	9.0	8.8	8.7	8.5	8.1	7.7	7.4	7.2	6.9	6.7
1.60	13.1	12.6	12.1	11.7	11.3	11.0	10.7	10.4	10.1	9.9	9.6	9.4	9.2	9.1	8.6	8.3	7.9	7.6	7.4	7.2
1.70	13.9	13.3	12.9	12.4	12.0	11.7	11.3	11.0	10.8	10.5	10.3	10.0	9.8	9.6	9.2	8.8	8.4	8.1	7.9	7.6
1.80	14.7	14.1	13.6	13.1	12.7	12.3	12.0	11.7	11.4	11.1	10.9	10.6	10.4	10.2	9.7	9.3	8.9	8.6	8.3	8.0
1.90	15.5	14.9	14.4	13.9	13.4	13.0	12.7	12.3	12.0	11.7	11.5	11.2	11.0	10.7	10.2	9.8	9.4	9.1	8.8	8.5
2.00	16.3	15.7	15.1	14.6	14.1	13.7	13.3	13.0	12.6	12.3	12.1	11.8	11.5	11.3	10.8	10.3	9.9	9.6	9.2	8.9
2.10	17.1	16.5	15.9	15.3	14.8	14.4	14.0	13.6	13.3	13.0	12.7	12.4	12.1	11.9	11.3	10.8	10.4	10.0	9.7	9.4
2.20	18.0	17.3	16.6	16.1	15.6	15.1	14.7	14.3	13.9	13.6	13.3	13.0	12.7	12.4	11.9	11.4	10.9	10.5	10.2	9.8
2.30	18.8	18.0	17.4	16.8	16.3	15.8	15.3	14.9	14.5	14.2	13.9	13.6	13.3	13.0	12.4	11.9	11.4	11.0	10.6	10.3
2.40	19.6	18.8	18.1	17.5	17.0	16.5	16.0	15.6	15.2	14.8	14.5	14.2	13.9	13.6	12.9	12.4	11.9	11.5	11.1	10.7
2.50	20.4	19.6	18.9	18.3	17.7	17.1	16.7	16.2	15.8	15.4	15.1	14.7	14.4	14.1	13.5	12.9	12.4	12.0	11.5	11.2
2.60	21.2	20.4	19.7	19.0	18.4	17.8	17.3	16.9	16.4	16.0	15.7	15.3	15.0	14.7	14.0	13.4	12.9	12.4	12.0	11.6
2.70	22.0	21.2	20.4	19.7	19.1	18.5	18.0	17.5	17.1	16.7	16.3	15.9	15.6	15.3	14.6	13.9	13.4	12.9	12.5	12.1
2.80	22.9	22.0	21.2	20.4	19.8	19.2	18.7	18.2	17.7	17.3	16.9	16.5	16.2	15.8	15.1	14.5	13.9	13.4	12.9	12.5
2.90	23.7	22.7	21.9	21.2	20.5	19.9	19.3	18.8	18.3	17.9	17.5	17.1	16.7	16.4	15.6	15.0	14.4	13.9	13.4	13.0
3.00	24.5	23.5	22.7	21.9	21.2	20.6	20.0	19.5	19.0	18.5	18.1	17.7	17.3	17.0	16.2	15.5	14.9	14.3	13.9	13.4
3.20	26.1	25.1	24.2	23.4	22.6	22.0	21.3	20.8	20.2	19.8	19.3	18.9	18.5	18.1	17.3	16.5	15.9	15.3	14.8	14.3
3.40	27.8	26.7	25.7	24.8	24.0	23.3	22.7	22.1	21.5	21.0	20.5	20.1	19.6	19.2	18.3	17.6	16.9	16.3	15.7	15.2
3.60	29.4	28.2	27.2	26.3	25.5	24.7	24.0	23.4	22.8	22.2	21.7	21.2	20.8	20.4	19.4	18.6	17.9	17.2	16.6	16.1
3.80	31.0	29.8	28.7	27.8	26.9	26.1	25.3	24.7	24.0	23.5	22.9	22.4	21.9	21.5	20.5	19.6	18.9	18.2	17.6	17.0
4.00	32.7	31.4	30.2	29.2	28.3	27.4	26.7	26.0	25.3	24.7	24.1	23.6	23.1	22.6	21.6	20.7	19.8	19.1	18.5	17.9
4.20	34.3	32.9	31.7	30.7	29.7	28.8	28.0	27.3	26.6	25.9	25.3	24.8	24.2	23.8	22.7	21.7	20.8	20.1	19.4	18.8
4.40	35.9	34.5	33.3	32.1	31.1	30.2	29.3	28.6	27.8	27.2	26.5	25.9	25.4	24.9	23.7	22.7	21.8	21.0	20.3	19.7
4.60	37.6	36.1	34.8	33.6	32.5	31.6	30.7	29.8	29.1	28.4	27.7	27.1	26.6	26.0	24.8	23.8	22.8	22.0	21.2	20.6
4.80	39.2	37.7	36.3	35.1	33.9	32.9	32.0	31.1	30.4	29.6	28.9	28.3	27.7	27.2	25.9	24.8	23.8	22.9	22.2	21.5
5.00	40.8	39.2	37.8	36.5	35.4	34.3	33.3	32.4	31.6	30.9	30.2	29.5	28.9	28.3	27.0	25.8	24.8	23.9	23.1	22.4
5.20	42.5	40.8	39.3	38.0	36.8	35.7	34.7	33.7	32.9	32.1	31.4	30.7	30.0	29.4	28.0	26.9	25.8	24.9	24.0	23.3
5.40	44.1	42.4	40.8	39.4	38.2	37.0	36.0	35.0	34.2	33.3	32.6	31.8	31.2	30.5	29.1	27.9	26.8	25.8	24.9	24.1
5.60	45.7	43.9	42.3	40.9	39.6	38.4	37.3	36.3	35.4	34.6	33.8	33.0	32.3	31.7	30.2	28.9	27.8	26.8	25.9	25.0
5.80	47.4	45.5	43.8	42.4	41.0	39.8	38.7	37.6	36.7	35.8	35.0	34.2	33.5	32.8	31.3	30.0	28.8	27.7	26.8	25.9
6.00	49.0	47.1	45.4	43.8	42.4	41.2	40.0	38.9	37.9	37.0	36.2	35.4	34.6	33.9	32.4	31.0	29.8	28.7	27.7	26.8
6.50	53.1	51.0	49.1	47.5	46.0	44.6	43.3	42.2	41.1	40.1	39.2	38.3	37.5	36.8	35.1	33.6	32.2	31.1	30.0	29.1
7.00	57.2	54.9	52.9	51.1	49.5	48.0	46.7	45.4	44.3	43.2	42.2	41.3	40.4	39.6	37.8	36.1	34.7	33.5	32.3	31.3
7.50		58.8	56.7	54.8	53.0	51.4	50.0	48.7	47.4	46.3	45.2	44.2	43.3	42.4	40.5	38.7	37.2	35.9	34.6	33.5
8.00			60.5	58.4	56.6	54.9	53.3	51.9	50.6	49.4	48.2	47.2	46.2	45.3	43.1	41.3	39.7	38.2	37.0	35.8
8.50				62.1	60.1	58.3	56.7	55.2	53.8	52.5	51.3	50.1	49.1	48.1	45.8	43.9	42.2	40.6	39.3	38.0
9.00						61.7	60.0	58.4	56.9	55.5	54.3	53.1	52.0	50.9	48.5	46.5	44.7	43.0	41.6	40.2
9.50									60.1	58.6	57.3	56.0	54.8	53.7	51.2	49.1	47.1	45.4	43.9	42.5
10.00										61.7	60.3	59.0	57.7	56.6	53.9	51.6	49.6	47.8	46.2	44.7
10.50												61.9	60.6	59.4	56.6	54.2	52.1	50.2	48.5	47.0

and calls, implied volatility v may be read directly for any combination of trading days remaining t, and option price expressed as a percentage of futures price p.

$$\frac{\text{Price of option}}{\text{Price of future}} \times 100 = \frac{11.5}{480} \times 100 = 2.39 \text{ percent}$$

Entering the table of Figure 4-7 with an option price ratio of 2.39 and a time remaining to expiry of 24 days, and interpolating, you arrive at an implied volatility of 19.5 percent.

***Example* 4-2.** On June 14, 1996, the September wheat future closed at $5.005 per bushel. The *September 500* put option, which had 50 trading days till expiry, closed at 25.5 cents. What is the implied volatility of this option?

$$\frac{\text{Price of option}}{\text{Price of future}} \times 100 = \frac{25.5}{500.5} \times 100 = 5.09 \text{ percent}$$

From the table of Figure 4-7, implied volatility is 28.9 percent.

***Example* 4-3.** On May 17, 1996, the July coffee future closed at $1.2865 cents per pound. The *July 130* call closed at 4.8 cents and the *July 130* put closed at 6.2 cents, for an *average* at-the-money premium of 5.5 cents. The options had 15 trading days till expiry. What is the implied volatility of *these* options?

$$\frac{\text{Price of option}}{\text{Price of future}} \times 100 = \frac{5.5}{128.65} \times 100 = 4.27 \text{ percent}$$

From the table of Figure 4-7, implied volatility is 44.2 percent.

***Example* 4-4.** On May 18, 1996, the September coffee future closed at $1.2435 cents per pound. The *September 125* put and call closed at an average premium of 12.7 cents. The options had 54 trading days till expiry. What is the implied volatility of these options?

$$\frac{\text{Price of option}}{\text{Price of future}} \times 100 = \frac{12.7}{124.35} \times 100 = 10.21 \text{ percent}$$

From the table of Figure 4-7, implied volatility is 54.4 percent.

From the last two examples above, it is clear that the September coffee option has a much higher implied volatility than the July coffee option (they are measured just 1 day apart). At-the-money options on *different* futures months need not imply the *same* volatility. The reasons for this seeming oddity are explored at length in Chapter 5.

Implied volatility v is a descriptive statistic with no intrinsic meaning; it is simply the standard deviation of the hypothetical normal distribution that would satisfy a particular pair of values of option price and time till expiry. Implied volatility is best thought of as a comparative number that allows options on different commodities and with different expiry times to be assessed for relative price.

The implied volatility of an option must not be confused with the *market volatility* of the underlying future, a statistic derived empirically from price change data. There is no necessary equivalence between the implied volatility of an option and the market volatility of its related commodity future (although a big divergence here would certainly point to a potential overvaluation or undervaluation situation). A coffee option with an implied volatility of 40 percent is clearly projecting a more variable futures price pattern for coffee than a gold option with an implied volatility of 10 percent is projecting for gold futures. There is no guarantee, however, that future market volatility will bear a close resemblance to an implied volatility projection. In reality, the true volatility of a market is very difficult to define and measure and can only ever be known in retrospect. The implied volatility of an option, however, is a calculable quantity known at every instant of time.

Implied volatility as a comparative statistic has attained such widespread currency amongst option traders that proprietary services have sprung up for the express purpose of searching out options where the objectively defined implied volatility from the options formula seems to be out of whack with some subjectively derived estimate of what upcoming market volatility is likely to be. Traders should be wary of using implied volatilities published by advisory services as absolute yardsticks for decisionmaking. An option with an apparently mispriced implied volatility does not necessarily point to a trading opportunity; the subjectively estimated market volatility may fail to reflect some key information that the option market has already discounted.

Understanding the subtleties in the relationship between implied and market volatility is the core problem in option evaluation. The relationship is fraught with conceptual pitfalls and is discussed in considerable detail in the next chapter.

CHAPTER FIVE

THE EMPEROR OF CHINA'S NOSE

It is January, say, and a quick check of the financial pages shows that the price of the March at-the-money coffee call is 5.25 cents. The implied volatility of this option (calculated either from the million dollar formula or Ockham's equation—or read from the table of Figure 4-7) turns out to be 41 percent. Does this implied volatility tell us anything useful? Can it be compared against anything?

We might look back in time and check the implied volatility of this same option on this same date in previous years. Suppose that in the previous two years the implied volatilities were 26 percent and 32 percent, respectively. Does the fact that *current* implied volatility is 41 percent suggest that the option is overvalued and a candidate for writing? Maybe, but not necessarily so, for we cannot make any assessment of the market's pricing of an option on the basis of its implied volatility alone. The implied volatility of an option only takes on real significance when it can be compared to the current market volatility of its underlying futures contract, and market volatility will always be a subjective estimate to some extent, because there are as many estimates of market volatility of a commodity future as there are players in the market. Consciously or subconsciously, whenever traders take positions in options, based on value considerations, they are making their own *independent estimates* of market volatility and comparing these independent estimates to the implied volatility of the options.

Option advisory services may tell you otherwise, but there is no such thing as an *obviously* overpriced or underpriced option; the market as a whole is much too smart to grant "freebies." That is not to say the market is always perfectly priced. But, when it isn't perfectly priced, it is certainly not going to advertise that fact. Some people seem to believe that the market is *always* fairly priced.

> There is, in fact, a way in which the strategist can let the market compute the volatility for him. This is called using the implied volatility—that is, the volatility that the market itself is implying. This concept makes the assumption that, for options with striking prices close to the current stock price and for options with relatively large trading volume, the market is fairly priced. [Lawrence McMillan, *Options as a Strategic Investment* (New York: NYIF Corp., 1993, p. 464)—one of the best-selling options books of all time.]

Now, it *is* true that the strategist can let the market compute implied volatility, but the strategist cannot expect the market to indicate whether an implied volatility fairly reflects market volatility. To suggest that the options market is always fairly priced is tantamount to saying there is no point in trying to independently place a value on an option; any estimate of market volatility would necessarily be inferior to the implied volatility already incorporated in the price of the option.

Perhaps McMillan's statement is expressing a different idea altogether. Could he be implying that at-the-money options *are* fairly priced (because of the large trading volume) while out-of-the-money options *may not* be fairly priced? Could this be his way of reconciling inconsistent implied volatilities at different prices? I believe what we have here is a piece of specious reasoning leading to a classic conundrum: *There is no reason ever to trade at-the-money options. If you make the assumption that these are always fairly priced, how could you then* disagree *with that assumption, which is exactly what you would be doing by taking a position in the market.*

Let me stress that I am talking here about taking an option position based on *perceived valuation,* for there are certainly *other* reasons to take an option position. A trader might buy options based on a strong fundamental feeling about the price trend of the underlying future, without particular concerns about whether the option appears "expensive" or "cheap." A trader so disposed would not be interested in option pricing models. Studying the relationship between option prices and futures prices is predicated on the belief, or at least the hope, that options are *not* always fairly priced. Now it may turn out that options *are* always fairly priced, which would be a disappointing discovery, to say the least. But why assume, as Lawrence McMillan does, that the question has been answered before the investigation has begun?

The failure to appreciate that the implied volatility of an option is simply a derivative of its price has produced some rather confusing terminology in the literature on option pricing. For example, it is quite common to see *separate* implied volatilities listed for *each* of the out-of-the-money strike prices on the *same* commodity future. The volatility that is being "implied" in an implied volatility calculation is, of course, the market volatility of the underlying future, and a commodity future would still "possess" a market volatility even if there *were* no options. The idea that a future can have more than one implied volatility does not really make sense. It is, nevertheless, common enough practice to talk about different implied volatilities on the same future, so I am compelled to do likewise—at least for the moment.

If the million dollar formula could accurately accommodate the *true* probability distribution of possible price changes instead of an *idealized* normal distribution of possible price changes, the implied volatilities of all options on a particular future would be the same. In the options pit, where prices are actually made, the true probability distribution makes itself felt through the experiences of traders betting with real money. The market knows from experience that option prices cannot possibly conform to the strictures of any formula based on a normal distribution, and it prices options according to true probabilities—as best it can. The fact that the million dollar formula comes up with inconsistent implied volatilities for different strike prices is a glaring indictment of its inadequacy as an option pricing model.

To calculate the implied volatility of an option one has to work backward from an *actual* option price instead of forward from an *actual* volatility toward an *implied* option price. If the calculations are performed forward, as they should be, the million dollar formula comes up with out-of-the-money option premiums well below actual values prevailing in the free market (Figure 5-1). If the market truly believed in the normal distribution, the vertical bars of Figure 5-1 would all be the same height. Volatility profiles vary by commodity and some implied volatility profiles are very much flatter than others. The nonlinear aspect of the implied volatility profile is sometimes referred to as the volatility *skew* or volatility *smile*. A volatility "frown" is never observed.

Working, it seems, on the theory that if you average a series of errors you will somehow wind up with a right answer, a number of authors—uncomfortable perhaps with the inconsistency in having more than one implied volatility—have suggested *averaging* implied volatilities to arrive at an *averaged implied volatility* or a *composite volatility*. No one has ever suggested a practical use for an averaged implied volatility, but that does not stop people from wanting to average it. For a detailed analysis of implied volatility averaging carried to its ludicrous extreme, including averaging along with *weighting by options trading volume*, see McMillan above.

> Nobody was permitted to see the Emperor of China, and the question was, What is the length of the Emperor of China's nose? To find out, you go all over the country asking people what they think the length of the Emperor of China's nose is, and you *average* it. And that would be very "accurate" because you averaged so many people. [Richard Feynman in *"Surely you're joking," Mr. Feynman* (New York: Norton 1987, p. 303)]

*

An inexperienced trader looking over a table of implied volatilities generated by the million dollar formula might be

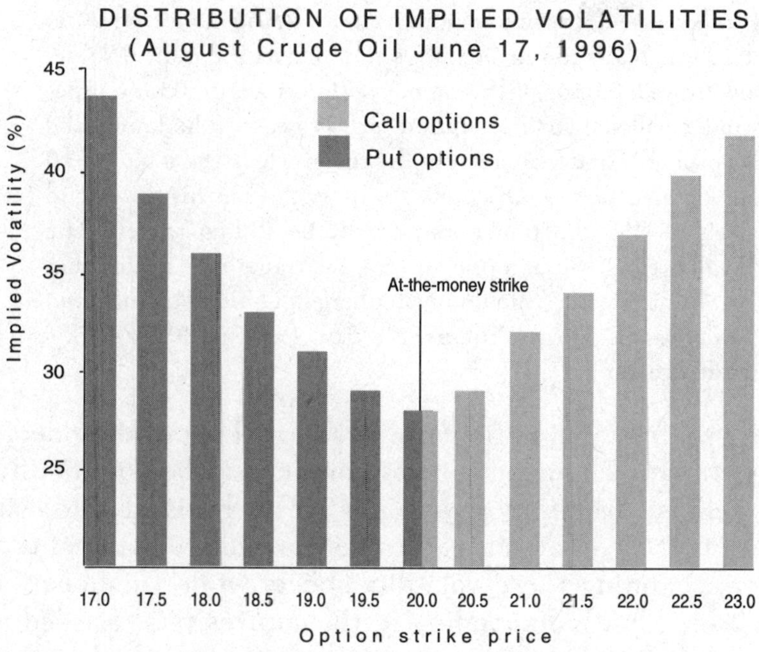

FIGURE 5-1. Implied volatilities calculated from option settlement prices typically follow the pattern above; the lowest value occurs *at the money* with values progressively increasing as the strike price move *out of the money.* Although implied volatilities are routinely calculated for *all* possible strikes, the only one that is useful for comparing different commodities or for comparing different futures of the same commodity is the *at-the-money* implied volatility.

seduced into a strategy of *buying* at-the-money options while *writing* out-of-the-money options, since the latter would appear to be overvalued relative to the former. This strategy might produce a lot of commission for the broker but probably little else, for the market is going to be rather astute in its relative pricing of options on the same future. Experienced traders know intuitively that there can be *only one volatility* associated with a commodity future. They also know from experience that the million dollar formula severely underestimates the fair value of out-of-the-money options. And they vote accordingly. Here's a former floor trader talking about the shortcomings of a generalized options pricing formula:

> Whatever the model says an option with an extreme exercise price is worth, it is probably worth more. How much more, nobody really

knows. But because of the apparent inaccuracy in the model, no experienced trader is likely to sell such an option for its theoretical value. If the model says a far out-of-the-money option is worth .05, no experienced trader will sell such an option for .05 because he knows the model has probably undervalued it in the real world. Even a bid of .10 or .15 may be insufficient. Of course, every trader has his price, and if someone bids .50 the trader may finally be willing to sell. The model may be wrong, but at a price of .50, the trader may decide that he can live with that risk. [Sheldon Natenberg in *Option Volatility and Pricing Strategies* (Chicago: Probus Pub. Co., 1988, p. 305)—highly recommended reading.]

To assist professional options traders in making trading decisions under rapidly changing futures conditions, the commodity exchanges publish "volatility sheets" on a daily basis. If you visit the options pit of a commodity exchange you will see many of the floor traders scanning these volatility sheets while they keep a close watch on what is happening in the futures pits. I asked a trader on the floor of the New York Cotton Exchange how he made use of his volatility sheet.

"So I know how much to bid or offer for an option," he replied. "I check the futures price on the board, check the volatility sheet at that price, and get the fair value of any option at that futures price. If I see a bid above fair value, I might sell it. If I see an offer below fair value, I might be a buyer."

He showed me the volatility sheet—about 8 pages of densely packed statistics. For every conceivable price that a future might trade at on that particular day, that is, for every other price tick from limit up to limit down, the sheet listed *fair value* put and call prices. And this for every option.

"Do you know where these numbers come from?" I asked.

"The exchange puts them out," he said. "They use a formula."

"What formula?"

"The Black Scholes Formula."

"What's that?

"You're writing a book on options and you don't know Black-Scholes. You got to be kidding, pal."

I was. "I'm trying a different approach, that's all."

He shook his head. "This business is ***built*** on the Black-Scholes model."

"Do you understand it?"

"Understand what?"

"The formula."

"I don't have to understand it. It's all done on a computer. It's very complicated."

Another trader butted in.

"You see all these option prices," he said, pointing to his sheet. "They're based on implied volatilities calculated from the previous day."

"And where do *these* implied volatilities come from?" I asked.

"From the implied volatilities of the day before that, I guess."

I borrowed the volatility sheets and studied them quickly—they were marked: "Confidential: For exclusive internal use of exchange personnel." The data were truly comprehensive and remarkably practical. The fair value option prices they listed had been calculated *not* from the million dollar formula but from *empirically observed relative pricing patterns prevailing in recent trading sessions.* It seemed as if actual options closing prices had been converted to implied volatilities via the million dollar formula—since different implied volatilities were listed for different strikes—and these implied volatilities then converted back to guideline option prices for use in the next trading session. There was even a built-in volatility correction factor, so that in the case of a *very* large price change in the future, *all* options would receive a boost in value. This was very logical, though exactly how it had been done I couldn't tell.

Still, the whole process had a circular feel to it. If all traders were to follow such guidelines, option prices (corrected for time decay and the inevitable shift in the at-the-money strike price) might never change at all, since each day's pricing would be determined absolutely from the previous day's pricing, and changes in the *market volatility* of the underlying future would not be reflected—at least through the actions of traders using the volatility sheets. It doesn't happen that way in the real world, of course. There are enough players tracking daily price swings in the futures markets, and enough players with an intuition for value, that any real change in futures market volatility will quickly be reflected in a change in overall option pricing structure.

While it may be argued, defensibly, that for any given future there can be only one true implied volatility, the same cannot be said of *different* futures on the *same* commodity; different futures on the same commodity can and do have different implied volatilities. In any logically constructed option formula (including the million dollar formula), the fair price of an at-the-money option will decrease in proportion as the square root of its time till expiry decreases. This is clear from Ockham's equation, for example, where:

$$\text{ATMO}_t = \frac{v \times \sqrt{t}}{40}$$

(This square-root time decay relationship is almost certainly valid for price change distributions that are *not* normal as well as distributions that *are* normal.)

Ockham's equation is certainly applicable to *any particular futures maturity* for the reason that if v is constant—which is to say, the probability distribution of daily price changes is unchanging—the only variable that can affect the price of the option is t, the time till expiry. Under conditions of constant volatility then, the fair value of an option can be expected to decline according to the geometry of Figure 5-2. In fact, with no change in volatility, the percentage amount that an at-the-money option can be expected to lose in value over the course of any period of time is given very simply as follows:

$$\begin{array}{c}\text{Expected percentage loss}\\\text{due to time decay alone}\end{array} = 100 \times (1 - \sqrt{t_e/t_s})$$

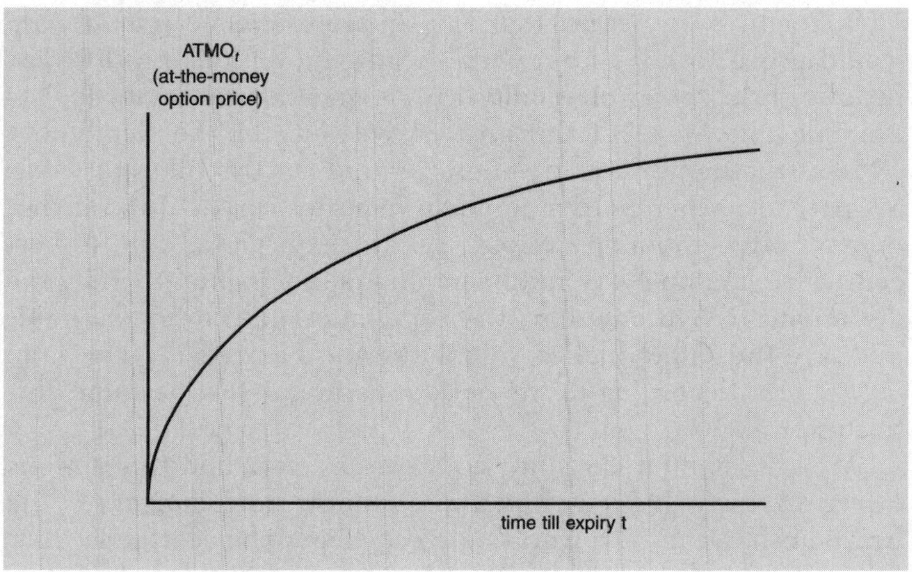

FIGURE 5-2. Assuming the volatility of a future remains constant, the price of the at-the-money option will diminish at an accelerating rate (moving from right to left along the curve) as the time to expiry approaches zero, according to the formula,

$$\text{ATMO}_t = \frac{v \times \sqrt{t}}{40}$$

Since different futures on the same commodity have, in general, different volatilities, each at-the-money option will follow its own particular decay curve.

where t_s is the number of days till expiry at the start of the period and t_e is the number of days at the end of the period. For example, between the tenth and ninth trading days till expiry,

Expected percentage loss due to time decay alone $= 100 \times [1 - \sqrt{(9/10)}] = 5.13$ percent

and between the tenth and fifth trading days till expiry, that is, during the second last week,

Expected percentage loss due to time decay alone $= 100 \times [1 - \sqrt{(5/10)}] = 29.3$ percent

It might be expected that the square-root time relationship would prove to hold true when comparing options on *different* futures of the *same* commodity. But, in general, this is not so. For example, on May 17, the implied volatility of the September 1996 at-the-money coffee option (54 trading days till expiry) was 54 percent, whereas the implied volatility of the July at-the-money coffee option (15 trading days till expiry) was only 44 percent. (See Example 4-3 and Example 4-4 in Chapter 4.) Why the discrepancy? Why shouldn't the September and July at-the-moneys have the same implied volatilities and be priced in the ratio of $\sqrt{(54/15)}$ according to the options formula? It's the same coffee, after all!

Well, it is and it isn't. July coffee is *old* crop, and July options expire in early June, before there is any frost danger to the Brazilian harvest—the world's largest. September coffee is *new* crop, and its options expire in early August, well through freeze-scare season. The market understands that there is greater potential for price volatility during the term of the September options than during the term of the July options and will therefore assign a higher relative price—or greater implied volatility—to the September options.

Frequently, it is the *nearby* option which exhibits the highest implied volatility. This is especially true in commodities where supply can be rapidly expanded or rapidly curtailed in response to price change. Crude oil is perhaps the best example. When oil demand exceeds supply, the nearby futures quickly go to a premium over the deferreds, and when demand falls short of supply the deferreds go to carrying charges over the nearbys. Consequently, price swings in the nearby crude oil future will always be larger than price swings in the deferred contracts. This characteristic of the crude oil futures market is reflected in the implied volatilities of its different option maturities. A similar configuration prevails in the grain market; the September soybean option regularly exhibits greater implied volatility than November soybean option. Both these options have the uncertain summer weather to contend with, but November encompasses a postharvest period where the uncertainty level drops, and a lowered overall uncertainty level results in a lowered option implied volatility.

Many commodities such as gold, silver, and stock index futures trade at carrying charges which only change when interest rates change, and in those markets you will find implied volatility to be relatively constant across different futures maturities. Sometimes an event with a massively uncertain outcome, but an outcome with large price implications, will distort the relative values of different option maturities on the same commodity. This can be a periodic event such as the "Hogs and Pigs Report" released quarterly by the U.S. Department of Agriculture, or a once-in-a-generation event (like the referendum on Quebec separation from Canada which created massive volatility in the price of the Canadian dollar).

A big surprise in a pig report can cause a sudden very large change in the price of hog and pork belly futures. The uncertainty preceding this report holds hog option prices way above what would be suggested by monitoring market volatility in hog futures. The large option premiums are a reflection of the collective understanding that just prior to the release of the report the market is not looking at a normal probability distribution of possible prices at all. If anything, the market is preoccupied with the likelihood of a sudden big price shift, either up *or* down. After a report of this type is released and the uncertainty is resolved, option prices will immediately shrink, though the degree of shrinkage will depend on the time to expiry of the option. As soon as uncertainty is removed from a futures market, its option prices almost always decline, *regardless of the magnitude of the impact the removal of the uncertainty may have on the futures price.* The time horizon should always be examined for the possibility of a major upcoming "event" whenever implied volatilities do not seem to line up in accordance with historical patterns.

Strictly speaking, then, an implied volatility is specific to one particular futures maturity. In practice you are not likely to encounter such a refinement in its definition. In the absence of information to the contrary, it is probably safe to assume that a stated implied volatility has been computed from option data pertinent to the the nearest future. It is indeed something of an oddity that where the implied volatility *ought* to be constant (different strikes on the same future), it is considered to be variable, whereas across different futures where implied volatility *ought* to be variable, it is usually (by omission) thought to be constant. So it goes.

*

Implied volatility is the quantity obtained when an option price is known, the time to expiry is known, and the option equation is solved for *v*, the unknown. Implied volatility is simply a way of expressing an option price so that it may be assessed in relation to market volatility—whatever that may be defined to be. Like implied volatility, market volatility is always expressed in annualized form, even though the data from which it is derived are measured on a daily basis. As discussed in Chapter 3, the standard deviation of 1-day price changes can be converted to a standard deviation on any time base by multiplying the standard deviation of daily price changes by the square root of the new time base, expressed in trading days. By convention 1 year is taken as the time base for specifying volatility.

If a full year's readings of actual daily price change (about 254 for the typical commodity) are assembled into a frequency distribution and the standard deviation of that distribution calculated, the resulting number is still a standard deviation of *daily* price changes. To convert this "daily" number to a reading of volatility it must be multiplied by $\sqrt{254}$, and the resulting product will be the *average volatility* observed over a 1-year period.

It is obvious that market conditions vary widely over a period as long as 1 year. Over the course of a year, all futures markets go through quiescent periods (where small daily price ranges are the norm) as well as through active periods (where large daily price ranges are the norm). These very different types of markets seem to come and go in more or less random fashion. Option values drop in unison during quiescent periods and rise in unison in active periods, but gradually rather than suddenly. The option pricing structure *can* change suddenly, but for other reasons.

The reason that option prices change gradually with time is straightforward enough; option traders are always wondering if an apparent change in the trading pattern of the future will be sustained, or if the apparent change is a temporary condition which will quickly revert to some longer-term norm. Because this question can be answered only after the fact, there will always be some option traders who vote in favor of a sustained change, and other option traders who vote in favor of *regression towards the mean*. Forecasting the market volatility of a commodity future from its recent or historic volatility is very much like forecasting the weather a few days in advance, say, without the benefit of any meteorological information.

Suppose you are in New York City in mid-July, in the middle of a heat wave, and that you are still able to breathe and think. Imagine yourself isolated in an apartment, with no access to any news whatsoever. The only information reaching you comes from a giant temperature indicator you can see out of the window, an indicator that has registered over 98° at noon every day for the past week. You know from experience that temperatures are way above normal (about 86°) and will eventually come down. But you are also aware that the heat wave has already lasted for a week and may well last for another week. Someone holds a gun to your head and asks you for your best estimate for the noon time temperature three days hence. Chances are you will opt for a temperature around 90°. And this will be a good estimate, for it makes maximum use of the information at your disposal—in this case an observed current high temperature, and prior experience of two opposing forces; the force of regression to the mean opposing the inertia of an established trend.

In the options market, exactly the same intuitions are at work, but the intuitions of thousands and thousands of individuals, each contributing a little bit of his own particular experience of how the future is linked to the past. Intuition is not instinct; it has to be learned. And some traders learn a great deal more from their experiences than others.

Market volatility exists in the eye of the beholder, and there are as many estimates of what market volatility really is as there are option traders playing the market. The trader best able to project upcoming market volatility from historical precedents—over the long haul—is the trader who will have the greatest trading edge in the market. The same historical data are available to all traders, but option data are notoriously hard to analyze because of the way prices are reported and records are kept. (Chapter 6 is devoted entirely to structuring historical option data in such a way that option prices can be related to futures volatility in a statistically meaningful way.)

Current market volatility may be estimated from historical volatility in two very different ways, each with its own set of advantages and disadvantages. First, let's be clear on the ways volatility is defined:

Implied volatility. The consensus of opinion on what the upcoming volatility of a future is going to be, as expressed through actual option prices.

Market volatility. What the volatility of a future has been in the recent or distant past, as expressed through a statistical analysis of actual futures price changes.

Market volatility may be subdivided into *short term*—measured from the most recent price behavior of the future—and *long term*—measured over a period as long as 1 year, say. The principal argument in favor of using short-term market volatility as the primary predictor of upcoming volatility is that commodity price profiles do change rather dramatically from month to month, or even week to week, and that to ignore this demonstrable fact is to ignore obviously useful information. It makes sense, the argument goes, to *increase* one's best estimate of market volatility in a commodity future as soon as the daily price swings in that future start to increase, and conversely, to *decrease* one's best estimate of market volatility as soon as daily price swings begin to decrease. There is, however, another argument which favors the longer-term view.

The argument in favor of using long-term volatility as a predictor rests on the observation that commodity prices always regress to typical behavior patterns, and that periods of unusually high or low activity in a futures market should therefore be viewed as *temporary aberrations* which ought to exert minimal influence on estimates of upcoming market volatility. A trader working on a long-term volatility model would be very slow to adjust an estimate of volatility in response to changing conditions in a futures market. Proponents of the long-term viewpoint can also argue that they are working with statistically more significant data, in that a long-term data set will contain up to a year's worth of readings—about 250—whereas a short-term data set may contain only 20 or so.

The short-term and long-term approaches to estimating market volatility can lead to conflicting conclusions on option valuation. For example, consider a futures market that has experienced a number of wild trading sessions and has now settled back into a trading pattern characterized by rather small daily price changes (Figure 5-3). The Japanese yen is a market with a tendency to generate such price patterns. A trader working with a short-term market volatility estimator will be focused on recent futures price data (perhaps the previous month's) and will be adjusting the volatility estimate downward, rather quickly, as the futures market quiets down. Actual option prices (implied volatilities) will be coming down more slowly and when compared with short-term volatility, may appear overvalued and therefore candidates for writing. A trader working with a long-term estimator of market volatility will be adjusting the estimate of market volatility very slowly, so that the implied volatility of the options may drop *below* the estimated market volatility. Under this scenario, the options may appear undervalued and candidates for buying.

One set of assumptions says buy, the other says sell. Which is correct? No one can say. The question of whether a short-term volatility estimator is superior to a long-term volatility estimator cannot be answered before-the-fact in any specific case. Can the question be answered in general terms? Possibly, but only through observation and analysis of a great deal of historical data. Before we get into drawing statistical inferences from empirical data, it will be helpful to look at ways in which market

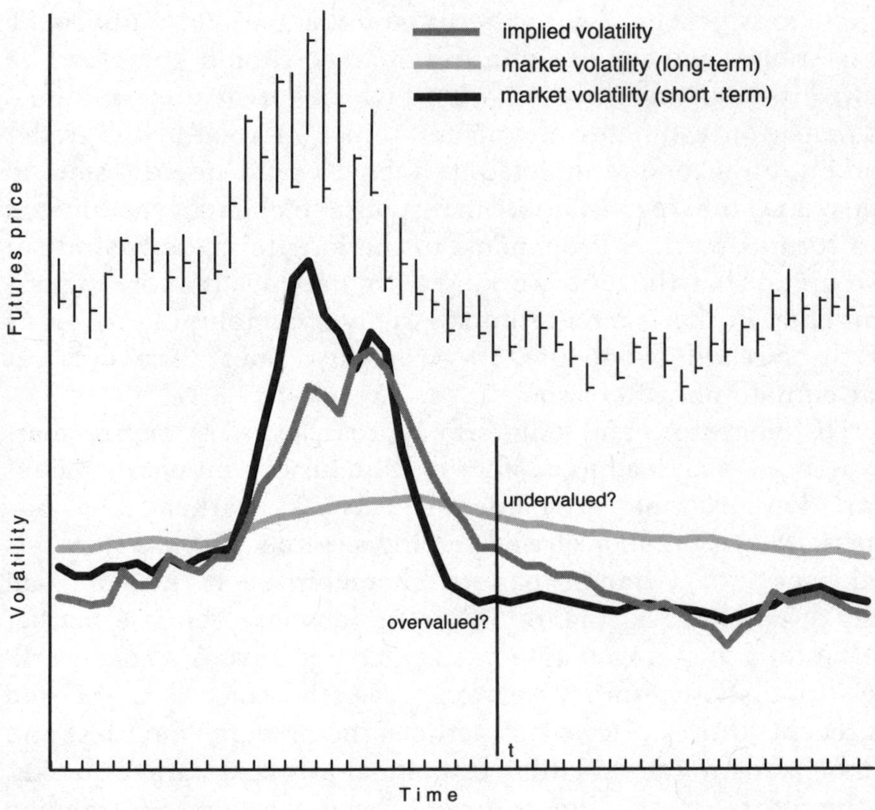

FIGURE 5-3. Estimating volatility from historical data is highly subjective and can produce very different interpretations of whether an option is overvalued or undervalued. In the example above, a futures market (daily high, low, close) moves rather quickly from a period characterized by large daily price swings to a period of much smaller daily price movement.

The short-term volatility estimator adjusts rapidly to changes in the daily price patterns of the future, while the long-term estimator hardly varies at all. If these market volatility estimators are compared with the implied volatility of the at-the-money option on the future, one estimator will be higher than the implied volatility while the other estimator will be lower; the option at time *t* appears *overvalued* by the short-term estimator, but *undervalued* by the long-term estimator.

volatility calculations are handled numerically, and in particular at some peculiar suggestions offered by certain people who appear to trade imaginary options from the confines of ivory towers.

*

Any statistically grounded attempt to forecast market volatility of a commodity future will involve calculating the standard deviation (or mean absolute deviation) of daily price changes, with the period chosen entirely at the discretion of the trader. A 6-week, continuously updated calculation of standard deviation would generally be considered a short-term volatility estimator. In Figure 5-4, the standard deviation of daily price changes for cocoa has been calculated using data from a 30-trading-day time interval. The procedure is straightforward enough. At the close of day 2, for example, you determine the price change from day 1, divide this number by the average of day 1 and day 2 futures closes, then multiply by 100 for a daily price change expressed as a percentage of its futures value. After calculating the standard deviation of these thirty observations and multiplying by $\sqrt{254}$, you arrive at a estimate of market volatility—in this case 33.3 percent. Were a time interval of 15 days or 60 days to be used instead of 30, the estimate of market volatility would, of course, be different.

In the calculations of Figure 5-4, equal weighting is given to each observation; that is, the price change 30 days back has the same degree of influence on the calculated volatility as the most recent price change. A good case can be made for assigning greater importance to recent observations, and this refinement can be easily incorporated into the basic calculation. Let's stick with the unweighted calculation for present, for there are some complicating suggestions from other writers regarding the calculation of market volatility that demand examination.

At some point in the development of option theory, the idea took hold that simple daily price changes could not be used directly to estimate daily volatility. This incorrect notion arose from the correct observation that while a price can never go below zero, it may double, triple, or go to any multiple on the upside. This latter observation is equivalent to postulating that the distribution of an absolute futures prices over the fullness of time is a *lognormal* distribution rather than a normal distribution. I have no argument with that.

However, the correct observation that absolute prices are not normally distributed provides no insight into the expected

Day	Price P_i	Change (ΔP_i)	(P_{av})	$\frac{100\,(\Delta P_i)}{(P_{av})}$	$R_i = \frac{P_i}{P_{i-1}}$	$100 \log_e(R_i)$
1	1364					
2	1347	-17.0	1356	-1.254	0.9875	-1.254
3	1335	-12.0	1341	-0.895	0.9911	-0.895
4	1321	-14.0	1328	-1.054	0.9895	-1.054
5	1346	25.0	1334	1.875	1.0189	1.875
6	1370	24.0	1358	1.767	1.0178	1.767
7	1411	41.0	1390	2.949	1.0299	2.949
8	1372	-39.0	1392	-2.803	0.9724	-2.803
9	1386	14.0	1379	1.015	1.0102	1.015
10	1427	41.0	1406	2.915	1.0296	2.915
11	1460	33.0	1444	2.286	1.0231	2.286
12	1441	-19.0	1450	-1.310	0.9870	-1.310
13	1447	6.0	1444	0.416	1.0042	0.416
14	1426	-21.0	1436	-1.462	0.9855	-1.462
15	1482	56.0	1454	3.851	1.0393	3.852
16	1513	31.0	1498	2.070	1.0209	2.070
17	1490	-23.0	1502	-1.532	0.9848	-1.532
18	1535	45.0	1512	2.975	1.0302	2.975
19	1497	-38.0	1516	-2.507	0.9752	-2.507
20	1522	25.0	1510	1.656	1.0167	1.656
21	1575	53.0	1548	3.423	1.0348	3.423
22	1540	-35.0	1558	-2.247	0.9778	-2.247
23	1511	-29.0	1526	-1.901	0.9812	-1.901
24	1495	-16.0	1503	-1.065	0.9894	-1.065
25	1470	-25.0	1482	-1.686	0.9833	-1.686
26	1488	18.0	1479	1.217	1.0122	1.217
27	1462	-26.0	1475	-1.763	0.9825	-1.763
28	1447	-15.0	1454	-1.031	0.9897	-1.031
29	1471	24.0	1459	1.645	1.0166	1.645
30	1432	-39.0	1452	-2.687	0.9735	-2.687
31	1460	28.0	1446	1.936	1.0196	1.936

Standard deviation = 2.09 percent
Volatility (SD x $\sqrt{254}$) = 33.31 percent

FIGURE 5-4. *Market volatility* projected for cocoa using the standard deviation calculation for daily price changes on a thirty-trading-day time base. Daily price changes are *first* divided by the average of the 'surrounding' daily closing prices (P_{av} above) and then multiplied by 100 to express them as percentages. To determine market volatility —by convention annualized—it is necessary to multiply the standard deviation of daily price changes by $\sqrt{254}$.

It has become common practice in options literature to calculate market volatility from "logarithmic returns." Using this method, each absolute price is divided by the preceding absolute price, and the standard deviation of the logarithm of these ratios is calculated. As is evident from the final two columns above, the logarithmic ratios are identical to the price changes expressed as percentages, which means the logarithmic volatility calculation will yield the same result as the simple price change volatility calculation. The logarithmic complication hardly seems worth the bother.

distribution of daily price changes, particularly when the latter are expressed as percentages of absolute values. Expressed as a percentage, a daily price change has a built-in compensator for radical shifts in the absolute price level. Furthermore, from purely practical considerations, a futures price is very unlikely to approach zero or double during the relatively short life span of an option.

Nevertheless, the fashion is to calculate market volatility via logarithms. (See the final two columns of Figure 5-4 for a comparison with the basic calculation.) Computationally, the logarithmic method goes something like this: You take the price on day 2, divide by the price on day 1, and call this a "return." You then calculate the natural logarithm of this "return" and finally compute the standard deviation of these logarithmic returns. And you wind up with exactly the same answer as the nonlogarithmic calculation, but by a considerably more devious route.

The classical standard deviation formula used in volatility calculations involves summing a series of squared terms, each of these terms being defined as the difference between an observed price change and the average of *all* the observed price changes:

$$(\text{Standard deviation})^2 = \frac{(\Delta P_i - \Delta P_{av})^2}{(N - 1)}$$

where ΔP_i = daily price change on the i th day

ΔP_{av} = average of all observations of ΔP_i

N = number of observations

In a trading market, or a market which ends up virtually unchanged in price between the first observation and last, the quantity ΔP_{av} will be very close to zero. But, in a strongly trending market of *comparable real volatility* the quantity ΔP_{av} will not be close to zero, since values of ΔP_i will be either mostly positive

Day	Price P_i	Change (ΔP_i)	$(\Delta P_i - \Delta P_{av})$	P_{av}	$\frac{100 \times (\Delta P_i - \Delta P_{av})}{(P_{av})}$	$\frac{100 \times \vert\Delta P_i\vert}{(P_{av})}$
1	1210					
2	1194	–16	–16	1202	–1.331	1.331
3	1160	–34	–34	1177	–2.689	2.889
4	1188	28	28	1174	2.385	2.385
5	1185	–3	–3	1186	–0.253	0.253
6	1170	–15	–15	1178	–1.274	1.274
7	1153	–17	–17	1162	–1.464	1.464
8	1178	25	25	1166	2.145	2.145
9	1172	–6	–6	1175	–0.511	0.511
10	1195	23	23	1184	1.943	1.943
11	1210	15	15	1202	1.247	1.247

$\Delta P_{av} = 0$ (MAD) = 1.544

Standard deviation (day) = 1.82%
Volatility (SD x $\sqrt{254}$) = 29.01%
Mean absolute deviatlon = 1.54%

Day	Price P_i	Change (ΔP_i)	$(\Delta P_i - \Delta P_{av})$	P_{av}	$\frac{100 \times (\Delta P_i - \Delta P_{av})}{(P_{av})}$	$\frac{100 \times \vert\Delta P_i\vert}{(P_{av})}$
1	1210					
2	1226	16	0	1218	0.000	1.314
3	1260	34	18	1243	1.448	2.735
4	1288	28	12	1274	0.942	2.198
5	1285	–3	–19	1286	–1.477	0.233
6	1300	15	–1	1292	–0.077	1.161
7	1317	17	1	1308	0.076	1.299
8	1342	25	9	1330	0.677	1.880
9	1336	–6	–22	1339	–1.643	0.448
10	1359	23	7	1348	0.519	1.707
11	1374	15	–1	1366	–0.073	1.098

$\Delta P_{av} = 16$ (MAD) = 1.407

Standard deviation (day) = 0.98%
Volatility (SD x $\sqrt{254}$) = 15.78%
Mean absolute deviatlon = 1.41%

FIGURE 5-5. A potentially serious error in the computation of volatility can result when the standard deviation of price changes is calculated in a runaway bull or bear trend. In the two price series above, daily price changes are of the *same magnitude*, indicating that volatility should be approximately the same. Yet, in the upward trending market, the calculated volatility is only half of what it is in the trading market.

In the limiting case, if a future were to advance by a constant amount every day, the variable $(\Delta P_i - \Delta P_{av})$ would tend toward zero, as would the standard deviation of daily price changes and the volatility. Using the mean absolute deviation, *MAD*, as a measure of volatility yields consistent results in both price series, the slightly lower value in the second series resulting from an increase in the absolute price level (a divisor).

or mostly negative. If ΔP_{av} turns out to be significantly nonzero, the standard deviation calculated from the formula above will not reflect the true volatility of the market (Figure 5-5).

In a strongly trending market, a reading of market volatility—as calculated by the standard deviation in the equation above—will be much lower than the implied volatility calculated from actual option prices, and a trader comparing these two volatilities might conclude that the options are overvalued and therefore be inclined to the sell side rather than the buy side. Were enough sellers to be drawn in for this reason, the net effect would be an artificial depression of option prices during runaway bull or bear phases in a futures market. Whether in reality this happens can only be answered empirically, if at all. It remains an interesting conjecture, though, and like all good conjectures it is based on reasoning, rather than on accidental observation.

In estimating market volatility from historical price data one must think clearly about what is being measured. In particular, it is crucial never to confuse *absolute* daily prices with daily price *changes.* Into this pothole, even the mightiest have stumbled (Figure 5-6).

In the development of Ockham's equation, it was shown that the *simple average* of a series of price change—taking all price changes to be positive—could be used instead of the standard deviation to estimate the fair value of an option. It was also demonstrated that the validity of this estimate was *independent* of the nature of the distribution of price changes. And furthermore, it has been shown in this chapter that using the mean absolute deviation of a set of price changes rather than the standard deviation of these price changes leads to market volatility estimates that are unaffected by trend. For the remainder of this manuscript, therefore, option fair value and futures market volatility will be estimated using the mean absolute deviation as the primary empirical statistic.

To estimate the fair value of an at-the-money option from empirical data, Eq. 3-1 from Chapter 3 is simply expanded to include t, the time till expiry of the option:

Some very peculiar advice. . .

*The computation of volatility is always a difficult problem for mathematical application. In the Black-Scholes model, volatility is defined as the annual standard deviation of the stock price. This is the regular statistical definition of the standard deviation.

$$s^2 = \frac{\sum_{i=1}^{n} (P_i - P)^2}{(n-1)}$$

$$v = \frac{s}{P}$$

where

P = average stock price of all P_i's

P_i = daily stock price

n = number of days observed

v = volatility

* From *Options as a Strategic Investment,* by Lawrence McMillan (NYIF Corp., 1993), p. 462.

FIGURE 5-6. The method of estimating historical volatility described above, lifted verbatim from a popular text on option trading, will produce very misleading results. At face value, the formula is plausible in that it seems to make use of all the available data, namely each price in the price series.

The error in using *absolute* prices rather than *daily price changes* arises when the *order* in which absolute prices occur is lost, as when using the formula above. In a strongly trending market, the quantity $\Sigma(P_i - P)^2$ will be a very large number, while in a trading market with the same magnitude of daily price swings, the quantity $\Sigma(P_i - P)^2$ will be relatively small. Same volatility, two very different answers. Something is clearly amiss. *Daily price changes must be used* when estimating volatility.

$$\text{Fair value of an at-the-money option} = 0.5 \times \sqrt{t} \times \text{MAD} \qquad \text{(Eq. 5-1)}$$

In Eq. 5-1, fair value and MAD may be expressed either in units of absolute price or as percentages of the base future price. To estimate market volatility (which you will recall is *defined* as annualized standard deviation) from a series of price changes, and to make this estimate *consistent* with the implied volatility in Ockham's equation, daily standard deviation is first related to mean absolute deviation, as before, by the formula:

$$SD_{daily} = 1.25 \times MAD$$

Next, annualized standard deviation is related to daily standard deviation, as before by the formula:

$$SD_{annual} = \sqrt{254} \times SD_{daily}$$

So that:

$$SD_{annual} = \sqrt{254} \times 1.25 \times MAD$$

Or, to a very good approximation:

$$\text{Market volatility} = 20 \times MAD \qquad \text{(Eq. 5-2)}$$

In Eq. 5-2, market volatility should be expressed as a percentage, if it is to be directly compared with an implied volatility calculated from an options formula. That is to say, MAD should be expressed as a percentage of futures price. Strictly speaking, the validity of Eq. 5-2 depends on the special relationship that exists between the standard deviation and the mean absolute deviation of a normal distribution. This equation may have to be modified later after empirical testing of actual market data.

This completes the theoretical discussion on options pricing. Some of the analysis may seem unnecessarily detailed—and it undoubtedly is—but it has been included so that the reader may correlate what I have to say with what has already been published by others in the field.

Options are not obliged to price themselves to conform to any mathematical theory, mine or anyone else's; the reality of the marketplace is what really counts. At this point, it will be appropriate to switch from theory to observation, for it can only be through empirical analysis, through an extensive investigation of what has happened in the past, that a systematically profitable approach to options trading—if it exists at all—is likely to be uncovered. Historical data on options are hard to get at and hard to structure for analysis. But the information is certainly there.

PART THREE

OPTION REALITY

CHAPTER SIX

PHANTOM OF THE OPTION

The difficulty in analyzing historical option data is that so many of the parameters seem to be changing at the same time. With a commodity future, the only variable that changes day to day is its price, so that any sequence of prices can be logically compared with any other sequence of prices. Not so with an option. Each day, the *difference* between a specific option's strike price and the price of its associated future changes, causing the option price itself to change in a rather complicated way (if this were not complicated there would be no need for the million dollar formula or any of its surrogates). Furthermore, the time to expiry of the option diminishes by 1 day, every day, also causing the price of the option to change in a nonlinear fashion.

For reasons that have been explained in previous chapters, the only option that merits empirical investigation is the *at-the-money* option—specifically, the put and the call whose strike price exactly equals the current futures price, whatever that price may turn out to be at the close of trading on any given day. What I propose developing, and comparing on a day-to-day basis, is a sequence of option prices, each related to a different strike price!

On first consideration, such a comparison might seem improbable. Prices of at-the-money options are not quoted as such, since the only time an at-the-money option can be measured is when a future closes exactly on an option strike price—a rather rare event, occurring, perhaps, no more than one time out of a hundred. Even the closest-to-the-money option is hard to pin down. One day the closest-to-the-money option may be—

in the case of the September S&P series, say—the September 950; the next day it may be the September 960. Apples and oranges, so to speak.

Now, it *is* true that during most trading sessions a future will trade at the strike price of one of its options, and theoretically therefore, if one were nimble enough and had ten sets of eyes, it would be possible to get an instantaneous fix on the relationship between an at-the-money option and its future on a more or less daily basis. Fine in theory, but hardly a practical proposition, and even then what would be established is a price relationship existing at one particular instant of time and specific to one specific option. What's more, the at-the-money option would most likely be one with a different strike price every day. All of which helps to explain why empirical research into option pricing remains virgin territory. Therefore, in exploring this territory for answers, what I *do* ask of the reader is a temporary suspension of disbelief.

Every day, closing prices *are* posted for the closest-to-the-money puts and calls. These options may not be identified explicitly as being the closest-to-the money options, but there is always a closest strike price by which to identify them as such. Imagine now that these closest-to-the-money option prices can somehow be corrected for the amount by which they are out-of-the money so that they become surrogate at-the-money options—*phantom options,* if you will. These phantom options will now be directly comparable on a day-to-day basis. For, although the strike price of the at-the-money option is certainly going to be changing almost every day, this parameter will now have been effectively removed as a variable. The key problem now reduces to whether close-to-the-money option prices be effectively corrected so that they express what true at-the-money option prices *would* have closed at.

*

As discussed in Chapter 3, the price of an at-the-money call *must* equal the price of the corresponding at-the-money put. If a put *and* a call having the same strike price are bought or written as a pair, the combination is called a *straddle,* and if the transaction is completed when the options are trading exactly at the money, the straddle premium paid or received will be exactly *double* the premium that would be paid or received for the put or the call separately.

Straddle prices may be calculated from option price tables published in the financial press simply by adding together the prices of the put and the call at any particular strike price. With rare exceptions, for any given future at any given time, *a straddle will have its minimum value when it is trading at the money* (Figure 6-1).

When straddle price is plotted against strike price, the resulting curve is parabolic with a rather flat base extending on either side of the minimum value. This flatness merely reflects the obvious reality that relatively small fluctuations in the price of a future are going to have similar but opposite effects on the put and call components of the straddle. For small price increases in the underlying future, what the call gains the put will lose, and vice-versa, of course, with small price decreases. Away from the money, the slope of the curve begins to rise steeply; with a large price change in a future and especially with a sustained series of price changes in the same direction one of the component options will begin to appreciate more rapidly than the other depreciates.

Due to the flatness of the straddle profile, the price of a close-to-the-money straddle will be almost identical to the price of the true at-the-money straddle. The question is how close does a futures settlement have to be to an option strike price before it is safe to take the nearest straddle as equivalent in price to the true at the money straddle? Whenever option strike prices are relatively close together—roughly speaking, when the separations between strike prices approximate the daily trading range of the future—the price of the closest-to-the-money straddle will be virtually equivalent to the price of the at-the-money straddle. The intervals between option strike prices are often sufficiently close that this equivalency prevails. However, in certain commodities the interval between strikes far exceeds the average daily trading range, and the true at-the-money straddle price must be estimated by applying a correction factor to the closest-to-the-money straddle.

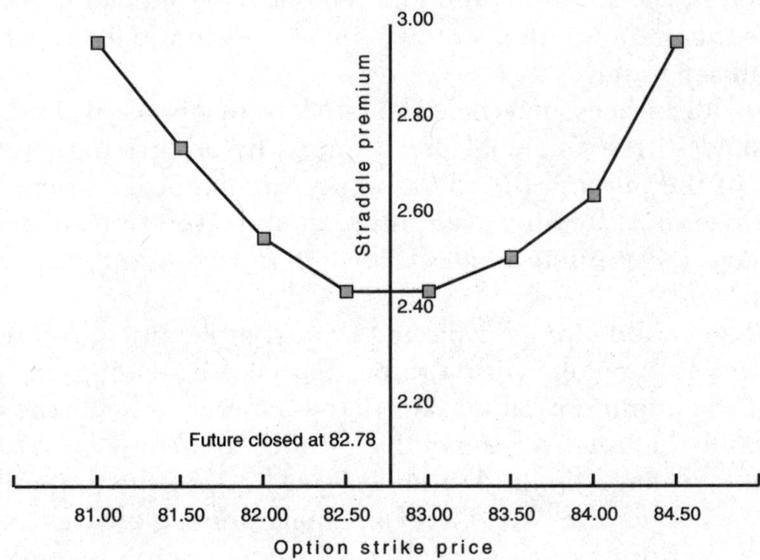

FIGURE 6-1. The straddle curve (straddle premium versus option strike price) is very flat at strike prices close to where the future is trading. Over a sizable range of futures price change, the price of straddles at different strikes will vary little, because the call will gain what the put loses and vice-versa. The market offers no prizes for information everyone knows—futures prices are *bound* to fluctuate.

In the example above—measured at one particular instant in time—the *true* at-the-money straddle implied at the futures price of 82.78 is almost identical to the actual straddle premiums registered at strikes of 82.50 and 83.00. In this particular configuration for the Japanese yen, it would take a fast move of about 100 points in the futures price to cause the at-the-money straddle price to increase by 10 points. In other words, the price of a straddle written close-to-the-money will change very slowly—at first. Of course, if the future embarks on a sustained move in one direction, either the put or call component of the straddle will begin to appreciate faster than the other side depreciates, and the total value of the straddle premium will increase at an accelerating rate given by the slope of the straddle curve.

The only way to tell what that correction factor ought to be is to search for instances where the true at-the-money option prices are known and to compare these prices with the also known prices of the nearest strike options. It is not common for a commodity future to close exactly on the strike price of one of its options, but it does happen. Here are three such instances from the historical record:

	AT THE MONEY			LOWER STRIKE			HIGHER STRIKE		
	Put	Call	Straddle	Put	Call	Straddle	Put	Call	Straddle
Swiss franc 6850	1.22	1.22	2.44	0.98	1.49	2.47	1.47	1.02	2.49
Cocoa 1450	0.59	0.59	1.18	0.34	0.89	1.23	0.82	0.40	1.22
Coffee 115	4.50	4.50	9.00	2.71	7.45	10.16	7.73	2.40	10.13

Because it has many strike prices at intervals comparable with the daily trading range of its future, the Swiss franc straddle premiums at strikes of *6800* and *6900* respectively are only slightly higher than the true at-the-money straddle premium at a strike price of *6850*. But, with cocoa and coffee, strike prices are relatively infrequent compared with the daily ranges of their respective futures prices, and the true straddle prices differ significantly from the straddle prices registered at the surrounding strikes.

Consider, in detail, the Swiss franc data above. If the two highest value option components of each of the *6800* and *6900* straddles are summed and divided by the sum of the two lowest value option components, the following ratio is obtained:

$$R_{\text{swiss}} = \frac{1.47 + 1.49}{0.98 + 1.02}$$

$$= 1.48$$

If, at the same time, the two equidistant and nearest-to-the-money straddle values, 2.47 and 2.49, are averaged, the correction multiplier *CM* necessary to produce the known at-the-money straddle price can be determined as follows:

$$CM_{\text{swiss}} = \frac{2.44}{2.48}$$

$$= 0.984$$

Repeating the procedure for cocoa and coffee produces the following sets of paired values:

$$CM_{swiss} = 0.984 \quad \text{with } R_{swiss} = 1.487$$
$$CM_{cocoa} = 0.963 \quad \text{with } R_{cocoa} = 2.311$$
$$CM_{coffee} = 0.887 \quad \text{with } R_{coffee} = 3.009$$

These preliminary observations suggest a possible empirical relationship between *CM* and *R*. An extensive search of the historical record uncovered about 30 instances where a commodity future had closed within a price tick of the strike price of one of its options. The search covered records from all actively traded options—grains, financials, metals, etcetera. When 30 or so *CM* and *R* values as defined above are calculated and plotted on a chart (Figure 6-2) they indicate a linear relationship between the variables, and a good straight-line fit to the data is given by the equation:

$$CM = 1.04 - (0.04 \times R)$$

Applying this correction multiplier to published option data, from which R can always be calculated, one can estimate the true at-the-money straddle value for *any* commodity future at *any* closing price. The correction may not be exact, but it will certainly be close.

*

Consider the correction suggested above applied on a daily basis to the closest-to-the-money straddle price of a given commodity future. The result will be a series of "phantom" straddle prices, since the corrected at-the-money straddle will have a theoretical strike price (the futures price) which does not, in general, correspond to any listed strike price. Does the phantom aspect of the price series make it any less valid as a data base for hypothetical testing?

I don't think so. For, though not explicitly stated, there *is* always an *implied* at-the-money put, call, and straddle with a strike price equal to the futures close on that day. Phantom

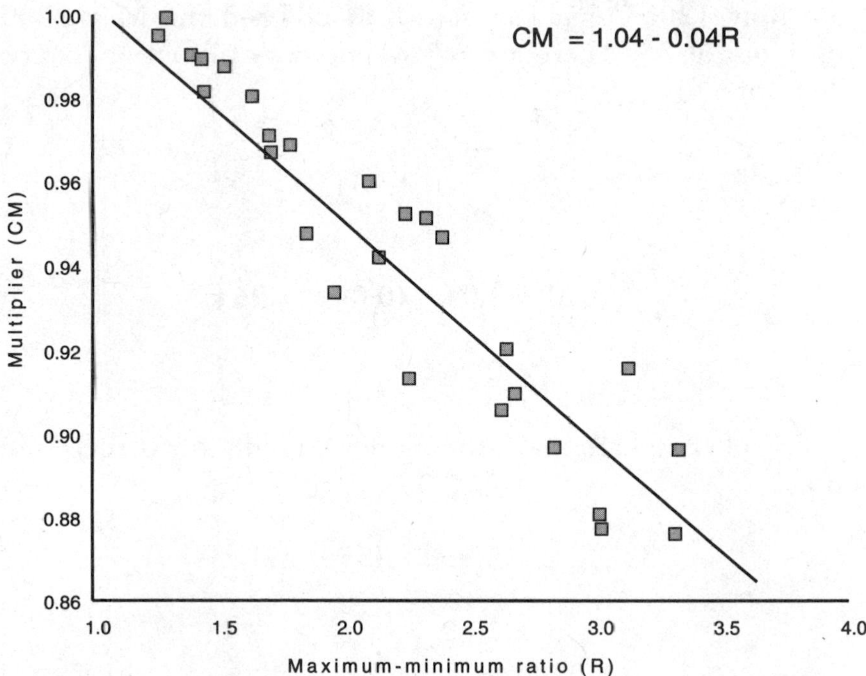

FIGURE 6-2. In order to establish a convincing relationship between *R* and *M*, it was necessary to search the historical record for instances where a commodity future closed exactly on one of its strike prices. Thirty or so such instances have been identified and plotted on a suitably scaled chart, the object being to approximate an empirical equation expressing the relationship. Fortunately, the plotted points fall more or less along a straight line, indicating a linear relationship conveniently expressed by the equation:

$$CM = 104 - (0.04 \times R)$$

The *CM* versus *R* relationship, derived from data where the at-the-money straddle price was ***known***, may now be applied as a correcting factor in situations where the at-the-money straddle price is *not* known.

options generate coherent price sequences whereas real options do not, and the phantom option possesses the one option statistic that can be compared directly with *that same option statistic* on the previous day or on any other day. Some numerical examples will help illustrate the point.

Example 6-1. On February 22, 1996, the May sugar future closes at 1179, making *1200* the closest option strike price.

The May 1200 sugar call settles at 28, and the May 1200 sugar put at 55. There are 37 trading days till option expiry. Therefore:

$$R = \frac{55}{28} = 1.964$$

$$CM = 1.04 - (0.04 \times 1.964)$$

$$= 0.962$$

The value of the phantom at-the-money straddle *PS* is therefore given by:

$$PS_{\text{Feb }22} = 0.962 \times (55 + 28)$$

$$= 79.8$$

***Example* 6-2.** One day later, February 23, 1996, the May sugar future closes at 1160, making 1150 the closest option strike price. The May 1150 sugar call closes at 46, and the May 1150 sugar put at 33. There are 36 trading days till expiry. As before:

$$R = \frac{46}{33} = 1.394$$

$$CM = 1.04 - (0.04 \times 1.394)$$

$$= 0.984$$

The value of the phantom at-the-money straddle *PS* is given by:

$$PS_{\text{Feb }23} = 0.984 \times (46 + 33)$$

$$= 77.8$$

The phantom straddles of February 22 and February 23 are directly comparable even though they are derived from option data pertaining to two *different* strike prices. By essentially freezing out strike price as a variable, the possibility of constructing a workable data base on which to test option hypotheses expands enormously.

It is a short step from estimating a phantom straddle price to calculating an implied volatility. Ockham's equation—the fundamental equation relating option price, time, and implied volatility—states that:

$$\text{ATMO}_t = \frac{v \times \sqrt{t}}{40}$$

where

ATMO_t = the at-the-money option price expressed as a percentage of the futures price

v = the option volatility also expressed as a percentage of the futures price

t = the number of days till option expiry

Since the at-the-money straddle is known to be exactly double the value of either the at-the-money put or the at-the-money call, Ockham's equation applied to a straddle may be restated thus:

$$\text{ATMS}_t = \frac{v \times \sqrt{t}}{20}$$

$$\text{or } v = \frac{20 \times \text{ATMS}_t}{\sqrt{t}} \qquad \text{(Eq. 6-1)}$$

where $ATMS_t$ = the at-the-money *straddle* price expressed as a percentage of the futures price

With *PS* now clearly synonymous with ATMS, the estimated at-the-money straddle prices for May sugar on February 22 and February 23 may now be converted to implied volatilities by application of Eq. 6-1, using the appropriate number of trading days to expiry, 37 and 36, respectively:

$$\text{Implied volatility for May sugar calculated on February 22} = \frac{20 \times ATMS_t}{\sqrt{t}}$$

$$= \frac{20}{\sqrt{37}} \times \frac{79.8 \times 100}{1179}$$

$$= 22.23 \text{ percent}$$

$$\text{And, by a similar calculation, implied volatility on February 23} = \frac{20}{\sqrt{36}} \times \frac{77.8 \times 100}{1160}$$

$$= 22.35 \text{ percent}$$

The calculations above are presented in this detailed way to clearly demonstrate the relationship between the three variables of paramount importance in option price evaluation—at-the-money straddle price, implied volatility, and time remaining to expiry.

In deriving the solutions above, time t was taken to be the number of trading days till option expiry. There is some debate about whether *trading* days or *calendar* days should be used in an implied volatility calculation. The million dollar formula uses calendar days expressed as a fraction of 365. For options with a long term to expiry the distinction between calendar days and trading days is inconsequential. But, for an option with a short term to expiry the difference can be significant.

The theoretical argument in favor of calendar days contends that the forces affecting a futures price are independent of whether the market is open or closed for trading, and that the two weekend days ought therefore to be considered as opportunities for the futures price to vary and ought therefore to be included in the time to expiry. There is some merit to this argument in the case of agricultural commodities but less merit when it comes to financial instruments. For pragmatic reasons alone, one standard has to be selected for use in all markets.

On balance, there are good practical reasons for preferring number of trading days over calendar days. In the first place, market volatility calculations cannot distinguish between weekdays and weekends. Therefore, neither, logically, should implied volatilities do so. Furthermore, the available empirical evidence strongly suggests that number of trading days more accurately reflects true variability.

Whether a weekend is equivalent to *two* trading days (implicit in using calendar days in an option pricing formula) or *no* trading days (implicit in using number of trading days in a formula) is a question that can be tested empirically, without reference to option prices at all. What is needed is a large database of futures price changes, and futures price change is a major component of the data base put together for this empirical research.

Of the almost 4000 futures price changes recorded in this data base, 80 percent occur weekday to weekday, with the remaining 20 percent occurring over a weekend (Figure 6-3). The ratio of average daily change occurring over a weekend to average daily change occurring between weekdays is measured at 1.08. If Saturday and Sundays are truly equivalent to weekdays—as far as opportunity for price variation to occur—then, in accordance with the square-root time relationship linking independent price variations over different time periods, the ratio of average daily changes (weekend versus weekday) ought to be $\sqrt{3}$ or approximately 1.714. If Saturdays and Sundays are *not* equivalent to weekdays, this ratio ought to be 1. The observed ratio of 1.08 *implies* a time multiplier of 1.17, or less than an hour's worth of open market trading.

	AVERAGE DAILY PRICE CHANGE (%)		
	Weekdays	Over weekend	Ratio
FINANCIALS			
S&P 500	0.622	0.672	1.080
T-Bonds	0.485	0.394	0.812
Swiss franc	0.409	0.395	0.966
Yen	0.367	0.381	1.038
RESOURCE			
Gold	0.262	0.338	1.290
Silver	0.805	0.834	1.036
Crude oil	1.434	1.615	1.126
Cotton	0.919	0.738	0.803
FOOD			
Soybeans	0.922	1.103	1.196
Wheat	1.345	1.307	0.972
Corn	1.099	1.381	1.257
Cattle	0.724	0.767	1.059
Cocoa	0.903	0.917	1.016
Coffee	1.476	2.140	1.450
Sugar	0.932	1.085	1.164
		Average →	1.084

FIGURE 6-3. The question of whether Saturdays and Sundays should be accorded equal weightings with weekdays can be answered by checking if the average price change over weekends is substantially higher from the average price change between regular weekdays.

A ratio of 1.714 (the square root of 3) would indicate that equal weighting be given to *all* days. A ratio of 1 would indicate that weekends should be ignored in the options formula. The observed average ratio from 3781 observations was 1.084.

In all the tables and calculations that follow, the time till expiry is taken as the number of trading days. By way of compromise, I do count a 3- or 4-day weekend or a midweek holiday as *one* additional trading day.

Using the techniques described in this chapter, it is now possible to determine, on a daily basis, the true value of the at-the-money straddle on *any* future on *any* commodity—from option tables published in the financial press. With the value of the straddle determined, the implied volatility is also determined.

The complicated matrixes of option data, where every parameter is changing day to day, has been simplified into two familiar price-time series—a strike independent at-the-money straddle versus time, and an implied volatility versus time. Figure 6-4 illustrates in tabular form samples of these two data series for crude oil. (Complete tabulations on this model for the 15 actively traded futures comprising the data base can be found under "Volatility Profiles" at the back of the book.)

Precisely how information can best be extracted from this data base is the subject of the next chapter. Suffice it to say that, in terms of price sequences versus time, we now have as much historical option data available as historical futures data. This data can be used to determine basic option trading expectations and to test different option trading strategies. Whether the data base will be large enough to convince the reader of the validity of any statistical inferences drawn from it, I cannot be sure. But of one thing, I *can* be sure. As far as data collecting and data processing is concerned, this is as far as I could reasonably go and still have a life.

CRUDE OIL April 1996 option and April 1996 future

Date	Futures price	Closest strike option max.	Closest strike option min.	$ATMS_t$	Trading days left	Implied volatility
Jan 2	1884	73	54	125	53	18.26
Jan 3	1890	68	58	125	52	18.36
Jan 4	1893	67	60	126	51	18.70
Jan 5	1928	73	57	129	50	18.86
Jan 9	1896	65	61	126	48	19.13
Jan 10	1878	73	51	122	47	18.93
Jan 11	1805	65	60	125	46	20.35
Jan 12	1774	78	53	129	45	21.60
Jan 15	1779	74	53	125	44	21.18
Jan 16	1743	72	65	136	43	23.87
Jan 17	1779	81	56	135	42	23.34
Jan 18	1796	70	68	138	41	23.97
Jan 19	1781	73	57	129	40	22.82
Jan 22	1774	81	56	135	39	24.29
Jan 23	1767	78	56	132	38	24.22
Jan 24	1788	71	59	129	37	23.71
Jan 25	1737	74	60	133	36	25.47
Jan 26	1736	75	60	134	35	26.03
Jan 29	1716	78	62	139	34	27.69
Jan 30	1724	81	57	136	33	27.40
Jan 31	1737	74	61	134	32	27.24
Feb 1	1731	79	59	136	31	28.25
Feb 2	1738	73	61	133	30	27.93
Feb 5	1717	80	62	140	29	30.36
Feb 6	1730	78	58	134	28	29.30
Feb 7	1731	74	55	127	27	28.29
Feb 8	1733	66	49	113	26	25.67
Feb 9	1738	60	48	107	25	24.61
Feb 12	1750	50	50	100	24	23.33
Feb 13	1835	61	46	106	23	24.00
Feb 14	1835	64	49	112	22	25.94
Feb 15	1837	64	51	114	21	27.04
Feb 16	1839	63	52	114	20	27.73
Feb 20	1927	74	47	118	18	28.92
Feb 21	1971	77	48	122	17	30.02
Feb 22	1985	77	62	138	16	34.67
Feb 23	1906	70	64	133	15	36.17
Feb 26	1939	71	60	130	14	35.85
Feb 27	1970	73	53	124	13	34.94
Feb 28	1928	71	50	119	12	35.63
Feb 29	1953	59	54	113	11	34.76
Mar 1	1944	58	52	109	10	35.62
Mar 4	1920				9	
Mar 5	1953				8	
Mar 6	2019				7	
Mar 7	1981				6	
Mar 8	1961				5	
Mar 11	1991				4	
Mar 12	2046				3	
Mar 13	2058				2	
Mar 14	2116				1	
Mar 15	2199 April option expires					

FIGURE 6-4. A sequence of at-the-money straddles and implied volatilities calculated for April crude oil over a 2-month time interval. Note how the implied volatility almost doubles between January 2 and March 1, even though the absolute price of the future rises only by a small amount.

The column headed $ATMS_i$ is the "corrected" at-the-money straddle price.

CHAPTER SEVEN

THE PROMISED LAND

Anyone who has seriously tested a "system" for trading commodity futures using historical price data knows that chance plays a large part in the outcome of any one hypothetical trade. One system is long gold with a sell stop at 295; another system is also long with a sell stop at 293. Gold comes down to 294, makes a bottom and immediately takes off on the upside. The first system is stopped out of its long and goes short, the second system stays long. The short-term performances for the two systems are radically different, even though the result is clearly a pure fluke. Savvy researches are well aware of the sensitivity of systems to fluke occurrences and take precautionary steps to eliminate chance from invalidating any general conclusions they are trying to draw.

First, they scrupulously avoid the temptation to start testing the system at a favorable time. It is a powerful temptation and may act even on a subliminal level. The way to avoid a bias of this kind is to choose one's initial conditions in a way that is *clearly* objective. To that end, to eliminate as far as possible any selectivity in choosing a period, I have dealt with one specific calendar year, 1996—beginning on the first trading day and ending on the last trading day (1996 is the latest calendar year for which data were available when the study began).

A second precautionary line to take in preparing to test a trading hypothesis is to *broaden the scope* of testing to cover as many different markets as possible, to take as large samples as are practicable, and to restrict one's conclusions to the market as a whole. To that end, I have selected 15 actively traded commodity futures markets with actively traded options, covering as wide a range of market types as possible; the selected markets include grains, meats, metals, tropical products, resources, and financial instruments. The goal is *not* to come to any conclusions about particular markets—the sample sizes cannot support this, but rather to come to particular conclusions about the market in general.

*

Suppose it were possible to obtain for every option ever written its residual value at expiry. If these residual values could then be summed and compared with the sum of the premiums received for writing them, it would be possible to answer, definitively, that most pressing of questions: Who has the edge in the market, the writer of options or the buyer of options?

It is only practical to look at a very small sample from the entire universe of options ever written. But this can still be a large absolute sample, and if made large enough should be representative of the universe of all options. How large is large? The data base available for testing here includes estimates of the true at-the-money straddle values and implied volatilities for 15 commodity contracts over 250 or so consecutive trading days—amounting to about 3750 observations in total.

Imagine that all 3750 of these at-the-money straddles were actually written—15 per day, every day, for an entire year, and that each straddle was held until it expired. Hold on, you say: How could these straddles possibly have been written? They have *implied* strike prices, not *real* strike prices. True enough. But, from a statistical perspective it makes no difference whether the straddle price is taken at a theoretical strike price or at a true strike price *as long as the correction multiplier is properly applied.*

Figure 7-1, an amplification of the information presented in Figure 6-4, lists the outcomes of writing phantom at-the-money straddles on the April 1996 crude oil futures contract over a 42-day trading period commencing January 2. Assume one straddle is written each day, at the close of trading, at the corrected at-the-money straddle price. As each day passes, the times to expiry of the straddles are continuously declining. The futures price is also continuously changing. The straddles are all bound to expire on the same date and be settled against the same futures close, but, since the straddles are contracted at very different prices and at very different times, as a group of hypothetical trades they are essentially independent and therefore when summed and averaged can be considered representative of the average outcome of option writing or option buying during the trading period in question.

Consider, for example, the statistics of Figure 7-1, beginning with the first line of the table. The implied strike price on January 2 is 1884. The option expires on March 15 with the futures price at 2199, leaving the option with an expired residual value (the call side of the straddle) of 315 points. Since the straddle premium at the time the option is written on January 2 was 125 points, this straddle transaction favors the buyer by the amount of 315 – 125, or 190 points.

Proceeding down the columns of Figure 7-1, it is evident that, in all 42 hypothetical straddle positions taken, the outcome favors the straddle buyer. The reason, of course, is that the future takes off sharply to the upside close to option expiry. (Whenever a strong trend develops in a futures market, unprotected option writers can expect to suffer.)

During the test period of 42 days, the *average* premium received by the writer of the straddle is 126 points, the average value of the straddle at option expiry 377 points, and the average gain to the buyer 251 points. How representative are these numbers of the crude oil futures market during January and February of 1996—as far as option writing and option buying are concerned? Pretty good, I think. A hypothetical straddle has been written at every possible futures price close, ensuring that no one rogue observation at some extreme futures close can exert undue influence on the overall result.

The final column of Figure 7-1 lists the implied volatilities of the at-the-money options. Notice how the the implied volatility increases from 18.62 to 35.82 and how the straddle premium on January 2 when there are 53 trading days to expiry is scarcely

CRUDE OIL April 1996 option and April 1996 future

Date	May future	Change (no sign)	(as %)	*Future at expiry	ATMSr expiry	ATMSt rec'd	ATMSt -ATMSr	Days left	Implied volatility
Jan 2	1884			2199	315	125	-190	53	18.26
Jan 3	1890	6	0.32	2199	309	125	-184	52	18.36
Jan 4	1893	3	0.16	2199	306	126	-180	51	18.70
Jan 5	1928	35	1.82	2199	271	129	-142	50	18.86
Jan 9	1896	32	1.69	2199	303	126	-177	48	19.13
Jan 10	1878	18	0.96	2199	321	122	-199	47	18.93
Jan 11	1805	73	4.04	2199	394	125	-269	46	20.35
Jan 12	1774	31	1.75	2199	425	129	-296	45	21.60
Jan 15	1779	5	0.28	2199	420	125	-295	44	21.18
Jan 16	1743	36	2.07	2199	456	136	-320	43	23.87
Jan 17	1779	36	2.02	2199	420	135	-285	42	23.34
Jan 18	1796	17	0.95	2199	403	138	-265	41	23.97
Jan 19	1781	15	0.84	2199	418	129	-289	40	22.82
Jan 22	1774	7	0.39	2199	425	135	-290	39	24.29
Jan 23	1767	7	0.40	2199	432	132	-300	38	24.22
Jan 24	1788	21	1.17	2199	411	129	-282	37	23.71
Jan 25	1737	51	2.94	2199	462	133	-329	36	25.47
Jan 26	1736	1	0.06	2199	463	134	-329	35	26.03
Jan 29	1716	20	1.17	2199	483	139	-344	34	27.69
Jan 30	1724	8	0.46	2199	475	136	-339	33	27.40
Jan 31	1737	13	0.75	2199	462	134	-328	32	27.24
Feb 1	1731	6	0.35	2199	468	136	-332	31	28.25
Feb 2	1738	7	0.40	2199	461	133	-328	30	27.93
Feb 5	1717	21	1.22	2199	482	140	-342	29	30.36
Feb 6	1730	13	0.75	2199	469	134	-335	28	29.30
Feb 7	1731	1	0.06	2199	468	127	-341	27	28.29
Feb 8	1733	2	0.12	2199	466	113	-353	26	25.67
Feb 9	1738	5	0.29	2199	461	107	-354	25	24.61
Feb 12	1750	12	0.69	2199	449	100	-349	24	23.33
Feb 13	1835	85	4.63	2199	364	106	-258	23	24.00
Feb 14	1835	0	0.00	2199	364	112	-252	22	25.94
Feb 15	1837	2	0.11	2199	362	114	-248	21	27.04
Feb 16	1839	2	0.11	2199	360	114	-246	20	27.73
Feb 20	1927	88	4.57	2199	272	118	-154	18	28.92
Feb 21	1971	44	2.23	2199	228	122	-106	17	30.02
Feb 22	1985	14	0.71	2199	214	138	-76	16	34.67
Feb 23	1906	79	4.14	2199	293	133	-160	15	36.17
Feb 26	1939	33	1.70	2199	260	130	-130	14	35.85
Feb 27	1970	31	1.57	2199	229	124	-105	13	34.94
Feb 28	1928	42	2.18	2199	271	119	-152	12	35.63
Feb 29	1953	25	1.28	2199	246	113	-133	11	34.76
Mar 1	1944	9	0.46	2199	255	109	-146	10	35.62
Averages →		23	1.26		377	126	-251		26.49

* On Mar 15, the Apr 96 option expired at 2199

FIGURE 7-1. The table above lists the outcomes of taking hypothetical at-the-money straddle positions on April crude oil on 42 consecutive trading days beginning January 2, 1996. It is assumed that a straddle once written is held until option expiry. Since an at-the-money straddle has to pay off on *one* side for sure, the straddle *must end up having residual value,* $ATMS_r$ (the difference between the phantom strike price and the price of the future at option expiry). The *writer's net gain* is the difference between the straddle premium received, $ATMS_t$, and the amount to be paid out, $ATMS_r$.

more than the straddle premium on March 1 when there are only 10 trading days till expiry.

As discussed in the chapters on option theory, the most important determinant of option premium (or implied volatility) is the size of the typical daily price changes in the futures contract and *not* the direction of the futures market. Did the implied volatility of April crude oil rise in response to a sharp rise in the market volatility of the future, as suggested by theory? To some extent, this is true, but visual inspection of the sequence of daily price changes does not suggest a *doubling* of market volatility corresponding to a doubling of implied volatility (daily price changes, and daily price changes expressed as percentages of absolute value are listed in the third and fourth columns of Figure 7-1). Is it possible that writers of crude oil options rather suddenly realized that the option market was underpriced for some other reason, and for that reason raised their asking prices? An interesting conjecture; if true, it supports the hypothesis that option markets may not always be fairly priced and that such conditions may persist for some considerable period.

In Figure 7-2, April crude oil numbers are replaced by the corresponding May silver numbers from the same 2 calendar months. With silver straddles it is the *writer* who wins on every hypothetical straddle, since on each occasion the straddle premium collected exceeds the residual value of the straddle at option expiry. The average premium received by the writer is 450 points, the average value of the straddle at option expiry is 123 points, and the average net gain to the writer 326 points. In contrast to crude oil, where the implied volatility doubles over the 2-month period, the implied volatility of silver remains fairly steady, fluctuating between 20 percent and 26 percent.

The crude oil and silver markets during January and February of 1996 represent polar extremes. In crude oil, the *buyer* wins all the time, and in silver the *writer* wins all the time. Does this indicate that crude oil is an option buyer's market while silver is an option writer's market? Hardly. The samples are much too small and unlikely to be representative of future patterns. In other periods, the outcomes could be completely different. Most of the time, which side a market is favoring at any particular moment

SILVER May1996 option and May 1996 future

Date	May future	Change (no sign)	Change (as %)	*Future at expiry	ATMSr expiry	ATMSt rec'd	ATMSt -ATMSr	Days left	Implied volatility
Jan 2	5443			5518	75	505	430	73	21.74
Jan 3	5440	3	0.06	5518	78	508	430	72	22.02
Jan 4	5463	23	0.42	5518	55	504	449	71	21.91
Jan 5	5603	140	2.50	5518	85	526	441	70	22.46
Jan 8	5603	0	0.00	5518	85	526	441	69	22.62
Jan 9	5610	7	0.12	5518	92	523	431	68	22.59
Jan 10	5673	63	1.11	5518	155	564	409	67	24.29
Jan 11	5583	90	1.61	5518	65	512	447	66	22.60
Jan 12	5523	60	1.09	5518	5	508	503	65	22.83
Jan 15	5498	25	0.45	5518	20	466	446	64	21.17
Jan 16	5540	42	0.76	5518	22	457	435	63	20.78
Jan 17	5568	28	0.50	5518	50	451	401	62	20.58
Jan 18	5513	55	1.00	5518	5	445	440	61	20.69
Jan 19	5523	10	0.18	5518	5	443	438	60	20.73
Jan 22	5648	125	2.21	5518	130	495	365	59	22.82
Jan 23	5628	20	0.36	5518	110	473	363	58	22.07
Jan 24	5580	48	0.86	5518	62	470	408	57	22.33
Jan 25	5638	58	1.03	5518	120	468	348	56	22.17
Jan 26	5598	40	0.71	5518	80	464	384	55	22.36
Jan 29	5598	0	0.00	5518	80	445	365	54	21.64
Jan 30	5616	18	0.32	5518	98	459	361	53	22.46
Jan 31	5641	25	0.44	5518	123	462	339	52	22.73
Feb 1	5848	207	3.54	5518	330	531	201	51	25.43
Feb 2	5893	45	0.76	5518	375	539	164	50	25.85
Feb 5	5867	26	0.44	5518	349	516	167	49	25.11
Feb 6	5829	38	0.65	5518	311	492	181	48	24.35
Feb 7	5763	66	1.15	5518	245	460	215	47	23.28
Feb 8	5780	17	0.29	5518	262	457	195	46	23.34
Feb 9	5720	60	1.05	5518	202	447	245	45	23.32
Feb 12	5723	3	0.05	5518	205	423	218	44	22.28
Feb 13	5772	49	0.85	5518	254	393	139	43	20.76
Feb 14	5790	18	0.31	5518	272	388	116	42	20.70
Feb 15	5699	91	1.60	5518	181	392	211	41	21.46
Feb 16	5776	77	1.33	5518	258	388	130	40	21.24
Feb 20	5583	193	3.46	5518	65	368	302	38	21.36
Feb 21	5633	50	0.89	5518	115	343	228	37	20.04
Feb 22	5577	56	1.00	5518	59	352	293	36	21.01
Feb 23	5504	73	1.33	5518	14	360	346	35	22.11
Feb 26	5530	26	0.47	5518	12	352	340	34	21.82
Feb 27	5504	26	0.47	5518	14	342	328	33	21.61
Feb 28	5535	31	0.56	5518	17	341	324	32	21.78
Feb 29	5545	10	0.18	5518	27	320	293	31	20.71
Averages →		50	0.88		123	450	326		22.23

* On Apr 12, the May 96 option expired at 5518

FIGURE 7-2. The table above lists the outcomes of taking hypothetical at-the-money straddle positions on May silver on 42 consecutive trading days beginning January 2, 1996. The outcomes are completely opposite to those for crude oil. The straddle writer is the clear winner; on every occasion, the premium collected exceeds the payout at option expiry.

will be unclear, and the results of serial straddle writing or buying will be very much a mixed bag (Figure 7-3).

S&P 500 INDEX January 1997 option and April 1997 future

Date	January future	Change (no sign)	Change (as %)	*Future at expiry	ATMSe expiry	ATMSr rec'd	ATMSt -ATMSr	Days left	Implied volatility
Nov 8	74080			78075	3995	3533	-462	49	13.63
Nov 11	74065	15	0.02	78075	4010	3510	-500	48	13.68
Nov 12	73855	210	0.28	78075	4220	3468	-752	47	13.70
Nov 13	74075	220	0.30	78075	4000	3349	-651	46	13.33
Nov 14	74585	510	0.68	78075	3490	3287	-203	45	13.14
Nov 15	74750	165	0.22	78075	3325	3218	-107	44	12.98
Nov 18	74705	45	0.06	78075	3370	3255	-115	43	13.29
Nov 19	75315	610	0.81	78075	2760	3283	523	42	13.45
Nov 20	75305	10	0.01	78075	2770	3464	694	41	14.37
Nov 21	75245	60	0.08	78075	2830	3334	504	40	14.01
Nov 22	75820	575	0.76	78075	2255	3288	1033	39	13.89
Nov 25	76700	880	1.15	78075	1375	3383	2008	38	14.31
Nov 26	76445	255	0.33	78075	1630	3571	1941	37	15.36
Nov 27	76305	140	0.18	78075	1770	3528	1758	36	15.41
Nov 29	76530	225	0.29	78075	1545	3518	1973	34	15.77
Dec 2	76510	20	0.03	78075	1565	3479	1914	33	15.83
Dec 3	75255	1255	1.67	78075	2820	3607	787	32	16.94
Dec 4	75475	220	0.29	78075	2600	3343	743	31	15.91
Dec 5	75245	230	0.31	78075	2830	3378	548	30	16.39
Dec 6	74755	490	0.66	78075	3320	3404	84	29	16.91
Dec 9	75855	1100	1.45	78075	2220	3178	958	28	15.84
Dec 10	75510	345	0.46	78075	2565	3089	524	27	15.75
Dec 11	74655	855	1.15	78075	3420	3202	-218	26	16.82
Dec 12	73450	1205	1.64	78075	4625	3386	-1239	25	18.44
Dec 13	73640	190	0.26	78075	4435	3378	-1057	24	18.73
Dec 16	72775	865	1.19	78075	5300	3263	-2037	23	18.70
Dec 17	73325	550	0.75	78075	4750	3000	-1750	22	17.45
Dec 18	73815	490	0.66	78075	4260	2809	-1451	21	16.61
Dec 19	75350	1535	2.04	78075	2725	2727	2	20	16.19
Dec 20	75725	375	0.50	78075	2350	2668	318	19	16.17
Dec 23	75410	315	0.42	78075	2665	2593	-72	18	16.21
Dec 24	75905	495	0.65	78075	2170	2437	267	17	15.57
Dec 26	76460	555	0.73	78075	1615	2377	762	15	16.05
Dec 27	76460	0	0.00	78075	1615	2377	762	14	16.62
Dec 30	75910	550	0.72	78075	2165	2283	118	13	16.68
Dec 31	74450	1460	1.96	78075	3625	2356	-1269	12	18.27
Averages ⟶		486	0.65		2972	3148	176		15.62

* On January 17, the Jan 97 option expired at 78075

FIGURE 7-3. In contrast to the previous examples of crude oil and silver, the S&P500 Index, over the period November 8 to December 31, generated mixed trading results slightly favoring the straddle writer.

To make any sound conclusion about the buyer or the writer's *expectation in general,* it will be necessary to look at the outcomes of hypothetical straddle positions taken in many different commodity markets and over a much longer period of time.

*

Option premiums begin to shrink rapidly as the option expiry date approaches, so, in order to keep the size of the hypothetical straddle premiums over an entire year roughly comparable, it is appropriate to switch to a new futures contract approximately every 2 months. (The final hypothetical straddles listed in Figures 7-1, 7-2, and 7-3 occur with at least 10 trading days remaining till option expiry.) There is no loss of continuity in switching months, since each hypothetical straddle is independent of all others, regardless of the future on which it is based.

It would be impractical to document here all the individual results from all the observations in the data base, though the entire data base is available for inspection—and possible independent testing by the reader—at the end of the book. The cumulative results of taking one hypothetical straddle position in 15 diverse commodity markets, every trading day of calendar year 1996—and holding that position till option expiry—are summarized in Figure 7-4. On average, there are 252 trading days per year per commodity, and the total number of observations turns out to be 3781. The precise number of trading days in a calendar year varies according to the holiday policies of different exchanges and can also vary due to occasional emergency shutdowns, as happened during severe weather in January of 1996. (And more extensively in a previous year when the World Trade Center in New York was bombed—an unexpected bonus for option writers.)

In order to make results directly comparable and compensate for vastly different contract sizes, *equal weightings* are given to the results from each of the 15 commodities, in the following way. The average payout received for buying a straddle and holding it till expiry is divided by the average premium collected for writing that straddle. A ratio of exactly 1 indicates that the market neither favors the writer nor the buyer. The payout ratio measured for the 15 commodities under study ranges from a low 0.50 in sugar (most favorable to the writer) to a high of 1.42 in wheat (most favorable to the buyer).

	* Trading days 1996	Average Premium	Average Payout	Payout / Premium
FINANCIALS				
S&P 500	254	2459	2160	0.878
T-Bonds	252	298	283	0.950
Swiss franc	254	219	251	1.146
Yen	254	228	222	0.974
RESOURCE				
Gold	252	107	134	1.252
Silver	252	369	261	0.707
Crude oil	251	167	232	1.389
Cotton	249	466	328	0.704
FOOD				
Soybeans	254	452	521	1.153
Wheat	254	364	517	1.420
Corn	254	281	379	1.349
Cattle	254	272	151	0.555
Cocoa	249	86	67	0.779
Coffee	249	1348	1671	1.240
Sugar	249	78	39	0.500
Total ⟶	3781		Average ⟶	1.000

* Different exchanges operate on slightly different business schedules

FIGURE 7-4. Average premiums received and average payouts made during calendar year 1996 have been calculated for straddle positions on 15 actively traded commodities—from a total of 3781 independent observations.

To make the results directly comparable and to accord the *same weighting* to each commodity in the overall result, the ratio of average payout to average premium has been calculated for each commodity, with a ratio of 1.0 indicating the break-even condition. Surprisingly, the *overall average* of this ratio turns out to be almost exactly 1.0 (a statistical fluke), indicating a *fairly priced overall market.*

These two extreme values of the payout ratio do *not* provide any information on the relative pricing of options on sugar and wheat. It just so happened that during the course of calendar year 1996 wheat experienced a major bull market followed by a major bear market, while sugar basically did nothing. Even if wheat options had been greatly overpriced in relation to wheat's average daily trading range, buyers of wheat options would probably still have come out winners; and even if sugar options had been underpriced, sugar option writers would probably still have come out on top.

The payout ratio that is truly meaningful is the overall payout ratio, and rather surprisingly, this turns out to be almost exactly equal to one. Of course, it is something of a fluke that the average ratio should be this close to unity. Nevertheless, it is the best estimate of the true ratio, and, if all 3781 independent straddles had, in fact, been written or purchased, the net result—ignoring transaction costs—would have balanced out very close to zero. No clear winner.

I have to rank this finding as something of a major surprise, because, if truly representative, it means that in general there *is* no intrinsic writer's edge in the options market, and I certainly was expecting to find some kind of edge. I believe most option traders would have expected the same thing. This rather surprising conclusion can be summarized as follows: *The conventional wisdom that indiscriminate option buying is a losing play is incorrect. At the most general level, the option market is remarkably efficient, neither favoring the buyer nor the writer, and equalizing their expectations at zero.*

I was sufficiently surprised by this finding to suspect some sort of computational error. There is none that I can see. One possibility which must be acknowledged is that even a sample size approaching 4000 may not be large enough to be truly representative of the universe of all option trades. Is there any precedent for nonrepresentative conditions prevailing over such a length of time and averaged over such a diverse group of commodities? The answer is yes, but it is a rather muted yes.

Suppose 1972 had been chosen instead of 1996. Almost every resource and food commodity was caught up that year in a general inflationary spiral precipitated by a sudden quadrupling of oil prices. (Not that a general bull or bear market guarantees a skewed result, for much depends on how option writers react, as a group, to a period of sustained option writing losses.) Regardless of which side a generally trending market finally favors, any deductions from a price data base derived from such a year would have to be interpreted with some caution—simply because it *is* an aberration. (The year 1972 has always been a favorite one for testing historical price data to back up a claim for a commodity trading system, since it always generates, retrospectively of course, such amazing returns.)

Ultimately, the reader must judge whether 1996 is typical or atypical of general commodity price behavior. To assist, detailed weekly price charts for all commodities are included in Chapter 10, under "Volatility Profiles." Generally, grains experienced both major bull and bear trends, gold drifted steadily lower as did the currencies and treasury bonds. The S&P 500 worked irregularly higher. Coffee, sugar, cocoa, silver, cattle, and crude oil experienced no major moves. In broad terms, an unexceptional year.

In the absence of any compelling reason to doubt the finding of equality of expectations for the buyer and the writer, I mean to take the result as valid until proven otherwise. One way to prove it otherwise would be to repeat the whole exercise for 1997, or any other year. But that is a task for someone else.

It is worth noting that equality of expectations in option trading does not imply that commodity prices are random in the long term. What equality of options expectations does say is that the options market, as a whole, manages to price itself fairly *after taking into consideration whatever trend component exists in commodity futures prices.* And doubtless, this balancing act occurs through that most elemental of self-correcting mechanisms, the reactions of the players to their experiences as winners and losers.

What does equality of expectations tell option buyers that they may not have known before? Most palpably this: The strategy of buying options to establish a fundamental position in a futures market now compares rather more favorably with the strategy of taking an outright futures position. Not that the expectations of the two strategies are necessarily any different—both are still 50-50 propositions. The option position does however have the feature of built-in stop-loss protection, or staying power, that the futures position lacks—a feature that now looks considerably more attractive.

What does equality of expectations tell option writers that they may not have known before? Most palpably this: The straightforward strategy of indiscriminate option writing is not automatically going to be a winning play. Even if a writer covers every option in every market, he or she will still wind up having no positive expectation—certainly no *significant* expectation. And this, too, before any transaction costs are considered.

*

Before exploring, in the next chapter, the implications of this "unexpected" finding of equality of expectations, it is worth reviewing, perhaps, how the most fundamental equations dealing with option option valuation tie together. None of these equations is difficult to apply, but it is not always immediately obvious which one is appropriate in a particular circumstance. A numerical example will be helpful at this point.

Consider the silver market, say, where the following information is known at a particular time.

At-the-money option price	=	21.6 cents
Corresponding futures price	=	$6.00
Trading days till expiry	=	36
Average daily price change (measured over 30 days)	=	5.4 cents

A trader wishes to know if this option is overvalued or undervalued in relation to the current market volatility. The time interval over which market volatility is measured is at the discretion of the trader, of course. (In this case, let us assume that price changes have been measured over 30 trading days.) The mean absolute deviation is the average daily price change taking all values as positive, and this deviation may be expressed either as an absolute price unit or as a percentage of the futures price depending on the equation in which it is used.

Overvaluation or undervaluation can be assessed by comparing volatilities (implied versus market). This exercise, naturally, only works for at-the-money options.

$$\text{Observed market volatility} = 20 \times \text{MAD} \qquad \text{(by Eq. 5-2)}$$

$$= \frac{20 \times 5.4 \times 100}{600}$$

$$= 18.0 \text{ percent}$$

$$\text{Implied volatility} = \frac{40 \times \text{ATMO}}{\sqrt{t}} \qquad \text{(by Eq. 3-8)}$$

$$= \frac{40 \times 21.6 \times 100}{600 \times \sqrt{36}}$$

$$= 24 \text{ percent}$$

By this comparison, the silver option would appear to be overvalued.

The limitations of the usefulness of valuation judgments using these equations should be well understood. First, the number of trading days used in the calculation of the mean absolute deviation is *always* arbitrary. Second, an option may appear to be substantially overvalued or undervalued relative to current market volatility, yet still be fairly priced in relation to other market imponderables weighing on the market—a crop forecast about to be released, or a major political uncertainty on the point of being resolved, say—forces whose potential impact on option prices may not be reflected in recent futures price action. The "unreflected uncertainty" component of an option pricing structure will be explored in detail in the next chapter.

CHAPTER EIGHT

BORN AGAIN

Can a finding of quality of expectations for option buyers and option writers be reconciled with common sense? It does seem only fair that option writers be awarded *something* for taking on risks with unlimited liability and that option buyers should have to pay *something* for the privilege of enjoying limited liability. Could this be happening, even under equivalence of basic expectations? I believe the answer is yes, for I was forgetting two things.

One is rather obvious: The writer gets to invest the proceeds received for writing the option, whereas the buyer has capital tied up in the options transaction until the option is exercised, thereby missing out on interest that could be earned elsewhere. If short-term interest is at 5 percent, the option writer has a built-in 10 percent advantage over the option buyer. In general, with $100,000 in equity, a well-diversified option writing account can garner an equivalent amount in option premium—funds that can be invested in short-term fixed interest securities and still be used to margin positions. At 5 percent nominal interest, then, a diversified option writer can expect a risk-free return of something like 10 percent on his invested capital. The option buyer is immediately behind to the extent that he receives no interest at all.

The second advantage accruing to the writer is not quite so obvious: It lies in his ability to take dynamic action *after* the option has been written. Let's consider, first, the option buyer's "options" after the option is bought. The buyer really has no follow-up strategy that makes sense; it is very much a case of buy, hold, and wait. Certainly, an option buyer may resell an option in the open market at any time, but under what rationale? If the option is appreciating in value, he will want to hold on to it, for to sell out an option whose price is going up is tantamount to selling into a trending market in the underlying future, a strategy known to be unsuccessful in the long run. If the option is declining in value, the loss may be due either to time decay or to an unfavorable move in the futures price. Regardless, the option will still reflect fair value (on average), and will certainly not be posing any immediate threat to the trader's equity, since the option will have already been paid for.

An option writer, on the other hand, faces starker choices when contemplating an option that is going against him. The reason is that when an option is going against an option writer, it is always due to a sustained trend developing in the underlying futures market. An option position which is allowed to appreciate unchecked will eventually become equivalent to a full-blown futures position and pose an unacceptably large risk to the trader's option-writing account. At the very least, a deep in-the-money option will mean large daily swings in account equity—a roller coaster effect that an astute option writer will strive to avoid.

It is prudent, therefore, for an option writer to have some kind of defensive plan drawn up in advance to handle an option going against him in a big way. The ability to take defensive action, the freedom to act dynamically, is an asset the option writer must be prepared to exploit. He is in much the same situation as the backgammon player who has been doubled by his opponent—down but not out.

Figure 8-1 shows the distribution of wins and losses associated with the hypothetical writing of the 3781 at-the-money straddles described in the previous chapter, where the overall result is known to be very close to break even. With individual straddles, the most favorable result for the option writer is a payout ratio of zero, while the most unfavorable result (theoretically unbounded) comes in at a payout ratio of around 6.0. A good number of payout ratios fall in the 2.0 to 3.0 range, and if a writer by some preemptive defensive action could bring down these large payouts, the *overall* payout ratio would drop substantially. The crucial question, of course, is this: Can the option writer take defensive action which will cut into losing transactions without reducing, proportionally, the payouts from

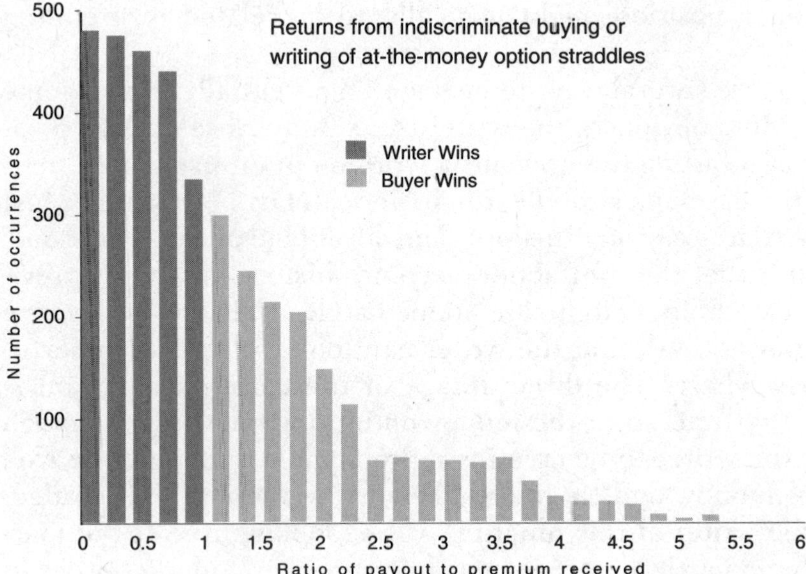

FIGURE 8-1. The frequency distribution above is compiled from 3781 independent observations of the outcome of buying or writing at-the-money straddles during calendar year 1996. The most a writer can gain on any one transaction is 100 percent of the premium (equivalent to zero on the ratio scale of the x axis). The buyer's gain on any one straddle is theoretically unlimited.

In the distribution above, the writer prevails in most of the transactions (about 2200 times out of 3781). The writer's overall expectation, however, is close to zero, since the *higher* percentage of winners is balanced by a *lower* average amount won.

winning transactions? If the answer to this question is yes, then the option edge can shift in favor of the writer.

An option writer who is going to employ a defensive strategy must be prepared to abide by some discipline that announces *when* action is necessary. Defensive action is necessary only in the event that the value of the straddle is increasing; the writer hopes, naturally, not to have to cover the straddle at all. To avoid excessive transaction costs, the writer must limit the number of straddles to be defended to those cases where there is a substantial adverse price move. If this rule is to be consistent in different commodity markets at different times, then the amount risked on a position ought, logically, to be related to premium received.

There are several ways to deal with a potentially troublesome option. Most obviously, the writer can simply close out the position by purchasing the previously written option in the free market. In the case of a straddle, the writer can buy both sides or just the side that is causing the loss. The advantage of the "close-out" solution is that the transaction becomes history, any funds previously tied up in margin are immediately available to finance other transactions, and the writer can look for writing opportunities elsewhere. The disadvantage of the close-out solution is that by the time an at-the-money option has moved far enough against the writer to be creating a problem, it is going to be well into the money, and therefore likely to be rather thinly traded. Since the writer at this juncture will be looking to exit the market rather smartly, he or she may have to enter a market order in an illiquid trading environment and may have an order filled well away from fair value. The writer may not even know what fair value is, since the option will no longer be close to the money, and the million dollar formula won't help. Whatever fair value is, the writer can be pretty sure of getting less. A writer who does not close out with a market order, or near market order, and tries to finesse for a predetermined price, could be stuck, unhedged, in a market that is running away.

An alternative to closing out a problem option is to "freeze" the loss by purchasing a more liquid option on the same future. This solution probably gets the seller a fairer price, but, although it does limit the loss, the complex options combination must be held until option expiry and the ultimate loss will not be known until option expiry. Trading capital will also be tied up to some extent.

A third way to temporarily neutralize a problem option is to initiate a position in the underlying futures contract. The appeal of *this* strategy is that market orders can be used, since the futures markets is going to be much more liquid than the options market. The downside of defending an option with a future is that the strategy may require additional defense if the futures price should whipsaw after the position is taken. This strategy also ties up capital.

If an option writer can set the levels at which to take protective action far enough from the market to ensure that relatively few options need be defended—and transaction costs thereby minimized, any of the defensive strategies described above will have the same long-run expectation, just as all logical trend-following "systems" for trading commodity futures have the same long-run expectation. There may be no hard evidence to back up this assertion, but it is one of the few assertions that I am happy to take on intuition alone.

It is virtually impossible to track, historically, the day-to-day price of any particular straddle after it has been written. Testing of defensive strategies based on option close-outs is therefore not a feasible proposition. The futures defensive strategy can, however, with some considerable difficulty, be put to the test. A system based on action at closing prices will give unbiased estimates of the prices at which transactions would have been made. In the exceptional instances where a market closes at a limit price, the opening price on the following day can be used instead of the closing price.

Historical opening, high, low, and closing prices *are* readily available for all actively traded future contracts. This information allows for the testing of hypothetical futures trades using good-till-cancelled *stop-loss* orders, which may be activated during a trading session. A problem with testing using stop-loss orders, however, is that under certain very volatile market conditions the opening, high, low, and closing prices do not unambiguously reveal whether the high or the low came first, and thus a hypothetical stop order might be hypothetically "missed" when, in hypothetical reality, it would have been elected!

Numbers in the financial press, too, have become less trustworthy because of the emergence of subsidiary futures markets (to satisfy the cravings of insomniacs) called Globex—where financial instruments such as stock index, interest rate, and currency futures can be traded almost round the clock. A Globex session on the S&P, for example, commences shortly after the main Chicago Mercantile Exchange trading pit finishes business for the day, and continues overnight, closing just 15 minutes before Chicago reopens on the following day. Opening, high, low, and closing prices quoted in the financial press reflect Globex values as well as Chicago values, and the former can be all over the map because of the thinness of trading. It is therefore impossible to trust results from hypothetical stop loss trading using these numbers. No such problem exists with using *closing prices*, however, as these always reflect the official exchange closings.

It goes almost without saying that any defensive system an option writer uses to limit losses on straddles that are going sour is bound to have *some* negative impact on transactions that *would have been* ultimately profitable at option expiry without intervention. You can't have your cake and eat it too.

*

Figure 8-2, which consists of a series of hypothetical straddles on crude oil—excerpted from the data base described in Chapter 6—shows how an option writer might employ a defensive strategy using a futures position to offset the losing option side of a straddle which has increased in value by a certain amount—a quantity to be determined ahead of time under some consistent rule equally valid in all commodities.

In testing the entire data base (Figure 8-2 contains just 43 hypothetical transactions out of a total of 3781), the size of an adverse price move at which an unrealized loss on a straddle was deemed sufficient to trigger an offsetting futures transaction was defined in this arbitrary, though consistent, way:

> If a commodity future closes at a price higher than the strike price of an at-the-money straddle *plus* the value of the straddle premium received, a hypothetical *long* futures will be initiated at that closing price. And likewise, if a commodity future closes at a price *lower* than the strike price of an at-the-money straddle *minus* the value of the straddle premium received, a hypothetical s*hort* futures will be initiated at that closing price.

This defensive rule is quite arbitrary, but it is not commodity specific and is chosen to strike a balance between taking too many premature protective positions and allowing the straddle loss on any one position to increase to a very large number.

	Futures price	Straddle premium	Exit on close above	below	Buy future	Exit future	Sell future	Exit future	Net gain to writer	
Sep 3	2205	265	*2470*	*1940*	2474				-4	53
Sep 4	2194	255	*2449*	*1939*	2474				-25	32
Sep 5	2221	251	*2472*	*1970*	2474				-2	55
Sep 6	2259	267	*2526*	*1992*	2534				-8	109
Sep 9	2247	254	*2501*	*1993*	2508				-7	84
Sep 10	2282	257	*2539*	*2025*	2546	2278			-146	122
Sep 11	2335	277	*2612*	*2058*					195	195
Sep 12	2355	287	*2642*	*2068*					225	225
Sep 13	2315	288	*2603*	*2027*					186	186
Sep 16	2231	253	*2484*	*1978*	2508				-24	67
Sep 17	2240	252	*2492*	*1988*	2508				-16	75
Sep 18	2294	270	*2564*	*2024*					147	147
Sep 19	2261	264	*2525*	*1997*	2534				-9	108
Sep 20	2274	261	*2535*	*2013*	2546	2264			-164	118
Sep 23	2284	257	*2541*	*2027*	2546	2278			-144	124
Sep 24	2353	269	*2622*	*2084*					205	205
Sep 25	2383	268	*2651*	*2115*					234	234
Sep 26	2358	261	*2619*	*2097*					202	202
Sep 27	2396	264	*2660*	*2132*					243	243
Sep 30	2377	249	*2626*	*2128*					209	209
Oct 1	2358	239	*2597*	*2119*					180	180
Oct 2	2352	240	*2592*	*2112*					175	175
Oct 3	2421	243	*2664*	*2178*					239	239
Oct 4	2424	230	*2654*	*2194*					223	223
Oct 7	2474	230	*2704*	*2244*					173	173
Oct 8	2508	234	*2742*	*2274*					143	143
Oct 9	2467	222	*2689*	*2245*					172	172
Oct 10	2395	203	*2598*	*2192*					181	181
Oct 11	2437	198	*2635*	*2239*					178	178
Oct 14	2521	201	*2722*	*2320*			2303		-17	97
Oct 15	2502	198	*2700*	*2304*			2303		-1	113
Oct 16	2478	186	*2664*	*2292*			2278		-14	125
Oct 17	2500	179	*2679*	*2321*			2303		-18	96
Oct 18	2534	187	*2721*	*2347*			2335		-12	70
Oct 21	2546	172	*2718*	*2374*			2335		-39	43
Oct 22	2553	169	*2722*	*2384*			2335		-49	33
Oct 23	2486	159	*2645*	*2327*			2303		-24	90
Oct 24	2450	153	*2603*	*2297*			2278		-19	120
Oct 25	2486	145	*2631*	*2341*			2335		-6	76
Oct 28	2485	140	*2625*	*2345*			2335		-10	72
Oct 29	2434	137	*2571*	*2297*			2278	2441	-43	120
Oct 30	2428	132	*2560*	*2296*			2278	2441	-42	121
Oct 31	2335	126	*2461*	*2209*					44	44
Nov 1	2303	106	*2409*	*2197*	2412				-3	-8
Nov 4	2278									
Nov 5	2264									
Nov 6	2269									
Nov 7	2274									
Nov 8	2359									
Nov 11	2337									
Nov 12	2335									
Nov 13	2412									
Nov 14	2441									
Nov 15	2417									

FIGURE 8-2. Testing a dynamic option writing strategy involving both options *and* futures is a complex procedure. In the example above, hypothetical at-the-money straddles are written on December crude oil futures on consecutive trading days between September 3 and November 4, 1996.

Each of these straddles has its own unique pair of futures "trigger levels" and must be tested against these trigger levels from the time they are written until the moment they expire to see if a defensive futures position must be initiated. The final column above is the net gain to the option writer when the strategy of no follow-up action is employed.

At the time a defensive futures position is taken, the straddle which it is aimed at protecting will have increased in value, perhaps by as much as 50 percent. *Exactly* how much it will have increased depends on two things: the magnitude of the move in the commodity future and the time remaining till option expiry at the time the futures position is taken.

An option writer who is following a defensive strategy based on buying or selling futures hopes, naturally, that the majority of the straddles written never have to be futures protected. But whether this happens is entirely beyond the writer's control, for there is no way that market behavior can be predicted in advance. The writer also hopes that once a futures position is taken, the momentum in the futures market continues in the same direction, for, if it does not, if the futures does a sudden about turn, the writer will have to think about protecting the futures position as well!

The rationale behind the defensive writing strategy is to limit the loss that will ensue from an unprotected straddle written in a futures market that has moved sharply, either up or down. An inevitable consequence of the defensive strategy is that a number of straddles which were profitable with indiscriminate (undefended) writing may now be rendered unprofitable with the purchase or sale of a future.

Consider the hypothetical crude oil straddle written on September 3 (Figure 8-2) at the phantom strike price of 2205, for which a premium of 265 points is received. According to the protocol previously described, the trigger levels on the December future will be:

$$\text{Upper trigger level} = 2205 + 265 = 2470$$
$$\text{Lower trigger level} = 2205 - 265 = 1940$$

These numbers appear opposite the September 3 futures price, in columns 4 and 5. The defensive strategy dictates that if, between September 3 and November 15—when the straddle expires—the December crude oil future should close above 2470 or below 1940, a future will be purchased or sold at that closing price.

On October 7, December crude oil closes at 2474, above the upper trigger level of 2470 established for the straddle written at strike 2205 on September 3. Assume, therefore, the purchase of a December crude oil future at 2474. At this point in time, it is clear that a loss (hopefully small) on this overall transaction is inevitable. Consider the possibilities after the futures position is taken. (The straddle itself will be held till option expiry.)

If all subsequent closes of December crude oil remain above the original strike price, 2205, there is no need for further action, and the overall loss on the transaction will be limited to the futures purchase price *less* the trigger level. To see why this is so, consider these two extreme cases: a futures price at option expiry of 3000 (major bull market) and a futures price at option expiry of 2245 (a reversal in market direction):

With future closing at 3000 at option expiry,

$$\begin{aligned}\text{Net gain to writer} &= \text{premium} - \text{payout} + \text{gain on future}\\ &= 265 - (3000 - 2205) + (3000 - 2474)\\ &= -4\end{aligned}$$

With the future closing at 2245 at option expiry,

$$\begin{aligned}\text{Net gain to writer} &= \text{premium} - \text{payout} + \text{gain on future}\\ &= 265 - (2245 - 2205) + (2245 - 2474)\\ &= -4\end{aligned}$$

At option expiry, for any futures price above the strike price, the loss on the overall transaction will be limited to 4 points—exactly what the defensive strategy is designed to do in such a case. At option expiry, the December future did in fact close at 2417, well above the option strike price of 2205. In checking all the futures prices occurring after the September 3 straddle is written, it is apparent that the price of the future never dips below 2205. But, had it done so, the option writer would be on the horns of a rather nasty dilemma, for the protective future at this juncture would be threatening to backfire, and the writer would be looking at a loss on the futures position alone greater than the total premium received on the straddle. And of course the straddle would still be open.

In the same way that option writers have to take protection against the losing side of a straddle, they must also take protection against a future that is incurring too big a loss. The amount of the loss they should be willing to take is again arbitrary, but a consistent amount would again be the total option premium received. The defensive rule needs to be expanded a little to include the case of a future that needs to be liquidated:

> A long futures position initiated to protect a call will, itself, be protected if it falls *below* the straddle strike price, and a short futures position initiated to protect a put will, itself, be protected if it rises *above* the straddle strike price.

When a defensive futures position is closed out, a loss is immediately realized, and the option writer is back in the position when the straddle was first written. The premium will have diminished due to time decay, but the writer has to be prepared to repeat the defensive strategy if necessary. It is quite unusual to have to take a second defensive futures position, but it does happen, and the option writer must be ready to deal with it when it does.

To appreciate the defensive futures strategy in action, consider (Figure 8-2) the crude oil straddle written on September 10, at a strike price of 2282 and with trigger levels of 2539 and 2025. On October 21, the upper trigger level is exceeded by the December crude oil future, and a futures contract must be assumed purchased at 2546, the closing price of the future on that day. On November 4, the original strike of 2280 is breached on the downside with a futures close at 2278, indicating that the long future has lost enough and warrants liquidation. The closing out of the long futures position results in a loss of (2546 – 2278), or 268 points. A second defensive strategy proves unnecessary, and when the option expires on November 15, with the future at 2417, the overall transaction can be summed up thus:

$$\begin{aligned}\text{Net gain to writer} &= \text{premium} - \text{payout} + \text{gain on future}\\ &= 257 - (2417 - 2282) - 268\\ &= -146 \text{ points}\end{aligned}$$

By way of contrast, all the straddles written between October 14 and November 3 require that short defensive futures positions be taken against them, and two of these short futures positions have, themselves, to be covered before option expiry.

The strategy of using futures in defensive way—in an awkward market—can be assessed by comparing the final two columns of Figure 8-2. The crude oil price sequence examined here is particularly choppy, with many apparent price breakouts which go nowhere—precisely the kind of market which makes an option writer wish he'd gone on vacation. In this particular time capsule, the defensive strategy compares unfavorably with the undefended strategy. In a more typical period, however, there would be many fewer futures positions initiated, and the two strategies would generate similar results. In strongly trending markets, the defensive strategy comes into its own, producing results that are still slightly negative but vastly superior to those of the "sell and hold" strategy.

Great care must be exercised when checking a dynamic trading system, so that no trades are "missed," that is, assumed not to have occurred when they would have occurred. It does not take many errors of this type to produce a seriously erroneous result. The reader will appreciate that the testing of 3781 straddles, each with its own unique set of contingencies, is a time-consuming and demanding exercise—even with the use of a computer. The devil, however, really *is* in the details!

It would not be practical to document all the details here, so the overall results, by commodity, are presented in Figure 8-3, from which it is immediately apparent that the effect of employing the defensive strategy is to *reduce the variability* of results across commodities. The trending markets, which scored heavily against the option writer under the sell-and-hold strategy are now much less unfavorable and even favor the writer in some instances. The trendless markets which formerly favored the writer, are now substantially *less* favorable. Meanwhile, the *overall edge* moves in the writer's favor, as the payout ratio drops from 1.000 to 0.902. Whether this shift in the ratio will be significant in the light of expected transaction costs remains to be seen.

The result is not unexpected, since the strategy of protecting an option against a runaway trend in the underlying future is a manifestation of the well-known market truism that losses should be cut and profits left to run. It will be interesting to see if this writer's edge—established for a defensive strategy—can be improved upon by any other means.

Taking dynamic action to limit large losses is an obvious strategy that must surely have occurred to every trader who has ever written a straddle that has seriously backfired. By dynamic action, I mean using futures for protection, covering the option with an identical offsetting trade, or covering the option with another option on the same future, all of which—the author avows—amount to the same thing in the long run. Running away to fight another day is a common-sense discipline (more spoken of than followed I might add), and it is welcome to see its usefulness confirmed, if only on a statistical basis.

A second strategy an option writer might employ to increase his edge is also fairly obvious, but much less easy to implement or test. This is the strategy of being selective about which straddles to write in the first place. If a writer can come up with a consistent method of comparing market volatility (measured) with implied volatility (computed), he may logically choose to write options only when they appear to be overvalued. Option valuation comparisons are accomplished by using the option volatility formulae given at the end of the previous chapter. As always, when calculating market volatility, the choice of time base is arbitrary.

To test for "overvaluation," I compared a simple reading of market volatility—calculated from the mean absolute deviation, MAD, over 30 days—with the implied volatility for each of the

	* Trading days 1996	Average premium	Average payout	Payout/Premium	Payout/Premium (previous)
FINANCIALS					
S&P 500	254	2459	2430	0.988	(0.878)
T-Bonds	252	298	302	1.013	(0.950)
Swiss franc	254	219	186	0.849	(1.146)
Yen	254	228	197	0.864	(0.974)
RESOURCE					
Gold	252	107	102	0.953	(1.252)
Silver	252	369	293	0.794	(0.707)
Crude oil	251	167	176	1.054	(1.389)
Cotton	249	466	325	0.697	(0.704)
FOOD					
Soybeans	254	452	443	0.980	(1.153)
Wheat	254	364	425	1.168	(1.420)
Corn	254	281	288	1.025	(1.349)
Cattle	254	272	223	0.820	(0.555)
Cocoa	249	86	68	0.791	(0.779)
Coffee	249	1348	1114	0.826	(1.240)
Sugar	249	78	55	0.705	(0.500)
Total ⟶	3781	Average ⟶		0.902	(1.000)

* Different exchanges operate on slightly different business schedules

FIGURE 8-3. Comparing the final two columns of the table above, it is apparent that the effect of employing a defensive futures strategy when writing straddles is to shift the edge in the writer's favor. Commodities such as the grains and coffee, which experienced large trends during 1996 and which previously, when unprotected, created large losses for the writer now generate much more favorable results. However, option writing results from the trendless markets, which previously favored the writer, are now considerably less favorable.

The number that truly matters is the overall payout-to-premium ratio, which is now 0.902, indicating that the trading edge has shifted in favor of the writer. There are additional costs associated with a defensive futures strategy, since there will be some increase in the number of transactions. Notwithstanding, the shift in the payout ratio does strike the author as significant.

at-the-money straddles in the data base. If the implied volatility exceeded the market volatility, I assumed the straddle written; otherwise, I excluded it from the summation. There is no special significance about choosing 30 days as the time base, other than that it falls in the general range of time intervals that strike a reasonable balance between long-term volatility and short-term volatility, and between data which go too far back in time and are possibly nonrepresentative and recent data which are certainly up-to-date but of rather small sample size. The important thing about choosing 30 is that I chose it in advance—*not* after testing 25 and 35 and finding that 30 gives the "optimum" result. If any results are in error here, it is most assuredly not on account of confirmation bias.

The results of the "selection by valuation" test—the kind of test which the advent of large spreadsheet computer programs now renders practicable—are documented in Figure 8-4. There is little to be read into the changes in the payout ratio *by commodity,* because falling sample sizes at the individual commodity level are bound to affect the results due to pure chance. There is also little significance to be attached to the wide disparity in the number of "overvaluations" observed in each commodity. For example, the disparity between gold (238 observations) and wheat (80 observations) is understandable in light of the atypical price variations occurring in the gold and wheat markets during 1996.

By the volatility comparison test, gold options were substantially overvalued on almost every trading day of 1996, even though implied volatilities were registering the lowest values seen in 20 years. The low implied volatilities were naturally tied to the day-to-day price variability in the gold futures market at that time. But, low as they were, implied volatilities refused to mirror short-term market volatility levels, because the option market was always expecting price variations to regress to their historical norms—and sooner rather than later. Reality is that "overvaluation" by mathematical calculation in a very quiet market is not really overvaluation at all, and a market registering unusually low levels of implied volatility will often seem falsely overvalued.

In contrast, the wheat option market of 1996 was falsely undervalued, since the option market was constantly (and not unreasonably) expecting the unusually high price variability to regress toward its historical mean. In a high-priced, volatile market, implied volatility normally stays below short-term market volatility, so that "undervaluation" goes hand in hand with high implied volatility.

Returning to Figure 8-4, it appears that selectivity by valuation has marginally improved the overall writer's edge from 0.902 to 0.884—not a great deal, perhaps, but at least a move in the

	* Trading days 1996	Average premium	Average payout	Number in sample	Payout / Premium
FINANCIALS					
S&P 500	254	2544	2597	189	1.021
T-Bonds	252	293	287	173	0.980
Swiss franc	254	226	199	221	0.881
Yen	254	245	198	195	0.808
RESOURCE					
Gold	252	105	103	238	0.981
Silver	252	371	291	243	0.784
Crude oil	251	175	174	90	0.994
Cotton	249	476	337	195	0.708
FOOD					
Soybeans	254	515	484	127	0.940
Wheat	254	359	476	80	1.326
Corn	254	302	298	137	0.987
Cattle	254	271	224	175	0.827
Cocoa	249	88	73	186	0.830
Coffee	249	1355	1118	165	0.825
Sugar	249	78	59	213	0.756
Total ⟶	3781	Average ⟶		2627	0.884

* Different exchanges operate on slightly different business schedules

FIGURE 8-4. As described in Figure 8-3, the effect of *introducing a defensive futures strategy* when writing straddles is to shift the payout ratio from 1.000 to 0.902.

The effect of *selecting* as writing candidates only those options that are overvalued (comparing market volatility with implied volatility) is to shift the payout ratio further in the writer's favor, but only by a small amount, from 0.902 to 0.884. The sample size drops from 3781 to 2627, and the number of sample observations is no longer constant by commodity. In the computation of the overall payout ratio, equal weighting is given to each observation, rather than each commodity.

Note the smaller sample size reduces somewhat the confidence level that can be placed on the overall result.

right direction. After eliminating all the "undervalued" straddles from the payout test, the number of observations drops from 3781 to 2627. It is a little bit of a puzzle that overvaluations and undervaluations don't occur in equal proportion, since the net outcome of writing *all* the straddles is already known to result in fair value.

In grasping for an explanation for this anomaly, I wondered if the small sample of 30 observations could be yielding a biased estimate of the mean absolute deviation, MAD. (Market volatility was calculated from Eq. 5-2, or 20 × MAD.) I also reconsidered a lingering reservation I have about using futures closing prices as the only basis for defining variability. It is true that the daily high price and daily low price of a future ought, logically, to influence the calculation of volatility. After all, a future may have a huge daily range, close unchanged, and count for zero in a volatility definition that encompasses only closing prices. Daily ranges are never used in volatility calculations because they cannot, as yet, be handled by any mathematical theory. (Now *here* is a problem are for an applied mathematician to direct his or her talents.) It is generally accepted—by omission, perhaps—that closing prices averaged over a sufficiently long period will work equally as well, because options, at expiry, are valued at a specific closing price. There is no doubt, however, that the failure to use highs and lows in a volatility calculation does represent a loss of information of unknown (hopefully small) dimension.

The empirical evidence based on the result of equality of expectations does suggest that Eq. 5-2 *underestimates* market volatility, or at least that estimate of market volatility which ought properly to be compared with implied volatility. If the overall options market is fairly priced, these volatilities should average out the same over a long time period and a large number of independent observations.

Could there be some way to modify Eq. 5-2 in the light of the empirical evidence that it estimates low? I think there is. The question can be formulated this way: If MAD multiplied by 20 yields 2627 "overvalueds" out of a total sample size of 3781, what multiplier of MAD would yield 1890 (exactly half of the total) "overvalueds"? The answer is a multiplier of 22, so that Eq. 5-2 when modified becomes:

$$\text{Market volatility} = 22 \times \text{MAD}$$

This is a wholly pragmatic definition of market volatility, but one that works where it matters; in a comparison with implied volatility. Rocket science this is not, but who cares?—if the thing flies.

It is less of a puzzle that a comprehensive test using valuation as the selection criterion should yield only a modest improvement in the overall payout ratio. The small improvement in the writer's edge, from 0.902 to 0.884 is, none the less, an unbiased estimate and deserves to be taken at face value. Maybe it is unrealistic to expect a larger improvement. As discussed above in reference to gold and wheat, option valuations are going to be out of whack for long periods in very atypical markets, since expectation of regression to the mean is certainly going to dominate at times, as are special factors governing uncertainty that cannot possibly be reflected in historical prices.

Is a writer's edge of 0.884 the best that can be expected through selectivity? Hard to say. Figure 8-5 shows the effect of selecting only those straddles where implied volatility is at least fifty percent higher than market volatility. The payout ratio here drops from 0.884 to 0.851, but the sample size is too small and the observations concentrated in too few commodities for the result to be considered reliable. One thing is clear from the valuation test; having an *after-the-fact* defensive strategy in place will be a lot more important to an option writer than having a system to spot which options to write in the first place.

In the testing of the valuation strategy above, MAD is calculated as a *simple average* of the 30 most recent price changes. This basic calculation may not necessarily give the most consistent and logical estimates. For example, a simple average ascribes the same *weighting* to each reading of price change whether that price change occurs 1 day or 30 days back in time. When a very large price change gets to be 30 days old, and drops off the list of readings to be averaged, the MAD can drop rather abruptly, and somewhat illogically.

A more dynamic, and more easily maintained running estimate of MAD is achievable via a calculation known as *exponential smoothing,* in which recent observations are given more import than distant observations. Whether a technique like exponential smoothing would change the outcome much is not a question I wish to probe (it probably improves it a little), for this is getting into boutique science of a kind that can lead to falsely optimized results. While in practice I recommend using exponential smoothing, as far as estimated payouts are concerned, I'll be happy to stick with the conservative no-frills estimate I got on the first pass.

	* Trading days 1996	Average premium	Average payout	Number in sample	Payout Premium
FINANCIALS					
S&P 500	254	2525	2967	22	1.175
T-Bonds	252	248	254	9	1.024
Swiss franc	254	299	253	40	0.846
Yen	254	330	181	46	0.548
RESOURCE					
Gold	252	105	103	88	0.981
Silver	252	492	96	22	0.195
Crude oil	251	143	233	15	1.629
Cotton	249			0	
FOOD					
Soybeans	254	681	100	7	0.147
Wheat	254	364	0	0	0.000
Corn	254	324	375	26	1.157
Cattle	254	291	346	2	1.189
Cocoa	249			0	
Coffee	249	1593	1057	38	0.664
Sugar	249			0	
Total →	3781	Average →		315	0.851

* Different exchanges operate on slightly different business schedules

FIGURE 8-5. When straddles with extremely high apparent overvaluations (a ratio of implied volatility to market volatility greater than 1.5) are selected as a subgroup, the sample size drops to 315, distributed very irregularly across the various commodities. For example, gold is highly overvalued 88 times, cotton, wheat, cocoa, and sugar not at all.

Although the payout ratio drops further, from 0.884 to 0.851, this result cannot be considered reliable because of the skewed weightings by commodity and the low overall sample size.

*

Since dynamic valuation using short-term market volatility appears to contribute so modestly to the writer's edge, it seems natural to ask whether comparing implied volatility with long-term market volatility is likely to be a superior selectivity strategy. If so, it is tantamount to saying that regression to the mean is a more powerful option valuation factor than current price action in the futures pit.

This question, however, has to remain unanswered—at least by me—since I can see no way to test selective option writing based on comparing implied volatilities with *absolute* or reference levels. Now it is true that long-term average implied volatilities can be calculated for all commodities and that comparison of a current implied volatility with its long-term average is a way of segregating hypothetical straddles into overvalued and undervalued categories.

But there are any number of problems associated with such a segregation. First, how do you handle commodities which exhibit strong seasonal patterns in the implied volatilities of their options? Second, how do you deal with commodities like stock index futures, which show a long-term secular increase in implied volatility? Furthermore, broad-stroke empirical evidence does not suggest that absolute volatility is likely to be a good discriminator. In the straddle tests carried out on 1996 data, wheat (unusually high implied volatility) is a big loser for the option writer, while cocoa and sugar (low implied volatilities) are big winners.

At one point during the research for this book, I did begin to test the 1996 data base for an absolute valuation strategy, first, by finding the average implied volatility by commodity during 1996 then by comparing daily implied volatilities with these averages. Naturally, half of the hypothetical straddles were defined as having above-average implied volatilities, while the other half were defined as having below-average implied volatilities. Hypothesizing straddle-writing on just the the "overvalued" options yielded very favorable option writing results, so favorable, in fact, that I knew something had to be wrong—and it most certainly was. I was committing the cardinal sin of hypothesis testing, which is to use information in a test that could not possibly have been available at the time the supposed test took place. An average implied volatility can only be computed after the fact, that is after the calendar year is over, and cannot, therefore, be used to segregate hypothetical straddles into overvalueds and undervalueds.

It seems imprudent now to have embarked on such a fundamentally unsound test, but it did not seem that way at the time. I mention this unfortunate detour as a reminder that it is rather easy to unintentionally concoct falsely optimized results. On common-sense as well as on practical grounds, therefore, I have chosen to reject for testing any strategy that is based on long-term valuation comparisons.

It did also occur to me to test the strategy of selectively writing options depending on whether the underlying futures market appeared to be in an uptrend, a downtrend, or stuck in a trading range. Everyone would love to write options in trading markets and buy options in trending markets, but this information is also not available until it is too late to capitalize upon it. While I don't discount the possibility that favorable *times* exist for writing options or buying options—on a purely technical basis—I don't see how such a hypothesis can be tested on a sound statistical basis. Therefore, again, on common-sense and practical grounds, I have rejected for testing any hypotheses based on forecasting futures market direction.

If the results of the hypothetical tests on the option and futures data from 1996 are representative—and there is no reason to suppose otherwise—it seems that a payout ratio of 0.88 is approaching the limit of the edge an option writer can expect to achieve by purely technical means. However, it will not necessarily be routine for even a well-disciplined trader to attain this level of edge, for an option writer, like a futures trader who is working a "system," is exposed to the same temptations to delay the taking of unpleasant decisions, any one of which can seriously affect overall expectation. In the case of straddle writing, the temptation is to delay covering the losing side, to give it "one more day," which, of course, easily becomes "one more week." Nevertheless, the numbers do suggest that with discipline and vigilance, a dedicated option writer can approach business with the confidence that his or her expectation is significantly positive.

If an option writer hopes to bring the payout ratio down much below 0.88, then it will almost certainly be through nontechnical means, and that implies *trade selectivity* based on fundamental judgments. These, by definition, are not amenable to statistical testing. Based on personal observation and trading experience, I believe that a dedicated option writer can, by judicious trade selectivity and shrewd timing, improve an already favorable edge of 0.88 by several points. I am not suggesting that in order to be a successful option writer, it is *necessary* to exercise fundamental judgment, only that the possibility exists for sharpening the edge and that the opportunity should not be dismissed.

An option writer who is cognizant of the fundamentals that affect option premiums—as opposed to the fundamentals that affect futures prices—should not be afraid to disagree with the market and from time to time take option positions based on a subjective estimate of uncertainty. However, a subjective disagreement with the uncertainty registered in the marketplace has to be more than a wild guess. It may be little more than a hunch, but a hunch which is still fundamentally based. I intend looking at some specific circumstances in which an option trader is likely to want to override his purely technical indicators. First, let's consider the components of uncertainty that contribute to an option's total value.

The price that the market places on a commodity option is a function of the uncertainty level surrounding the price outlook for its underlying commodity future. Most of this uncertainty is already reflected in the long-term and short-term volatilities observable in the price history of the commodity future. As already discussed in great detail, current market volatility, modified by historical norms, is the key to the fair pricing of a commodity option—under most circumstances. Historical average values of volatility—by individual commodity—are especially relevant when *current* volatility in a commodity future is unusually high or unusually low.

Coffee, for example, is consistently the most volatile commodity of all, with a long-term average implied volatility for its options around the 40 percent level. In contrast, the implied volatility of a currency option is usually below 10 percent. The market is well aware of what is "normal" volatility for each commodity and will reflect this normal value to some extent in the options, regardless of current market volatility in the futures. However, the option market cannot ignore what is happening in the futures market and will find a compromise pricing structure which takes into consideration both what is normal and what is current.

From a purely technical standpoint, then, an option writer can always obtain an objective fix on the current price of an option by determining where its implied volatility lies in relation to both its average level and the level implied by the current fluctuations in its future. Nothing new here, yet. These comparisons—current implied volatility versus historical average implied volatility, and current implied volatility versus current market volatility—can suggest potential overvaluation or undervaluation. For instance, an option that appears to be overvalued on *both* comparisons would clearly be a candidate for writing and certainly a candidate worthy of further investigation.

Whenever an option appears to be overvalued on both long-term and short-term volatility comparisons, there will usually be an identifiable fundamental reason: a source of uncertainty that is known to exist but is not being reflected in recent variability of the futures price. When unreflected uncertainty (let's call it the *U* factor) is a dominant component in an option premium structure, it is a prime opportunity for the fundamentally motivated option trader to exercise fundamental judgment.

The essential feature of a U-factor in operation is an *upcoming resolution of uncertainty* at a very specific and precisely known point in future time. This uncertainty component of an option premium typically reaches a peak just prior to the release of fundamental information from a government report or just prior to a decision by some quasi-political body wielding significant economic clout. Guesses as to the impact of the fundamental information to be released will be wildly divergent, but this divergence of opinion need not be reflected in a high volatility of the price of the commodity future in question. In fact, upcoming resolution of a major uncertainty may lead to subdued futures trading just prior to the event. The opposite is true of options, which will usually command premiums way in excess of those indicated on a purely technical basis. Apparent overvaluation in such cases is therefore not overvaluation at all. Worth remembering: *Prior to the release of important fundamental information affecting a commodity, futures volatility typically* falls *while option implied volatilities typically* rise. *After the release of fundamental information, futures prices often sustain large moves, whereas option premiums almost always shrink substantially.*

Although the above statement is most certainly true, it is really no more than a self-evident, if not so obvious, truth, and no strategy can be devised to exploit in any systematic way that which is already known. It *is* true that when uncertainty is about to be resolved, more opportunity exists for a cool head to prevail in turbulent conditions, but remember that it is only by *registering superior fundamental judgment in specific circumstances* that a trader can hope to add to his or her trading edge.

An option trader may choose to play the U-factor *before* the release of fundamental information (second-guessing its contents or its probable impact) or *after* the release of fundamental information (by analyzing and reacting to the market's reaction). To get a feel for how fundamental judgment may be exercised, it will be useful to review how particular options have reacted in the past, in the days leading up to and in the days following the release of significant news.

A regular resolver of uncertainty is the Federal Open Market Committee (FOMC) meeting of the Federal Reserve Board, which meets every other month to decide whether to raise interest rates, lower interest rates, or leave interest rates unchanged. A change in the prime rate can have a major impact on the whole economy and can affect currencies, the stock market, the yield curve, and all interest-rate-sensitive commodity futures. The reason that the uncertainty surrounding a FOMC meeting *cannot* be quantified is that the economic conditions prevailing at the time of the meeting change from month to month, as does the likelihood of a policy change and the impact of any such change.

If inflation is low, the unemployment rate steady, and wage pressures subdued, there is a strong probability that the Fed will do nothing. Under this scenario, the U-factor going into the meeting will be low. If, however, there is fundamental evidence that the economy may be overheating, there will be a good number of players who believe that the Fed will tighten. Under this second scenario, the U-factor will be much more important. Regardless of the outcome of a FOMC meeting, and regardless of the impact of any FOMC decision on futures prices, option premiums on interest-sensitive financial instruments will almost always drop as soon as the Fed's decision is announced. The at-the-money strike price may change, and change in a big way, but the at-the-money option premium will decline, simply because uncertainty has been removed.

How much option premium should the Fed command? Nobody knows, of course, but it is a question on which a fundamentally motivated option trader who trades volatility might have an opinion. Where would such an opinion come from? From observations of past market reactions, perhaps. From intuition, too, or from a correct assessment of the political climate. There are many, many reasons why a trader might disagree with the implied volatility of an option. One thing is fairly certain: The days surrounding the release of major information are often prime opportunities for a trader to exercise fundamental judgment.

Option writers are interested in trading "volatility." They would like to sell volatility when it is too high and avoid selling volatility (or even buy it) when they feel it is too low. A trader who can identify a market which is vastly overvalued might feel that there *must* be a way to capitalize on an assessment of overvaluation—a way to *lock in* a profit as it were. Unfortunately, even under conditions of large positive expectation, a negative result from an option trade is always possible. There are ways of improving the odds that a trade will turn out to be profitable, but no way of guaranteeing that it will be profitable, for there is always something the market can do to confound the best-laid strategy of the most astute option writer—on any one trade, that is.

Of course, the option writer is not going to be unduly concerned over the outcome of one trade, any more than a bookmaker is going to worry about paying off a single punter, or an insurance company is going to be jeopardized by any one claim. All these activities depend on spreading the risk and letting the power of high volume ensure a predictable overall return. For different ways in which a trader can buy and sell volatility using a variety of inter-option spreading techniques, I refer the reader to Sheldon Natenberg's *Option Volatility and Pricing.* This book, written by a floor trader with expert knowledge, covers a great deal of interesting territory I have tread but lightly upon.

*

There may not seem much connection between the interest-rate policy of the FOMC and the release of grain data by the United States Department of Agriculture. In terms of the U-factor, however, the potential impact on option premiums is much the same—just substitute corn and soybeans for currencies and bonds.

As a specific case in point, consider the action in the corn markets (futures and options) following the release of the important "Stocks in All Positions" report after the close of trading on January 15, 1996. At the close of trading that day, the closest-to-the-money March corn options were registering an implied volatility of 23.61, a relatively high number for that time of year. (Compare years 1993 through 1997 on page 238 of the reference section.) January is usually a low volatility month for corn, simply because not much can affect the supply/demand balance at that time: It is the middle of the marketing season, the old crop has been harvested and is known in size, and the new crop is still to be planted.

The relatively high volatility in corn futures in January 1996 was understandable, however, in light of the low carryover stocks that were almost certainly going to be a fact-of-life later that summer, and the stocks report scheduled for release in mid-January was being anticipated with more than usual interest. The question for options traders was whether an implied volatility of

23.61 was ascribing too much or too little option premium to the U-factor about to be resolved with the release of the stocks figure. Here's the *Wall Street Journal* (January 16, 1996, p. C16) reporting *after* the news was out and the market had had an opportunity to react:

> According to the Agricultural Department's report, released yesterday morning after a three-day delay caused by last weekend's east coast snowstorms, corn stockpiles at December 1, totalled only 6.101 billion bushels down from 8.081 billion a year ago, signalling that high prices have yet to curb consumption levels.
>
> More important, ending stocks—the amount of corn expected to be available by August 31, when this summer's crop is harvested—were trimmed to 507 million bushels, the lowest level in 20 years. That's down 110 million bushels.
>
> While these kinds of bullish data might have been expected to send prices soaring to fresh highs, traders said speculators had already factored in that kind of report in their recent buying.

The market had in fact dropped substantially that day—from $3.65 to $3.54 a bushel for March corn futures, a typically perverse response to allegedly bullish news, and the largest price move in corn in 2 months. Yet, despite this relatively large move in the futures price—usually accompanied by an *increase* in option implied volatility—the implied volatility of the new at-the-money option dropped from 23.61 to 18.72, an extremely large move for one day's trading. For option premiums, the effect of removing the uncertainty in the fundamentals (the release of the stocks figure) had overwhelmed any tendency toward an increase in volatility resulting from the price move in the futures. This is the normal reaction of option implied volatility to new supply information when the futures market turns lower.

If, after the report, corn futures had turned higher instead of lower, it is less clear what would have happened to the implied volatility of corn options. Most probably, option premiums would also have shrunk, but to a lesser degree. And, if the upside move had been extremely large, it is possible that option premiums would have increased. The important point here is that the reaction of option implied volatility to price action in crop futures is substantially asymmetrical, and the trader must be aware of what are viewed as "normal" changes in implied volatility in such situations, for it is the abnormal response—the occasion when the market does not respond according to its historical norm—that the option trader seeking an additional edge should be searching for.

*

Sometimes, fundamental judgment is appropriate in circumstances that are completely without precedent. In April 1996, the implied volatility of options on cattle futures shot up rather suddenly from under 15 percent to almost 30 percent, in a declining futures market. The volatility of cattle futures does have a tendency to increase in a falling market—in contrast to grains, say—but a large component of the increase in option implied volatility at that time was a large U-factor associated with "mad cow" disease.

How much option premium is a mad cow worth? Rather a lot it seems, or seemed at the time. Consider what was going through traders' minds when the mad cow rumors were flying: fear of the unknown, of course. Traders were reluctant to hold long futures positions in American cattle contracts, even though the problem seemed to be confined to Europe, specifically Britain. Although the mad cow story was not new, it received broad media coverage, which created a climate of great uncertainty, not necessarily supported by the facts at hand but with large potential implications. What if the public's appetite for beef were to vanish rather suddenly? What if cattle ranchers were to panic, rush their cattle to market and liquidate breeding stock? In the cattle futures market, prices fell precipitously, but it was not clear how the situation would be resolved. There was even a *bullish* case to be made: What if a preemptive slaughtering of cattle were to lead to a shortage of healthy deliverable animals later on, after the scare had passed—as scares almost always have done?

One commodity was in great supply—confusion. And a confusion that led to a doubling of the option implied volatility on the nearby cattle contract. All this is retrospective, of course, but looking back, was there any opportunity for an option trader to grab a fundamental edge in such a confused situation? Possibly. Cattle futures traders would have noticed that the volatility of the nearest future was much greater than the volatility of the more distant contracts. Experienced traders knew that the confusion would not last and that the bullish and bearish arguments would probably cancel each other out over the longer term.

The market, therefore, was clever enough not to permit the implied volatilities of options on deferred contracts to rise to the same extent as the implied volatility of the nearby. Nevertheless, the former *were* dragged substantially higher, with the implied volatility of the August at-the-money option increasing at the peak of the scare by almost the same amount as the June at-the-money—at that time, the lead contract. (On April 9, 1996, the implied volatilities of the June and August options were 15.18 and 15.22, respectively; by April 26, June implied volatility had increased to 28.31, and August to 26.80.)

Should the implied volatility of August have risen almost as much as the implied volatility for June? Probably not—at least that seems to be what *I'm* implying. While I could be legitimately accused of taking unreasonable advantage of hindsight, I offer this cattle story as an example of "opportunity in confusion" of the kind that an option fundamentalist might want to try and exploit.

Another market where the U-factor is always present to some degree is crude oil. Here, the trick is to guess when political intervention is likely to occur. Supply is in the hands of a cartel which makes periodic attempts to prop up falling prices by reducing production. The implied volatilities of crude oil options will expand or contract according to the consensus of opinion about when "intervention" will occur and how successful it is likely to be if it takes place. The cartel members usually get together in crisis situations, which to them is a declining price for crude oil. There is no record of them ever getting together to expand supplies in a rising oil market. The net effect of cartel interference is to make crude oil rather more volatile on the downside than on the upside. Given the general venality of the regimes that make up OPEC, and the propensity of individual members to cheat on their self-imposed production quotas, past attempts at propping up oil prices have only been marginally successful.

Consider the market action in crude oil futures during March and April of 1998, a typical bear market positively crying out for OPEC support (Figure 8-6). All during March of 1998, as crude oil was dropping in price, the implied volatility of the May crude oil option was increasing—from an already above average 32.01 percent on March 2 to 37.94 percent on March 16. Technically, both on a long-term and short-term comparison basis, the May crude oil option was overvalued. But the market was anticipating OPEC interference and incorporating a high U-factor into the option premium structure.

On Tuesday, March 17, implied volatility jumped to a new high of 42.32 percent. The reason was quickly forthcoming; after the close of trading that day, the oil producing countries announced that a special meeting would be held in very short order. This news produced a typical sharp rally in crude oil futures on March 18, accompanied by a further increase in option implied volatility to 46.60 percent. The *New York Times* (March 19, 1998, p. D7) commented on the rally, as follows:

> Crude oil prices rebounded 8.6 percent yesterday as the market was encouraged by news that there might soon be a special meeting of the big oil producing countries to discuss reductions in output.
>
> Reductions of 1.5 to 2 million barrels per day are reportedly being considered. Such cuts, some analysts have said could increase the price of crude oil by $4 to $5 per barrel.

Did the increase in option implied volatility *after* the announcement of an upcoming meeting make sense? Yes, it did. Although it was true that the market had been half *expecting* some such announcement, its *confirmation* did not reduce uncertainty, for no one yet knew the extent of the measures that would be proposed. Three days later the hard news came out. Crude oil futures soared by $2 a barrel, and option implied

Date	May crude oil futures High	Low	Close	At-the-money straddle premium	Days left	Implied Volatility
Mar 2	1599	1565	1566	144	33	32.01
Mar 3	1590	1552	1561	146	32	33.07
Mar 4	1580	1544	1565	141	31	32.36
Mar 5	1588	1563	1567	135	30	31.46
Mar 6	1574	1526	1530	133	29	32.28
Mar 9	1529	1441	1472	126	28	32.35
Mar 10	1488	1460	1463	128	27	33.68
Mar 11	1486	1455	1456	132	26	35.56
Mar 12	1478	1438	1457	137	25	37.61
Mar 13	1472	1440	1443	133	24	37.63
Mar 16	1442	1360	1385	126	23	37.94
Mar 17	1374	1315	1350	134	22	42.32
Mar 18	1475	1356	1461	156	21	46.60
Mar 19	1490	1441	1460	145	20	44.42
Mar 20	1484	1430	1461	155	19	48.68
Mar 23	1750	1575	1651	149	18	42.54
Mar 24	1597	1573	1592	132	17	40.22
Mar 25	1651	1570	1648	127	16	38.53
Mar 26	1770	1648	1683	137	15	42.04
Mar 27	1704	1668	1676	139	14	44.33
Mar 30	1690	1607	1621	123	13	42.09
Mar 31	1626	1556	1561		12	
Apr 1	1578	1531	1554		11	
Apr 2	1580	1548	1574		10	
Apr 3	1608	1575	1599		9	
Apr 6	1595	1534	1545		8	
Apr 7	1548	1517	1522		7	
Apr 8	1568	1516	1555		6	
Apr 9	1580	1552	1556		5	
Apr 13	1568	1528	1532		3	
Apr 14	1535	1510	1512		2	
Apr 15	1560	1502	1546		1	
Apr 16	1600	1547	1590		May option expires	

FIGURE 8-6. Price action on May 1998 crude oil futures, and the May 1998 at-the-money crude oil straddle, during March and April of 1998. Premiums on options were unusually high, reflecting uncertainty about what OPEC might try to do to stem a major price decline.

volatility dropped, though not by very much. Again, from the *New York Times* (March 24, 1998, p. D10):

> The price of crude oil rose 13 percent yesterday in world petroleum markets, the biggest one day surge since the Persian Gulf War more than seven years ago; in reaction to weekend promises by producing nations to reduce their exports.

> By yesterday, seven other major producers had joined Saudi Arabia, Venezuela, and Mexico, the three that led the drive to reduce exports, which they announced on Sunday.

In the days following the agreement, the implied volatility of the May crude oil option fell slightly, but by Friday March 27, it was back near its highest level at 44.33 percent. Here we have a situation where the *news is out,* and the U-factor has been *resolved,* yet option premiums have not declined appreciably: in other words, the atypical response, and a *potential* overvaluation situation.

The corn, cattle, and crude oil examples described above are not offered as *obvious* cases of option overvaluation, but rather as pointers towards potential overvaluation. As stressed earlier, the outcome of any one option trade—be it a buy or a sell, a put or a call, a straddle or a strangle—will depend very much on fortuitous timing. For example, in the crude oil scenario above—an implied straddle-writing situation due to possible overvaluation—crude oil futures made a subsequent large move before the expiry of the May option; a move which would have demanded a *covering response* from a disciplined option writer (Figure 8-6). *That* outcome does not mean that writing a straddle on March 27 would have been a bad idea; it just would not have worked out in this particular case due to unlucky timing. Had the straddle been written on any of the subsequent five trading days, it would, if held to expiry, have been rather profitable.

No discussion of volatility would be complete without some reference to the "mother of all futures contracts"—the S&P500 Index. Not only has this contract the largest daily trading range, in dollar terms, it has become, along with its options, one of the most liquid to trade. The S&P options market is one of the few where it can truly be said that commission charges are not going to have a serious impact upon the profitability of option trading. Of course, the S&P futures and options complex has benefitted enormously from the huge bull market in stocks over the last fifteen years. The options, in particular, have gained great popularity with the general increase in the volatility of stock prices.

I can't pretend to be able to read much into the day-to-day changes in the implied volatility of S&P options, or to have correctly identified many cases of potential overvaluation or undervaluation; the S&P futures contract is still a relative newcomer on the trading scene. In addition, because of the secular bull market that has been in place since the inception of the contract, there is some question as to whether past history is going to be representative of the future.

Certainly, the same U-factors that affect interest rate and currency futures are going to impact upon the stock market. However, there *may* be a U-factor particular to stocks, stock indexes, and futures. With the broad-based public participation that is unique to stock trading, there is some reason to suppose that price action there may be fundamentally different from price action in conventional commodities. (More of this, shortly, when I discuss my own uncorroborated theories on what makes the stock market tick.)

During its fifteen-year bull run, the stock market has experienced two very large one-day price declines, neither of which was followed by any further downside action. The first of these drops occurred in October of 1987, and the second almost exactly ten years later in October of 1997. In percentage terms, the 1987 plunge was almost four times as large as the 1997 plunge; it came so suddenly and was of such a magnitude that it probably wiped out a generation of option writers; certainly those option writers who were not employing very strict defensive strategies to protect any puts they had written.

Huge stock market declines are bound to be accompanied by greatly expanded option prices on stock index futures, simply because the uncertainty following such an event is so acute. Figures 8-7 and 8-8 show how S&P options and futures reacted in the days leading up to and following the days of the large price declines. In the debacle of 1987, on the Friday preceding "Crash Monday," the implied volatility of the at-the-money S&P option expanded from 22.90 to 27.22, a steep rise, to be sure, but not a surprising increase in view of the larger than normal drop in the futures market that day. The S&P options market has always been very sensitive to even slightly larger than usual daily price declines in stock futures, for there is a constant and justifiable fear among option writers of a sudden downside washout in stock prices. (Memories of 1929 still lingered in 1987.)

No one, of course—including the holders of put options who may claim great after-the-fact wisdom—could have foreseen what would happen on Monday, October 20. Not even in 1929 had a one-day decline of 25 percent—or anything like that—been experienced. The crash was of such unprecedented proportions that settlement prices on S&P options could not be published, the first and only time this has occurred. On the day following the crash, Tuesday, October 21, S&P futures closed higher, and option settlement prices *were* available, but only on the December series (November was still the front month). Option implied volatility had shot up from 27.23 to 83.51. The next day, futures rallied again, and implied volatility shrank to 56.08.

What happened subsequently is rather curious. A couple of days later, on Friday, October 23, a quietish day in which futures declined from 244 to 241, implied volatility shot up again to 85 percent, and on the following day to 93 percent. It was as if option traders had all woken up to a new reality and decided collectively, overnight, that options were way too cheap. I find this a curious reaction, because, in a high-priced environment, especially an environment in which stability appears to be returning, option implied volatility usually drops quite sharply.

Within a few days, implied volatility had dropped back to the 40 to 50 percent range. To a lesser extent, the same option implied volatility pattern emerged after in the plunge of 1997: a rapid increase in implied volatility due to the decline in futures, a pullback in implied volatility as the market appeared to be stabilizing, then an increase in implied volatility to new heights *for no apparent reason,* followed by a rapid decline. Clearly, in a highly unstable futures market, ideas of what constitutes fair option value can shift substantially from day to day. In circumstances such as these, the trader who can come up with an independent estimate of option fair value may want to bid or offer at

Date	Futures(1) High	Low	Close	Option Month	Straddle(2) Premium	Days	Volatility (3),(4) Implied	Market
Oct 1	332	326	331	Nov	18.90	36	19.03	20.93
Oct 2	333	330	331	Nov	18.40	35	18.79	19.88
Oct 5	332	328	330	Nov	18.00	34	18.71	19.22
Oct 6	330	319	319	Nov	19.35	33	21.12	22.05
Oct 7	322	317	320	Nov	17.35	32	19.17	21.29
Oct 8	321	313	315	Nov	17.30	31	19.73	21.97
Oct 9	317	311	312	Nov	17.30	30	20.25	21.93
Oct 12	314	308	311	Nov	17.20	29	20.54	21.19
Oct 13	317	312	315	Nov	16.65	28	19.98	21.53
Oct 14	313	304	305	Nov	16.60	27	20.95	24.06
Oct 15	307	297	298	Nov	17.40	26	22.90	25.44
Oct 16	301	277	282	Nov	19.20	25	27.23	30.41
Oct 19	269	198	201	Nov	Not available			73.22
Oct 20	242	181	216	Dec	57.75	41	83.51	77.19
Oct 21	259	239	258	Dec	45.75	40	56.08	91.24
Oct 22	250	195	244	Dec	47.25	39	62.02	92.99
Oct 23	253	234	241	Dec	63.50	38	85.49	89.71
Oct 26	237	218	220	Dec	62.25	37	93.03	95.73
Oct 27	242	223	228	Dec	47.40	36	69.30	94.80
Oct 28	234	218	231	Dec	43.25	35	63.30	91.49
Oct 29	249	235	245	Dec	38.50	34	53.90	93.20
Oct 30	260	252	259	Dec	36.65	33	49.27	94.48
Nov 2	258	251	257	Dec	32.50	32	44.71	90.62
Nov 3	254	240	250	Dec	34.35	31	49.36	89.17
Nov 4	253	246	250	Dec	32.85	30	47.98	84.71
Nov 5	258	247	255	Dec	30.60	29	44.57	82.63
Nov 6	258	242	249	Dec	30.10	28	45.69	81.15
Nov 9	248	242	245	Dec	29.70	27	46.66	78.89
Nov 10	243	237	239	Dec	29.80	26	48.91	77.70
Nov 11	245	240	242	Dec	28.25	25	46.69	75.18
Nov 12	251	247	249	Dec	27.05	24	44.35	74.07

FIGURE 8-7. The December 1987 S&P futures contract, showing how option premiums and implied volatilities fluctuated before and after the "crash of '87." The final column shows market volatility derived by exponentially smoothing the mean absolute deviation of daily price changes. In chaotic conditions, the relationship between implied volatility and market volatility is tenuous, to say the least. Notes (1) and (2) below, and notes (3) and (4) under Figure 8-8 pertain to both Figure 8-7 and Figure 8-8.

[1] Futures prices have been rounded to nearest whole number.

[2] Straddle premium is the combined value of the put and call premiums available at the closest-to-the-money strike price.

a fixed price, especially if the quoted bid–asked spread is very wide or not quoted at all. The fixed price order may be filled against a market order on the other side—just because no one else is brave enough to declare.

Date	Futures(1) High	Low	Close	Option Month	Straddle(2) Premium	Days	Volatility(3),(4) Implied	Market
Oct 1	967	954	963	Nov	57.40	37	19.60	17.80
Oct 2	970	961	969	Nov	56.20	36	19.33	17.60
Oct 5	986	961	975	Nov	54.95	35	19.05	17.39
Oct 6	983	976	981	Nov	53.80	34	18.81	17.20
Oct 7	992	979	989	Nov	51.40	33	18.09	17.23
Oct 8	991	975	982	Nov	50.75	32	18.27	17.15
Oct 9	983	969	978	Nov	49.75	31	18.27	16.74
Oct 12	980	965	976	Nov	48.85	30	18.28	16.13
Oct 13	982	974	976	Nov	47.30	29	18.00	15.32
Oct 14	981	968	978	Nov	46.70	28	18.05	14.78
Oct 15	977	968	973	Nov	45.60	27	18.04	14.61
Oct 16	981	956	960	Nov	45.80	26	18.71	15.37
Oct 19	959	935	948	Nov	45.75	25	19.30	15.99
Oct 20	963	947	962	Nov	43.50	24	18.46	16.79
Oct 21	980	962	979	Nov	40.65	23	17.32	17.86
Oct 22	980	970	974	Nov	40.30	22	17.64	17.53
Oct 23	976	948	955	Nov	43.70	21	19.97	18.85
Oct 26	969	942	944	Nov	44.65	20	21.15	19.19
Oct 27	944	874	874	Nov	59.40	19	31.18	27.04
Oct 28	932	844	924	Nov	49.50	18	25.25	31.64
Oct 29	941	917	924	Nov	49.75	17	26.12	30.06
Oct 30	929	902	903	Nov	57.90	16	32.06	31.11
Nov 2	926	899	924	Nov	50.30	15	28.11	32.06
Nov 3	946	921	945	Nov	43.90	14	24.83	32.90
Nov 4	946	936	942	Nov	43.50	13	25.62	31.60
Nov 5	955	938	947	Nov	41.00	12	25.00	30.60
Nov 6	947	937	942	Nov	40.40	11	25.86	29.66
Nov 9	943	916	931	Nov	44.90	10	30.50	29.47
Nov 10	941	923	926	Nov	42.20	9	30.38	28.59
Nov 11	933	922	926	Nov	37.00	8	28.25	27.16
Nov 12	929	905	908	Nov	37.70	7	31.39	27.99

FIGURE 8-8. The December 1997 S&P futures contract, showing how option premiums and implied volatilities fluctuated around the time of the record one-day point loss in the Dow Jones industrial average. Compared to 1987, the options market reacted in a much more orderly fashion. Option-implied volatilities stayed pretty much in line with calculated market volatility.

[3] Implied volatilities may be obtained from the table entries of Figure 4-7 or from the equation: $iv = 20 \times p/\sqrt{t}$.

[4] Market volatility on October 1 is calculated from the MAD of observed values during September and updated thereafter by exponential smoothing, using a smoothing constant of 0.05, according to:

$$MAD_2 = 0.95 \times MAD_1 + 0.05 \times |\text{price change}_2|$$

and

$$mv_2 = 22.0 \times MAD_2$$

From close observation of the way stock index futures trade, I have come to the belief that stock averages generate price patterns that are rather different from all other traded commodities. The most striking difference, in my view, is the speed with which the S&P (the one I watch most closely) moves between what technicians call support and resistance levels—with very little trading in between. Either everybody seems to want it, or nobody seems to want it. The usual middle ground appears to be missing. What's more, this on-again off-again love-hate affair is occurring on an ever-shortening time horizon. What are the implications, apart from the obvious one that the whole thing may suddenly implode in some bizarre unimaginable way?

My assessment of the current frenzy on Wall Street (August 1998) is that short-term stock market volatility may be increasing, while long-term volatility may be staying the same. If true, this could present an opportunity in options. The volatility of a true random variable does not depend on the time horizon over which it is observed, and that is why the option pricing structure on the carrying-charge commodities, such as currencies and metals, follows the square-root-time equation almost exactly. Does the S&P option pricing structure also follow the square-root-time law? Yes, it does. And that means one of two things. Either my suggestion that short-term volatility is greater than long-term volatility is incorrect, or options on deferred S&P contracts are overvalued in relation to nearbys. If the latter is the case, a trading opportunity may exist.

What psychology could account for a market becoming more volatile only in the short-term? I think the answer may lie in the composition of the players playing the game and in the technology these players are using in their attempts to outsmart each other. It is well known that, in the last few years, index funds, that is, mutual funds which try to mimic the performance of the S&P Index, have become major players in the S&P futures trading pit. In other words, more big players can influence—if only in the short-term—the direction of the market. These large players may also be able to create their own bandwagon effects. I think it would definitely be fair to conjecture that markets dominated by the actions of a few large players are going to be more volatile than markets dominated by a large number of small players, even when the total trading volumes are the same. With the possible exception of Alan Greenspan, however, no individual or consortium is large enough to influence prices over the longer term.

It is also fair to conjecture that the amount of computer and telecommunications gadgetry employed at the present time—by traders desperate to divine the next 10-minute trend—is also destabilizing to the market, since a "high-tech" psychology promotes decisionmaking based on observing price patterns rather than decisionmaking based on economics. It does not surprise me in the least that the implied volatility of S&P options continues on its long-term secular uptrend. In such a crap-shoot environment as Wall Street 1998, it may be hard to see how any kind of fundamental judgment on option valuations can be brought to bear. But, there are always hidden truths waiting to be discovered by an astute and patient observer.

How much of an additional edge can an option writer hope to achieve through the exercise of fundamental judgment? Based on my own trading experience, I would cautiously suggest that a sound fundamental override can reduce the option writer's payout ratio from 0.88 (purely technical) to around 0.85, equivalent to a trading edge of 15 percent. It is now time to investigate whether a gross trading edge of 15 percent can translate into a respectable return on the investment required to finance the appropriate transactions.

CHAPTER NINE

THE ARMCHAIR BROKER

After completing Chapter 5, the last of the theoretical chapters of this book, I sent the manuscript to a friend, for his comments. He pronounced it a "good read" but reminded me that my stated goal was to explore the available empirical evidence, with the objective of answering some questions that had long gone unanswered. He wrote down these questions, rather succinctly:

> Being a pragmatic kind of a guy, I am looking forward to the second part of the book, to see the answer to my three-part question, which, to review, is:
>
> 1. Applying a purely systematic and objective approach to trading options, is it possible to obtain a long-term positive mathematical expectation?
> 2. Is the edge large enough to overcome a series of impediments that we must cope with, the most important being transaction costs and "slippage" associated with each trade?
> 3. Finally, will the edge provide a worthwhile return on the "true and necessary" trading capital?

Well, I do believe I have answered the first question; the other two still require a bit of work, but I will get to these before this final chapter is over.

From the hypothetical trading results detailed in previous chapters, and from personal experience writing option straddles in many different markets, I feel confident in asserting that a 15 percent trading edge can be attained by any disciplined option writer using a little bit of imagination. I am not aware of any trading technique that can produce a positive expectation through the systematic buying of options. Therefore, in these few remaining pages, I am going to concentrate exclusively on option-writing strategy, expectations, and return on invested capital. In the process, I will be drawing on my own practical experience as an option trader (nonspecialist) as well as on information gathered from individuals with first-hand knowledge of what actually happens on the option trading floor.

First, a 15 percent trading edge does not translate into a 15 percent return on equity. To understand what an edge does mean, let's review how the cash flows in an options-writing program. An option writer operating with a gross 15 percent trading edge can expect to keep $150 out of every $1000 received in premiums; the other $850 will be paid back to the option buyers. These, however, are the cash flows that would prevail in a "Goldilocks" trading environment. In real trading, the writer is going to keep less than $150. The key question is how much less.

*

For all option traders, there are going to be significant costs associated with executing trades. Commission costs are relatively straightforward to estimate, and I'll deal with those shortly. Less obvious, and sometimes hidden, are the costs incurred by the trader who pays more to purchase an option and receives less for selling an option than the true equilibrium trading price.

In all the calculations leading up to the estimated 15 percent trading edge, it was assumed that hypothetical trades were executed at the closing prices posted by the option exchanges. These are the numbers that appear in option tables in the financial press, and are unbiased estimates of the true trading values of options—as distinct from fair value, which is another concept altogether. Because of their low trading volumes compared to futures, it will frequently be the case that with certain options no actual trades are made on the close—or at any time during a session for that matter. With illiquid and nontraded options, it is the job of the exchanges to *estimate* closing prices and to maintain option values in logical proportions to each other. They have to estimate prices, because brokerage firms need to know, on a daily basis, the market value of each and every listed option to properly calculate clients' equities.

The settlement committees of the different options exchanges are made up of traders with extensive first-hand knowledge of the trading pits and with a good understanding of relative values, and these committees do a pretty good job of settling prices at close to their true trading values. Far out-of-the-money options, for example, will be keyed mostly off the at-the-money option, according to recent historical proportions. So, whether actual trades are made on the close or not, it is safe to assume that posted prices are at least unbiased and that no inherent error should arise in using posted prices to test a hypothetical trading system. In practice, naturally, it is not likely that a trader will execute a trade right on the close, and it is also true that option premiums are continuously declining, even as the trading session progresses. These considerations, however, do not make the closing price any less relevant as a reference point. In hypothesis testing, one point in time is as valid as any other.

Yet, even with unbiased closing price estimates, the option trader is still going to be faced with execution costs. As all active traders know, posted option closing prices represent the middle point between a hypothetical *bid* and a hypothetical *asking* price. As a buyer, you will, in reality, have to pay an asking price higher than the true value, and as a seller you will have to take a bid price lower than the true value—that is, if you want your order to be executed right away, or, *at the market,* to use the technical term. The spread between the bid price and the asking price can have serious long-run consequences for traders using market orders, since an option writer is already working with a rather small edge to begin with. It is important, therefore, to have an idea of the size of this spread and the conditions under which the use of market orders may be acceptable.

Many option traders would recoil at the thought of using market orders in the somewhat illiquid option pits, fearing that the dearth of volume would all but guarantee lousy fills, thereby negating any hard-won edge achieved through the exercise of good discipline and a little creative imagination. I had some of these concerns myself. So, to understand the trading process a little better, I paid a visit to the New York Cotton Exchange, where Jurgens Bauer, an options floor trader of some considerable experience and reputation, agreed, goodnaturedly, to answer some of my layman's questions.

*

"One of my real problems with options," I said, "is not being able to act fast and get a reasonable price. I trade a lot of futures, often with market orders, and I don't feel I'm giving too much away. But here?

"That's a common fear," said Bauer. "But an exaggerated one."

"Sometimes an option will not trade for hours," I said. "What if there is no one around to take the other side of my trade, at the time *I* want it done?"

"There's always a bid and an asking price," he said. "The numbers may not show up on your quotation monitor, but you can always get them off the floor." Bauer pointed out some intense-looking individuals on the other side of the pit, who appeared to be checking the futures boards while punching data into pocket calculators. "One of these guys will give me a price on any option or combination I want," he added.

"But what if I give *you,* as my broker, say, a big sell order *at the market*? Won't the other guy drop his bid, knowing that you have a market order which you will have to keep offering lower until somebody bites?"

"It's not quite like that," said Bauer, smiling. "Watch, you said selling a hundred of the *December seventy-ones,* didn't you?"

Before I could answer, he had boomed out a request.

"I'm talking hypothetically," I said, just slightly alarmed.

"Don't worry," he said. "So am I."

Seconds later, a shout came back from the other side of the pit: "One sixty-five bid, one seventy-two offered."

"That's fine," I said. "But he still doesn't know whether you want to buy or sell, does he?"

"That's right," said Bauer.

"And he doesn't know how many contracts?

"Right again. Why should I tip my hand?"

"Okay, I'm getting the idea," I said. "But how is the trade finally executed? Surely, somebody has to declare eventually?"

"He already has. *He* has to take what *I* give him now.

"Buy or sell?"

"Buy or sell."

"And the quantity?"

"Whatever I want."

"One contract or ten?"

"Or a thousand, for that matter."

"And what if the guy on the floor takes a thousand lot position and the market starts to move against *him?*

"Don't worry about him. There are plenty of ways he can hedge with futures. Now, are you still afraid to go with a big market order?"

"Not as much as I was," I had to concede.

"Just one thing, though," said Bauer. "Make sure you know your broker." At least, I think that's what I heard him say.

*

Since my visit to the Cotton Exchange, I have been less reluctant to use market orders in the options pit, especially when exiting from a position—which, as an option writer, is usually when the futures market is accelerating against me. I try to enter new positions, particularly straddles, with limit orders, and try to estimate this limit, or fixed price, as the midpoint between what I think the bid and the asked ought to be. That way, *I* become the offer, and an antsy buyer may be tempted to grab me. But, sometimes, even with a straddle, I will go at the market—if I absolutely don't want to miss the trade or if the apparent premium available even at the bid strikes me as unusually favorable and I don't expect it to stay there long.

An option trader should always be familiar with the "mood" of the futures market, before deciding on which way to have an order executed. In volatile conditions—where futures are trading at the daily price limit, say—option asking prices may rise above their true trading values, simply because writers choose to stand back and give themselves time to assess the situation. These are not the conditions in which to enter market orders. They are, however, exactly the conditions where a well-thought-out fixed-price order may find a taker. Where chaos reigns, it sometimes pays to be bold.

Whether one uses market orders or not, there is no way of avoiding execution costs, and these have to be viewed simply as costs of doing business. With a market order, the execution cost—sometimes called *slippage*—can be estimated from the typical bid-asked spread associated with the option in question. If, for example, you are quoted a straddle price of 2.35 bid, 2.45 offered, you are going to be giving away 0.05, either as a buyer or as a seller, because the true value is going to be 2.40. The 15 percent edge was calculated, remember, on true values. Of the 2.40 premium received, you "expect" to keep 15 percent, or 0.36. In fact, because of the slippage of 0.05, you can expect to keep only 0.31, which, in this case, would bring the trading edge down well below 15 percent.

If you try to avoid slippage by splitting the bid and the asked, and offer 2.40, the true value, instead of taking the bid at 2.35, you may or may not get the transaction completed, and if you don't, there will be a "hidden" execution cost, since the gross trading edge is predicated upon getting all hypothetical positions transacted.

In estimating potential returns from option writing, I prefer to be conservative and assume that orders are filled at the market, in which case, from my own experience, the overall gross trading edge will come down to a net of around 13 percent. Bear in mind, too, that in the systematic writing of straddles there are going to be exit as well as entry execution costs. I'm referring to those cases where defensive follow-up action is necessary. If the losing side of a straddle is to be covered either by direct offset or by the purchase of another option, there will be a further execution cost incurred. Furthermore, even with a successfully written straddle that is held till option expiry, it is axiomatic that one side of the straddle will end up having residual value, and *that* option will be exercised and will require a futures offset to cancel it out. Consequently, a further small slippage charge will be incurred. All things considered, I would suggest that execution costs, conservatively, are going to knock 3 percentage points of the option writer's edge, bringing net expectation down from 15 percent to around 12 percent.

*

In all the hypothetical trading results from the 1996 data base, it was assumed that whenever it was necessary to "protect" the losing side of a straddle, this protection was accomplished via an offsetting position in the futures market. Using futures was the simplest way (computationally) to evaluate the effects of employing a defensive strategy. In actual trading, two problems are associated with the defensive futures strategy. First, the futures position requires continuous monitoring to see if further defensive action will be necessary. And second, a futures position is going to tie up additional trading capital in margin.

An equally effective defensive strategy is accomplished with the purchase of an at-the-money put or call, instead of a future. It should be clear that, since the purchase of an offsetting option will only be necessary where one side of the original straddle is already incurring a large loss, the at-the-money strike price of a partially offsetting option will now be some considerable distance away from the strike price of the original straddle. While essentially locking in a loss, the at-the-money offset still affords protection and is still an effective way of neutralizing the straddle.

Now, it is true that the "neatest" way out of the losing leg of a straddle is to buy back the original straddle, or at least the option component that is incurring the loss. The problem here is that the losing option will be so deep in the money that it will be extremely illiquid, and it will therefore be difficult to get a reasonable execution price. On balance, it seems to me that the purchase of the *current* at-the-money or closest-to-the-money option is the best way out of a problem straddle. The covering trade is going to be made in the most liquid option, and, once completed, the straddle is basically shut down, allowing the writer to explore new writing opportunities in that same commodity.

If a straddle is to be offset by the purchase of a put or a call, the writer has the choice of either going at the market or going with a limit order. Whenever a trader wishes to offset a losing position via a relatively liquid (at-the-money) option, it is safer to go at the market. A lot of money can be given away fast, when an attempt to finesse a covering option fails and the futures market roars away. In option writing, there's a lot to be said for getting in slow and getting out fast.

Execution-wise, there is a subtle difference between going with a limit order on a straddle and going with a limit order on a put or a call—if the order is to be left *resting* in the pit. Because the straddle curve is very flat, close to the money, even a sudden large move in the futures price is not going to change the true value of the straddle very much. So, there is a wide range of futures prices where a resting straddle may be fairly filled on a resting limit order. However, with a limit order on a put or a call, a sharp move in the futures price may cause this order to be filled at the limit price, even though the true value may now be quite different—another good reason for using market orders on exit. The floor trader who is looking after a resting limit order may or may not get a better price than the limit specified, but he is not obliged to get a better price just because the futures have moved. With a resting option limit order, the trader would do well to keep an eye on the futures price and be prepared to cancel quickly if an unwelcome fill looms as a distinct possibility.

*

The other cost associated with trading is, of course, commission. For floor traders, commission is negligible, but for armchair bookmakers commission is a major cost. Commission costs are usually the same regardless of the commodity or the size of contract. For the retail customer, I reckon that the commission cost of executing a straddle to completion will average out at around $130, broken down as follows: $30 for the put, $30 for the call, $50 for the offsetting futures trade, and an additional $20 (averaged) to cover situations where one or both sides of a straddle have to offset. (On occasions, a massive whipsaw move in a futures price may call for offsetting both sides of a straddle. It is a rare occurrence, but it does happen.) Large traders may be able to negotiate lower commission rates for doing multiple contracts. For now, I want to consider the small trader doing one or two contracts, who will definitely be looking at commission of around $130.

Since the commission for trading a straddle position is basically fixed, its effect upon the profitability of the overall trade changes dramatically with the dollar amount of premium received, which in turn varies with the size of the contract, the volatility of the contract, and the time till expiry of the options. Typical dollar amounts of premium available for writing straddles on different commodities, and for options with different expiry times, are shown in Figure 9-1.

First, let's consider the extreme cases. The sale of a 7-week S&P straddle will net the option writer over $10,000, from which the writer can "expect" to keep 12 percent, say, or $1200. Here, a commission charge of $130 will reduce the writer's edge by a little over 1 percentage point (Figure 9-2). At the other extreme, consider sugar options, where a 6-month straddle will generate a premium of about $1200, from which the writer can "expect" to keep $144. Here, the commission charge of $130 will reduce the writer's edge to almost nothing, so that the only winners will be the brokerage houses and the exchanges.

Clearly, commission cost has to be a major consideration for the nonfloor trader who is trying to decide whether a low-priced option is worth trading in the first place. At some level of premium received, a straddle cannot possibly be worth trading—even with a net positive expectation of 12 percent. I would put the lower limit at around $2500, which would still leave the writer a positive expectation of 6.5 percent.

With that restriction, it is obvious from Figure 9-1 that some commodities will only rarely be candidates for writing, specifically, sugar, cocoa, cattle, corn, and gold. When wheat, silver, and crude oil are active, it will usually be possible to net $2500 by writing a straddle with a longish time till expiry. For the

	OPTION MATURITY					
	May	June	July	Aug.	Sept.	Oct.
S&P Index	10,500	13,500				
T-Bonds	1,800	2,900	3,700			
Swiss Franc	2,600	3,500				
Japanese Yen	2,800	3,800				
Gold		1,100		1,500		
Silver		1,600	2,200			
Crude Oil		1,600	2,100			
Cotton			2.300			3,800
Soybeans	3,000		4,600	5,700		
Wheat			2,300		2,700	
Corn			1,700		2,500	
Cattle		1,200		1,500		
Cocoa		1,000		1,500		
Sugar		600				1,200
Coffee	4.100		11,000			

FIGURE 9-1. Straddle premiums, expressed in dollars, available on selected commodities, as of March 27, 1997. At one extreme, $10,500 is available on a 7-week S&P straddle. At the other extreme, a sugar straddle with 6 months till expiry yields only $1200.

remaining commodities of Figure 9-1, it will almost always be possible to net at least $3000. In cotton, this will require the writing of an option with as much as a 6-month term. In the S&P, $3000 can be had from a straddle with as little as 2 weeks till expiry.

With ($) receipts of:	10,000	5,000	4,000	3,000	2,000	1,000
Retained before commission	1,200	600	480	360	240	120
Commission per straddle	130	130	130	130	130	130
Retained after commission	1,070	470	350	230	110	−10
Net expectation (%)	10.7	9.4	8.7	7.7	5.5	<0

FIGURE 9-2. The expected profitability from writing options is highly sensitive to the dollar amount of premium received. Low-priced options, where the straddle premium is less than $2500, say, are simply not worth writing—at least, for the general public. For large traders able to negotiate lower commission rates, the cut-off point at which profitability will be compromised is lower.

One very good reason for writing straddles (at-the-money strikes) as opposed to strangles (out-of-the-money strikes) is that the straddle yields the ***maximum premium possible.***

Since the amount of premium received per option is so critical to the profitability of option writing, it is especially important to receive the maximum premium possible. For this reason, it is better for the writer to concentrate on writing straddles (puts and calls with the same strike price) rather than strangles (options with the call price higher than the put price). Although a strangle has a winning zone where the writer can, with a bit of luck, retain *all* the premium, the lower total premium received in the first place makes the strangle an inferior choice to the straddle. (It should be noted in passing that the commission charge problem affects option writers much more than option buyers, who are usually going after profits many times larger than their initial investments, and not buying options in any systematic way.

Does it make any sense to have a fixed commission charge for trading an option? That it should cost the same to trade an S&P option as a sugar option? I can't see it. At current price and volatility levels, the daily price range of an S&P future, in dollar terms, is approaching $5000. In sugar, $300 would be a big day. There is no reason why an option on a low-priced low-volatility contract—like sugar, cocoa, gold, and cattle—could not be resized to cover five contracts, say, with the same commission charge. If this were done, a great many more players would enter the game, because at least they would have a shot at beating the house edge. As things stand, the option-writing public is essentially excluded from writing options on certain exchanges. Could it be that these exchanges only want the public as *buyers,* that option writing is to be the preserve of floor traders who pay little or no commission? It sure looks that way, but one has to wonder why.

*

Many commodity-related trading systems have been devised with convincingly demonstrated high expectations—sometimes with returns of over 100 percent per annum. These systems all suffer from one rather unfortunate drawback. With convincingly demonstrable regularity, they get wiped out.

Brokerage firms will not margin on "positive expectations" alone. They are only interested in positive equity balances, and it is a simple fact of life that trying to force more than 20 percent return per annum out of a futures trading system will run too high a risk of incurring an eventual equity drawdown that will cripple the account for good.

In Chapter 8, I showed that the single most important step that an option writer can take to ensure long-run profitability is to systematically employ defensive action in cases where one side of a straddle position starts to go sour in a big way. I showed that defensive action alone shifts the payout ratio from 1.00 (break even) to 0.90 (a 10 percent writer's edge). The *difference* between defended option writing and undefended option writing was accomplished by trading futures—nothing else. A skeptic might argue that since profitability was achieved purely on the strength of futures positions, why not forget the whole option rigmarole and just trade the futures. Since "defensive" futures positions were always initiated *with* the trend and liquidated also *with* the trend, omission of the straddles would leave a pure trend-following futures portfolio, which, as I demonstrated in *Winner Takes All,* has a substantial positive expectation.

True enough. But one crucial detail is missing: In futures trading, even diversified futures trading, capital requirements will be large, and equity variations will be large. The extraordinary feature about diversified straddle writing is that extraordinarily large positions can be financed with rather small amounts of money, because variations in account equity can be kept at almost incredibly low levels. Let's see how this is accomplished.

The key to low equity variability is diversification. At the individual commodity level, a straddle-writing portfolio is going to achieve diversification through the trading of options that are independently variable in the first place. On a second level, diversification comes from the very nature of the straddle itself. Because the value of a straddle—a *liability* to the writer once written—can only increase with a relatively large movement in its corresponding future, the odds of a straddle going against the writer in a very short time are not great. And the odds against 10 independent straddles all going sour at the same time is correspondingly that much less. Option writers should be aware that this powerful brake against sudden large equity drawdowns does *not* exist to the same extent when options are written on only *one* side of a market.

Returning now to the second of the three questions posed at the beginning of the chapter: *Is the edge large enough to overcome a series of impediments that we must cope with, the most important being transaction costs and "slippage" associated with each trade?* The answer has to be, yes, with the proviso that a straddle yields a premium of at least $2500. From the numbers of Figure 9-2, the writer's edge, net of all charges, should average, conservatively, about 8 percent. And how does a trading edge of 8 percent translate into return on investment? In other words, what is the answer to my friend from Missouri's third and most important question: *Is the whole exercise worthwhile when the return on "true and necessary" capital is considered?*

To get the level of dollar premium necessary to overcome execution and commission costs—that is, to maintain an average edge of 8 percent—the average time to expiry of the straddles is going to vary between 6 weeks and 6 months, with a conservative estimate of the average being about 4 months. If $100,000, say, is the total amount of premium collected from writing straddles with an average of 4 months to expiry, an 8 percent trading edge should net the writer $8000 three times per year, for a total return of $24,000 per annum.

The crucial question now becomes: How much equity does one need to finance a short option position of $100,000? And the answer, which is defined by margin requirements, is approximately $100,000. A well-diversified short option portfolio is able to margin a surprisingly large number of option positions. Brokerage firms use a sophisticated program (SPAN) to calculate the margin requirements of an account, based on the true degree of risk to the equity of that account. In the case of an account which concentrates exclusively on the writing of option straddles, the true degree of risk is very much diminished through diversification and symmetry.

An initial equity of $100,000 deposited in a brokerage account will allow the writing of sufficient straddles to pull in $100,000 cash from option buyers, and most of this cash—at least 60 percent—may safely be deposited, as margin collateral, in short-term treasury bills. So, too, can the entire original investment. Taking 5 percent as a typical short-term yield on treasury bills (it used to be considerably higher), the interest return on an investment of $100,000 will therefore be in the region of $8000. Adding this amount to the annualized return from the trader's edge, you wind up with a total annual cash return of $32,000.

Admittedly, an annual rate of return of 32 percent may not look so spectacular to investors who have had their money parked in an S&P-indexed mutual fund for the past several years. At some point though, double-digit stock market returns will be the stuff of fond memories—a refrain I seem to have been singing for longer than I care to remember. Five years ago, in *Winner Takes All*, I made a singularly unprophetic forecast:

> At this time of writing (summer 1993) stock market "bears" rightly point out that earnings and dividends in relation to stock prices are at historically low levels. Stock prices reflect public attitudes towards money and investments, even though, logically, stock prices ought to be related to company asset

values. Even if the economy *does* recover with some vigor, there is no guarantee that stock prices will go up from here.

Well, did I ever get a wrong number! The Dow Jones Industrial Index was under 4000 at the time. (To be fair, I did also point out that if you religiously enter a stop-loss order after a trade is made, you can dial a lot of wrong numbers, and still eventually get through.)

In the great post–bull market era which will come to pass sooner or later, a rate of return from option writing of 32 percent, let's say, a rate of return certainly between 20 percent and 40 percent, is going to look very attractive, especially if it can be achieved with minimum equity variability, as I am suggesting is possible from systematic straddle writing. Human nature and human frailty being what they are, I am not suggesting that very many people would be able to achieve anything like this level of performance, because even the best-intentioned and hardest-headed of traders would have many obstacles to surmount along the way.

Consider the evidence. It is generally understood and accepted as truth that the key to long-run success in trading—be it in soybeans, spiders, or seashells—is to cut losses and let profits run. Yet, were you to look at the open positions in 95 percent of all futures accounts you would see that unrealized losses far exceed unrealized profits. Why? Why do people persist in behaviors they *know* to be detrimental to their interests? Who knows? But fact is, they do, and in a remarkably consistent way.

I have a long-suffering friend who trades a lot of stocks, sometimes on the recommendations of "insiders." He keeps price histories on every stock he follows for "technical signals," so he has an objective system for cutting losses when the market tells him he is wrong. He bought a stock recently at $4—because it was "going to $10"—and he was risking a recently established low on the price chart.

"Look, it was so obvious," he said, showing me one of his meticulously maintained charts. "There was huge support at $3.75. I *knew* when it took out this low there was something seriously wrong."

"Where did you get out?" I asked him.

"I didn't," he said.

"And what's it at now?"

"A buck forty."

"What are you going to do?"

"Sell half of it. If it goes up to eight dollars, I'll break even."

I've been down that road before and so have most of the people reading this book.

The somewhat paradoxical truth about option writing is that despite its extraordinary attractions as an investment—the promise of exceptional returns combined with low risk, and despite the powerful empirical evidence in support of this promise, it will remain for most people a difficult feat to accomplish—and I include myself in this group of potential underachievers. In learning option writing by doing, I have to confess to numerous false starts already, and I have not been involved with the problem long enough to have generated conclusive proof from actual trading results that option writing is as profitable as I am suggesting it should be. Yet, the evidence is there. It is not a question of being lucky or unlucky, and not a question of having tremendous insight; it is truly a question of mastering one's own psychological weakness.

It can be done. The numbers say so.

*

For the last several chapters, it seems I have been talking almost exclusively about the merits of option *writing* as opposed to option *buying*. That is the way the wind has blown, because all the empirical evidence points to the conclusion that, although systematic option writing *may* be a winning play, systematic option buying (that is routine buying without fundamental insight) can *never* be a winning play. But, I would not care to leave the reader with the impression that I am promoting just one idea. People may trade options for any number of reasons that I cannot imagine, and I would like to think that the results of my research may be generally useful, whether the interests of the reader lie in the area of armchair bookmaking or in simply getting a better understanding of option valuation. There is a great deal of data in the reference section of this book, data which should be useful to anyone pursuing his or her own independent line of investigation.

Perhaps, I have shown scant respect for the works of acclaimed theoreticians on this topic, but as Truman Capote observed: If you're afraid of going too far, you may not go far enough. And doubtless, I shall be slammed in academic circles for lack of rigor, for rounding out numbers, for simplifying formulae by omitting unnecessary terms, and for generally cutting to the chase where the trail seemed hot. However, I stand by this pragmatic approach.

Better this, surely, than to be skewered on a rigid mathematical model divorced from all reality, as appears to have been the fate of one of the world's largest hedge funds, *Long Term Capital Growth,* which bet heavily on the validity of the million dollar formula and found itself victim of the billion-dollar blowout. As the *Wall Street Journal* (September 24, 1998, p.1) reported:

> Much of Long Term Capital's success in previous years was the result of its sophisticated models, devised by its Nobel laureates (Scholes and Merton) to predict how various markets would react in essentially normal times. While Long Term Capital won't comment, banks who were present at the meeting (organized by the Federal Reserve) to craft the bailout say that the firm's models failed to take into account what might happen in the event of a world-wide financial crisis that caused reactions in the market.

So, the normal distribution of price charges turned out to be not so normal after all. Big surprise, and doubtless this blunder will be rationalized as a once-in-a-lifetime 'unforseeable' event, beyond the scope of conventional mathematical analysis.

But the money's gone, all the same.

Many financial commentators expressed shock that a giant fund managed by such a concentration of brain power could produce such brainless results. They shouldn't have been so surprised. Had they probed behind the numbers a little, they would have seen that the Black-Scholes option pricing model has, for years, been an accident looking for a place to happen.

To calculate the implied volatility *iv* of an at-the-money put or call trading at price *p* (expressed as a percentage of futures price) and having *t* trading days till expiry, read from the tables of Figure 4-7 or use:

$$iv = \frac{40 \times p}{\sqrt{t}}$$

To calculate a futures market volatility *mv* from a mean absolute deviation *MAD* (expressed as a percentage of futures price) that will be directly comparable with *iv* above, use:

$$mv = 22 \times MAD$$

To calculate mean absolute deviation of a series of *N* price changes Δp_i (all readings taken as positive and expressed as a percentage of the futures price) use:

$$MAD = \frac{[\Sigma(\Delta p_i)]}{N}$$

To maintain an exponentially smoothed mean absolute deviation, update *MAD* daily with a new $|\Delta p|$, using:

$$MAD = 0.95 \times MAD_{prev} + 0.05 \times |\Delta p|$$

To convert the nearest at-the-money straddle price to a true at-the-money straddle price, calculate the correction multiplier *CM* from the straddle ratio *R*, using:

$$CM = 1.04 - 0.04 \times R \quad \text{(see Figure 6-3)}$$

FIGURE 9-3. A summary of some important formulae an option trader might wish to have at hand.

What, then, does the aspiring trader really need? At the very least, an active trader needs a straightforward method of calculating option volatilities, both implied and market, and of comparing these numbers with historical patterns and averages. All of this information is contained in the equation summary of Figure 9-3 or in the statistical reference section of Chapter 10.

My best advice to the aspiring option trader is to clear his or her thinking of all the superfluous complications which obfuscate this fascinating subject and to focus only on those things that are truly relevant to trading. Let's pack up all the betas, thetas, gammas, and deltas and send them back on a slow boat to Greece.

It's about time *somebody* called it.

PART FOUR

REFERENCE

CHAPTER TEN

VOLATILITY PROFILES

The data base which follows covers 15 diverse futures markets on which options are actively traded:

The S&P500 stock index	Silver	Corn
Treasury bonds	Crude oil	Cattle
Swiss franc	Cotton	Cocoa
Japanese yen	Soybeans	Coffee
Gold	Wheat	Sugar

For each commodity is listed:

A five-year history of implied volatilities, sampled monthly

A weekly high/low/close chart for 1996 based on a nearby future

Detailed daily statistics for calendar year 1996

FIVE-YEAR HISTORIES

Over a time period as long as 5 years, it is only practical to sample implied volatilities periodically. Here, the implied volatilities for 15 commodities are measured at the beginning of each month based on a nearby option and future.

Because implied volatility is *option specific*, its value can jump suddenly when switching between options. This primarily seasonal effect is found in crop commodities—in particular, grains, cotton, and coffee.

Over a 5-year period, each commodity is going to experience a wide range of supply-demand configurations, and a correspondingly wide range of implied volatilities. The tables which follow show, historically, how volatility has varied with absolute price, giving some indication of what can reasonably be expected in the future.

WEEKLY CHARTS

These charts have been developed from daily statistics. Implied volatilities, which were calculated weekly, may disagree slightly with the volatilities in the 5-year summaries, as the latter were sampled at the beginning of each calendar month.

DAILY STATISTICS

For each trading day of calendar year 1996, the following data are available:

1. Futures price of a nearby contract
2. Value of the put and call at the nearest strike price
3. Corrected value of the at-the-money straddle
4. The number of trading days till expiry
5. The implied volatility of the at-the-money straddle

Regarding items 1 and 2, to maintain continuity as options approach expiry it is necessary to switch to a new future every 2 months or so. Note that all readings of implied volatility are related to a specific option on a specific future.

Historical daily futures prices are readily available from commercial data banks. Option prices in general must be extracted from the pages of the financial press.

The data contained in the following tables come from sources the author considers reliable. In certain instances—where the author had good reason to believe published data to be inaccurate, or where overlapping futures prices required interpolation—numbers in these tables may disagree with those published in the financial press or stored in commercial data banks.

S&P500 INDEX

Calendar month	Year	Based on Option	Nearest strike	Implied volatility
JANUARY	1993	Feb	*435*	11.88
FEBRUARY	1993	Mar	*445*	10.07
MARCH	1993	Apr	*445*	10.61
APRIL	1993	May	*450*	12.03
MAY	1993	Jun	*440*	11.40
JUNE	1993	Jul	*455*	10.93
JULY	1993	Aug	*445*	10.37
AUGUST	1993	Sep	*450*	10.20
SEPTEMBER	1993	Oct	*465*	10.07
OCTOBER	1993	Nov	*460*	10.02
NOVEMBER	1993	Dec	*470*	9.88
DECEMBER	1993	Jan	*465*	11.40
JANUARY	1994	Feb	*466*	10.10
FEBRUARY	1994	Mar	*480*	8.56
MARCH	1994	Apr	*465*	12.56
APRIL	1994	May	*440*	18.34
MAY	1994	Jun	*455*	11.54
JUNE	1994	Jul	*460*	9.76
JULY	1994	Aug	*445*	12.74
AUGUST	1994	Sep	*465*	9.25
SEPTEMBER	1994	Oct	*475*	10.00
OCTOBER	1994	Nov	*465*	12.36
NOVEMBER	1994	Dec	*470*	12.27
DECEMBER	1994	Jan	*450*	15.24
JANUARY	1995	Feb	*465*	10.61
FEBRUARY	1995	Mar	*470*	9.62
MARCH	1995	Apr	*490*	10.08
APRIL	1995	May	*505*	10.80
MAY	1995	Jun	*515*	9.92
JUNE	1995	Jul	*540*	10.44
JULY	1995	Aug	*545*	10.56
AUGUST	1995	Sep	*560*	11.03
SEPTEMBER	1995	Oct	*570*	9.69
OCTOBER	1995	Nov	*585*	11.24
NOVEMBER	1995	Dec	*590*	11.14
DECEMBER	1995	Jan	*615*	9.36
JANUARY	1996	Mar	*625*	10.78
FEBRUARY	1996	Mar	*640*	10.52
MARCH	1996	Apr	*655*	14.40
APRIL	1996	Jun	*655*	14.62
MAY	1996	Jun	*655*	13.77
JUNE	1996	Jun	*670*	13.45
JULY	1996	Aug	*680*	12.34
AUGUST	1996	Aug	*655*	15.40
SEPTEMBER	1996	Sep	*655*	15.69
OCTOBER	1996	Nov	*695*	13.97
NOVEMBER	1996	Nov	*705*	15.19
DECEMBER	1996	Jan	*765*	15.83
JANUARY	1997	Feb	*745*	18.08
FEBRUARY	1997	Mar	*790*	17.19
MARCH	1997	Apr	*800*	19.34
APRIL	1997	May	*765*	17.84
MAY	1997	Jun	*800*	17.77
JUNE	1997	Jul	*855*	18.32
JULY	1997	Aug	*900*	18.51
AUGUST	1997	Sep	*955*	20.65
SEPTEMBER	1997	Oct	*945*	22.02
OCTOBER	1997	Nov	*965*	20.70
NOVEMBER	1997	Dec	*945*	25.27
DECEMBER	1997	Jan	*990*	21.72

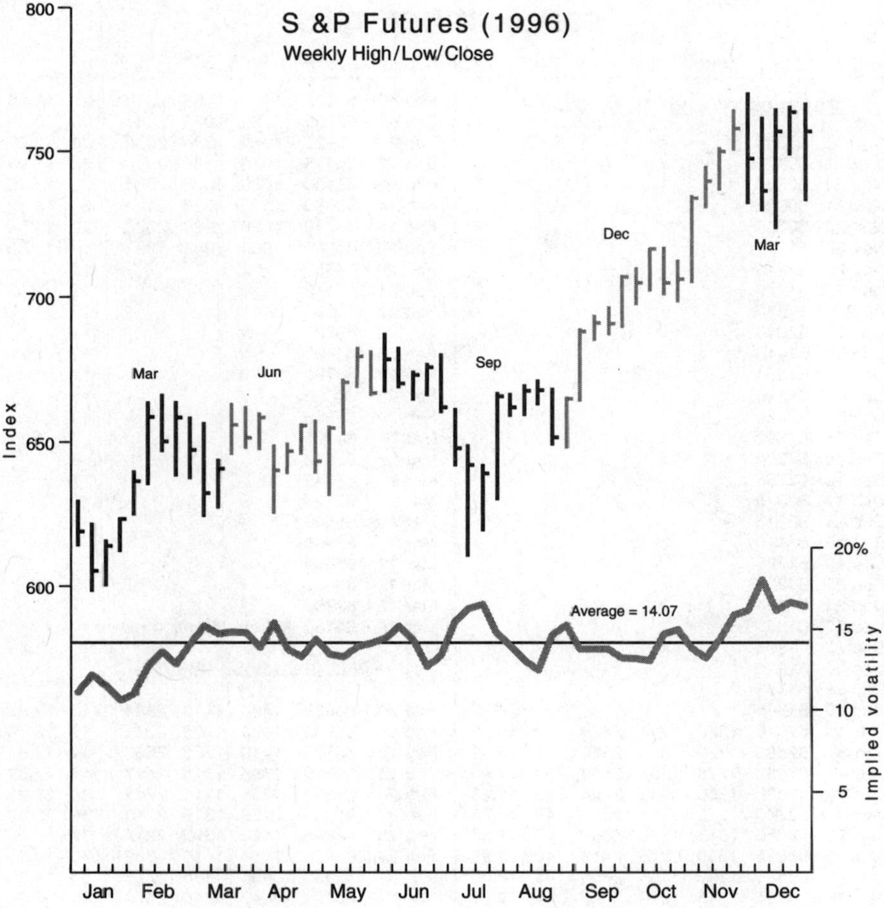
S &P Futures (1996)
Weekly High/Low/Close
800
750
700
650
600
Index
Mar
Jun
Sep
Dec
Mar
Average = 14.07
20%
15
10
5
Implied volatility
Jan
Feb
Mar
Apr
May
Jun
Jul
Aug
Sep
Oct
Nov
Dec

S&P500 INDEX 1996

March option and March future

	fp	max	min	s	td	iv
Nov 20	60365					
Nov 21	60705					
Nov 22	60565					
Nov 24	60685					
Nov 27	60705					
Nov 28	61325					
Nov 29	61345					
Nov 30	61275					
Dec 1	61380					
Dec 4	62040					
Dec 5	62445					
Dec 6	62550					
Dec 7	62240					
Dec 8	62420					
Dec 11	62590					
Dec 12	62500					
Dec 13	62755					
Dec 14	62375					
Dec 15	62275					
Dec 18	61160					
Dec 19	61785					
Dec 20	61305					
Dec 21	61595					
Dec 22	61835					
Dec 26	61955					
Dec 27	61920					
Dec 28	61775					
Dec 29	61845					
Jan 2	62510	1220	1210	2429	52	10.78
Jan 3	62695	1325	1025	2322	51	10.37
Jan 4	61980	1270	1250	2518	50	11.49
Jan 5	61930	1250	1180	2424	49	11.18
Jan 8	62240	1275	1055	2311	48	10.72
Jan 9	60850	1315	1165	2467	47	11.83
Jan 10	60075	1350	1275	2619	46	12.85
Jan 11	60565	1260	1195	2450	45	12.06
Jan 12	60495	1215	1210	2425	44	12.08
Jan 15	60320	1230	1170	2395	43	12.11
Jan 16	61090	1220	1130	2343	42	11.83
Jan 17	60830	1245	1075	2305	41	11.84
Jan 18	61050	1170	1120	2286	40	11.84
Jan 19	61415	1120	1035	2148	39	11.20
Jan 22	61370	1135	1005	2129	38	11.25
Jan 23	61615	1130	1015	2135	37	11.39
Jan 24	62195	1120	925	2028	36	10.87
Jan 25	61900	1070	970	2032	35	11.10
Jan 26	62415	995	910	1898	34	10.43
Jan 29	62620	995	875	1860	33	10.34
Jan 30	63195	1040	845	1868	32	10.45
Jan 31	63795	1025	820	1827	31	10.28
Feb 1	63965	940	905	1842	30	10.52
Feb 2	63835	1045	880	1911	29	11.12
Feb 5	64190	1070	880	1933	28	11.38
Feb 6	64820	1120	940	2044	27	12.14
Feb 7	65175	1100	955	2043	26	12.29
Feb 8	65835	1080	970	2041	25	12.40
Feb 9	65925	1060	985	2039	24	12.63
Feb 12	66425	1070	995	2059	23	12.93
Feb 13	66180	1090	1005	2088	22	13.45
Feb 14	65590	1110	1020	2122	21	14.12
Feb 15	65140	1120	980	2088	20	14.34
Feb 16	65040	985	945	1927	19	13.59
Feb 20	64350				17	
Feb 21	65170				16	
Feb 22	65995				15	
Feb 23	65925				14	
Feb 26	64885				13	
Feb 27	64760				12	
Feb 28	64350				11	
Feb 29	63825				10	
Mar 1	64725				9	
Mar 4	65070				8	
Mar 5	65745				7	
Mar 6	65120				6	
Mar 7	65415				5	
Mar 8	63205				4	
Mar 11	63885				3	
Mar 12	63480				2	
Mar 13	63750				1	
Mar 14	64160	March 96 option expires				

April option and June future

	fp	max	min	s	td	iv
Feb 20	64930	1480	1410	2884	43	13.55
Feb 21	65765	1470	1205	2651	42	12.44
Feb 22	66605	1410	1255	2652	41	12.44
Feb 23	66540	1355	1315	2667	40	12.67
Feb 26	65500	1395	1315	2703	39	13.22
Feb 27	65380	1435	1315	2740	38	13.60
Feb 28	64965	1425	1390	2812	37	14.23
Feb 29	64425	1485	1410	2889	36	14.95
Mar 1	65330	1455	1285	2726	35	14.10
Mar 4	65690	1440	1250	2674	34	13.96
Mar 5	66365	1340	1205	2534	33	13.29
Mar 6	65725	1435	1160	2570	32	13.83
Mar 7	66030	1295	1285	2579	31	14.03
Mar 8	63800	1570	1370	2923	30	16.73
Mar 11	64495	1350	1345	2695	29	15.52
Mar 12	64090	1395	1305	2693	28	15.88
Mar 13	64375	1350	1225	2564	27	15.33
Mar 14	64750	1350	1075	2400	26	14.54
Mar 15	64700	1275	1075	2333	25	14.42
Mar 18	65950	1170	1120	2286	24	14.15
Mar 19	65730	1340	1080	2397	23	15.21
Mar 20	65615	1245	1130	2365	22	15.37
Mar 21	65465	1140	1105	2242	21	14.95
Mar 22	65635	1145	1010	2143	20	14.60
Mar 25	65590	1105	1015	2112	19	14.78
Mar 26	65880	1080	960	2030	18	14.52
Mar 27	65130	1095	965	2049	17	15.26

LEGEND: *fp* = futures price, *max* = closest strike high option price, *min* = closest strike low option price, *s* = price corrected at-the-money-straddle, *td* = number of trading days till expiry, *iv* = implied volatility.

S&P500 INDEX 1996

	fp	max	min	s	td	iv
Mar 28	65475	1020	995	2013	16	15.37
Mar 29	65125	1070	945	2004	15	15.89
Apr 1	65740	1030	790	1798	14	14.62
Apr 2	65860	835	695	1518	13	12.78
Apr 3	65910	785	695	1472	12	12.90
Apr 4	65960				11	
Apr 8	64700				9	
Apr 9	64500				8	
Apr 10	63325				7	
Apr 11	63360				6	
Apr 12	64060				5	
Apr 15	64580				4	
Apr 16	64730				3	
Apr 17	64485				2	
Apr 18	64595				1	
Apr 19	64705	April 96 option expires				

June option and June future

	fp	max	min	s	td	iv
Apr 4	65960	1755	1715	3467	55	14.17
Apr 8	64700	1855	1655	3493	53	14.83
Apr 9	64500	1715	1715	3430	52	14.75
Apr 10	63325	2095	1775	3842	51	16.99
Apr 11	63360	1890	1750	3628	50	16.20
Apr 12	64060	1725	1665	3385	49	15.10
Apr 15	64580	1670	1590	3253	48	14.54
Apr 16	64730	1725	1435	3134	47	14.13
Apr 17	64485	1595	1580	3174	46	14.51
Apr 18	64595	1595	1500	3087	45	14.25
Apr 19	64705	1570	1365	2917	44	13.59
Apr 22	65205	1540	1335	2857	43	13.37
Apr 23	65500	1380	1380	2760	42	13.00
Apr 24	65170	1490	1320	2796	41	13.40
Apr 25	65505	1360	1355	2715	40	13.10
Apr 26	65645	1415	1275	2678	39	13.07
Apr 29	65515	1355	1340	2694	38	13.34
Apr 30	65485	1365	1350	2714	37	13.63
May 1	65645	1435	1290	2713	36	13.77
May 2	64585	1460	1375	2828	35	14.80
May 3	64350	1410	1260	2657	34	14.16
May 6	64290	1475	1225	2678	33	14.50
May 7	63905	1385	1290	2667	32	14.76
May 8	64750	1395	1105	2474	31	13.72
May 9	64735	1390	1175	2546	30	14.36
May 10	65490	1200	1190	2389	29	13.55
May 13	66375	1185	1060	2234	28	12.72
May 14	66730	1245	1015	2240	27	12.92
May 15	66735	1240	1030	2251	26	13.23
May 16	66705	1145	1035	2171	25	13.02
May 17	67150	1250	995	2222	24	13.51
May 20	67625	1150	1025	2164	23	13.35
May 21	67580	1110	1030	2133	22	13.46
May 22	68090	1090	1000	2082	21	13.35
May 23	67845	1115	960	2062	20	13.59
May 24	68060	1035	975	2005	19	13.52
May 28	67380	1080	960	2030	17	14.61
May 29	66910	1025	935	1952	16	14.59
May 30	67340	960	800	1746	15	13.39
May 31	66695	1010	815	1808	14	14.49
Jun 3	66945	895	840	1730	13	14.34
Jun 4	67320	910	730	1624	12	13.93
Jun 5	67875	855	730	1574	11	13.99
Jun 6	67325	895	720	1599	10	15.02
Jun 7	67380	780	660	1430	9	14.14
Jun 10	67130	765	635	1389	8	14.63
Jun 11	67145	725	580	1292	7	14.54
Jun 12	66970	645	615	1258	6	15.33
Jun 13	66875	635	510	1134	5	15.16
Jun 14	66475	535	510	1043	4	15.69
Jun 17	66570				3	
Jun 18	66170				2	
Jun 19	66290				1	
Jun 20	66120	June 96 option expires				

August option and September future

	fp	max	min	s	td	iv
Jun 17	67150	1740	1590	3317	44	14.90
Jun 18	66750	1770	1520	3268	43	14.93
Jun 19	66870	1705	1575	3269	42	15.09
Jun 20	66685	1695	1510	3189	41	14.94
Jun 21	67345	1595	1440	3022	40	14.19
Jun 24	67515	1485	1470	2954	39	14.01
Jun 25	67415	1455	1370	2818	38	13.56
Jun 26	66865	1445	1310	2744	37	13.49
Jun 27	67305	1475	1170	2617	36	12.96
Jun 28	67680	1350	1170	2504	35	12.51
Jul 1	68080	1295	1165	2449	34	12.34
Jul 2	67880	1265	1145	2400	33	12.31
Jul 3	67610	1275	1165	2431	32	12.71
Jul 5	66110	1315	1190	2494	30	13.78
Jul 8	65630	1345	1215	2549	29	14.42
Jul 9	65915	1240	1155	2388	28	13.69
Jul 10	66170	1235	1065	2285	27	13.29
Jul 11	64835	1300	1135	2421	26	14.65
Jul 12	64805	1280	1085	2348	25	14.49
Jul 15	63025	1360	1335	2693	24	17.44
Jul 16	63210	1450	1240	2672	23	17.63
Jul 17	63780	1330	1115	2426	22	16.22
Jul 18	64745	1190	965	2135	21	14.39
Jul 19	64200	1220	1020	2222	20	15.48
Jul 22	63755	1295	1050	2323	19	16.72
Jul 23	62815	1335	1150	2469	18	18.53
Jul 24	63070	1195	1125	2314	17	17.80
Jul 25	63520	1040	1020	2058	16	16.20
Jul 26	63935	1040	980	2015	15	16.28
Jul 29	63100	1040	940	1972	14	16.70
Jul 30	63770	1025	795	1799	13	15.65
Jul 31	64240	1020	780	1778	12	15.98
Aug 1	65305	940	745	1667	11	15.40
Aug 2	66635	780	645	1413	10	13.41
Aug 5	66170				9	
Aug 6	66425				8	

LEGEND: *fp* = futures price, *max* = closest strike high option price, *min* = closest strike low option price, *s* = price corrected at-the-money-straddle, *td* = number of trading days till expiry, *iv* = implied volatility.

S&P500 INDEX 1996

	fp	max	min	s	td	iv
Aug 7	66620				7	
Aug 8	66620				6	
Aug 9	66245				5	
Aug 12	66775				4	
Aug 13	66180				3	
Aug 14	66360				2	
Aug 15	66360				1	
Aug 16	66810	August 96 option expires				

September option and September future

	fp	max	min	s	td	iv
Aug 5	66170	1490	1320	2796	33	14.71
Aug 6	66425	1390	1315	2699	32	14.36
Aug 7	66620	1365	1245	2600	31	14.02
Aug 8	66620	1330	1210	2530	30	13.87
Aug 9	66245	1440	1195	2613	29	14.65
Aug 12	66775	1315	1070	2363	28	13.38
Aug 13	66180	1335	1085	2398	27	13.94
Aug 14	66360	1305	1055	2338	26	13.82
Aug 15	66360	1250	1000	2228	25	13.43
Aug 16	66810	1190	935	2102	24	12.84
Aug 19	66820	1160	915	2053	23	12.81
Aug 20	66795	1120	870	1967	22	12.56
Aug 21	66600	990	890	1872	21	12.26
Aug 22	67185	970	860	1821	20	12.12
Aug 23	66880	950	830	1770	19	12.14
Aug 26	66420	965	885	1843	18	13.08
Aug 27	66670	975	805	1765	17	12.84
Aug 28	66570	895	825	1714	16	12.87
Aug 29	65715	1000	755	1732	15	13.61
Aug 30	65135	995	860	1843	14	15.13
Sep 3	65585	940	845	1777	12	15.64
Sep 4	65660	960	800	1746	11	16.03
Sep 5	64900	970	870	1832	10	17.85
Sep 6	65825	845	595	1416	9	14.34
Sep 9	66505				8	
Sep 10	66510				7	
Sep 11	66700				6	
Sep 12	67215				5	
Sep 13	68285				4	
Sep 16	68470				3	
Sep 17	68395				2	
Sep 18	68120				1	
Sep 19	68405	September 96 option expires				

November option and December future

	fp	max	min	s	td	iv
Sep 9	67105	1710	1605	3306	49	14.08
Sep 10	67115	1690	1575	3255	48	14.00
Sep 11	67300	1785	1500	3260	47	14.13
Sep 12	67810	1775	1445	3191	46	13.87
Sep 13	68885	1770	1390	3125	45	13.53
Sep 16	69075	1655	1465	3104	44	13.55
Sep 17	68995	1595	1540	3131	43	13.84
Sep 18	68720	1685	1440	3104	42	13.94
Sep 19	68985	1520	1525	3045	41	13.79
Sep 20	69190	1595	1405	2984	40	13.64
Sep 23	69240	1625	1385	2989	39	13.83
Sep 24	69205	1580	1375	2937	38	13.77
Sep 25	69105	1510	1405	2906	37	13.83
Sep 26	69195	1565	1215	2748	36	13.24
Sep 27	69140	1485	1345	2818	35	13.78
Sep 30	69140	1495	1355	2838	34	14.08
Oct 1	69510	1400	1390	2789	33	13.97
Oct 2	69935	1385	1320	2700	32	13.65
Oct 3	69770	1485	1235	2698	31	13.89
Oct 4	70720	1365	1145	2491	30	12.86
Oct 7	70820	1310	1130	2424	29	12.71
Oct 8	70475	1235	1210	2443	28	13.10
Oct 9	70050	1260	1210	2466	27	13.55
Oct 10	69840	1300	1140	2426	26	13.63
Oct 11	70590	1175	1085	2253	25	12.76
Oct 14	70750	1250	1000	2228	24	12.85
Oct 15	70665	1210	1045	2241	23	13.22
Oct 16	70860	1145	1005	2138	22	12.87
Oct 17	71100	1120	1020	2132	21	13.08
Oct 18	71585	1065	980	2038	20	12.73
Oct 21	71440	1045	985	2025	19	13.01
Oct 22	70910	1075	985	2052	18	13.64
Oct 23	71105	1060	955	2006	17	13.69
Oct 24	70375	1105	980	2074	16	14.74
Oct 25	70535	1005	970	1972	15	14.44
Oct 28	70035	1040	1005	2042	14	15.59
Oct 29	70625	1030	905	1924	13	15.11
Oct 30	70280	1060	840	1880	12	15.44
Oct 31	70965	935	900	1832	11	15.57
Nov 1	70650	930	780	1697	10	15.19
Nov 4	71125	835	710	1534	9	14.38
Nov 5	71540	800	660	1448	8	14.31
Nov 6	72940	740	630	1360	7	14.10
Nov 7	73095	685	590	1267	6	14.15
Nov 8	73425				5	
Nov 11	73410				4	
Nov 12	73200				3	
Nov 13	73415				2	
Nov 14	73925				1	
Nov 15	74090	November 96 option expires				

January option and March future

	fp	max	min	s	td	iv
Nov 8	74080	1810	1730	3533	49	13.63
Nov 11	74065	1790	1725	3510	48	13.68
Nov 12	73855	1870	1620	3468	47	13.70
Nov 13	74075	1715	1640	3349	46	13.33
Nov 14	74585	1730	1570	3287	45	13.14
Nov 15	74750	1745	1495	3218	44	12.98
Nov 18	74705	1785	1495	3255	43	13.29
Nov 19	75315	1810	1500	3283	42	13.45
Nov 20	75305	1895	1595	3464	41	14.37
Nov 21	75245	1800	1555	3334	40	14.01
Nov 22	75820	1780	1530	3288	39	13.89
Nov 25	76700	1800	1600	3383	38	14.31

LEGEND: *fp* = futures price, *max* = closest strike high option price, *min* = closest strike low option price, *s* = price corrected at-the-money-straddle, *td* = number of trading days till expiry, *iv* = implied volatility.

S&P500 INDEX 1996

	fp	max	min	s	td	iv	fp	max	min	s	td	iv
Nov 26	76445	1815	1760	3571	37	15.36						
Nov 27	76305	1900	1650	3528	36	15.41						
Nov 29	76530	1775	1745	3518	34	15.77						
Dec 2	76510	1745	1735	3479	33	15.83						
Dec 3	75255	1920	1705	3607	32	16.94						
Dec 4	75475	1685	1660	3343	31	15.91						
Dec 5	75245	1825	1575	3378	30	16.39						
Dec 6	74755	1835	1590	3404	29	16.91						
Dec 9	75855	1695	1500	3178	28	15.84						
Dec 10	75510	1550	1540	3089	27	15.75						
Dec 11	74655	1685	1530	3202	26	16.82						
Dec 12	73450	1720	1670	3386	25	18.44						
Dec 13	73640	1765	1625	3378	24	18.73						
Dec 16	72775	1800	1490	3263	23	18.70						
Dec 17	73325	1595	1420	3000	22	17.45						
Dec 18	73815	1505	1320	2809	21	16.61						
Dec 19	75350	1445	1295	2727	20	16.19						
Dec 20	75725	1470	1220	2668	19	16.17						
Dec 23	75410	1345	1255	2593	18	16.21						
Dec 24	75905	1270	1175	2437	17	15.57						
Dec 26	76460	1210	1170	2377	15	16.05						
Dec 27	76460	1210	1170	2377	14	16.62						
Dec 30	75910	1190	1100	2283	13	16.68						
Dec 31	74450	1205	1155	2356	12	18.27						
Jan 2	74470				11							
Jan 3	75720				10							
Jan 6	75070				9							
Jan 7	75965				8							
Jan 8	75550				7							
Jan 9	75890				6							
Jan 10	76660				5							
Jan 13	76430				4							
Jan 14	77320				3							
Jan 15	77165				2							
Jan 16	77525				1							
Jan 17	78075	January 97 option expires										

LEGEND: *fp* = futures price, *max* = closest strike high option price, *min* = closest strike low option price, *s* = price corrected at-the-money-straddle, *td* = number of trading days till expiry, *iv* = implied volatility.

T-BONDS

Calendar month	Year	Based on Option	Nearest strike	Implied volatility
JANUARY	1993	Mar	*105*	8.60
FEBRUARY	1993	Mar	*107*	8.51
MARCH	1993	Jun	*110*	9.15
APRIL	1993	Jun	*109*	8.74
MAY	1993	Sep	*111*	9.23
JUNE	1993	Sep	*110*	8.76
JULY	1993	Sep	*114*	8.04
AUGUST	1993	Dec	*115*	8.60
SEPTEMBER	1993	Dec	*118*	8.07
OCTOBER	1993	Dec	*119*	8.77
NOVEMBER	1993	Mar	*118*	8.72
DECEMBER	1993	Mar	*115*	9.95
JANUARY	1994	Mar	*113*	9.15
FEBRUARY	1994	Mar	*106*	8.24
MARCH	1994	Jun	*109*	9.66
APRIL	1994	Jun	*103*	11.50
MAY	1994	Sep	*104*	11.27
JUNE	1994	Sep	*103*	11.60
JULY	1994	Sep	*101*	12.65
AUGUST	1994	Dec	*104*	10.82
SEPTEMBER	1994	Dec	*103*	10.27
OCTOBER	1994	Dec	*99*	10.56
NOVEMBER	1994	Mar	*97*	9.59
DECEMBER	1994	Mar	*98*	9.98
JANUARY	1995	Mar	*99*	9.58
FEBRUARY	1995	Mar	*101*	9.40
MARCH	1995	Jun	*103*	8.84
APRIL	1995	Jun	*104*	8.71
MAY	1995	Sep	*105*	8.47
JUNE	1995	Sep	*113*	9.65
JULY	1995	Sep	*114*	10.82
AUGUST	1995	Sep	*110*	10.56
SEPTEMBER	1995	Dec	*113*	9.66
OCTOBER	1995	Dec	*114*	9.70
NOVEMBER	1995	Mar	*117*	9.97
DECEMBER	1995	Mar	*120*	9.38
JANUARY	1996	Mar	*121*	9.39
FEBRUARY	1996	Apr	*120*	10.56
MARCH	1996	Jun	*116*	9.64
APRIL	1996	Jun	*118*	10.31
MAY	1996	Jun	*109*	11.43
JUNE	1996	Jul	*107*	10.85
JULY	1996	Sep	*110*	9.94
AUGUST	1996	Sep	*111*	11.16
SEPTEMBER	1996	Dec	*107*	10.27
OCTOBER	1996	Dec	*110*	10.40
NOVEMBER	1996	Dec	*113*	9.01
DECEMBER	1996	Jan	*116*	10.25
JANUARY	1997	Mar	*111*	10.58
FEBRUARY	1997	Mar	*112*	9.79
MARCH	1997	Jun	*110*	9.48
APRIL	1997	Jun	*107*	8.84
MAY	1997	Sep	*109*	9.00
JUNE	1997	Sep	*110*	8.57
JULY	1997	Sep	*112*	8.30
AUGUST	1997	Sep	*115*	8.53
SEPTEMBER	1997	Dec	*113*	8.41
OCTOBER	1997	Dec	*116*	8.33
NOVEMBER	1997	Dec	*118*	8.26
DECEMBER	1997	Mar	*119*	9.13

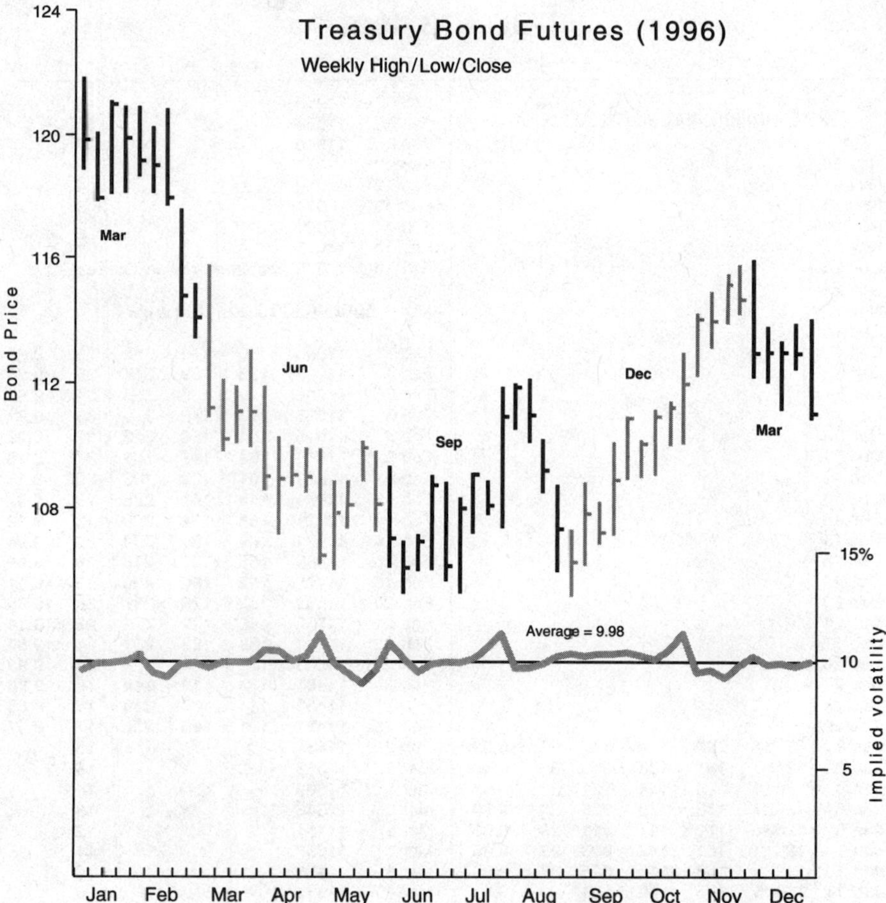
Treasury Bond Futures (1996)
Weekly High/Low/Close
124
120
116
112
108
Bond Price
Mar
Jun
Sep
Dec
Mar
15%
10
5
Implied volatility
Average = 9.98
Jan
Feb
Mar
Apr
May
Jun
Jul
Aug
Sep
Oct
Nov
Dec

T-BONDS 1996

March option and March future

	fp	max	min	s	td	iv
Nov 20						
Nov 21						
Nov 22						
Nov 24						
Nov 27						
Nov 28						
Nov 29						
Nov 30						
Dec 1						
Dec 4						
Dec 5						
Dec 6						
Dec 7						
Dec 8						
Dec 11						
Dec 12						
Dec 13						
Dec 14						
Dec 15						
Dec 18						
Dec 19						
Dec 20						
Dec 21						
Dec 22						
Dec 26						
Dec 27						
Dec 28						
Dec 29						
Jan 2	12134	200	134	327	33	9.39
Jan 3	12156	181	138	315	32	9.16
Jan 4	12065	180	144	321	31	9.55
Jan 5	12028	178	150	326	30	9.88
Jan 8	12034	173	141	311	29	9.60
Jan 9	12012	161	148	308	28	9.69
Jan 10	11878	158	148	305	27	9.89
Jan 11	11896	153	148	301	26	9.91
Jan 12	11896	148	145	293	25	9.84
Jan 15	11896	145	144	289	24	9.92
Jan 16	12003	142	141	283	23	9.83
Jan 17	12112	142	141	283	22	9.96
Jan 18	12131	153	122	272	21	9.79
Jan 19	12150	158	108	261	20	9.61
Jan 22	12053	152	105	252	19	9.61
Jan 23	12009	130	122	251	18	9.87
Jan 24	12090	128	119	246	17	9.88
Jan 25	11959	145	105	246	16	10.29
Jan 26	12053	145	98	238	15	10.21
Jan 29	11990	123	114	236	14	10.53
Jan 30	12068	134	102	233	13	10.71
Jan 31	12093	112	106	218	12	10.38
Feb 1	12040				11	
Feb 2	11953				10	
Feb 5	11959				9	
Feb 6	11975				8	
Feb 7	11965				7	
Feb 8	11968				6	
Feb 9	11971				5	
Feb 12	12059				4	
Feb 13	12071				3	
Feb 14	12021				2	
Feb 15	11915				1	
Feb 16	11825	March 96 option expires				

April option and June future

	fp	max	min	s	td	iv
Feb 1	11990	180	173	352	36	9.80
Feb 2	11903	175	169	344	35	9.76
Feb 5	11909	170	166	336	34	9.67
Feb 6	11925	173	148	319	33	9.31
Feb 7	11915	164	150	313	32	9.28
Feb 8	11918	164	141	303	31	9.13
Feb 9	11921	161	139	298	30	9.13
Feb 12	12009	148	141	288	29	8.92
Feb 13	12021	158	134	290	28	9.12
Feb 14	11971	159	131	288	27	9.24
Feb 15	11868	155	123	275	26	9.09
Feb 16	11775	152	130	280	25	9.51
Feb 20	11562	162	128	287	23	10.35
Feb 21	11562	156	122	275	22	10.14
Feb 22	11603	133	125	257	21	9.68
Feb 23	11503	131	125	256	20	9.93
Feb 26	11481	138	112	248	19	9.90
Feb 27	11456	144	100	240	18	9.86
Feb 28	11421	131	106	235	17	9.97
Feb 29	11434				16	
Mar 1	11553				15	
Mar 4	11609				14	
Mar 5	11546				13	
Mar 6	11481				12	
Mar 7	11459				11	
Mar 8	11159				10	
Mar 11	11231				9	
Mar 12	11187				8	
Mar 13	11156				7	
Mar 14	11150				6	
Mar 15	11059				5	
Mar 18	11109				4	
Mar 19	11112				3	
Mar 20	11187				2	
Mar 21	11212				1	
Mar 22	11184	April 96 option expires				

June option and June future

	fp	max	min	s	td	iv
Feb 29	11434	225	194	416	56	9.73
Mar 1	11553	231	186	413	55	9.64
Mar 4	11609	209	200	408	54	9.57
Mar 5	11546	233	180	408	53	9.71
Mar 6	11481	212	195	406	52	9.80

LEGEND: *fp* = futures price, *max* = closest strike high option price, *min* = closest strike low option price, *s* = price corrected at-the-money-straddle, *td* = number of trading days till expiry, *iv* = implied volatility.

T-BONDS 1996

	fp	max	min	s	td	iv
Mar 7	11459	217	180	394	51	9.62
Mar 8	11159	259	124	366	50	9.28
Mar 11	11231	212	181	390	49	9.93
Mar 12	11187	202	189	390	48	10.06
Mar 13	11156	216	170	382	47	9.98
Mar 14	11150	214	164	373	46	9.88
Mar 15	11059	220	161	375	45	10.12
Mar 18	11109	233	142	365	44	9.92
Mar 19	11112	231	144	366	43	10.04
Mar 20	11187	186	173	358	42	9.87
Mar 21	11212	180	167	346	41	9.64
Mar 22	11184	180	162	340	40	9.63
Mar 25	11278	210	133	335	39	9.51
Mar 26	11268	203	134	330	38	9.50
Mar 27	11131	205	136	334	37	9.87
Mar 28	11071	214	142	349	36	10.50
Mar 29	11146	198	145	338	35	10.25
Apr 1	11178	180	158	336	34	10.31
Apr 2	11231	183	152	332	33	10.30
Apr 3	11209	172	162	333	32	10.51
Apr 4	11162	188	150	335	31	10.77
Apr 8	10893	203	109	301	29	10.27
Apr 9	10943	173	119	287	28	9.90
Apr 10	10862	183	120	297	27	10.51
Apr 11	10818	159	141	298	26	10.82
Apr 12	10990	145	136	280	25	10.20
Apr 15	11028	150	122	270	24	9.98
Apr 16	11031	147	116	260	23	9.84
Apr 17	10984	132	119	250	22	9.70
Apr 18	10943	150	106	252	21	10.04
Apr 19	10993	125	119	244	20	9.91
Apr 22	11050	144	95	234	19	9.72
Apr 23	11025	130	108	236	18	10.09
Apr 24	10975	130	108	236	17	10.43
Apr 25	10996	117	114	231	16	10.49
Apr 26	11028	127	98	222	15	10.41
Apr 29	10984	119	103	221	14	10.74
Apr 30	10915	136	100	233	13	11.82
May 1	10912	114	103	216	12	11.43
May 2	10743	133	89	218	11	12.21
May 3	10675	103	78	179	10	10.59
May 6	10715	86	70	155	9	9.62
May 7	10693	78	72	150	8	9.89
May 8	10793				7	
May 9	10759				6	
May 10	10868				5	
May 13	10887				4	
May 14	10946				3	
May 15	10956				2	
May 16	10893				1	
May 17	10959	June 96 option expires				

<u>July option and September future</u>

	fp	max	min	s	td	iv
May 8	10737	167	130	294	32	9.67
May 9	10703	150	134	283	31	9.49
May 10	10812	148	136	283	30	9.56
May 13	10831	153	122	272	29	9.33
May 14	10890	139	133	272	28	9.42
May 15	10900	134	133	267	27	9.43
May 16	10837	148	109	253	26	9.17
May 17	10903	128	125	253	25	9.27
May 20	10922	131	109	238	24	8.90
May 21	10900	116	116	232	23	8.88
May 22	10959	131	91	218	22	8.49
May 23	10884	120	106	225	21	9.01
May 24	10944	136	83	213	20	8.72
May 28	10928	123	92	212	18	9.15
May 29	10825	122	94	213	17	9.56
May 30	10847	136	86	217	16	10.00
May 31	10750	139	89	223	15	10.71
Jun 3	10740	131	91	218	14	10.85
Jun 4	10753	130	83	208	13	10.74
Jun 5	10815	111	95	205	12	10.92
Jun 6	10881	109	91	198	11	11.00
Jun 7	10700	89	89	178	10	10.52
Jun 10	10656	108	64	167	9	10.46
Jun 11	10628	91	65	154	8	10.21
Jun 12	10587	79	66	144	7	10.27
Jun 13	10621	77	53	128	6	9.81
Jun 14	10681	64	45	107	5	8.97
Jun 17	10734				4	
Jun 18	10703				3	
Jun 19	10678				2	
Jun 20	10681				1	
Jun 21	10700	July 96 option expires				

<u>September option and September future</u>

	fp	max	min	s	td	iv
Jun 17	10734	211	145	350	49	9.30
Jun 18	10703	228	131	348	48	9.40
Jun 19	10678	219	141	352	47	9.62
Jun 20	10681	220	139	351	46	9.68
Jun 21	10700	227	127	343	45	9.55
Jun 24	10715	217	133	341	44	9.60
Jun 25	10759	195	155	346	43	9.82
Jun 26	10771	188	159	344	42	9.87
Jun 27	10840	195	155	346	41	9.98
Jun 28	10953	197	150	343	40	9.89
Jul 1	10956	194	150	340	39	9.94
Jul 2	10906	189	145	330	38	9.82
Jul 3	10925	184	142	322	37	9.70
Jul 5	10640	180	139	315	35	10.02
Jul 8	10643	175	131	302	34	9.73
Jul 9	10693	152	145	296	33	9.65
Jul 10	10746	175	128	299	32	9.82
Jul 11	10775	166	141	305	31	10.16
Jul 12	10834	164	130	291	30	9.81
Jul 15	10781	158	139	295	29	10.18
Jul 16	10850	173	123	291	28	10.14
Jul 17	10837	167	130	294	27	10.43
Jul 18	10971	152	123	272	26	9.74

LEGEND: *fp* = futures price, *max* = closest strike high option price, *min* = closest strike low option price, *s* = price corrected at-the-money-straddle, *td* = number of trading days till expiry, *iv* = implied volatility.

T-BONDS 1996

	fp	max	min	s	td	iv
Jul 19	10906	138	133	271	25	9.92
Jul 22	10856	156	112	264	24	9.92
Jul 23	10909	138	128	265	23	10.14
Jul 24	10818	150	131	279	22	11.01
Jul 25	10843	162	119	277	21	11.15
Jul 26	10856	159	119	274	20	11.30
Jul 29	10781	152	133	283	19	12.06
Jul 30	10843	159	116	271	18	11.78
Jul 31	10912	136	123	258	17	11.46
Aug 1	11068	141	109	247	16	11.16
Aug 2	11184				15	
Aug 5	11175				14	
Aug 6	11159				13	
Aug 7	11143				12	
Aug 8	11128				11	
Aug 9	11206				10	
Aug 12	11206				9	
Aug 13	11090				8	
Aug 14	11103				7	
Aug 15	11068				6	
Aug 16	11128				5	
Aug 19	11090				4	
Aug 20	11087				3	
Aug 21	11062				2	
Aug 22	11056				1	
Aug 23	10953	September 96 options expire				

December option and December future

	fp	max	min	s	td	iv
Aug 2	11131	270	191	453	73	9.53
Aug 5	11122	267	189	448	72	9.50
Aug 6	11106	281	177	447	71	9.56
Aug 7	11090	277	184	452	70	9.74
Aug 8	11075	267	191	451	69	9.80
Aug 9	11153	242	200	438	68	9.53
Aug 12	11153	242	198	436	67	9.55
Aug 13	11037	239	198	433	66	9.67
Aug 14	11050	242	192	429	65	9.64
Aug 15	11015	223	205	426	64	9.68
Aug 16	11075	222	203	423	63	9.63
Aug 19	11037	220	203	422	62	9.70
Aug 20	11034	219	203	421	61	9.76
Aug 21	11009	217	203	419	60	9.82
Aug 22	11003	216	203	418	59	9.89
Aug 23	10900	216	202	417	58	10.04
Aug 26	10809	214	202	415	57	10.17
Aug 27	10840	230	186	412	56	10.16
Aug 28	10825	219	191	408	55	10.15
Aug 29	10759	222	184	403	54	10.19
Aug 30	10678	242	164	398	53	10.25
Sep 3	10737	217	180	394	51	10.27
Sep 4	10696	198	195	393	50	10.39
Sep 5	10640	222	181	399	49	10.72
Sep 6	10675	197	173	368	48	9.95
Sep 9	10721	194	172	364	47	9.91
Sep 10	10665	200	170	367	46	10.16
Sep 11	10678	198	177	373	45	10.42
Sep 12	10725	200	175	373	44	10.48
Sep 13	10871	220	147	360	43	10.09
Sep 16	10881	220	139	351	42	9.94
Sep 17	10812	184	172	355	41	10.26
Sep 18	10806	180	173	352	40	10.31
Sep 19	10765	195	161	353	39	10.50
Sep 20	10775	188	164	350	38	10.54
Sep 23	10809	175	166	340	37	10.35
Sep 24	10862	200	138	332	36	10.19
Sep 25	10921	172	152	322	35	9.98
Sep 26	10981	170	153	322	34	10.04
Sep 27	10946	191	144	331	33	10.52
Sep 30	10918	173	155	326	32	10.57
Oct 1	10990	164	155	318	31	10.40
Oct 2	11031	170	139	306	30	10.14
Oct 3	11031	172	141	310	29	10.45
Oct 4	11168	164	133	294	28	9.96
Oct 7	11115	153	138	290	27	10.03
Oct 8	11109	148	141	288	26	10.18
Oct 9	11056	169	125	290	25	10.49
Oct 10	11003	144	141	285	24	10.57
Oct 11	11059	155	112	263	23	9.91
Oct 15	11050	158	108	261	22	10.07
Oct 16	11031	141	111	249	21	9.86
Oct 17	11112	128	116	243	20	9.78
Oct 18	11128	134	106	237	19	9.79
Oct 21	11106	122	116	238	18	10.08
Oct 22	11062	138	102	237	17	10.38
Oct 23	11084	125	109	233	16	10.49
Oct 24	11059	139	97	232	15	10.83
Oct 25	11100	114	114	228	14	10.98
Oct 28	11090	119	109	227	13	11.36
Oct 29	11259	136	95	227	12	11.64
Oct 30	11259	134	92	222	11	11.88
Oct 31	11300	106	106	212	10	11.87
Nov 1	11275	95	70	163	9	9.62
Nov 4	11300	75	72	147	8	9.18
Nov 5	11378	79	67	145	7	9.63
Nov 6	11362	86	48	130	6	9.32
Nov 7	11428	72	46	115	5	9.03
Nov 8	11406	58	52	109	4	9.60
Nov 12	11490				3	
Nov 13	11471				2	
Nov 14	11528				1	
Nov 15	11493	December 96 option expires				

January option and March future

	fp	max	min	s	td	iv
Nov 12	11449	175	127	297	28	9.82
Nov 13	11430	162	131	290	27	9.77
Nov 14	11487	144	131	274	26	9.35
Nov 15	11452	159	116	271	25	9.46
Nov 18	11443	152	108	256	24	9.12
Nov 19	11480	131	112	241	23	8.77
Nov 20	11530	141	106	244	22	9.01

LEGEND: *fp* = futures price, *max* = closest strike high option price, *min* = closest strike low option price, *s* = price corrected at-the-money-straddle, *td* = number of trading days till expiry, *iv* = implied volatility.

T-BONDS 1996

	fp	max	min	s	td	iv
Nov 21	11512	130	114	243	21	9.20
Nov 22	11490	123	117	240	20	9.32
Nov 25	11505	125	116	240	19	9.58
Nov 26	11493	122	122	244	18	10.01
Nov 27	11490	119	116	235	17	9.91
Nov 29	11580	122	109	230	15	10.25
Dec 2	11587	117	105	221	14	10.19
Dec 3	11600	105	105	210	13	10.04
Dec 4	11534	119	84	200	12	9.99
Dec 5	11409	105	95	199	11	10.53
Dec 6	11384	97	81	177	10	9.81
Dec 9	11443				9	
Dec 10	11437				8	
Dec 11	11290				7	
Dec 12	11250				6	
Dec 13	11325				5	
Dec 16	11275				4	
Dec 17	11253				3	
Dec 18	11206				2	
Dec 19	11315				1	
Dec 20	11331	January 97 option expires				

March 97 option and March 97 future

	fp	max	min	s	td	iv
Dec 9	11443	222	178	396	52	9.60
Dec 10	11437	217	178	392	51	9.59
Dec 11	11290	220	175	391	50	9.79
Dec 12	11250	225	173	393	49	9.99
Dec 13	11325	208	183	389	48	9.91
Dec 16	11275	200	175	373	47	9.65
Dec 17	11253	212	166	374	46	9.80
Dec 18	11206	191	184	374	45	9.96
Dec 19	11315	195	180	374	44	9.96
Dec 20	11331	197	166	360	43	9.70
Dec 23	11343	198	155	349	42	9.50
Dec 24	11340	195	155	346	41	9.54
Dec 26	11334	187	155	339	39	9.58
Dec 27	11393	177	170	346	38	9.87
Dec 30	11387	178	166	343	37	9.90
Dec 31	11262	192	153	341	36	10.11
Jan 2	11137				35	
Jan 3	11156				34	
Jan 6	11128				33	
Jan 7	11087				32	
Jan 8	11071				31	
Jan 9	11140				30	
Jan 10	11034				29	
Jan 13	11040				28	
Jan 14	11140				27	
Jan 15	11128				26	
Jan 16	11071				25	
Jan 17	11093				24	
Jan 21	11150				23	
Jan 22	11103				22	
Jan 23	11084				21	
Jan 24	11025				20	
Jan 27	10978				19	
Jan 28	11006				18	
Jan 29	11025				17	
Jan 30	11056				16	
Jan 31	11143				15	
Feb 3	11209				14	
Feb 4	11221				13	
Feb 5	11203				12	
Feb 6	11190				11	
Feb 7	11246				10	
Feb 10	11246				9	
Feb 11	11246				8	
Feb 12	11240				7	
Feb 13	11334				6	
Feb 14	11393				5	
Feb 18	11384				3	
Feb 19	11362				2	
Feb 20	11303				1	
Feb 21	11293	March 97 option expires				

LEGEND: *fp* = futures price, *max* = closest strike high option price, *min* = closest strike low option price, *s* = price corrected at-the-money-straddle, *td* = number of trading days till expiry, *iv* = implied volatility.

SWISS FRANC

Calendar month	Year	Based on Option	Nearest strike	Implied volatility
JANUARY	1993	Feb	*6700*	12.31
FEBRUARY	1993	Mar	*6550*	14.42
MARCH	1993	Apr	*6450*	15.48
APRIL	1993	May	*6750*	15.29
MAY	1993	Jun	*7000*	13.13
JUNE	1993	Jul	*7000*	14.68
JULY	1993	Aug	*6600*	13.10
AUGUST	1993	Sep	*6700*	11.95
SEPTEMBER	1993	Oct	*6800*	13.23
OCTOBER	1993	Nov	*7000*	13.24
NOVEMBER	1993	Dec	*6650*	12.08
DECEMBER	1993	Jan	*6650*	11.75
JANUARY	1994	Feb	*6700*	12.38
FEBRUARY	1994	Mar	*6900*	10.17
MARCH	1994	Apr	*6950*	12.77
APRIL	1994	May	*7000*	10.48
MAY	1994	Jun	*7100*	10.03
JUNE	1994	Jul	*7150*	9.63
JULY	1994	Aug	*7500*	11.30
AUGUST	1994	Sep	*7500*	12.71
SEPTEMBER	1994	Oct	*7550*	12.25
OCTOBER	1994	Nov	*7800*	10.93
NOVEMBER	1994	Dec	*8050*	10.48
DECEMBER	1994	Jan	*7550*	10.25
JANUARY	1995	Feb	*7650*	9.44
FEBRUARY	1995	Mar	*7800*	9.73
MARCH	1995	Apr	*8100*	11.01
APRIL	1995	May	*8950*	20.20
MAY	1995	Jun	*8750*	16.99
JUNE	1995	Jul	*8650*	17.84
JULY	1995	Aug	*8750*	14.32
AUGUST	1995	Sep	*8800*	13.18
SEPTEMBER	1995	Oct	*8350*	13.12
OCTOBER	1995	Nov	*8800*	14.79
NOVEMBER	1995	Dec	*8800*	14.56
DECEMBER	1995	Jan	*8550*	12.66
JANUARY	1996	Mar	*8700*	12.87
FEBRUARY	1996	Apr	*8350*	11.24
MARCH	1996	Apr	*8400*	10.79
APRIL	1996	Jun	*8450*	10.09
MAY	1996	Jun	*8050*	9.88
JUNE	1996	Jul	*8050*	9.15
JULY	1996	Sep	*8350*	8.73
AUGUST	1996	Sep	*8350*	9.71
SEPTEMBER	1996	Oct	*8350*	8.19
OCTOBER	1996	Dec	*8050*	8.23
NOVEMBER	1996	Dec	*7900*	9.27
DECEMBER	1996	Jan	*7650*	9.30
JANUARY	1997	Feb	*7500*	11.61
FEBRUARY	1997	Mar	*7100*	12.18
MARCH	1997	Apr	*6850*	11.74
APRIL	1997	May	*7000*	11.95
MAY	1997	Jun	*6850*	10.25
JUNE	1997	Jul	*7050*	11.58
JULY	1997	Aug	*6900*	10.30
AUGUST	1997	Sep	*6600*	10.87
SEPTEMBER	1997	Oct	*6650*	11.52
OCTOBER	1997	Nov	*6900*	10.87
NOVEMBER	1997	Dec	*7100*	11.78
DECEMBER	1997	Jan	*7050*	10.88

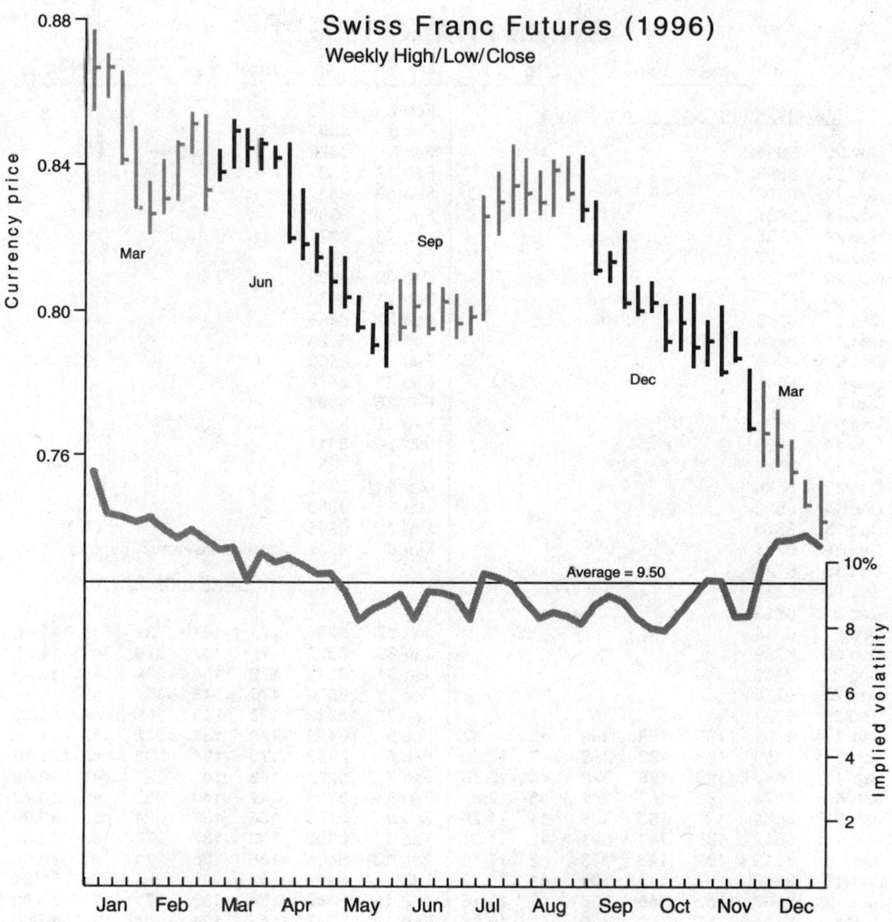
Swiss Franc Futures (1996)
Weekly High/Low/Close
0.88
0.84
0.80
0.76
Currency price
Mar
Jun
Sep
Dec
Mar
Average = 9.50
10%
8
6
4
2
Implied volatility
Jan
Feb
Mar
Apr
May
Jun
Jul
Aug
Sep
Oct
Nov
Dec

SWISS FRANC 1996

March option and March future

	fp	max	min	s	td	iv
Nov 20	8898					
Nov 21	8898					
Nov 22	8902					
Nov 24	8837					
Nov 27	8738					
Nov 28	8737					
Nov 29	8670					
Nov 30	8578					
Dec 1	8575					
Dec 4	8644					
Dec 5	8644					
Dec 6	8647					
Dec 7	8612					
Dec 8	8636					
Dec 11	8633					
Dec 12	8587					
Dec 13	8578					
Dec 14	8686					
Dec 15	8678					
Dec 18	8797					
Dec 19	8722					
Dec 20	8717					
Dec 21	8713					
Dec 22	8714					
Dec 26	8739					
Dec 27	8716					
Dec 28	8724					
Dec 29	8731					
Jan 2	8702	195	193	388	48	12.87
Jan 3	8650	193	192	385	47	12.98
Jan 4	8648	190	188	378	46	12.88
Jan 5	8674	192	167	357	45	12.27
Jan 8	8664	177	163	339	44	11.79
Jan 9	8642	165	157	321	43	11.34
Jan 10	8673	169	146	313	42	11.14
Jan 11	8666	163	147	309	41	11.12
Jan 12	8667	162	145	306	40	11.15
Jan 15	8631	158	139	295	39	10.96
Jan 16	8538	159	141	298	38	11.34
Jan 17	8467	160	143	302	37	11.71
Jan 18	8459	151	142	292	36	11.52
Jan 19	8424	158	132	288	35	11.55
Jan 22	8464	143	128	270	34	10.93
Jan 23	8462	140	128	267	33	10.99
Jan 24	8430	144	124	266	32	11.17
Jan 25	8391	135	126	260	31	11.14
Jan 26	8296	133	129	262	30	11.52
Jan 29	8321				29	
Jan 30	8262				28	
Jan 31	8277				27	
Feb 1	8269				26	
Feb 2	8267				25	
Feb 5	8392				24	
Feb 6	8373				23	
Feb 7	8330				22	
Feb 8	8332				21	
Feb 9	8309				20	
Feb 12	8330				19	
Feb 13	8332				18	
Feb 14	8399				17	
Feb 15	8377				16	
Feb 16	8448				15	
Feb 20	8503				13	
Feb 21	8470				12	
Feb 22	8486				11	
Feb 23	8525				10	
Feb 26	8500				9	
Feb 27	8478				8	
Feb 28	8382				7	
Feb 29	8344				6	
Mar 1	8311				5	
Mar 4	8332				4	
Mar 5	8342				3	
Mar 6	8330				2	
Mar 7	8341				1	
Mar 8	8307	March 1996 option expires				

April option and June future

	fp	max	min	s	td	iv
Jan 29	8386	171	161	331	48	11.40
Jan 30	8327	172	157	328	47	11.48
Jan 31	8342	172	154	324	46	11.47
Feb 1	8334	170	143	311	45	11.11
Feb 2	8332	172	139	308	44	11.15
Feb 5	8458	179	137	312	43	11.26
Feb 6	8438	173	134	303	42	11.10
Feb 7	8397	148	145	293	41	10.89
Feb 8	8399	142	143	285	40	10.73
Feb 9	8375	155	131	284	39	10.86
Feb 12	8398	139	137	276	38	10.66
Feb 13	8400	136	135	271	37	10.60
Feb 14	8467	153	121	271	36	10.67
Feb 15	8446	138	133	271	35	10.83
Feb 16	8517	142	124	264	34	10.65
Feb 20	8573	151	128	277	32	11.42
Feb 21	8541	137	128	264	31	11.11
Feb 22	8557	133	126	258	30	11.03
Feb 23	8598	126	124	250	29	10.79
Feb 26	8575	121	120	241	28	10.62
Feb 27	8552	117	115	232	27	10.43
Feb 28	8456	138	94	228	26	10.56
Feb 29	8417	123	106	228	25	10.81
Mar 1	8383	120	103	222	24	10.79
Mar 4	8403	129	82	206	23	10.23
Mar 5	8414	107	93	199	22	10.07
Mar 6	8402	98	96	194	21	10.07
Mar 7	8414	104	90	193	20	10.25
Mar 8	8382	108	90	196	19	10.75
Mar 11	8405	127	72	193	18	10.82
Mar 12	8464	99	84	182	17	10.41

LEGEND: *fp* = futures price, *max* = closest strike high option price, *min* = closest strike low option price, *s* = price corrected at-the-money-straddle, *td* = number of trading days till expiry, *iv* = implied volatility.

SWISS FRANC 1996

	fp	max	min	s	td	iv
Mar 13	8494	94	88	182	16	10.68
Mar 14	8494	86	80	166	15	10.06
Mar 15	8505	81	76	157	14	9.84
Mar 18	8472	81	59	138	13	9.03
Mar 19	8475	79	55	132	12	8.97
Mar 20	8463	73	60	132	11	9.39
Mar 21	8425	76	52	126	10	9.43
Mar 22	8444	65	59	123	9	9.75
Mar 25	8458				8	
Mar 26	8447				7	
Mar 27	8417				6	
Mar 28	8475				5	
Mar 29	8464				4	
Apr 1	8436				3	
Apr 2	8437				2	
Apr 3	8425				1	
Apr 4	8441	April 1996 option expires				

June option and June future

	fp	max	min	s	td	iv
Mar 25	8458	165	157	321	54	10.34
Mar 26	8447	159	156	315	53	10.24
Mar 27	8417	171	154	324	52	10.66
Mar 28	8475	171	145	314	51	10.37
Mar 29	8464	159	145	303	50	10.12
Apr 1	8436	155	141	295	49	9.99
Apr 2	8437	150	137	286	48	9.78
Apr 3	8425	153	129	280	47	9.69
Apr 4	8441	146	137	282	46	9.86
Apr 8	8424	149	125	272	44	9.73
Apr 9	8317	149	132	280	43	10.25
Apr 10	8288	147	135	281	42	10.46
Apr 11	8246	138	133	271	41	10.25
Apr 12	8200	130	130	260	40	10.03
Apr 15	8147	132	125	256	39	10.08
Apr 16	8185	134	119	252	38	9.98
Apr 17	8195	125	120	245	37	9.81
Apr 18	8258	124	116	239	36	9.66
Apr 19	8189	123	113	235	35	9.71
Apr 22	8182	124	106	228	34	9.58
Apr 23	8157	117	110	226	33	9.66
Apr 24	8166	117	101	217	32	9.38
Apr 25	8125	123	98	219	31	9.67
Apr 26	8142	112	104	215	30	9.66
Apr 29	8116	113	97	209	29	9.55
Apr 30	8072	115	93	206	28	9.65
May 1	8030	112	92	202	27	9.69
May 2	8064	108	94	201	26	9.77
May 3	8087	103	90	192	25	9.49
May 6	8071	103	82	183	24	9.26
May 7	8072	97	75	170	23	8.78
May 8	8133	98	81	177	22	9.31
May 9	8098	85	83	168	21	9.05
May 10	8037	85	73	157	20	8.73
May 13	8027	86	63	147	19	8.39
May 14	8014	75	61	135	18	7.93

	fp	max	min	s	td	iv
May 15	8000	65	65	130	17	7.88
May 16	7878	76	55	129	16	8.19
May 17	7953	64	61	125	15	8.10
May 20	7939				14	
May 21	7880				13	
May 22	7900				12	
May 23	7916				11	
May 24	7905				10	
May 28	7871				8	
May 29	7948				7	
May 30	7946				6	
May 31	8012				5	
Jun 3	7962				4	
Jun 4	7964				3	
Jun 5	7964				2	
Jun 6	7950				1	
Jun 7	7884	June 1996 option expires				

July option and September future

	fp	max	min	s	td	iv
May 20	8003	102	99	201	34	8.60
May 21	7944	104	98	202	33	8.83
May 22	7964	118	83	198	32	8.77
May 23	7980	105	85	188	31	8.47
May 24	7967	109	77	183	30	8.38
May 28	7931	106	75	178	28	8.48
May 29	8009	96	87	182	27	8.76
May 30	8003	95	92	187	26	9.15
May 31	8070	102	82	182	25	9.03
Jun 3	8041	95	86	180	24	9.15
Jun 4	8023	103	78	179	23	9.29
Jun 5	8024	98	74	170	22	9.02
Jun 6	8010	87	77	163	21	8.89
Jun 7	7942	79	72	150	20	8.47
Jun 10	7952	72	70	142	19	8.18
Jun 11	7964	76	62	137	18	8.09
Jun 12	7972	76	56	130	17	7.92
Jun 13	8035	73	58	130	16	8.07
Jun 14	8017	77	60	135	15	8.72
Jun 17	8045				14	
Jun 18	8088				13	
Jun 19	8039				12	
Jun 20	8013				11	
Jun 21	7942				10	
Jun 24	7974				9	
Jun 25	7980				8	
Jun 26	8009				7	
Jun 27	8074				6	
Jun 28	8030				5	
Jul 1	8050				4	
Jul 2	8048				3	
Jul 3	8028				2	
Jul 5	7964	July 1996 option expires				

LEGEND: *fp* = futures price, *max* = closest strike high option price, *min* = closest strike low option price, *s* = price corrected at-the-money-straddle, *td* = number of trading days till expiry, *iv* = implied volatility.

SWISS FRANC 1996

September option and September future

	fp	max	min	s	td	iv
Jun 17	8045	172	128	296	59	9.58
Jun 18	8088	154	142	295	58	9.58
Jun 19	8039	140	129	268	57	8.83
Jun 20	8013	138	125	262	56	8.74
Jun 21	7942	155	113	264	55	8.96
Jun 24	7974	144	118	260	54	8.86
Jun 25	7980	140	120	258	53	8.89
Jun 26	8009	136	127	262	52	9.08
Jun 27	8074	148	123	269	51	9.32
Jun 28	8030	139	119	256	50	9.03
Jul 1	8050	123	123	246	49	8.73
Jul 2	8048	123	121	244	48	8.75
Jul 3	8028	130	109	237	47	8.62
Jul 5	7964	121	106	226	45	8.45
Jul 8	7957	112	105	216	44	8.20
Jul 9	7957	113	106	218	43	8.37
Jul 10	7962	111	99	209	42	8.10
Jul 11	8000	105	105	210	41	8.20
Jul 12	7981	113	94	205	40	8.14
Jul 15	8039	108	98	205	39	8.17
Jul 16	8277	150	127	275	38	10.78
Jul 17	8297	139	136	275	37	10.89
Jul 18	8242	131	123	253	36	10.25
Jul 19	8267	126	109	234	35	9.55
Jul 22	8316	126	110	235	34	9.68
Jul 23	8284	122	106	227	33	9.52
Jul 24	8269	120	101	219	32	9.38
Jul 25	8325	127	101	226	31	9.74
Jul 26	8300	105	104	209	30	9.19
Jul 29	8322	111	89	198	29	8.84
Jul 30	8352	104	102	206	28	9.32
Jul 31	8388	115	103	217	27	9.96
Aug 1	8353	105	102	207	26	9.71
Aug 2	8357	101	94	194	25	9.31
Aug 5	8350	93	92	185	24	9.04
Aug 6	8322	97	75	170	23	8.52
Aug 7	8297	84	81	165	22	8.47
Aug 8	8292	85	77	161	21	8.49
Aug 9	8331	91	72	161	20	8.66
Aug 12	8335	83	68	150	19	8.24
Aug 13	8373	86	63	147	18	8.27
Aug 14	8300	70	70	140	17	8.18
Aug 15	8309	73	64	136	16	8.20
Aug 16	8297	67	64	131	15	8.14
Aug 19	8303				14	
Aug 20	8313				13	
Aug 21	8346				12	
Aug 22	8298				11	
Aug 23	8395				10	
Aug 26	8392				9	
Aug 27	8395				8	
Aug 28	8402				7	
Aug 29	8387				6	
Aug 30	8337				5	
Sep 3	8287				3	
Sep 4	8297				2	
Sep 5	8289				1	
Sep 6	8208	September 1996 option expires				

October option and December future

	fp	max	min	s	td	iv
Aug 19	8369	116	88	201	34	8.25
Aug 20	8378	117	95	210	33	8.73
Aug 21	8411	110	99	208	32	8.75
Aug 22	8363	117	80	193	31	8.31
Aug 23	8462	103	95	197	30	8.52
Aug 26	8462	104	92	195	29	8.56
Aug 27	8464	103	87	189	28	8.42
Aug 28	8472	104	82	184	27	8.36
Aug 29	8457	93	86	178	26	8.27
Aug 30	8407	87	80	166	25	7.92
Sep 3	8359	87	78	164	23	8.19
Sep 4	8369	88	69	155	22	7.91
Sep 5	8362	83	71	153	21	7.98
Sep 6	8278	89	68	155	20	8.38
Sep 9	8263				19	
Sep 10	8163				18	
Sep 11	8175				17	
Sep 12	8148				16	
Sep 13	8114				15	
Sep 16	8130				14	
Sep 17	8110				13	
Sep 18	8125				12	
Sep 19	8117				11	
Sep 20	8141				10	
Sep 23	8164				9	
Sep 24	8227				8	
Sep 25	8128				7	
Sep 26	8050				6	
Sep 27	8025				5	
Sep 30	8039				4	
Oct 1	8039				3	
Oct 2	8013				2	
Oct 3	8025				1	
Oct 4	8009	October 1996 option expires				

December option and December future

	fp	max	min	s	td	iv
Sep 9	8263	163	126	286	64	8.64
Sep 10	8163	162	125	284	63	8.75
Sep 11	8175	156	131	285	62	8.85
Sep 12	8148	162	115	272	61	8.56
Sep 13	8114	148	133	280	60	8.90
Sep 16	8130	148	128	274	59	8.78
Sep 17	8110	142	132	273	58	8.85
Sep 18	8125	153	128	279	57	9.09
Sep 19	8117	147	130	276	56	9.07
Sep 20	8141	141	132	272	55	9.02
Sep 23	8164	143	128	270	54	8.99

LEGEND: *fp* = futures price, *max* = closest strike high option price, *min* = closest strike low option price, *s* = price corrected at-the-money-straddle, *td* = number of trading days till expiry, *iv* = implied volatility.

SWISS FRANC 1996

	fp	max	min	s	td	iv
Sep 24	8227	147	120	265	53	8.84
Sep 25	8128	139	117	254	52	8.67
Sep 26	8050	123	123	246	51	8.56
Sep 27	8025	135	110	243	50	8.56
Sep 30	8039	124	113	236	49	8.39
Oct 1	8039	120	110	229	48	8.23
Oct 2	8013	117	104	220	47	8.01
Oct 3	8025	125	101	224	46	8.23
Oct 4	8009	116	107	222	45	8.27
Oct 7	8027	120	97	215	44	8.07
Oct 8	8057	111	104	214	43	8.12
Oct 9	8032	113	95	206	42	7.93
Oct 10	8057	105	98	202	41	7.85
Oct 11	8030	107	87	192	40	7.57
Oct 14	8038	103	91	193	39	7.69
Oct 15	7932	104	86	188	38	7.71
Oct 16	7939	102	91	192	37	7.95
Oct 17	7923	109	84	191	36	8.02
Oct 18	7917	108	91	198	35	8.43
Oct 21	7961	102	91	192	34	8.28
Oct 22	8025	109	84	191	33	8.27
Oct 23	8024	109	85	192	32	8.45
Oct 24	7998	97	95	192	31	8.62
Oct 25	7970	103	83	184	30	8.44
Oct 28	7973	103	80	181	29	8.43
Oct 29	8003	100	96	196	28	9.24
Oct 30	8006	101	95	196	27	9.40
Oct 31	7914	101	78	177	26	8.77
Nov 1	7908	96	88	183	25	9.27
Nov 4	7927	103	77	178	24	9.14
Nov 5	7869	98	79	175	23	9.29
Nov 6	7859	92	83	174	22	9.45
Nov 7	7877	101	78	177	21	9.80
Nov 8	7930	96	76	170	20	9.60
Nov 11	7989	90	80	169	19	9.71
Nov 12	7909	88	79	166	18	9.91
Nov 13	7909	82	73	154	17	9.46
Nov 14	7863	79	66	144	16	9.15
Nov 15	7839	71	61	131	15	8.64
Nov 18	7909	65	56	120	14	8.13
Nov 19	7888	65	53	117	13	8.22
Nov 20	7914	66	51	116	12	8.44
Nov 21	7914	63	48	110	11	8.35
Nov 22	7889	57	46	102	10	8.18
Nov 25	7778				9	
Nov 26	7762				8	
Nov 27	7750				7	
Nov 29	7683				5	
Dec 2	7560				4	
Dec 3	7582				3	
Dec 4	7580				2	
Dec 5	7619				1	
Dec 6	7606	December 1996 option expires				

	fp	max	min	s	td	iv
January option and March future						
Nov 25	7842	90	83	172	27	8.46
Nov 26	7825	99	74	171	26	8.55
Nov 27	7814	88	73	160	25	8.17
Nov 29	7747	82	78	160	24	8.41
Dec 2	7622	85	85	170	23	9.30
Dec 3	7645	88	93	181	22	10.12
Dec 4	7642	96	88	183	21	10.47
Dec 5	7681	106	87	191	20	11.14
Dec 6	7667	99	81	178	19	10.68
Dec 9	7600	87	87	174	18	10.79
Dec 10	7609	86	77	162	17	10.34
Dec 11	7699	85	84	169	16	10.97
Dec 12	7677	91	66	155	15	10.40
Dec 13	7622	88	67	153	14	10.73
Dec 16	7625				13	
Dec 17	7610				12	
Dec 18	7578				11	
Dec 19	7538				19	
Dec 20	7550				9	
Dec 23	7534				8	
Dec 24	7484				7	
Dec 26	7492				5	
Dec 27	7464				4	
Dec 30	7464				3	
Dec 31	7520				2	
Jan 2	7488				1	
Jan 3	7416	January 1997 option expires				
February option and March future						
Dec 16	7625	164	90	246	38	10.45
Dec 17	7610	171	82	242	37	10.46
Dec 18	7578	136	107	240	36	10.57
Dec 19	7538	128	116	243	35	10.90
Dec 20	7550	122	121	243	34	11.04
Dec 23	7534	125	109	233	33	10.75
Dec 24	7484	121	105	225	32	10.61
Dec 26	7492	114	107	220	30	10.74
Dec 27	7464	129	94	220	29	10.93
Dec 30	7464	125	90	212	28	10.72
Dec 31	7520	123	88	208	27	10.63
Feb 7	7021	February 1997 option expires				

LEGEND: *fp* = futures price, *max* = closest strike high option price, *min* = closest strike low option price, *s* = price corrected at-the-money-straddle, *td* = number of trading days till expiry, *iv* = implied volatility.

JAPANESE YEN

Calendar month	Year	Based on Option	Nearest strike	Implied volatility
JANUARY	1993	Feb	*7950*	7.99
FEBRUARY	1993	Mar	*8000*	7.54
MARCH	1993	Apr	*8400*	10.71
APRIL	1993	May	*8750*	11.35
MAY	1993	Jun	*9000*	10.32
JUNE	1993	Jul	*9350*	11.24
JULY	1993	Aug	*9200*	14.62
AUGUST	1993	Sep	*9600*	13.83
SEPTEMBER	1993	Oct	*9600*	14.75
OCTOBER	1993	Nov	*9450*	11.89
NOVEMBER	1993	Dec	*9250*	8.90
DECEMBER	1993	Jan	*9200*	10.27
JANUARY	1994	Feb	*8900*	10.45
FEBRUARY	1994	Mar	*9300*	11.93
MARCH	1994	Apr	*9600*	13.80
APRIL	1994	May	*9750*	12.19
MAY	1994	Jun	*9850*	12.19
JUNE	1994	Jul	*9650*	9.22
JULY	1994	Aug	*10200*	13.02
AUGUST	1994	Sep	*10100*	12.54
SEPTEMBER	1994	Oct	*10100*	10.78
OCTOBER	1994	Nov	*10200*	10.12
NOVEMBER	1994	Dec	*10400*	9.19
DECEMBER	1994	Jan	*10200*	8.02
JANUARY	1995	Feb	*9950*	9.15
FEBRUARY	1995	Mar	*10100*	8.38
MARCH	1995	Apr	*10450*	8.68
APRIL	1995	May	*11750*	16.33
MAY	1995	Jun	*12050*	15.65
JUNE	1995	Jul	*11950*	13.66
JULY	1995	Aug	*11900*	11.27
AUGUST	1995	Sep	*11400*	12.97
SEPTEMBER	1995	Oct	*10400*	14.82
OCTOBER	1995	Nov	*10050*	16.41
NOVEMBER	1995	Dec	*9750*	14.83
DECEMBER	1995	Jan	*10000*	12.36
JANUARY	1996	Mar	*9700*	12.92
FEBRUARY	1996	Apr	*9500*	10.94
MARCH	1996	Apr	*9600*	10.27
APRIL	1996	Jun	*9400*	10.25
MAY	1996	Jun	*9550*	9.81
JUNE	1996	Jul	*9350*	8.62
JULY	1996	Sep	*9200*	7.93
AUGUST	1996	Sep	*9400*	9.03
SEPTEMBER	1996	Oct	*9300*	6.47
OCTOBER	1996	Dec	*9100*	7.14
NOVEMBER	1996	Dec	*8850*	8.37
DECEMBER	1996	Jan	*8850*	6.83
JANUARY	1997	Feb	*8700*	9.25
FEBRUARY	1997	Mar	*8250*	11.86
MARCH	1997	Apr	*8450*	11.93
APRIL	1997	May	*8300*	10.79
MAY	1997	Jun	*7950*	8.82
JUNE	1997	Jul	*8700*	9.97
JULY	1997	Aug	*8800*	10.53
AUGUST	1997	Sep	*8500*	11.43
SEPTEMBER	1997	Oct	*8250*	13.11
OCTOBER	1997	Nov	*8350*	12.31
NOVEMBER	1997	Dec	*8300*	11.74
DECEMBER	1997	Jan	*7900*	14.01

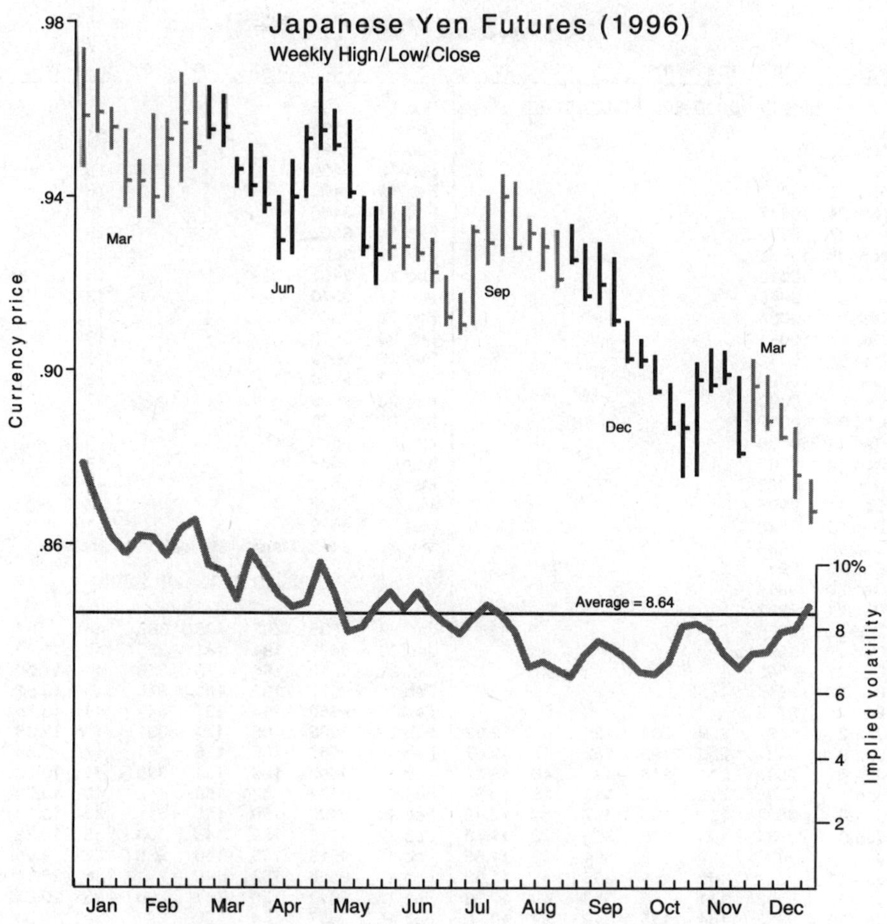
Japanese Yen Futures (1996)
Weekly High/Low/Close
Currency price
.98
.94
.90
.86
Mar
Jun
Sep
Dec
Mar
Average = 8.64
10%
8
6
4
2
Implied volatility
Jan
Feb
Mar
Apr
May
Jun
Jul
Aug
Sep
Oct
Nov
Dec

JAPANESE YEN 1996

March option and March future

	fp	max	min	s	td	iv
Nov 20	10057					
Nov 21	10028					
Nov 22	10097					
Nov 24	10017					
Nov 27	9998					
Nov 28	10032					
Nov 29	10010					
Nov 30	9948					
Dec 1	10035					
Dec 4	10041					
Dec 5	10032					
Dec 6	10020					
Dec 7	10000					
Dec 8	10017					
Dec 11	10036					
Dec 12	9963					
Dec 13	9978					
Dec 14	9988					
Dec 15	9928					
Dec 18	9983					
Dec 19	9937					
Dec 20	9944					
Dec 21	9937					
Dec 22	9906					
Dec 26	9898					
Dec 27	9842					
Dec 28	9845					
Dec 29	9773					
Jan 2	9721	229	208	435	48	12.92
Jan 3	9637	236	199	432	47	13.07
Jan 4	9595	221	216	437	46	13.42
Jan 5	9589	213	202	414	45	12.88
Jan 8	9592	203	195	397	44	12.49
Jan 9	9631	195	176	369	43	11.70
Jan 10	9637	189	176	364	42	11.65
Jan 11	9631	188	169	355	41	11.53
Jan 12	9592	171	163	333	40	10.99
Jan 15	9592	164	156	319	39	10.66
Jan 16	9537	171	158	328	38	11.16
Jan 17	9563	169	156	324	37	11.14
Jan 18	9550	155	155	310	36	10.82
Jan 19	9569	157	138	293	35	10.36
Jan 22	9531	153	134	285	34	10.27
Jan 23	9519	148	129	275	33	10.07
Jan 24	9413	149	136	284	32	10.66
Jan 25	9420	148	128	274	31	10.46
Jan 26	9439	138	127	264	30	10.22
Jan 29	9425				29	
Jan 30	9387				28	
Jan 31	9402				27	
Feb 1	9417				26	
Feb 2	9448				25	
Feb 5	9575				24	
Feb 6	9557				23	
Feb 7	9492				22	
Feb 8	9394				21	
Feb 9	9386				20	
Feb 12	9408				19	
Feb 13	9403				18	
Feb 14	9456				17	
Feb 15	9502				16	
Feb 16	9527				15	
Feb 20	9491				13	
Feb 21	9570				12	
Feb 22	9548				11	
Feb 23	9573				10	
Feb 26	9619				9	
Feb 27	9610				8	
Feb 28	9589				7	
Feb 29	9525				6	
Mar 1	9503				5	
Mar 4	9531				4	
Mar 5	9517				3	
Mar 6	9502				2	
Mar 7	9509				1	
Mar 8	9442	March 1996 option expires				

April option and June future

	fp	max	min	s	td	iv
Jan 29	9535	203	165	365	48	11.04
Jan 30	9497	184	181	365	47	11.20
Jan 31	9512	184	173	356	46	11.04
Feb 1	9527	187	161	346	45	10.82
Feb 2	9558	194	151	341	44	10.76
Feb 5	9685	188	174	361	43	11.36
Feb 6	9667	188	156	341	42	10.89
Feb 7	9602	166	164	330	41	10.73
Feb 8	9504	160	158	318	40	10.58
Feb 9	9496	160	152	311	39	10.50
Feb 12	9518	159	145	303	38	10.32
Feb 13	9513	149	140	288	37	9.96
Feb 14	9566	152	140	291	36	10.14
Feb 15	9612	150	141	290	35	10.21
Feb 16	9637	164	130	291	34	10.35
Feb 20	9601	150	150	300	32	11.05
Feb 21	9680	165	144	307	31	11.40
Feb 22	9658	178	135	309	30	11.68
Feb 23	9683	162	144	304	29	11.68
Feb 26	9729	161	142	301	28	11.71
Feb 27	9720	160	140	298	27	11.81
Feb 28	9699	146	145	291	26	11.76
Feb 29	9635	139	123	261	25	10.82
Mar 1	9613	128	115	242	24	10.27
Mar 4	9641	122	113	234	23	10.13
Mar 5	9628	126	104	228	22	10.10
Mar 6	9613	112	99	210	21	9.53
Mar 7	9621	113	92	203	20	9.44
Mar 8	9559	112	103	214	19	10.28
Mar 11	9609	106	97	202	18	9.92
Mar 12	9627	114	91	203	17	10.22

LEGEND: *fp* = futures price, *max* = closest strike high option price, *min* = closest strike low option price, *s* = price corrected at-the-money-straddle, *td* = number of trading days till expiry, *iv* = implied volatility.

JAPANESE YEN 1996

	fp	max	min	s	td	iv
Mar 13	9634	105	91	195	16	10.11
Mar 14	9596	88	84	172	15	9.24
Mar 15	9567	89	72	159	14	8.91
Mar 18	9549	74	73	147	13	8.53
Mar 19	9528	81	59	138	12	8.36
Mar 20	9514	76	62	137	11	8.67
Mar 21	9473	83	60	141	10	9.40
Mar 22	9462	74	62	135	9	9.51
Mar 25	9522				8	
Mar 26	9491				7	
Mar 27	9489				6	
Mar 28	9514				5	
Mar 29	9425				4	
Apr 1	9394				3	
Apr 2	9389				2	
Apr 3	9453				1	
Apr 4	9435	April 1996 option expires				

June option and June future

	fp	max	min	s	td	iv
Mar 25	9522	197	175	370	54	10.58
Mar 26	9491	187	178	364	53	10.54
Mar 27	9489	188	177	364	52	10.64
Mar 28	9514	188	173	360	51	10.59
Mar 29	9425	186	162	346	50	10.38
Apr 1	9394	170	164	334	49	10.14
Apr 2	9389	158	148	305	48	9.38
Apr 3	9453	159	156	315	47	9.71
Apr 4	9435	160	145	304	46	9.49
Apr 8	9380	154	134	286	44	9.20
Apr 9	9322	155	133	286	43	9.36
Apr 10	9311	146	135	280	42	9.28
Apr 11	9303	136	132	268	41	8.99
Apr 12	9294	132	126	258	40	8.76
Apr 15	9291	130	121	250	39	8.63
Apr 16	9319	133	114	245	38	8.54
Apr 17	9312	125	113	237	37	8.37
Apr 18	9448	129	127	256	36	9.03
Apr 19	9394	124	118	242	35	8.69
Apr 22	9448	120	118	238	34	8.63
Apr 23	9446	121	117	238	33	8.76
Apr 24	9450	119	118	237	32	8.86
Apr 25	9439	120	109	228	31	8.68
Apr 26	9533	129	112	240	30	9.18
Apr 29	9608	141	133	273	29	10.57
Apr 30	9583	142	125	266	28	10.47
May 1	9550	120	119	239	27	9.63
May 2	9633	138	121	258	26	10.49
May 3	9567	128	110	236	25	9.89
May 6	9589	122	111	232	24	9.88
May 7	9569	113	94	205	23	8.95
May 8	9549	98	97	195	22	8.70
May 9	9596	101	97	198	21	8.99
May 10	9528	100	79	177	20	8.31
May 13	9564	91	76	166	19	7.95
May 14	9481	90	71	159	18	7.92
May 15	9392	80	72	151	17	7.82
May 16	9407	76	69	144	16	7.68
May 17	9400	71	70	141	15	7.74
May 20	9375				14	
May 21	9364				13	
May 22	9373				12	
May 23	9381				11	
May 24	9294				10	
May 28	9208				8	
May 29	9269				7	
May 30	9303				6	
May 31	9266				5	
Jun 3	9239				4	
Jun 4	9203				3	
Jun 5	9191				2	
Jun 6	9167				1	
Jun 7	9164	June 1996 option expires				

July option and September future

	fp	max	min	s	td	iv
May 20	9489	117	107	223	34	8.07
May 21	9481	118	99	215	33	7.91
May 22	9489	114	103	216	32	8.05
May 23	9497	111	107	218	31	8.23
May 24	9409	112	103	214	30	8.31
May 28	9323	118	95	211	28	8.55
May 29	9384	116	100	215	27	8.80
May 30	9421	119	98	215	26	8.96
May 31	9384	111	95	205	25	8.72
Jun 3	9356	102	96	198	24	8.62
Jun 4	9320	114	94	206	23	9.23
Jun 5	9307	107	100	206	22	9.46
Jun 6	9283	113	96	208	21	9.76
Jun 7	9280	104	84	186	20	8.97
Jun 10	9296	87	83	170	19	8.37
Jun 11	9252	85	83	168	18	8.55
Jun 12	9289	88	78	165	17	8.62
Jun 13	9312	85	73	157	16	8.43
Jun 14	9282	88	70	156	15	8.70
Jun 17	9289				14	
Jun 18	9400				13	
Jun 19	9378				12	
Jun 20	9356				11	
Jun 21	9271				10	
Jun 24	9286				9	
Jun 25	9281				8	
Jun 26	9241				7	
Jun 27	9263				6	
Jun 28	9221				5	
Jul 1	9222				4	
Jul 2	9153				3	
Jul 3	9147				2	
Jul 5	9124	July 1996 option expires				

LEGEND: *fp* = futures price, *max* = closest strike high option price, *min* = closest strike low option price, *s* = price corrected at-the-money-straddle, *td* = number of trading days till expiry, *iv* = implied volatility.

JAPANESE YEN 1996

<u>September option and September future</u>

	fp	max	min	s	td	iv
Jun 17	9289	172	162	333	59	9.34
Jun 18	9400	173	172	345	58	9.64
Jun 19	9378	176	155	329	57	9.30
Jun 20	9356	158	152	310	56	8.84
Jun 21	9271	164	143	305	55	8.88
Jun 24	9286	151	137	287	54	8.41
Jun 25	9281	149	130	277	53	8.21
Jun 26	9241	146	137	282	52	8.47
Jun 27	9263	148	135	282	51	8.52
Jun 28	9221	152	131	281	50	8.63
Jul 1	9222	140	118	256	49	7.93
Jul 2	9153	128	124	252	48	7.94
Jul 3	9147	126	123	249	47	7.93
Jul 5	9124	136	112	246	45	8.03
Jul 8	9114	128	114	241	44	7.97
Jul 9	9156	125	119	244	43	8.11
Jul 10	9159	120	111	230	42	7.76
Jul 11	9150	112	111	223	41	7.61
Jul 12	9100	109	108	217	40	7.54
Jul 15	9146	109	105	214	39	7.48
Jul 16	9232	128	110	236	38	8.31
Jul 17	9278	130	109	237	37	8.40
Jul 18	9292	132	124	255	36	9.16
Jul 19	9331	136	117	251	35	9.11
Jul 22	9373	138	115	251	34	9.18
Jul 23	9339	129	119	247	33	9.21
Jul 24	9291	119	110	228	32	8.69
Jul 25	9296	109	105	214	31	8.26
Jul 26	9292	105	98	202	30	7.95
Jul 29	9311	100	94	194	29	7.72
Jul 30	9323	111	88	197	28	7.98
Jul 31	9437	134	97	227	27	9.28
Aug 1	9391	113	104	216	26	9.03
Aug 2	9414	110	96	205	25	8.70
Aug 5	9432	107	89	194	24	8.41
Aug 6	9414	100	86	185	23	8.19
Aug 7	9312	91	79	169	22	7.74
Aug 8	9284	81	73	153	21	7.21
Aug 9	9283	82	65	145	20	7.01
Aug 12	9336	77	63	139	19	6.82
Aug 13	9337	74	61	134	18	6.76
Aug 14	9300	65	65	130	17	6.78
Aug 15	9298	64	62	126	16	6.77
Aug 16	9321	72	51	121	15	6.70
Aug 19	9311				14	
Aug 20	9261				13	
Aug 21	9250				12	
Aug 22	9267				11	
Aug 23	9282				10	
Aug 26	9309				9	
Aug 27	9311				8	
Aug 28	9248				7	
Aug 29	9247				6	
Aug 30	9200				5	
Sep 3	9170				3	
Sep 4	9210				2	
Sep 5	9171				1	
Sep 6	9148	September 1996 option expires				

<u>October option and December future</u>

	fp	max	min	s	td	iv
Aug 19	9428	113	91	202	34	7.35
Aug 20	9377	110	85	193	33	7.15
Aug 21	9367	103	85	186	32	7.04
Aug 22	9384	100	84	183	31	6.99
Aug 23	9399	86	85	171	30	6.64
Aug 26	9427	101	76	175	29	6.88
Aug 27	9428	103	82	183	28	7.34
Aug 28	9367	90	73	161	27	6.64
Aug 29	9366	85	69	153	26	6.39
Aug 30	9319	86	67	151	25	6.49
Sep 3	9291	77	68	144	23	6.47
Sep 4	9331	85	66	149	22	6.82
Sep 5	9292	75	67	141	21	6.64
Sep 6	9267	74	56	128	20	6.19
Sep 9	9281				19	
Sep 10	9233				18	
Sep 11	9196				17	
Sep 12	9189				16	
Sep 13	9170				15	
Sep 16	9191				14	
Sep 17	9185				13	
Sep 18	9278				12	
Sep 19	9250				11	
Sep 20	9205				10	
Sep 23	9209				9	
Sep 24	9267				8	
Sep 25	9153				7	
Sep 26	9139				6	
Sep 27	9117				5	
Sep 30	9075				4	
Oct 1	9071				3	
Oct 2	9028				2	
Oct 3	9061				1	
Oct 4	9030	October 1996 option expires				

<u>December option and December future</u>

	fp	max	min	s	td	iv
Sep 9	9281	148	129	275	64	7.42
Sep 10	9233	152	119	268	63	7.31
Sep 11	9196	136	132	268	62	7.39
Sep 12	9189	137	127	263	61	7.33
Sep 13	9170	149	119	265	60	7.47
Sep 16	9191	138	129	266	59	7.54
Sep 17	9185	142	127	268	58	7.65
Sep 18	9278	151	126	275	57	7.85
Sep 19	9250	132	132	264	56	7.63
Sep 20	9205	131	126	257	55	7.52
Sep 23	9209	131	122	252	54	7.46

LEGEND: *fp* = futures price, *max* = closest strike high option price, *min* = closest strike low option price, *s* = price corrected at-the-money-straddle, *td* = number of trading days till expiry, *iv* = implied volatility.

JAPANESE YEN 1996

	fp	max	min	s	td	iv
Sep 24	9267	136	119	254	53	7.52
Sep 25	9153	122	118	240	52	7.26
Sep 26	9139	124	113	236	51	7.23
Sep 27	9117	128	110	236	50	7.34
Sep 30	9075	130	106	234	49	7.36
Oct 1	9071	128	99	224	48	7.14
Oct 2	9028	121	100	219	47	7.08
Oct 3	9061	112	101	212	46	6.90
Oct 4	9030	113	93	204	45	6.74
Oct 7	9084	110	94	203	44	6.72
Oct 8	9056	104	98	202	43	6.79
Oct 9	9041	102	93	194	42	6.63
Oct 10	9075	108	83	189	41	6.49
Oct 11	9039	99	88	186	40	6.51
Oct 14	9038	97	85	181	39	6.41
Oct 15	8987	99	86	184	38	6.64
Oct 16	8982	100	82	180	37	6.60
Oct 17	8980	99	79	176	36	6.54
Oct 18	8957	94	87	180	35	6.81
Oct 21	8937	94	81	174	34	6.67
Oct 22	8966	98	82	179	33	6.93
Oct 23	8914	98	84	181	32	7.17
Oct 24	8920	98	78	174	31	7.01
Oct 25	8874	102	76	176	30	7.22
Oct 28	8813	102	89	190	29	8.00
Oct 29	8806	103	97	200	28	8.56
Oct 30	8830	104	84	186	27	8.12
Oct 31	8822	104	82	184	26	8.18
Nov 1	8874	106	82	186	25	8.37
Nov 4	8833	96	79	173	24	8.02
Nov 5	8812	93	81	173	23	8.19
Nov 6	8822	89	67	154	22	7.44
Nov 7	8958	96	88	183	21	8.93
Nov 8	8984	89	73	161	20	7.99
Nov 11	9053	84	81	165	19	8.35
Nov 12	9006	81	75	156	18	8.14
Nov 13	8991	79	70	148	17	8.00
Nov 14	9028	79	58	135	16	7.48
Nov 15	9038	72	60	131	15	7.48
Nov 18	9000	60	69	130	14	7.70
Nov 19	8994	59	53	111	13	6.88
Nov 20	8991	59	50	108	12	6.95
Nov 21	9011	58	47	104	11	6.96
Nov 22	8992	55	48	102	10	7.20
Nov 25	8899				9	
Nov 26	8906				8	
Nov 27	8844				7	
Nov 29	8802				5	
Dec 2	8737				4	
Dec 3	8841				3	
Dec 4	8858				2	
Dec 5	8911				1	
Dec 6	8860	December 1996 option expires				

January option and March future

	fp	max	min	s	td	iv
Nov 25	9012	88	76	163	27	6.96
Nov 26	9019	88	69	155	26	6.75
Nov 27	8957	76	69	144	25	6.45
Nov 29	8914	77	63	139	24	6.35
Dec 2	8849	73	72	145	23	6.83
Dec 3	8953	77	73	150	22	7.13
Dec 4	8972	86	64	148	21	7.20
Dec 5	9025	95	70	163	20	8.06
Dec 6	8974	90	66	154	19	7.86
Dec 9	8939	72	61	132	18	6.96
Dec 10	8939	70	59	128	17	6.95
Dec 11	8967	74	56	128	16	7.16
Dec 12	8938	68	56	123	15	7.10
Dec 13	8892	68	61	128	14	7.72
Dec 16	8833				13	
Dec 17	8894				12	
Dec 18	8908				11	
Dec 19	8878				19	
Dec 20	8853				9	
Dec 23	8871				8	
Dec 24	8841				7	
Dec 26	8803				5	
Dec 27	8750				4	
Dec 30	8700				3	
Dec 31	8713				2	
Jan 2	8742				1	
Jan 3	8678	January 1997 option expires				

February option and March future

	fp	max	min	s	td	iv
Dec 16	8833	116	99	214	38	7.84
Dec 17	8894	110	104	214	37	7.89
Dec 18	8908	113	105	217	36	8.13
Dec 19	8878	119	90	206	35	7.86
Dec 20	8853	105	101	206	34	7.97
Dec 23	8871	109	88	195	33	7.66
Dec 24	8841	101	92	192	32	7.69
Dec 26	8803	101	98	199	30	8.24
Dec 27	8750	124	84	204	29	8.66
Dec 30	8700	104	104	208	28	9.04
Dec 31	8713	102	101	203	27	8.96
Feb 7	8173	February 1997 option expires				

LEGEND: *fp* = futures price, *max* = closest strike high option price, *min* = closest strike low option price, *s* = price corrected at-the-money-straddle, *td* = number of trading days till expiry, *iv* = implied volatility.

GOLD

Calendar month	Year	Based on Option	Nearest strike	Implied volatility
JANUARY	1993	Apr	*325*	9.59
FEBRUARY	1993	Apr	*330*	9.03
MARCH	1993	Jun	*330*	8.69
APRIL	1993	Jun	*340*	9.50
MAY	1993	Aug	*355*	14.21
JUNE	1993	Oct	*375*	18.03
JULY	1993	Oct	*390*	18.25
AUGUST	1993	Dec	*410*	19.69
SEPTEMBER	1993	Dec	*375*	14.16
OCTOBER	1993	Dec	*360*	15.28
NOVEMBER	1993	Feb	*365*	16.34
DECEMBER	1993	Apr	*380*	16.47
JANUARY	1994	Apr	*395*	17.35
FEBRUARY	1994	Jun	*385*	14.50
MARCH	1994	Jun	*380*	13.39
APRIL	1994	Aug	*390*	13.86
MAY	1994	Aug	*380*	11.34
JUNE	1994	Oct	*390*	13.17
JULY	1994	Oct	*390*	12.51
AUGUST	1994	Dec	*390*	10.91
SEPTEMBER	1994	Dec	*390*	9.71
OCTOBER	1994	Feb	*400*	10.99
NOVEMBER	1994	Feb	*390*	8.76
DECEMBER	1994	Apr	*385*	8.03
JANUARY	1995	Apr	*380*	8.09
FEBRUARY	1995	Jun	*380*	8.25
MARCH	1995	May	*380*	7.79
APRIL	1995	Aug	*400*	12.15
MAY	1995	Aug	*395*	10.75
JUNE	1995	Oct	*390*	7.79
JULY	1995	Oct	*390*	7.43
AUGUST	1995	Dec	*390*	7.02
SEPTEMBER	1995	Dec	*385*	7.52
OCTOBER	1995	Feb	*385*	6.96
NOVEMBER	1995	Feb	*385*	7.44
DECEMBER	1995	Apr	*390*	8.38
JANUARY	1996	Apr	*395*	7.98
FEBRUARY	1996	Apr	*415*	14.14
MARCH	1996	Jun	*404*	9.90
APRIL	1996	Jun	*400*	8.64
MAY	1996	Aug	*400*	7.68
JUNE	1996	Oct	*395*	7.35
JULY	1996	Oct	*385*	6.92
AUGUST	1996	Dec	*390*	6.17
SEPTEMBER	1996	Dec	*390*	5.66
OCTOBER	1996	Feb	*385*	5.79
NOVEMBER	1996	Feb	*380*	4.94
DECEMBER	1996	Apr	*375*	6.64
JANUARY	1997	Apr	*370*	7.73
FEBRUARY	1997	Jun	*350*	10.32
MARCH	1997	Jun	*365*	11.18
APRIL	1997	Aug	*355*	9.02
MAY	1997	Aug	*345*	8.92
JUNE	1997	Oct	*345*	8.43
JULY	1997	Oct	*375*	9.12
AUGUST	1997	Dec	*365*	10.09
SEPTEMBER	1997	Dec	*325*	12.92
OCTOBER	1997	Feb	*338*	9.66
NOVEMBER	1997	Feb	*315*	15.78
DECEMBER	1997	Apr	*300*	15.16

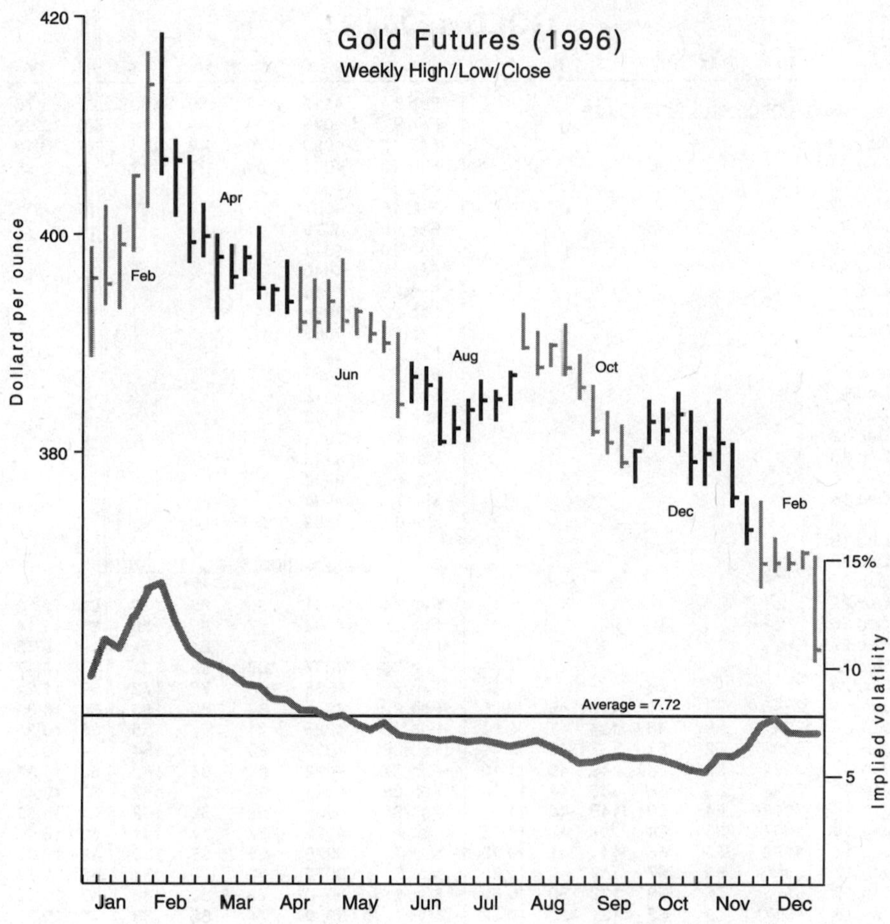
Gold Futures (1996)
Weekly High/Low/Close
420
400
380
Dollard per ounce
Feb
Apr
Jun
Aug
Oct
Dec
Feb
15%
10
5
Implied volatility
Average = 7.72
Jan
Feb
Mar
Apr
May
Jun
Jul
Aug
Sep
Oct
Nov
Dec

GOLD 1996

April option and April future

	fp	max	min	s	td	iv
Nov 20						
Nov 21						
Nov 22						
Nov 27						
Nov 28						
Nov 29						
Nov 30						
Dec 1						
Dec 4						
Dec 5						
Dec 6						
Dec 7						
Dec 8						
Dec 11						
Dec 12						
Dec 13						
Dec 14						
Dec 15						
Dec 18						
Dec 19						
Dec 20						
Dec 21						
Dec 22						
Dec 26						
Dec 27						
Dec 28						
Dec 29						
Jan 2	3948	77	38	110	48	8.06
Jan 3	3991	79	48	124	47	9.04
Jan 4	3983	82	57	137	46	10.11
Jan 5	3994	82	68	149	45	11.10
Jan 8	3994	83	68	150	44	11.30
Jan 9	3998	84	66	148	43	11.32
Jan 10	4031	85	64	147	42	11.26
Jan 11	4022	77	65	141	41	10.95
Jan 12	3996	83	67	149	40	11.76
Jan 15	3990	78	56	132	39	10.59
Jan 16	4017	69	63	131	38	10.62
Jan 17	4029	76	58	132	37	10.80
Jan 18	4005	65	62	127	36	10.55
Jan 19	4028	75	55	128	35	10.75
Jan 22	4064	97	59	152	34	12.83
Jan 23	4065	89	53	138	33	11.83
Jan 24	4064	94	55	145	32	12.59
Jan 25	4096	87	62	147	31	12.86
Jan 26	4087	81	67	147	30	13.11
Jan 29	4087	79	65	143	29	12.97
Jan 30	4070	84	63	145	28	13.47
Jan 31	4085	89	61	147	27	13.87
Feb 1	4137	95	58	149	26	14.14
Feb 2	4177	96	57	149	25	14.25
Feb 5	4159	98	57	151	24	14.78
Feb 6	4146	94	48	137	23	13.74
Feb 7	4114	75	61	135	22	13.97
Feb 8	4115	73	58	130	21	13.75
Feb 9	4078	71	49	118	20	12.92
Feb 12	4033	76	43	115	19	13.12
Feb 13	4051	84	39	117	18	13.65
Feb 14	4065				17	
Feb 15	4057				16	
Feb 16	4075				15	
Feb 20	4011				13	
Feb 21	4040				12	
Feb 22	4015				11	
Feb 23	3999				10	
Feb 26	4006				9	
Feb 27	3996				8	
Feb 28	4021				7	
Feb 29	4012				6	
Mar 1	4002				5	
Mar 4	3952				4	
Mar 5	3946				3	
Mar 6	3944				2	
Mar 7	3964				1	
Mar 8	3982	April 96 option expires				

June option and June future

	fp	max	min	s	td	iv
Feb 14	4091	95	85	179	62	11.12
Feb 15	4083	97	82	178	61	11.14
Feb 16	4101	87	84	171	60	10.75
Feb 20	4037	102	63	161	58	10.47
Feb 21	4066	103	72	172	57	11.21
Feb 22	4041	97	69	163	56	10.80
Feb 23	4025	91	66	155	55	10.36
Feb 26	4032	90	66	154	54	10.38
Feb 27	4022	88	66	152	53	10.38
Feb 28	4047	93	62	152	52	10.41
Feb 29	4038	98	58	152	51	10.52
Mar 1	4028	87	57	141	50	9.90
Mar 4	3978	85	57	139	49	10.00
Mar 5	3972	82	55	134	48	9.76
Mar 6	3970	78	60	136	47	10.02
Mar 7	3990	74	65	138	46	10.22
Mar 8	4008	71	71	142	45	10.56
Mar 11	3993	69	66	135	44	10.18
Mar 12	4001	67	62	129	43	9.80
Mar 13	4003	65	58	122	42	9.44
Mar 14	3991	62	57	119	41	9.28
Mar 15	3995	59	58	117	40	9.25
Mar 18	3989	60	55	115	39	9.20
Mar 19	3986	61	51	111	38	9.04
Mar 20	3991	59	53	111	37	9.19
Mar 21	4013	62	51	112	36	9.31
Mar 22	4015	65	48	111	35	9.38
Mar 25	4016	63	45	106	34	9.08
Mar 26	4031	72	39	107	33	9.26
Mar 27	4030	71	39	106	32	9.33
Mar 28	3995	51	48	99	31	8.88
Mar 29	3984	57	41	96	30	8.84

LEGEND: *fp* = futures price, *max* = closest strike high option price, *min* = closest strike low option price, *s* = price corrected at-the-money-straddle, *td* = number of trading days till expiry, *iv* = implied volatility.

GOLD 1996

	fp	max	min	s	td	iv
Apr 1	3977	59	36	93	29	8.64
Apr 2	3966	63	28	86	28	8.24
Apr 3	3968	62	29	87	27	8.43
Apr 4	3976	56	31	84	26	8.31
Apr 8	4007	46	39	84	24	8.60
Apr 9	3971	57	28	81	23	8.56
Apr 10	3975	54	29	80	22	8.60
Apr 11	3983	49	32	79	21	8.69
Apr 12	3971	53	24	73	20	8.25
Apr 15	3955	52	21	69	19	7.97
Apr 16	3935	52	18	65	18	7.75
Apr 17	3930	47	18	61	17	7.51
Apr 18	3924	46	22	65	16	8.29
Apr 19	3927	47	20	63	15	8.33
Apr 22	3936				14	
Apr 23	3934				13	
Apr 24	3927				12	
Apr 25	3953				11	
Apr 26	3922				10	
Apr 29	3924				9	
Apr 30	3935				8	
May 1	3949				7	
May 2	3957				6	
May 3	3941				5	
May 6	3957				4	
May 7	3958				3	
May 8	3948				2	
May 9	3945				1	
May 10	3920 June 96 option expires					

August option and August future

	fp	max	min	s	td	iv
Apr 22	3969	86	46	127	58	8.43
Apr 23	3967	86	43	124	57	8.27
Apr 24	3960	83	40	118	56	7.94
Apr 25	3986	81	38	114	55	7.69
Apr 26	3955	78	35	107	54	7.39
Apr 29	3957	80	34	108	53	7.49
Apr 30	3968	78	37	110	52	7.68
May 1	3982	69	42	108	51	7.61
May 2	3990	67	46	111	50	7.86
May 3	3974	75	38	109	49	7.81
May 6	3990	62	45	105	48	7.62
May 7	3991	63	46	107	47	7.85
May 8	3981	67	42	106	46	7.88
May 9	3978	70	38	104	45	7.82
May 10	3953	72	34	101	44	7.72
May 13	3960	75	30	99	43	7.60
May 14	3962	74	30	98	42	7.63
May 15	3968	65	30	91	41	7.13
May 16	3968	64	29	89	40	7.05
May 17	3963	66	27	88	39	7.08
May 20	3946	63	24	81	38	6.69
May 21	3947	63	23	80	37	6.67
May 22	3953				36	
May 23	3951				35	
May 24	3942				34	
May 28	3949				32	
May 29	3945				31	
May 30	3938				30	
May 31	3942				29	
Jun 3	3936				28	
Jun 4	3908				27	
Jun 5	3889				26	
Jun 6	3884				25	
Jun 7	3876				24	
Jun 10	3885				23	
Jun 11	3869				22	
Jun 12	3868				21	
Jun 13	3865				20	
Jun 14	3871				19	
Jun 17	3873				18	
Jun 18	3877				17	
Jun 19	3865				16	
Jun 20	3863				15	
Jun 21	3868				14	
Jun 24	3867				13	
Jun 25	3856				12	
Jun 26	3847				11	
Jun 27	3836				10	
Jun 28	3816				9	
Jul 1	3827				8	
Jul 2	3833				7	
Jul 5	3825				5	
Jul 8	3821				4	
Jul 9	3835				3	
Jul 10	3834				2	
Jul 11	3846				1	
Jul 12	3844 August 96 option expires					

October option and October future

	fp	max	min	s	td	iv
May 22	3975	75	56	129	80	7.27
May 23	3973	76	56	130	79	7.37
May 24	3964	81	53	131	78	7.49
May 28	3971	76	55	129	76	7.45
May 29	3967	78	50	125	75	7.28
May 30	3960	80	50	127	74	7.45
May 31	3964	77	52	127	73	7.47
Jun 3	3958	80	47	123	72	7.35
Jun 4	3930	85	36	114	71	6.91
Jun 5	3911	62	45	105	70	6.44
Jun 6	3906	58	48	105	69	6.48
Jun 7	3898	54	52	106	68	6.59
Jun 10	3907	60	49	108	67	6.76
Jun 11	3891	55	52	107	66	6.75
Jun 12	3890	55	52	107	65	6.81
Jun 13	3887	56	50	105	64	6.78
Jun 14	3893	53	53	106	63	6.86
Jun 17	3895	53	51	104	62	6.77
Jun 18	3899	55	49	103	61	6.80
Jun 19	3887	55	48	102	60	6.80

LEGEND: *fp* = futures price, *max* = closest strike high option price, *min* = closest strike low option price, *s* = price corrected at-the-money-straddle, *td* = number of trading days till expiry, *iv* = implied volatility.

GOLD 1996

	fp	max	min	s	td	iv
Jun 20	3885	54	46	99	59	6.66
Jun 21	3890	51	47	98	58	6.59
Jun 24	3889	51	46	97	57	6.58
Jun 25	3878	57	41	96	56	6.65
Jun 26	3869	61	35	93	55	6.49
Jun 27	3858	68	31	94	54	6.65
Jun 28	3838	71	29	94	53	6.74
Jul 1	3849	75	28	96	52	6.92
Jul 2	3855	69	28	91	51	6.63
Jul 5	3847	73	24	89	49	6.62
Jul 8	3843	71	24	88	48	6.58
Jul 9	3857	64	27	86	47	6.51
Jul 10	3856	65	26	86	46	6.54
Jul 11	3868	57	31	85	45	6.56
Jul 12	3866	58	28	82	44	6.42
Jul 15	3879				43	
Jul 16	3864				42	
Jul 17	3864				41	
Jul 18	3868				40	
Jul 19	3875				39	
Jul 22	3877				38	
Jul 23	3877				37	
Jul 24	3885				36	
Jul 25	3879				35	
Jul 26	3879				34	
Jul 29	3872				33	
Jul 30	3866				32	
Jul 31	3897				31	
Aug 1	3894				30	
Aug 2	3906				29	
Aug 5	3923				28	
Aug 6	3917				27	
Aug 7	3914				26	
Aug 8	3917				25	
Aug 9	3905				24	
Aug 12	3906				23	
Aug 13	3904				22	
Aug 14	3889				21	
Aug 15	3888				20	
Aug 16	3885				19	
Aug 19	3895				18	
Aug 20	3900				17	
Aug 21	3889				16	
Aug 22	3896				15	
Aug 23	3902				14	
Aug 26	3914				13	
Aug 27	3909				12	
Aug 28	3900				11	
Aug 29	3894				10	
Aug 30	3883				9	
Sep 3	3875				7	
Sep 4	3869				6	
Sep 5	3867				5	
Sep 6	3860				4	
Sep 9	3844				3	
Sep 10	3840				2	

Date	fp	max	min	s	td	iv
Sep 11	3838				1	
Sep 12	3830	October 96 option expires				
December option and December future						
Jul 15	3907	66	55	120	84	6.70
Jul 16	3892	64	58	121	83	6.85
Jul 17	3892	62	56	117	82	6.67
Jul 18	3896	58	58	116	81	6.62
Jul 19	3903	59	55	114	80	6.51
Jul 22	3905	60	53	112	79	6.48
Jul 23	3905	59	54	113	78	6.53
Jul 24	3913	64	49	112	77	6.50
Jul 25	3907	60	50	109	76	6.41
Jul 26	3907	61	51	111	75	6.57
Jul 29	3900	56	54	110	74	6.55
Jul 30	3894	54	52	106	73	6.36
Jul 31	3925	68	38	103	72	6.16
Aug 1	3922	62	42	102	71	6.17
Aug 2	3934	66	39	102	70	6.20
Aug 5	3951	78	35	107	69	6.55
Aug 6	3945	81	32	106	68	6.52
Aug 7	3942	81	32	106	67	6.58
Aug 8	3945	81	30	103	66	6.46
Aug 9	3933	81	30	103	65	6.53
Aug 12	3934	82	30	104	64	6.62
Aug 13	3932	81	30	103	63	6.63
Aug 14	3917	80	30	103	62	6.66
Aug 15	3916	80	30	103	61	6.71
Aug 16	3913	78	29	100	60	6.58
Aug 19	3923	78	27	97	59	6.44
Aug 20	3928	75	26	93	58	6.24
Aug 21	3917	75	26	93	57	6.32
Aug 22	3924	75	25	92	56	6.27
Aug 23	3930	73	24	89	55	6.11
Aug 26	3942	73	24	89	54	6.15
Aug 27	3937	72	23	87	53	6.06
Aug 28	3928	72	22	85	52	6.03
Aug 29	3922	73	23	88	51	6.26
Aug 30	3911	45	33	77	50	5.56
Sep 3	3903	41	36	77	48	5.66
Sep 4	3897	39	36	75	47	5.60
Sep 5	3895	37	33	70	46	5.27
Sep 6	3888	41	29	69	45	5.28
Sep 9	3872	51	23	70	44	5.48
Sep 10	3868	54	22	72	43	5.64
Sep 11	3866	56	22	73	42	5.84
Sep 12	3858	65	16	71	41	5.75
Sep 13	3857	65	16	71	40	5.83
Sep 16	3863				39	
Sep 17	3861				38	
Sep 18	3863				37	
Sep 19	3856				36	
Sep 20	3839				35	
Nov 8	3805	December 96 option expires				

LEGEND: *fp* = futures price, *max* = closest strike high option price, *min* = closest strike low option price, *s* = price corrected at-the-money-straddle, *td* = number of trading days till expiry, *iv* = implied volatility.

GOLD 1996

February option and February future

	fp	max	min	s	td	iv
Sep 16	3883	58	45	102	82	5.79
Sep 17	3881	58	44	101	81	5.77
Sep 18	3883	55	44	98	80	5.64
Sep 19	3876	61	43	102	79	5.94
Sep 20	3859	71	37	104	78	6.10
Sep 23	3864	69	38	104	77	6.11
Sep 24	3877	61	41	100	76	5.92
Sep 25	3873	63	38	98	75	5.86
Sep 26	3856	69	31	95	74	5.73
Sep 27	3848	76	27	96	73	5.81
Sep 30	3825	61	36	94	72	5.81
Oct 1	3830	64	33	93	71	5.79
Oct 2	3843	75	27	95	70	5.89
Oct 3	3847	75	26	93	69	5.84
Oct 4	3846	74	26	93	68	5.84
Oct 7	3846	74	25	91	67	5.80
Oct 8	3854	75	24	91	66	5.79
Oct 9	3855	73	24	89	65	5.73
Oct 10	3865	63	31	90	64	5.83
Oct 11	3854	77	25	94	63	6.11
Oct 14	3858	73	24	89	62	5.86
Oct 15	3853	71	22	85	61	5.63
Oct 16	3850	72	21	84	60	5.63
Oct 17	3846	71	21	83	59	5.64
Oct 18	3841	68	21	81	58	5.54
Oct 21	3859	69	20	80	57	5.51
Oct 22	3881	49	32	79	56	5.46
Oct 23	3879	51	32	81	55	5.63
Oct 24	3869	55	26	77	54	5.44
Oct 25	3866	58	25	79	53	5.59
Oct 28	3866	55	25	76	52	5.46
Oct 29	3836	55	20	70	51	5.09
Oct 30	3833	54	21	70	50	5.19
Oct 31	3811	40	29	68	49	5.09
Nov 1	3812	39	30	68	48	5.16
Nov 4	3816	40	26	65	47	4.94
Nov 5	3816	41	26	65	46	5.06
Nov 6	3807	36	31	67	45	5.21
Nov 7	3816	41	27	67	44	5.26
Nov 8	3825	46	23	66	43	5.28
Nov 11	3848				42	

Jan 10 3602 February 97 option expires

April option and April future

	fp	max	min	s	td	iv
Nov 11	3869	68	44	110	87	6.07
Nov 12	3875	67	43	108	86	5.99
Nov 13	3883	63	48	110	85	6.12
Nov 14	3853	81	33	107	84	6.08
Nov 15	3859	81	32	106	83	6.03
Nov 18	3838	79	32	104	82	6.01
Nov 19	3825	58	39	95	81	5.53
Nov 20	3831	64	36	97	80	5.66
Nov 21	3806	52	50	102	79	6.02
Nov 22	3804	52	51	103	78	6.13
Nov 25	3786	62	46	106	77	6.41
Nov 26	3788	61	49	109	76	6.60
Nov 27	3771	74	44	115	75	7.03
Dec 2	3730	69	40	106	73	6.64
Dec 3	3725	72	40	108	72	6.86
Dec 4	3746	86	41	121	71	7.69
Dec 5	3751	90	40	124	70	7.87
Dec 6	3729	77	49	123	69	7.95
Dec 9	3718	70	53	121	68	7.92
Dec 10	3726	73	47	117	67	7.70
Dec 11	3727	74	47	118	66	7.81
Dec 12	3729	71	42	110	65	7.31
Dec 13	3725	67	42	106	64	7.14
Dec 16	3720	63	42	103	63	6.97
Dec 17	3726	66	39	102	62	6.96
Dec 18	3734	71	36	103	61	7.05
Dec 19	3732	68	36	100	60	6.94
Dec 20	3726	63	38	98	59	6.87
Dec 23	3727	64	37	98	58	6.91
Dec 24	3727	64	37	98	57	6.97
Dec 26	3732	66	35	97	55	7.04
Dec 27	3732	65	34	95	54	6.96
Dec 30	3733	64	32	92	53	6.78
Dec 31	3713	57	40	95	52	7.12
Jan 2	3687				51	
Jan 3	3641				50	
Jan 6	3608				49	
Jan 7	3618				48	
Jan 8	3589				47	
Jan 9	3609				46	
Jan 10	3623				45	
Jan 13	3618				44	
Jan 14	3568				43	
Jan 15	3553				42	
Jan 16	3571				41	
Jan 17	3585				40	
Jan 20	3567				39	
Jan 21	3567				38	
Jan 22	3538				37	
Jan 23	3546				36	
Jan 24	3555				35	
Jan 27	3594				34	
Jan 28	3561				33	
Jan 29	3539				32	
Jan 30	3483				31	
Jan 31	3470				30	
Feb 3	3495				29	
Feb 4	3477				28	
Feb 5	3477				27	
Feb 6	3464				26	
Feb 7	3451				25	

Mar 14 3530 April 97 option expires

LEGEND: *fp* = futures price, *max* = closest strike high option price, *min* = closest strike low option price, *s* = price corrected at-the-money-straddle, *td* = number of trading days till expiry, *iv* = implied volatility.

SILVER

Calendar month	Year	Based on Option	Nearest strike	Implied volatility
JANUARY	1993	May	*375*	16.39
FEBRUARY	1993	May	*375*	14.88
MARCH	1993	Jul	*350*	15.96
APRIL	1993	Jul	*400*	20.94
MAY	1993	Sep	*425*	29.03
JUNE	1993	Sep	*450*	34.80
JULY	1993	Dec	*500*	34.25
AUGUST	1993	Dec	*550*	35.81
SEPTEMBER	1993	Dec	*475*	29.38
OCTOBER	1993	Mar	*400*	30.50
NOVEMBER	1993	Mar	*425*	31.68
DECEMBER	1993	Mar	*475*	30.48
JANUARY	1994	May	*525*	32.32
FEBRUARY	1994	May	*525*	29.36
MARCH	1994	Jul	*525*	30.35
APRIL	1994	Jul	*550*	31.63
MAY	1994	Jul	*550*	24.37
JUNE	1994	Sep	*550*	29.27
JULY	1994	Dec	*550*	27.28
AUGUST	1994	Dec	*525*	24.01
SEPTEMBER	1994	Dec	*550*	22.39
OCTOBER	1994	Mar	*575*	21.93
NOVEMBER	1994	Mar	*550*	20.59
DECEMBER	1994	Mar	*500*	20.85
JANUARY	1995	May	*475*	23.22
FEBRUARY	1995	May	*475*	21.76
MARCH	1995	Jul	*450*	19.58
APRIL	1995	Jul	*525*	33.07
MAY	1995	Sep	*600*	35.45
JUNE	1995	Sep	*550*	31.03
JULY	1995	Dec	*500*	26.73
AUGUST	1995	Dec	*525*	22.31
SEPTEMBER	1995	Dec	*525*	24.83
OCTOBER	1995	Mar	*525*	23.49
NOVEMBER	1995	Mar	*550*	23.13
DECEMBER	1995	Mar	*525*	20.18
JANUARY	1996	May	*550*	21.59
FEBRUARY	1996	May	*575*	25.43
MARCH	1996	May	*550*	19.53
APRIL	1996	Jul	*550*	20.33
MAY	1996	Sep	*550*	20.90
JUNE	1996	Sep	*550*	18.79
JULY	1996	Sep	*500*	19.08
AUGUST	1996	Dec	*525*	18.51
SEPTEMBER	1996	Dec	*525*	15.86
OCTOBER	1996	Mar	*500*	17.61
NOVEMBER	1996	Mar	*475*	17.17
DECEMBER	1996	Mar	*475*	17.28
JANUARY	1997	May	*475*	18.34
FEBRUARY	1997	May	*500*	21.43
MARCH	1997	Jul	*550*	23.14
APRIL	1997	Jul	*500*	21.34
MAY	1997	Sep	*475*	19.24
JUNE	1997	Sep	*475*	20.44
JULY	1997	Dec	*475*	19.49
AUGUST	1997	Dec	*450*	23.30
SEPTEMBER	1997	Dec	*475*	23.59
OCTOBER	1997	Mar	*525*	22.45
NOVEMBER	1997	Mar	*500*	24.21
DECEMBER	1997	Mar	*525*	25.10

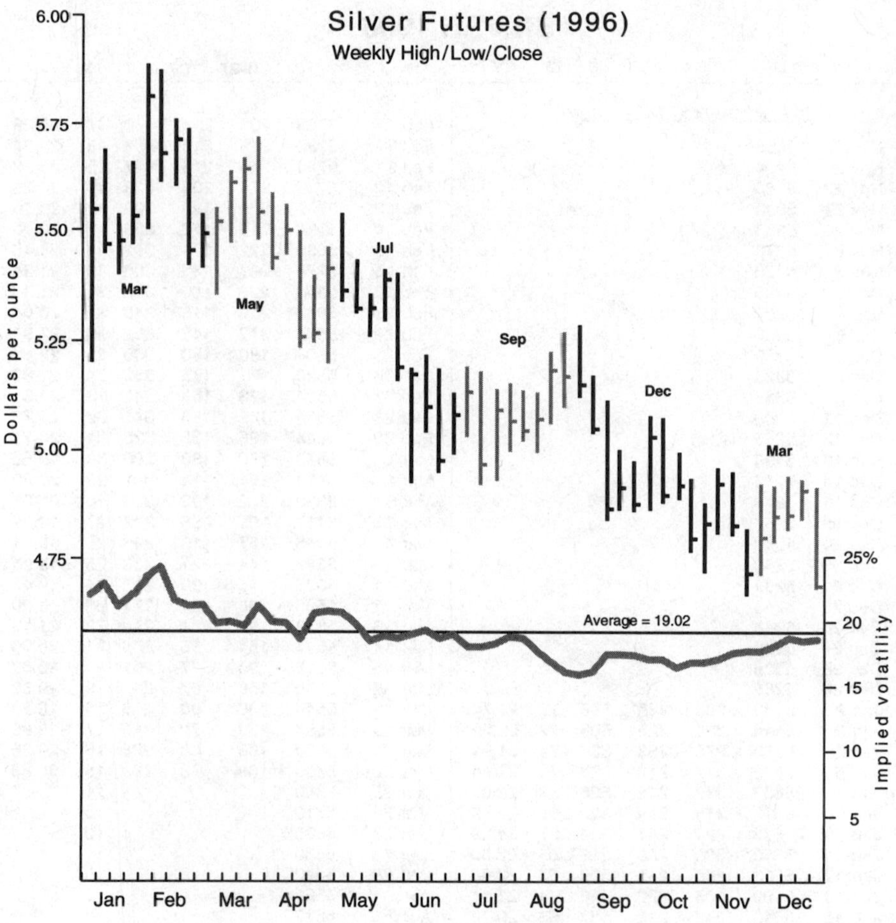
Silver Futures (1996)
Weekly High/Low/Close
6.00
5.75
5.50
5.25
5.00
4.75
Dollars per ounce
Mar
May
Jul
Sep
Dec
Mar
Average = 19.02
25%
20
15
10
5
Implied volatility
Jan
Feb
Mar
Apr
May
Jun
Jul
Aug
Sep
Oct
Nov
Dec

SILVER 1996

May option and May future

	fp	max	min	s	td	iv
Nov 20	5466					
Nov 21	5404					
Nov 22	5283					
Nov 27	5330					
Nov 28	5333					
Nov 29	5270					
Nov 30	5320					
Dec 1	5295					
Dec 4	5290					
Dec 5	5330					
Dec 6	5353					
Dec 7	5325					
Dec 8	5315					
Dec 11	5308					
Dec 12	5253					
Dec 13	5198					
Dec 14	5215					
Dec 15	5215					
Dec 18	5250					
Dec 19	5218					
Dec 20	5240					
Dec 21	5233					
Dec 22	5243					
Dec 26	5248					
Dec 27	5230					
Dec 28	5225					
Dec 29	5260					
Jan 2	5443	286	225	505	73	21.74
Jan 3	5440	289	225	508	72	22.02
Jan 4	5463	275	233	504	71	21.91
Jan 5	5603	317	219	526	70	22.46
Jan 8	5603	317	219	526	69	22.62
Jan 9	5610	319	214	523	68	22.59
Jan 10	5673	324	247	564	67	24.29
Jan 11	5583	300	220	512	66	22.60
Jan 12	5523	265	245	508	65	22.83
Jan 15	5498	236	230	466	64	21.17
Jan 16	5540	248	212	457	63	20.78
Jan 17	5568	260	197	451	62	20.58
Jan 18	5513	227	219	445	61	20.69
Jan 19	5523	232	213	443	60	20.73
Jan 22	5648	303	202	495	59	22.82
Jan 23	5628	291	192	473	58	22.07
Jan 24	5580	288	192	470	57	22.33
Jan 25	5638	285	192	468	56	22.17
Jan 26	5598	281	192	464	55	22.36
Jan 29	5598	272	182	445	54	21.64
Jan 30	5616	283	186	459	53	22.46
Jan 31	5641	284	188	462	52	22.73
Feb 1	5848	330	213	531	51	25.43
Feb 2	5893	336	215	539	50	25.85
Feb 5	5867	336	195	516	49	25.11
Feb 6	5829	311	193	492	48	24.35
Feb 7	5763	237	224	460	47	23.28
Feb 7	5763	237	224	460	47	23.28
Feb 8	5780	245	215	457	46	23.34
Feb 9	5720	240	210	447	45	23.32
Feb 12	5723	225	200	423	44	22.28
Feb 13	5772	210	185	393	43	20.76
Feb 14	5790	216	176	388	42	20.70
Feb 15	5699	222	174	392	41	21.46
Feb 16	5776	207	183	388	40	21.24
Feb 20	5583	225	150	368	38	21.36
Feb 21	5633	243	116	343	37	20.04
Feb 22	5577	212	146	352	36	21.01
Feb 23	5504	180	180	360	35	22.11
Feb 26	5530	177	175	352	34	21.82
Feb 27	5504	173	169	342	33	21.61
Feb 28	5535	189	155	341	32	21.78
Feb 29	5545	185	139	320	31	20.71
Mar 1	5540	170	130	296	30	19.53
Mar 4	5417	194	115	301	29	20.60
Mar 5	5390	212	102	300	28	21.07
Mar 6	5407	191	98	278	27	19.79
Mar 7	5455	157	113	266	26	19.11
Mar 8	5522	144	121	263	25	19.05
Mar 11	5525	145	120	263	24	19.42
Mar 12	5595	180	100	271	23	20.20
Mar 13	5632	198	94	279	22	21.13
Mar 14	5597	184	85	256	21	20.00
Mar 15	5612	190	77	251	20	20.03
Mar 18	5570	158	87	237	19	19.52
Mar 19	5540	130	90	216	18	18.39
Mar 20	5587	158	70	217	17	18.80
Mar 21	5630	186	62	228	16	20.26
Mar 22	5650	168	73	228	15	20.88
Mar 25	5650				14	
Mar 26	5710				13	
Mar 27	5685				12	
Mar 28	5530				11	
Mar 29	5540				10	
Apr 1	5550				9	
Apr 2	5517				8	
Apr 3	5522				7	
Apr 4	5435				6	
Apr 8	5565				4	
Apr 9	5467				3	
Apr 10	5492				2	
Apr 11	5562				1	
Apr 12	5518	May 96 option expires				

July option and July future

	fp	max	min	s	td	iv
Mar 25	5699	263	210	468	59	21.39
Mar 26	5759	239	232	470	58	21.45
Mar 27	5734	259	219	475	57	21.92
Mar 28	5579	260	185	438	56	20.97
Mar 29	5589	260	175	427	55	20.58
Apr 1	5599	264	168	422	54	20.52

LEGEND: *fp* = futures price, *max* = closest strike high option price, *min* = closest strike low option price, *s* = price corrected at-the-money-straddle, *td* = number of trading days till expiry, *iv* = implied volatility.

SILVER 1996

	fp	max	min	s	td	iv
Apr 2	5566	227	165	386	53	19.06
Apr 3	5571	230	160	383	52	19.08
Apr 4	5484	201	185	385	51	19.64
Apr 8	5614	255	142	384	49	19.56
Apr 9	5516	202	185	386	48	20.18
Apr 10	5541	212	170	378	47	19.91
Apr 11	5611	254	145	387	46	20.34
Apr 12	5567	222	153	368	45	19.72
Apr 15	5529	185	155	337	44	18.40
Apr 16	5340	209	120	319	43	18.23
Apr 17	5354	215	111	314	42	18.09
Apr 18	5316	192	127	312	41	18.36
Apr 19	5306	192	135	321	40	19.16
Apr 22	5374				39	
Apr 23	5364				38	
Apr 24	5341				37	
Apr 25	5414				36	
Apr 26	5311				35	
Apr 29	5261				34	
Apr 30	5340				33	
May 1	5425				32	
May 2	5420				31	
May 3	5470				30	
May 6	5490				29	
May 7	5515				28	
May 8	5465				27	
May 9	5447				26	
May 10	5375				25	
May 13	5395				24	
May 14	5400				23	
May 15	5412				22	
May 16	5377				21	
May 17	5337				20	
May 20	5275				19	
May 21	5298				18	
May 22	5343				17	
May 23	5335				16	
May 24	5323				15	
May 28	5358				13	
May 29	5335				12	
May 30	5343				11	
May 31	5403				10	
Jun 3	5380				9	
Jun 4	5185				8	
Jun 5	5155				7	
Jun 6	5195				6	
Jun 7	5173				5	
Jun 10	5177				4	
Jun 11	5100				3	
Jun 12	5090				2	
Jun 13	5050				1	
Jun 14	5172	July 96 option expires				

September option and September future

	fp	max	min	s	td	iv
Apr 22	5430	298	220	511	78	21.30
Apr 23	5420	298	213	503	77	21.15
Apr 24	5397	310	200	499	76	21.20
Apr 25	5470	265	230	492	75	20.77
Apr 26	5367	292	185	466	74	20.19
Apr 29	5317	265	205	464	73	20.45
Apr 30	5396	301	192	482	72	21.05
May 1	5481	255	231	484	71	20.96
May 2	5476	257	228	483	70	21.06
May 3	5526	253	232	483	69	21.06
May 6	5546	259	218	473	68	20.70
May 7	5571	270	203	467	67	20.47
May 8	5521	240	223	462	66	20.58
May 9	5503	230	230	460	65	20.74
May 10	5431	264	190	447	64	20.57
May 13	5451	248	194	437	63	20.20
May 14	5456	244	195	435	62	20.23
May 15	5468	230	192	419	61	19.61
May 16	5433	240	171	404	60	19.22
May 17	5393	260	150	398	59	19.21
May 20	5331	227	150	369	58	18.19
May 21	5354	239	139	367	57	18.16
May 22	5399	226	152	371	56	18.35
May 23	5391	261	125	369	55	18.47
May 24	5379	255	130	370	54	18.73
May 28	5414	235	146	372	52	19.04
May 29	5391	246	135	368	51	19.14
May 30	5399	239	137	365	50	19.11
May 31	5459	203	162	361	49	18.91
Jun 3	5436	212	148	354	48	18.79
Jun 4	5241	205	148	348	47	19.35
Jun 5	5211	185	145	326	46	18.47
Jun 6	5251	163	162	325	45	18.45
Jun 7	5229	171	150	319	44	18.41
Jun 10	5233	162	145	306	43	17.81
Jun 11	5156	216	120	325	42	19.47
Jun 12	5146	216	110	313	41	19.02
Jun 13	5106	212	108	308	40	19.06
Jun 14	5228	179	155	332	39	20.33
Jun 17	5238	165	152	316	38	19.57
Jun 18	5231	164	145	307	37	19.32
Jun 19	5168	192	110	293	36	18.90
Jun 20	5178	183	111	286	35	18.70
Jun 21	5163	193	107	290	34	19.29
Jun 24	5191	167	109	270	33	18.12
Jun 25	5203	158	110	263	32	17.89
Jun 26	5111	157	112	265	31	18.60
Jun 27	5038	155	115	266	30	19.30
Jun 28	5035	147	115	259	29	19.11
Jul 1	5082	174	92	257	28	19.08
Jul 2	5112	187	75	246	27	18.55
Jul 5	5130	194	75	252	25	19.64
Jul 8	5067	182	67	232	24	18.68
Jul 9	5115	170	60	213	23	17.38

LEGEND: *fp* = futures price, *max* = closest strike high option price, *min* = closest strike low option price, *s* = price corrected at-the-money-straddle, *td* = number of trading days till expiry, *iv* = implied volatility.

SILVER 1996

	fp	max	min	s	td	iv
Jul 10	5115	168	58	209	22	17.41
Jul 11	5145	166	61	211	21	17.93
Jul 12	5142	162	55	200	20	17.40
Jul 15	5165				19	
Jul 16	4943				18	
Jul 17	4960				17	
Jul 18	5000				16	
Jul 19	4965				15	
Jul 22	5015				14	
Jul 23	4970				13	
Jul 24	5010				12	
Jul 25	4987				11	
Jul 26	5103				10	
Jul 29	5068				9	
Jul 30	5068				8	
Jul 31	5148				7	
Aug 1	5110				6	
Aug 2	5075				5	
Aug 5	5087				4	
Aug 6	5035				3	
Aug 7	5042				2	
Aug 8	5098				1	
Aug 9	5040	September 96 option expires				

December option and December future

	fp	max	min	s	td	iv
Jul 15	5241	211	213	424	84	17.66
Jul 16	5019	225	200	423	83	18.50
Jul 17	5036	229	193	419	82	18.37
Jul 18	5076	249	174	416	81	18.20
Jul 19	5041	228	188	412	80	18.30
Jul 22	5091	250	165	406	79	17.96
Jul 23	5046	228	183	407	78	18.26
Jul 24	5086	247	162	400	77	17.94
Jul 25	5063	240	172	405	76	18.37
Jul 26	5179	250	183	427	75	19.03
Jul 29	5144	270	168	427	74	19.32
Jul 30	5144	264	162	415	73	18.90
Jul 31	5224	214	193	405	72	18.28
Aug 1	5186	235	175	404	71	18.51
Aug 2	5151	259	162	411	70	19.07
Aug 5	5163	268	145	399	69	18.61
Aug 6	5111	266	143	395	68	18.74
Aug 7	5118	264	139	389	67	18.55
Aug 8	5174	264	141	391	66	18.60
Aug 9	5116	264	140	390	65	18.90
Aug 12	5143	258	135	379	64	18.41
Aug 13	5161	250	128	364	63	17.75
Aug 14	5121	244	120	349	62	17.31
Aug 15	5163	242	119	346	61	17.16
Aug 16	5153	239	116	340	60	17.03
Aug 19	5286	253	128	366	59	18.03
Aug 20	5286	252	116	351	58	17.43
Aug 21	5246	163	162	325	57	16.41
Aug 22	5296	187	145	328	56	16.56
Aug 23	5273	173	144	314	55	16.08
Aug 26	5329	205	123	319	54	16.31
Aug 27	5314	195	130	318	53	16.47
Aug 28	5248	157	156	313	52	16.54
Aug 29	5251	150	145	295	51	15.71
Aug 30	5250	145	145	290	50	15.62
Sep 3	5208	166	124	286	48	15.86
Sep 4	5230	152	132	282	47	15.75
Sep 5	5193	173	117	284	46	16.15
Sep 6	5158	210	86	279	45	16.12
Sep 9	5128	206	83	272	44	15.99
Sep 10	5143	204	81	268	43	15.87
Sep 11	5140	205	81	268	42	16.12
Sep 12	5060	162	102	258	41	15.91
Sep 13	5053	155	102	252	40	15.75
Sep 16	5085				39	
Nov 8	4838	December option expires				

March option and March future

	fp	max	min	s	td	iv
Sep 16	5156	297	177	461	107	17.29
Sep 17	5149	299	174	459	106	17.33
Sep 18	5169	295	172	454	105	17.13
Sep 19	5011	233	215	446	104	17.47
Sep 20	4934	260	200	454	103	18.15
Sep 23	4966	238	206	441	102	17.60
Sep 24	5006	228	217	444	101	17.65
Sep 25	4993	220	217	437	100	17.49
Sep 26	4956	240	200	436	99	17.70
Sep 27	4991	215	210	425	98	17.19
Sep 30	4948	238	190	424	97	17.39
Oct 1	4981	223	208	430	96	17.61
Oct 2	4998	214	213	427	95	17.53
Oct 3	4976	220	202	420	94	17.43
Oct 4	4946	239	185	419	93	17.57
Oct 7	4959	226	185	407	92	17.13
Oct 8	4969	216	185	398	91	16.81
Oct 9	5044	223	178	397	90	16.59
Oct 10	5131	280	152	417	89	17.25
Oct 11	5129	280	152	417	88	17.35
Oct 14	5106	278	151	415	87	17.41
Oct 15	5116	277	149	411	86	17.34
Oct 16	5091	270	144	400	85	17.02
Oct 17	4973	208	180	386	84	16.92
Oct 18	4968	207	173	377	83	16.66
Oct 21	5008	188	182	370	82	16.30
Oct 22	5061	218	158	370	81	16.26
Oct 23	5059	216	158	369	80	16.29
Oct 24	4989	193	181	373	79	16.82
Oct 25	4996	185	180	365	78	16.53
Oct 28	5001	183	183	366	77	16.68
Oct 29	4891	248	125	358	76	16.81
Oct 30	4899	249	126	360	75	16.99
Oct 31	4879	247	125	357	74	17.03
Nov 1	4869	248	124	357	73	17.17
Nov 4	4879	243	121	349	72	16.88

LEGEND: *fp* = futures price, *max* = closest strike high option price, *min* = closest strike low option price, *s* = price corrected at-the-money-straddle, *td* = number of trading days till expiry, *iv* = implied volatility.

SILVER 1996

	fp	max	min	s	td	iv		fp	max	min	s	td	iv
Nov 5	4864	243	118	346	71	16.87	Jan 28	4963				13	
Nov 6	4784	182	153	332	70	16.61	Jan 29	4940				12	
Nov 7	4904	246	122	353	69	17.33	Jan 30	4955				11	
Nov 8	4909	237	112	333	68	16.47	Jan 31	4920				10	
Nov 11	4964	193	153	342	67	16.85	Feb 3	4902				9	
Nov 12	4951	201	149	345	66	17.16	Feb 4	4857				8	
Nov 13	4969	192	158	347	65	17.32	Feb 5	4872				7	
Nov 14	4911	242	117	344	64	17.49	Feb 6	4857				6	
Nov 15	5009	178	170	347	63	17.47	Feb 7	4942				5	
Nov 18	4954	197	151	344	62	17.63	Feb 10	4960				4	
Nov 19	4944	202	145	342	61	17.69	Feb 11	4838				3	
Nov 20	5016	177	163	339	60	17.44	Feb 12	5135				2	
Nov 21	4911	233	113	331	59	17.57	Feb 13	5142				1	
Nov 22	4906	239	112	335	58	17.94	Feb 14	5252	March 97 option expires				
Nov 25	4791	182	142	320	57	17.71							
Nov 26	4785	186	145	327	56	18.28							
Nov 27	4785	175	140	312	55	17.58							
Dec 2	4742	154	145	298	53	17.28							
Dec 3	4845	190	124	307	52	17.59							
Dec 4	4862	227	104	315	51	18.16							
Dec 5	4892	226	102	312	50	18.04							
Dec 6	4805	179	125	299	49	17.76							
Dec 9	4807	177	120	291	48	17.50							
Dec 10	4872	222	100	306	47	18.34							
Dec 11	4860	221	98	303	46	18.38							
Dec 12	4860	220	96	300	45	18.38							
Dec 13	4850	221	96	300	44	18.68							
Dec 16	4835	217	102	305	43	19.22							
Dec 17	4893	212	108	308	42	19.41							
Dec 18	4893	212	92	288	41	18.39							
Dec 19	4885	212	88	283	40	18.33							
Dec 20	4858	211	87	281	39	18.53							
Dec 23	4863	209	85	277	38	18.47							
Dec 24	4873	206	84	273	37	18.43							
Dec 26	4928	206	83	272	35	18.65							
Dec 27	4913	204	82	269	34	18.78							
Dec 30	4815	160	100	254	33	18.35							
Dec 31	4790	147	107	250	32	18.47							
Jan 2	4732				31								
Jan 3	4685				30								
Jan 6	4652				29								
Jan 7	4710				28								
Jan 8	4660				27								
Jan 9	4735				26								
Jan 10	4765				25								
Jan 13	4717				24								
Jan 14	4675				23								
Jan 15	4685				22								
Jan 16	4740				21								
Jan 17	4772				20								
Jan 20	4732				19								
Jan 21	4715				18								
Jan 22	4723				17								
Jan 23	4875				16								
Jan 24	4977				15								
Jan 27	5047				14								

LEGEND: *fp* = futures price, *max* = closest strike high option price, *min* = closest strike low option price, *s* = price corrected at-the-money-straddle, *td* = number of trading days till expiry, *iv* = implied volatility.

CRUDE OIL

Calendar month	Year	Based on Option	Nearest strike	Implied volatility
JANUARY	1993	Apr	*1950*	17.23
FEBRUARY	1993	May	*2050*	21.47
MARCH	1993	Jun	*2050*	20.05
APRIL	1993	Jul	*2100*	17.44
MAY	1993	Aug	*2100*	15.01
JUNE	1993	Sep	*2050*	16.47
JULY	1993	Oct	*1850*	20.95
AUGUST	1993	Nov	*1850*	21.53
SEPTEMBER	1993	Dec	*1850*	22.94
OCTOBER	1993	Jan	*1900*	22.61
NOVEMBER	1993	Feb	*1800*	24.27
DECEMBER	1993	Mar	*1600*	27.07
JANUARY	1994	Apr	*1500*	30.58
FEBRUARY	1994	May	*1600*	24.94
MARCH	1994	May	*1500*	25.03
APRIL	1994	Jul	*1600*	23.47
MAY	1994	Aug	*1700*	26.84
JUNE	1994	Sep	*1750*	24.22
JULY	1994	Oct	*1850*	25.76
AUGUST	1994	Nov	*2000*	32.11
SEPTEMBER	1994	Dec	*1750*	26.55
OCTOBER	1994	Jan	*1850*	29.22
NOVEMBER	1994	Feb	*1850*	30.36
DECEMBER	1994	Mar	*1800*	22.85
JANUARY	1995	Apr	*1750*	22.00
FEBRUARY	1995	May	*1800*	21.44
MARCH	1995	Jun	*1800*	20.06
APRIL	1995	Jul	*1850*	17.77
MAY	1995	Aug	*2000*	24.45
JUNE	1995	Sep	*1850*	20.82
JULY	1995	Oct	*1700*	20.93
AUGUST	1995	Nov	*1750*	21.56
SEPTEMBER	1995	Dec	*1750*	20.86
OCTOBER	1995	Jan	*1700*	20.63
NOVEMBER	1995	Feb	*1750*	20.56
DECEMBER	1995	Mar	*1800*	17.13
JANUARY	1996	Apr	*1900*	18.26
FEBRUARY	1996	Apr	*1750*	27.93
MARCH	1996	Apr	*1950*	35.62
APRIL	1996	Mar	*2050*	28.43
MAY	1996	Aug	*1900*	26.91
JUNE	1996	Aug	*1950*	24.73
JULY	1996	Oct	*2000*	20.38
AUGUST	1996	Oct	*2050*	23.00
SEPTEMBER	1996	Dec	*2200*	32.95
OCTOBER	1996	Dec	*2350*	35.34
NOVEMBER	1996	Dec	*2300*	29.22
DECEMBER	1996	Feb	*2450*	33.26
JANUARY	1997	Apr	*2450*	32.74
FEBRUARY	1997	May	*2350*	25.42
MARCH	1997	Jun	*2000*	28.23
APRIL	1997	Jul	*2000*	27.24
MAY	1997	Aug	*2000*	27.00
JUNE	1997	Sep	*2100*	27.47
JULY	1997	Oct	*2000*	29.92
AUGUST	1997	Nov	*2050*	28.32
SEPTEMBER	1997	Dec	*2000*	26.71
OCTOBER	1997	Jan	*2100*	26.54
NOVEMBER	1997	Feb	*2100*	31.24
DECEMBER	1997	Mar	*1900*	25.81

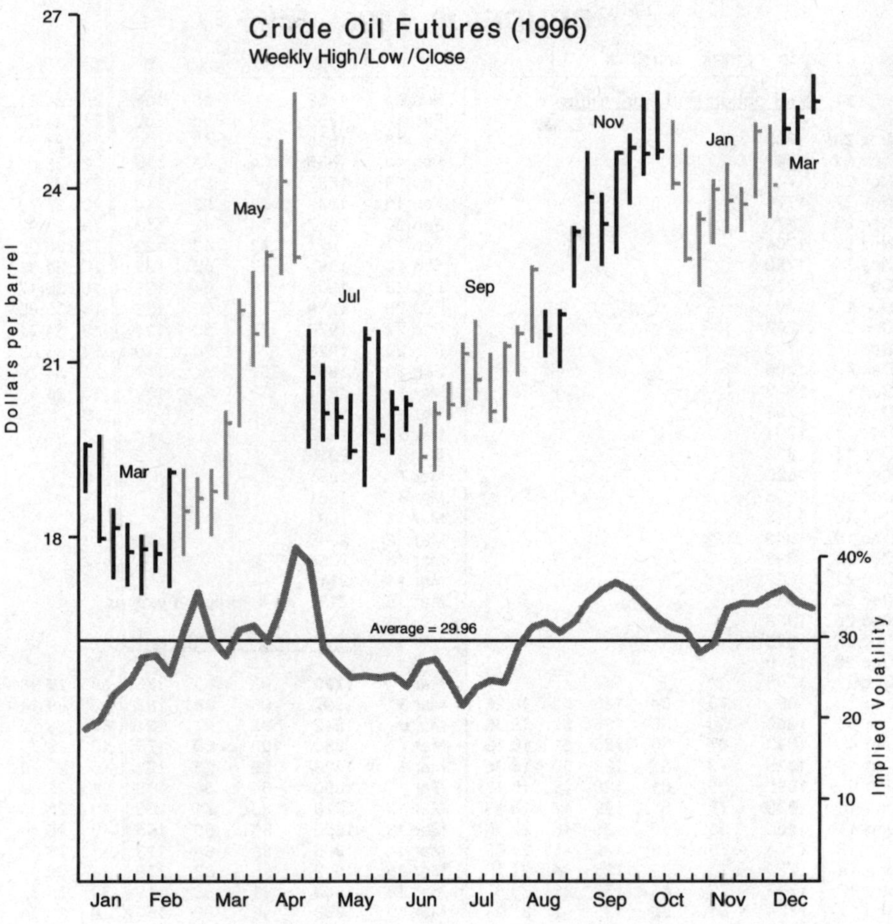
Crude Oil Futures (1996)
Weekly High/Low/Close
Dollars per barrel
27
24
21
18
Mar
May
Jul
Sep
Nov
Jan
Mar
Average = 29.96
40%
30
20
10
Implied Volatility
Jan
Feb
Mar
Apr
May
Jun
Jul
Aug
Sep
Oct
Nov
Dec

CRUDE OIL 1996

April option and April future

	fp	max	min	s	td	iv
Nov 20	1753					
Nov 21	1747					
Nov 22	1743					
Nov 27	1778					
Nov 28	1770					
Nov 29	1764					
Nov 30	1759					
Dec 1	1778					
Dec 4	1791					
Dec 5	1793					
Dec 6	1796					
Dec 7	1796					
Dec 8	1812					
Dec 11	1795					
Dec 12	1801					
Dec 13	1832					
Dec 14	1825					
Dec 15	1835					
Dec 18	1843					
Dec 19	1840					
Dec 20	1833					
Dec 21	1832					
Dec 22	1842					
Dec 26	1853					
Dec 27	1865					
Dec 28	1856					
Dec 29	1868					
Jan 2	1884	73	54	125	53	18.26
Jan 3	1890	68	58	125	52	18.36
Jan 4	1893	67	60	126	51	18.70
Jan 5	1928	73	57	129	50	18.86
Jan 9	1896	65	61	126	48	19.13
Jan 10	1878	73	51	122	47	18.93
Jan 11	1805	65	60	125	46	20.35
Jan 12	1774	78	53	129	45	21.60
Jan 15	1779	74	53	125	44	21.18
Jan 16	1743	72	65	136	43	23.87
Jan 17	1779	81	56	135	42	23.34
Jan 18	1796	70	68	138	41	23.97
Jan 19	1781	73	57	129	40	22.82
Jan 22	1774	81	56	135	39	24.29
Jan 23	1767	78	56	132	38	24.22
Jan 24	1788	71	59	129	37	23.71
Jan 25	1737	74	60	133	36	25.47
Jan 26	1736	75	60	134	35	26.03
Jan 29	1716	78	62	139	34	27.69
Jan 30	1724	81	57	136	33	27.40
Jan 31	1737	74	61	134	32	27.24
Feb 1	1731	79	59	136	31	28.25
Feb 2	1738	73	61	133	30	27.93
Feb 5	1717	80	62	140	29	30.36
Feb 6	1730	78	58	134	28	29.30
Feb 7	1731	74	55	127	27	28.29
Feb 8	1733	66	49	113	26	25.67
Feb 9	1738	60	48	107	25	24.61
Feb 12	1750	50	50	100	24	23.33
Feb 13	1835	61	46	106	23	24.00
Feb 14	1835	64	49	112	22	25.94
Feb 15	1837	64	51	114	21	27.04
Feb 16	1839	63	52	114	20	27.73
Feb 20	1927	74	47	118	18	28.92
Feb 21	1971	77	48	122	17	30.02
Feb 22	1985	77	62	138	16	34.67
Feb 23	1906	70	64	133	15	36.17
Feb 26	1939	71	60	130	14	35.85
Feb 27	1970	73	53	124	13	34.94
Feb 28	1928	71	50	119	12	35.63
Feb 29	1953	59	54	113	11	34.76
Mar 1	1944	58	52	109	10	35.62
Mar 4	1920				9	
Mar 5	1953				8	
Mar 6	2019				7	
Mar 7	1981				6	
Mar 8	1961				5	
Mar 11	1991				4	
Mar 12	2046				3	
Mar 13	2058				2	
Mar 14	2116				1	
Mar 15	2199	April 96 option expires				

June option and June future

	fp	max	min	s	td	iv
Mar 4	1790	93	83	175	49	27.96
Mar 5	1807	95	88	182	48	29.14
Mar 6	1842	95	87	181	47	28.72
Mar 7	1830	100	80	178	46	28.71
Mar 8	1826	98	75	171	45	27.90
Mar 11	1850	84	84	168	44	27.38
Mar 12	1879	96	71	165	43	26.73
Mar 13	1895	85	80	165	42	26.80
Mar 14	1905	89	84	173	41	28.30
Mar 15	1913	95	82	176	40	29.07
Mar 18	1953	91	88	179	39	29.31
Mar 19	1958	96	90	186	38	30.74
Mar 20	1961	101	91	191	37	32.05
Mar 21	1977	107	84	189	36	31.85
Mar 22	2030	113	83	193	35	32.17
Mar 25	2074	109	85	192	34	31.72
Mar 26	2052	94	92	186	33	31.53
Mar 27	2028	99	79	176	32	30.72
Mar 28	1997	91	88	179	31	32.15
Mar 29	2015	91	76	166	30	30.02
Apr 1	2062	86	73	158	29	28.43
Apr 2	2085	87	72	158	28	28.58
Apr 3	2060	82	72	153	27	28.61
Apr 4	2089	83	72	154	26	28.93
Apr 8	2108	87	79	165	24	32.02
Apr 9	2131	92	73	163	23	31.95
Apr 10	2210	93	83	175	22	33.79
Apr 11	2280	108	88	194	21	37.18

LEGEND: *fp* = futures price, *max* = closest strike high option price, *min* = closest strike low option price, *s* = price corrected at-the-money-straddle, *td* = number of trading days till expiry, *iv* = implied volatility.

CRUDE OIL 1996

	fp	max	min	s	td	iv
Apr 12	2191	101	93	193	20	39.46
Apr 15	2248	99	97	196	19	39.97
Apr 16	2159	105	95	199	18	43.48
Apr 17	2134	103	87	189	17	42.87
Apr 18	2081	96	77	171	16	41.16
Apr 19	2103	82	80	162	15	39.74
Apr 22	2153	79	76	155	14	38.42
Apr 23	2270	99	79	176	13	43.06
Apr 24	2239	84	74	157	12	40.52
Apr 25	2220	81	61	140	11	38.07
Apr 26	2232	72	54	124	10	35.23
Apr 29	2242				9	
Apr 30	2120				8	
May 1	2081				7	
May 2	2086				6	
May 3	2117				5	
May 6	2103				4	
May 7	2111				3	
May 8	2100				2	
May 9	2067				1	
May 10	2100	June 96 option expires				

August option and August future

	fp	max	min	s	td	iv
Apr 29	1999	98	97	195	53	26.79
Apr 30	1949	99	98	197	52	28.02
May 1	1922	106	81	185	51	26.91
May 2	1928	107	81	186	50	27.23
May 3	1941	95	88	182	49	26.85
May 6	1938	100	86	185	48	27.53
May 7	1937	97	87	183	47	27.58
May 8	1940	94	84	177	46	26.93
May 9	1979	95	75	168	45	25.34
May 10	1947	84	83	167	44	25.85
May 13	1957	84	76	159	43	24.83
May 14	1967	86	70	155	42	24.25
May 15	1965	82	68	149	41	23.65
May 16	1901	86	72	157	40	26.08
May 17	1884	83	68	150	39	25.44
May 20	1998	79	77	156	38	25.31
May 21	1978	85	65	148	37	24.63
May 22	2042	82	74	155	36	25.36
May 23	2024	91	64	152	35	25.45
May 24	2032	84	66	148	34	25.04
May 28	2016	80	63	141	32	24.81
May 29	1993	72	64	135	31	24.39
May 30	1925	78	53	129	30	24.38
May 31	1910	75	54	127	29	24.69
Jun 3	1920	73	54	125	28	24.65
Jun 4	1962	69	58	126	27	24.73
Jun 5	1903	65	62	127	26	26.13
Jun 6	1924	76	52	126	25	26.12
Jun 7	1942	65	55	119	24	25.04
Jun 10	1944	59	52	110	23	23.68
Jun 11	1930	66	46	110	22	24.31
Jun 12	1928	62	42	102	21	23.09
Jun 13	1922	62		100	20	23.21
Jun 14	1950	52		101	19	23.71
Jun 17	2070	70		118	18	26.89
Jun 18	2021	67		113	17	27.16
Jun 19	1985	65		114	16	28.62
Jun 20	2009	57		104	15	26.79
Jun 21	1992	56		104	14	28.01
Jun 24	1998	47		93	13	25.80
Jun 25	1996	45		85	12	24.46
Jun 26	2064	55		94	11	27.34
Jun 27	2102	50		98	10	29.44
Jun 28	2092	50		89	9	28.39
Jul 1	2153				8	
Jul 2	2113				7	
Jul 3	2121				6	
Jul 8	2127				4	
Jul 9	2141				3	
Jul 10	2155				2	
Jul 11	2195				1	
Jul 12	2189	August 96 option expires				

October option and October future

	fp	max	min	s	td	iv
Jul 1	1986	81	67	147	53	20.38
Jul 2	1959	79	69	148	52	20.89
Jul 3	1969	85	66	150	51	21.34
Jul 8	1979	87	61	146	49	21.15
Jul 9	2005	75	70	145	48	20.85
Jul 10	2023	87	63	149	47	21.43
Jul 11	2054	80	76	156	46	22.37
Jul 12	2051	78	74	152	45	22.07
Jul 15	2106	86	80	166	44	23.73
Jul 16	2097	84	81	165	43	23.98
Jul 17	2057	83	77	160	42	23.97
Jul 18	2056	82	76	158	41	23.96
Jul 19	2031	93	67	159	40	24.68
Jul 22	2029	92	67	158	39	24.87
Jul 23	2041	82	74	156	38	24.74
Jul 24	2017	86	69	154	37	25.13
Jul 25	2023	86	63	148	36	24.34
Jul 26	1969	80	61	140	35	24.03
Jul 29	1977	83	58	140	34	24.21
Jul 30	1984	78	60	137	33	24.05
Jul 31	1991	72	65	137	32	24.27
Aug 1	2048	64	67	131	31	23.00
Aug 2	2073	88	63	150	30	26.34
Aug 5	2067	88	71	158	29	28.42
Aug 6	2064	83	71	153	28	28.10
Aug 7	2087	85	72	156	27	28.84
Aug 8	2100	81	82	163	26	30.45
Aug 9	2106	84	78	162	25	30.72
Aug 12	2164	92	77	168	24	31.75
Aug 13	2184	88	76	163	23	31.21
Aug 14	2158	84	76	160	22	31.54
Aug 15	2139	80	70	150	21	30.51
Aug 16	2205	80	75	155	20	31.39

LEGEND: *fp* = futures price, *max* = closest strike high option price, *min* = closest strike low option price, *s* = price corrected at-the-money-straddle, *td* = number of trading days till expiry, *iv* = implied volatility.

CRUDE OIL 1996

	fp	max	min	s	td	iv
Aug 19	2247	85	61	145	19	29.53
Aug 20	2211	85	74	158	18	33.79
Aug 21	2172	83	61	143	17	31.89
Aug 22	2230	84	64	147	16	32.94
Aug 23	2196	69	64	133	15	31.22
Aug 26	2162	70	57	126	14	31.24
Aug 27	2156	68	51	118	13	30.38
Aug 28	2171	67	46	112	12	29.71
Aug 29	2214	64	49	112	11	30.56
Aug 30	2225	66	42	106	10	30.25
Sep 3	2339				8	
Sep 4	2324				7	
Sep 5	2344				6	
Sep 6	2385				5	
Sep 9	2373				4	
Sep 10	2412				3	
Sep 11	2475				2	
Sep 12	2500				1	
Sep 13	2450	October 96 option expires				

December and December future

	fp	max	min	s	td	iv
Sep 3	2205	135	130	265	53	32.97
Sep 4	2194	130	125	255	52	32.18
Sep 5	2221	137	116	251	51	31.67
Sep 6	2259	139	129	267	50	33.45
Sep 9	2247	128	126	254	49	32.28
Sep 10	2282	142	117	257	48	32.48
Sep 11	2335	143	135	277	47	34.65
Sep 12	2355	146	141	287	46	35.89
Sep 13	2315	152	137	288	45	37.06
Sep 16	2231	137	118	253	44	34.24
Sep 17	2240	131	122	252	43	34.35
Sep 18	2294	138	132	270	42	36.26
Sep 19	2261	138	127	264	41	36.48
Sep 20	2274	144	119	261	40	36.27
Sep 23	2284	137	121	257	39	35.98
Sep 24	2353	136	133	269	38	37.06
Sep 25	2383	143	126	268	37	36.92
Sep 26	2358	135	127	261	36	36.94
Sep 27	2396	134	130	264	35	37.20
Sep 30	2377	139	112	249	34	35.87
Oct 1	2358	124	116	239	33	35.34
Oct 2	2352	121	119	240	32	36.05
Oct 3	2421	133	112	243	31	36.08
Oct 4	2424	128	104	230	30	34.63
Oct 7	2474	128	104	230	29	34.51
Oct 8	2508	120	114	234	28	35.19
Oct 9	2467	120	103	222	27	34.56
Oct 10	2395	104	99	203	26	33.18
Oct 11	2437	106	93	198	25	32.48
Oct 14	2521	112	91	201	24	32.57
Oct 15	2502	100	98	198	23	32.98
Oct 16	2478	105	83	186	22	32.01
Oct 17	2500	90	89	179	21	31.23
Oct 18	2534	102	86	187	20	32.93

	fp	max	min	s	td	iv
Oct 21	2546	88	84	172	19	30.94
Oct 22	2553	86	83	169	18	31.16
Oct 23	2486	87	73	159	17	30.98
Oct 24	2450	77	76	153	16	31.21
Oct 25	2486	80	66	145	15	30.07
Oct 28	2485	78	63	140	14	30.04
Oct 29	2434	77	61	137	13	31.12
Oct 30	2428	82	53	132	12	31.40
Oct 31	2335	71	56	126	11	32.45
Nov 1	2303	67	42	106	10	29.22
Nov 4	2278				9	
Nov 5	2264				8	
Nov 6	2269				7	
Nov 7	2274				6	
Nov 8	2359				5	
Nov 11	2337				4	
Nov 12	2335				3	
Nov 13	2412				2	
Nov 14	2441				1	
Nov 15	2417	December 96 option expires				

February option and February future

	fp	max	min	s	td	iv
Nov 4	2223	121	98	218	47	28.59
Nov 5	2209	112	103	215	46	28.65
Nov 6	2219	116	97	212	45	28.50
Nov 7	2236	105	91	195	44	26.34
Nov 8	2306	106	100	206	43	27.21
Nov 11	2293	108	101	209	42	28.09
Nov 12	2295	104	99	203	41	27.60
Nov 13	2365	116	101	216	40	28.92
Nov 14	2394	120	114	234	39	31.27
Nov 15	2370	126	106	231	38	31.63
Nov 18	2337	124	111	234	37	32.98
Nov 19	2387	125	117	242	36	33.75
Nov 20	2302	114	112	226	35	33.18
Nov 21	2348	119	117	236	34	34.46
Nov 22	2333	126	109	234	33	34.95
Nov 25	2305	115	109	224	32	34.32
Nov 26	2313	114	101	214	31	33.30
Nov 27	2334	119	103	221	30	34.62
Dec 2	2427	121	94	214	28	33.26
Dec 3	2433	122	89	209	27	33.09
Dec 4	2426	118	93	210	26	33.91
Dec 5	2494	113	107	220	25	35.24
Dec 6	2502	112	100	211	24	34.50
Dec 9	2480	114	94	207	23	34.81
Dec 10	2396	100	96	196	22	34.85
Dec 11	2293	97	90	187	21	35.53
Dec 12	2323	106	80	185	20	35.54
Dec 13	2399	94	93	187	19	35.76
Dec 16	2509	103	94	197	18	36.94
Dec 17	2510	95	95	190	17	36.72
Dec 18	2526	104	80	183	16	36.17
Dec 19	2546	91	86	177	15	35.86
Dec 20	2508	84	76	160	14	34.02

LEGEND: *fp* = futures price, *max* = closest strike high option price, *min* = closest strike low option price, *s* = price corrected at-the-money-straddle, *td* = number of trading days till expiry, *iv* = implied volatility.

CRUDE OIL 1996

	fp	max	min	s	td	iv	fp	max	min	s	td	iv
Dec 23	2479	90	65	154	13	34.36						
Dec 24	2510	75	65	140	12	32.10						
Dec 26	2492	73	65	138	10	34.93						
Dec 27	2522	76	54	129	9	34.03						
Dec 30	2537	67	54	120	8	33.54						
Dec 31	2592	64	55	119	7	34.58						
Jan 2	2569				6							
Jan 3	2559				5							
Jan 6	2637				4							
Jan 7	2623				3							
Jan 8	2662				2							
Jan 9	2637				1							
Jan 10	2609	February 97 option expires										

LEGEND: *fp* = futures price, *max* = closest strike high option price, *min* = closest strike low option price, *s* = price corrected at-the-money-straddle, *td* = number of trading days till expiry, *iv* = implied volatility.

COTTON

Calendar month	Year	Based on Option	Nearest strike	Implied volatility
JANUARY	1993	Mar	*5800*	17.28
FEBRUARY	1993	May	*6000*	20.74
MARCH	1993	May	*6300*	17.38
APRIL	1993	Jul	*6100*	18.97
MAY	1993	Jul	*6000*	20.44
JUNE	1993	Oct	*5900*	18.10
JULY	1993	Oct	*5600*	17.74
AUGUST	1993	Oct	*5900*	20.30
SEPTEMBER	1993	Dec	*5600*	20.20
OCTOBER	1993	Dec	*5800*	19.01
NOVEMBER	1993	Mar	*5900*	16.43
DECEMBER	1993	Mar	*6200*	16.68
JANUARY	1994	Mar	*6800*	18.40
FEBRUARY	1994	May	*7700*	21.78
MARCH	1994	May	*7900*	21.44
APRIL	1994	Jul	*7800*	17.60
MAY	1994	Jul	*8300*	22.70
JUNE	1994	Oct	*7800*	20.23
JULY	1994	Oct	*7200*	18.80
AUGUST	1994	Oct	*7000*	23.12
SEPTEMBER	1994	Dec	*6900*	19.06
OCTOBER	1994	Dec	*6700*	19.81
NOVEMBER	1994	Mar	*7400*	16.89
DECEMBER	1994	Mar	*8100*	17.16
JANUARY	1995	Mar	*9000*	23.11
FEBRUARY	1995	May	*9000*	20.91
MARCH	1995	May	*10800*	31.01
APRIL	1995	Jul	*9100*	31.43
MAY	1995	Jul	*10600*	41.46
JUNE	1995	Oct	*8500*	29.75
JULY	1995	Oct	*8600*	29.57
AUGUST	1995	Oct	*7400*	27.56
SEPTEMBER	1995	Dec	*8600*	30.59
OCTOBER	1995	Dec	*9000*	30.19
NOVEMBER	1995	Mar	*8500*	20.11
DECEMBER	1995	Mar	*8600*	22.22
JANUARY	1996	Mar	*8100*	20.72
FEBRUARY	1996	May	*8600*	21.30
MARCH	1996	May	*8300*	19.20
APRIL	1996	Jul	*8600*	19.36
MAY	1996	Jul	*8600*	21.45
JUNE	1996	Oct	*7900*	20.40
JULY	1996	Oct	*7300*	22.30
AUGUST	1996	Oct	*7200*	22.10
SEPTEMBER	1996	Dec	*7700*	24.12
OCTOBER	1996	Dec	*7600*	21.37
NOVEMBER	1996	Mar	*7400*	16.80
DECEMBER	1996	Mar	*7600*	16.18
JANUARY	1997	Mar	*7500*	14.21
FEBRUARY	1997	May	*7600*	14.43
MARCH	1997	May	*7600*	16.86
APRIL	1997	Jul	*7300*	17.01
MAY	1997	Jul	*7200*	18.96
JUNE	1997	Oct	*7500*	15.86
JULY	1997	Oct	*7600*	15.21
AUGUST	1997	Oct	*7500*	17.02
SEPTEMBER	1997	Dec	*7300*	15.51
OCTOBER	1997	Dec	*7200*	15.19
NOVEMBER	1997	Mar	*7400*	12.94
DECEMBER	1997	Mar	*7000*	18.01

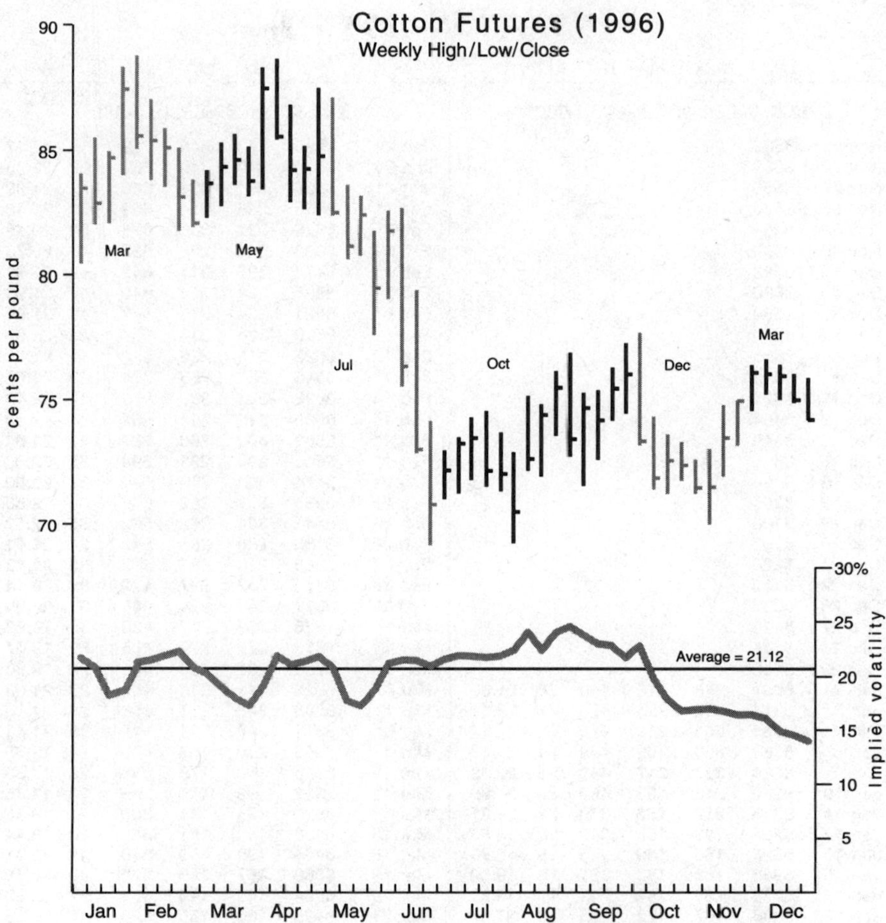
Cotton Futures (1996)
Weekly High/Low/Close
90
85
80
75
70
cents per pound
Mar
May
Jul
Oct
Dec
Mar
30%
25
20
15
10
5
Implied volatility
Average = 21.12
Jan
Feb
Mar
Apr
May
Jun
Jul
Aug
Sep
Oct
Nov
Dec

COTTON 1996

March option and March future

	fp	max	min	s	td	iv
Nov 21	8630					
Nov 22	8688					
Nov 27	8530					
Nov 28	8420					
Nov 29	8464					
Nov 30	8509					
Dec 1	8583					
Dec 4	8630					
Dec 5	8580					
Dec 6	8460					
Dec 7	8555					
Dec 8	8610					
Dec 11	8621					
Dec 12	8464					
Dec 13	8545					
Dec 14	8566					
Dec 15	8484					
Dec 18	8295					
Dec 19	8103					
Dec 20	8105					
Dec 21	8228					
Dec 22	8110					
Dec 26	8033					
Dec 27	8116					
Dec 28	8145					
Dec 29	8105					
Jan 2	8067	243	210	450	28	21.09
Jan 3	8214	249	223	470	27	22.01
Jan 4	8335	254	219	470	26	22.12
Jan 5	8363	250	203	449	25	21.47
Jan 9	8389	227	217	443	23	22.03
Jan 10	8280	216	193	407	22	20.96
Jan 11	8247	212	163	370	21	19.61
Jan 12	8264	193	158	348	20	18.83
Jan 15	8325	185	160	343	19	18.90
Jan 16	8203	168	163	331	18	19.00
Jan 17	8275	169	144	311	17	18.22
Jan 18	8246	167	122	285	16	17.27
Jan 19	8450	170	120	285	15	17.43
Jan 22	8432	157	126	280	14	17.76
Jan 23	8456	162	118	276	13	18.09
Jan 24	8642	170	128	294	12	19.65
Jan 25	8774	161	130	288	11	19.81
Jan 26	8750	162	112	269	10	19.45
Jan 29	8805				9	
Jan 30	8708				8	
Jan 31	8569				7	
Feb 1	8600				6	
Feb 2	8560				5	
Feb 5	8586				4	
Feb 6	8410				3	
Feb 7	8442				2	
Feb 8	8560				1	
Feb 9	8538	March 96 option expires				

May option and May future

	fp	max	min	s	td	iv
Jan 29	8825	373	348	719	54	22.17
Jan 30	8730	370	340	707	53	22.26
Jan 31	8620	351	331	680	52	21.89
Feb 1	8633	348	314	659	51	21.38
Feb 2	8626	327	300	625	50	20.49
Feb 5	8638	334	296	627	49	20.73
Feb 6	8478	333	311	642	48	21.87
Feb 7	8525	334	308	640	47	21.90
Feb 8	8621	334	310	642	46	21.96
Feb 9	8610	324	314	637	45	22.06
Feb 12	8525	319	295	612	44	21.65
Feb 13	8545	325	283	604	43	21.57
Feb 14	8522	321	300	619	42	22.43
Feb 15	8535	315	291	604	41	22.10
Feb 16	8583	309	280	587	40	21.61
Feb 20	8605	299	295	594	38	22.38
Feb 21	8474	303	279	580	37	22.50
Feb 22	8355	307	262	565	36	22.55
Feb 23	8442	304	262	562	35	22.52
Feb 26	8480	280	263	542	34	21.91
Feb 27	8355	273	237	507	33	21.12
Feb 28	8373	252	227	477	32	20.14
Feb 29	8320	243	224	465	31	20.09
Mar 1	8325	233	207	438	30	19.20
Mar 4	8278	225	202	425	29	19.07
Mar 5	8238	231	193	421	28	19.30
Mar 6	8325	241	216	455	27	21.03
Mar 7	8386	238	221	458	26	21.40
Mar 8	8371	240	211	449	25	21.43
Mar 11	8333	220	188	405	24	19.85
Mar 12	8294	180	176	356	23	17.88
Mar 13	8339	198	155	349	22	17.85
Mar 14	8520	194	174	366	21	18.76
Mar 15	8428	189	161	348	20	18.44
Mar 18	8464	190	153	340	19	18.41
Mar 19	8389	167	156	322	18	18.10
Mar 20	8564	180	145	322	17	18.23
Mar 21	8425	160	135	293	16	17.38
Mar 22	8469	160	130	287	15	17.52
Mar 25	8505	140	132	271	14	17.05
Mar 26	8459	144	120	262	13	17.17
Mar 27	8384	130	118	247	12	17.01
Mar 28	8386	132	118	249	11	17.89
Mar 29	8356	138	94	228	10	17.23
Apr 1	8478				9	
Apr 2	8486				8	
Apr 3	8580				7	
Apr 4	8755				6	
Apr 8	8722				4	
Apr 9	8689				3	
Apr 10	8737				2	
Apr 11	8675				1	
Apr 12	8599	May 96 option expires				

LEGEND: *fp* = futures price, *max* = closest strike high option price, *min* = closest strike low option price, *s* = price corrected at-the-money-straddle, *td* = number of trading days till expiry, *iv* = implied volatility.

COTTON 1996

July option and July future

	fp	max	min	s	td	iv
Apr 1	8578	317	295	610	54	19.36
Apr 2	8586	319	304	622	53	19.89
Apr 3	8696	315	310	625	52	19.92
Apr 4	8883	342	308	647	51	20.40
Apr 8	8864	370	307	671	49	21.64
Apr 9	8827	355	329	682	48	22.30
Apr 10	8859	370	330	697	47	22.94
Apr 11	8814	351	336	686	46	22.94
Apr 12	8737	328	292	617	45	21.05
Apr 15	8525	335	308	641	44	22.66
Apr 16	8405	285	280	565	43	20.49
Apr 17	8467	299	266	562	42	20.49
Apr 18	8559	311	260	567	41	20.67
Apr 19	8534	305	268	570	40	21.12
Apr 22	8523	290	267	555	39	20.86
Apr 23	8453	298	252	546	38	20.96
Apr 24	8462	297	260	554	37	21.52
Apr 25	8564	303	269	569	36	22.15
Apr 26	8564	295	259	551	35	21.75
Apr 29	8436	286	251	534	34	21.71
Apr 30	8512	275	264	538	33	22.01
May 1	8635	281	246	524	32	21.45
May 2	8583	275	257	531	31	22.20
May 3	8614	265	251	515	30	21.82
May 6	8697	253	250	503	29	21.47
May 7	8687	251	238	488	28	21.23
May 8	8650	260	210	466	27	20.71
May 9	8544	249	204	449	26	20.61
May 10	8275	205	189	393	25	18.98
May 13	8292	195	189	384	24	18.88
May 14	8287	183	171	353	23	17.76
May 15	8250	194	148	338	22	17.46
May 16	8106	160	154	314	21	16.88
May 17	8120	163	143	304	20	16.76
May 20	8088	160	148	307	19	17.42
May 21	8092	151	140	290	18	16.90
May 22	8152	172	120	287	17	17.07
May 23	8159	164	124	284	16	17.42
May 24	8255	169	124	289	15	18.06
May 28	8130	152	122	271	13	18.51
May 29	7962	155	110	261	12	18.90
May 30	7839	144	114	255	11	19.64
May 31	7928	142	112	251	10	20.05
Jun 3	8032				9	
Jun 4	8139				8	
Jun 5	8055				7	
Jun 6	8053				6	
Jun 7	8195				5	
Jun 10	8172				4	
Jun 11	8003				3	
Jun 12	7996				2	
Jun 13	7707				1	
Jun 14	7628	July 96 option expires				

October option and October future

	fp	max	min	s	td	iv
Jun 3	7917	355	335	688	73	20.35
Jun 4	7955	395	348	739	72	21.90
Jun 5	7914	365	350	714	71	21.41
Jun 6	7855	388	339	723	70	22.00
Jun 7	7860	373	334	704	69	21.56
Jun 10	7900	402	304	697	68	21.40
Jun 11	7845	367	322	685	67	21.34
Jun 12	7782	355	335	688	66	21.78
Jun 13	7642	351	312	660	65	21.41
Jun 14	7700	333	333	666	64	21.62
Jun 17	7730	351	330	679	63	22.14
Jun 18	7630	345	310	652	62	21.71
Jun 19	7595	317	314	631	61	21.27
Jun 20	7616	319	303	621	60	21.04
Jun 21	7555	330	287	613	59	21.14
Jun 24	7570	318	290	606	58	21.01
Jun 25	7286	284	280	564	57	20.49
Jun 26	7292	288	279	566	56	20.75
Jun 27	7300	280	280	560	55	20.69
Jun 28	7209	293	280	572	54	21.59
Jul 1	7235	301	284	584	53	22.16
Jul 2	7237	301	284	584	52	22.37
Jul 3	7207	284	282	566	51	21.99
Jul 8	7238	290	260	547	49	21.61
Jul 9	7383	289	273	561	48	21.92
Jul 10	7208	276	267	542	47	21.95
Jul 11	7271	287	259	544	46	22.05
Jul 12	7328	287	257	541	45	22.03
Jul 15	7230	277	244	518	44	21.61
Jul 16	7280	273	253	524	43	21.97
Jul 17	7245	280	240	517	42	22.00
Jul 18	7275	270	245	513	41	22.02
Jul 19	7352	278	228	502	40	21.57
Jul 22	7425	260	236	494	39	21.31
Jul 23	7264	263	230	490	38	21.89
Jul 24	7264	263	230	490	37	22.19
Jul 25	7197	241	241	482	36	22.32
Jul 26	7207	231	224	454	35	21.32
Jul 29	7170	245	215	457	34	21.88
Jul 30	7273	244	216	458	33	21.91
Jul 31	7320	238	218	454	32	21.94
Aug 1	7248	249	200	445	31	22.03
Aug 2	7228	236	206	439	30	22.20
Aug 5	7253	238	191	425	29	21.75
Aug 6	7208	213	194	405	28	21.26
Aug 7	7000	201	200	401	27	22.04
Aug 8	7030	219	189	405	26	22.62
Aug 9	7025	238	199	434	25	24.69
Aug 12	7325	225	225	450	24	25.08
Aug 13	7475	228	202	428	23	23.87
Aug 14	7385	213	197	409	22	23.60
Aug 15	7347	225	177	398	21	23.62
Aug 16	7272	200	182	380	20	23.40

LEGEND: *fp* = futures price, *max* = closest strike high option price, *min* = closest strike low option price, *s* = price corrected at-the-money-straddle, *td* = number of trading days till expiry, *iv* = implied volatility.

COTTON 1996

	fp	max	min	s	td	iv
Aug 19	7212	195	186	380	19	24.19
Aug 20	7300	178	175	353	18	22.78
Aug 21	7252	196	145	336	17	22.49
Aug 22	7292	147	140	286	16	19.64
Aug 23	7430	174	144	315	15	21.92
Aug 26	7378	149	145	294	14	21.28
Aug 27	7585	168	157	324	13	23.70
Aug 28	7531	175	146	318	12	24.41
Aug 29	7632	175	158	332	11	26.20
Aug 30	7564	175	145	317	10	26.54
Sep 3	7639				8	
Sep 4	7491				7	
Sep 5	7272				6	
Sep 6	7310				5	
Sep 9	7175				4	
Sep 10	7189				3	
Sep 11	7489				2	
Sep 12	7481				1	
Sep 13	7480	October 96 option expires				

<u>December option and December future</u>

	fp	max	min	s	td	iv
Sep 3	7725	337	313	648	48	24.22
Sep 4	7562	324	287	608	47	23.45
Sep 5	7364	312	278	587	46	23.51
Sep 6	7417	300	284	583	45	23.42
Sep 9	7285	290	275	564	44	23.33
Sep 10	7307	284	277	560	43	23.39
Sep 11	7607	318	284	599	42	24.31
Sep 12	7596	301	297	598	41	24.58
Sep 13	7585	291	277	567	40	23.63
Sep 16	7548	285	245	527	39	22.34
Sep 17	7405	264	264	528	38	23.13
Sep 18	7445	283	238	517	37	22.84
Sep 19	7528	275	247	520	36	23.01
Sep 20	7539	278	240	515	35	23.08
Sep 23	7610	258	255	513	34	23.11
Sep 24	7722	265	243	506	33	22.82
Sep 25	7721	265	243	506	32	23.18
Sep 26	7684	256	240	495	31	23.13
Sep 27	7619	238	218	454	30	21.77
Sep 30	7567	235	206	439	29	21.52
Oct 1	7616	224	208	431	28	21.37
Oct 2	7775	232	209	439	27	21.74
Oct 3	7678	224	203	425	26	21.72
Oct 4	7673	229	202	429	25	22.35
Oct 7	7764	235	200	432	24	22.71
Oct 8	7585	217	203	419	23	23.03
Oct 9	7623	223	195	416	22	23.25
Oct 10	7539	225	195	417	21	24.16
Oct 11	7320	186	166	350	20	21.40
Oct 14	7342	189	145	330	19	20.62
Oct 15	7412	171	159	329	18	20.92
Oct 16	7312	150	140	289	17	19.18
Oct 17	7278	145	128	272	16	18.66
Oct 18	7164	147	112	256	15	18.44
Oct 21	7192	132	124	255	14	18.98
Oct 22	7288	125	113	237	13	18.04
Oct 23	7308	120	112	231	12	18.28
Oct 24	7220	115	95	208	11	17.39
Oct 25	7253	117	70	182	10	15.87
Oct 28	7275				9	
Oct 29	7273				8	
Oct 30	7295				7	
Oct 31	7205				6	
Nov 1	7247				5	
Nov 4	7252				4	
Nov 5	7227				3	
Nov 6	7137				2	
Nov 7	7153				1	
Nov 8	7131	December 96 option expires				

<u>March option and March future</u>

	fp	max	min	s	td	iv
Oct 28	7430	288	259	545	76	16.81
Oct 29	7445	294	251	541	75	16.79
Oct 30	7470	288	265	551	74	17.15
Oct 31	7375	276	261	536	73	17.01
Nov 1	7417	284	252	533	72	16.95
Nov 4	7445	287	243	526	71	16.77
Nov 5	7423	270	250	518	70	16.69
Nov 6	7345	281	237	514	69	16.85
Nov 7	7359	280	240	517	68	17.02
Nov 8	7341	276	237	510	67	16.96
Nov 11	7278	273	252	523	66	17.70
Nov 12	7264	264	230	491	65	16.77
Nov 13	7308	249	241	489	64	16.74
Nov 14	7374	260	234	492	63	16.81
Nov 15	7342	264	223	483	62	16.72
Nov 18	7407	245	238	482	61	16.68
Nov 19	7410	245	236	480	60	16.73
Nov 20	7423	250	227	475	59	16.66
Nov 21	7573	256	230	484	58	16.78
Nov 22	7510	242	234	475	57	16.77
Nov 25	7489	233	223	455	56	16.24
Nov 26	7514	226	213	438	55	15.72
Nov 27	7607	231	224	454	54	16.26
Dec 2	7649	251	202	449	52	16.27
Dec 3	7578	235	213	446	51	16.49
Dec 4	7475	232	210	440	50	16.65
Dec 5	7560	241	201	438	49	16.57
Dec 6	7611	214	214	428	48	16.23
Dec 9	7630	228	200	426	47	16.27
Dec 10	7653	237	191	424	46	16.33
Dec 11	7617	214	197	410	45	16.03
Dec 12	7645	227	182	405	44	15.97
Dec 13	7610	201	191	391	43	15.68
Dec 16	7585	192	177	368	42	14.96
Dec 17	7553	195	150	341	41	14.10
Dec 18	7553	201	155	352	40	14.73
Dec 19	7580	189	169	356	39	15.05
Dec 20	7600	177	172	349	38	14.88

LEGEND: *fp* = futures price, *max* = closest strike high option price, *min* = closest strike low option price, *s* = price corrected at-the-money-straddle, *td* = number of trading days till expiry, *iv* = implied volatility.

COTTON 1996

	fp	max	min	s	td	iv	fp	max	min	s	td	iv
Dec 23	7571	179	149	325	37	14.13						
Dec 26	7553	185	140	321	35	14.36						
Dec 27	7507	156	149	304	34	13.91						
Dec 30	7431	150	146	296	33	13.85						
Dec 31	7514	153	138	290	32	13.63						
Jan 2	7538				31							
Jan 3	7408				30							
Jan 6	7414				29							
Jan 7	7363				28							
Jan 8	7396				27							
Jan 9	7356				26							
Jan 10	7377				25							
Jan 13	7417				24							
Jan 14	7389				23							
Jan 15	7455				22							
Jan 16	7421				21							
Jan 17	7408				20							
Jan 20	7384				19							
Jan 21	7300				18							
Jan 22	7410				17							
Jan 23	7464				16							
Jan 24	7460				15							
Jan 27	7525				14							
Jan 28	7511				13							
Jan 29	7535				12							
Jan 30	7464				11							
Jan 31	7495				10							
Feb 3	7500				9							
Feb 4	7450				8							
Feb 5	7485				7							
Feb 6	7445				6							
Feb 7	7458				5							
Feb 10	7425				4							
Feb 11	7385				3							
Feb 12	7342				2							
Feb 13	7321				1							
Feb 14	7310	March 97 option expires										

LEGEND: *fp* = futures price, *max* = closest strike high option price, *min* = closest strike low option price, *s* = price corrected at-the-money-straddle, *td* = number of trading days till expiry, *iv* = implied volatility.

SOYBEANS

Calendar month	Year	Based on Option	Nearest strike	Implied volatility
JANUARY	1993	May	*575*	11.65
FEBRUARY	1993	May	*575*	11.24
MARCH	1993	Jul	*575*	15.66
APRIL	1993	Jul	*600*	18.11
MAY	1993	Jul	*600*	15.84
JUNE	1993	Sep	*575*	19.19
JULY	1993	Sep	*650*	39.73
AUGUST	1993	Nov	*700*	29.85
SEPTEMBER	1993	Mar	*675*	18.66
OCTOBER	1993	Mar	*625*	12.69
NOVEMBER	1993	Mar	*625*	12.56
DECEMBER	1993	Mar	*675*	16.38
JANUARY	1994	May	*700*	17.49
FEBRUARY	1994	May	*700*	16.99
MARCH	1994	Jul	*675*	15.29
APRIL	1994	Jul	*650*	14.48
MAY	1994	Jul	*675*	19.21
JUNE	1994	Sep	*675*	34.96
JULY	1994	Sep	*560*	30.57
AUGUST	1994	Nov	*550*	16.56
SEPTEMBER	1994	Mar	*600*	13.34
OCTOBER	1994	Mar	*550*	14.12
NOVEMBER	1994	Mar	*575*	12.98
DECEMBER	1994	Mar	*575*	12.98
JANUARY	1995	May	*550*	12.71
FEBRUARY	1995	May	*550*	10.70
MARCH	1995	Jul	*575*	13.54
APRIL	1995	Jul	*600*	18.74
MAY	1995	Jul	*600*	20.88
JUNE	1995	Sep	*600*	27.12
JULY	1995	Sep	*600*	25.99
AUGUST	1995	Nov	*625*	20.72
SEPTEMBER	1995	Mar	*650*	17.75
OCTOBER	1995	Mar	*650*	17.44
NOVEMBER	1995	Mar	*700*	16.60
DECEMBER	1995	Mar	*700*	14.92
JANUARY	1996	Mar	*750*	18.84
FEBRUARY	1996	May	*750*	15.09
MARCH	1996	May	*750*	14.16
APRIL	1996	Jul	*775*	20.07
MAY	1996	Jul	*825*	30.10
JUNE	1996	Sep	*750*	23.82
JULY	1996	Sep	*750*	26.36
AUGUST	1996	Sep	*725*	21.09
SEPTEMBER	1996	Nov	*800*	24.85
OCTOBER	1996	Jan	*750*	16.41
NOVEMBER	1996	Jan	*675*	19.37
DECEMBER	1996	Mar	*700*	14.94
JANUARY	1997	May	*700*	16.67
FEBRUARY	1997	May	*725*	15.67
MARCH	1997	Jul	*800*	22.10
APRIL	1997	Jul	*875*	29.09
MAY	1997	Jul	*875*	27.35
JUNE	1997	Sep	*725*	28.94
JULY	1997	Sep	*600*	21.14
AUGUST	1997	Nov	*650*	29.74
SEPTEMBER	1997	Mar	*650*	18.23
OCTOBER	1997	Mar	*625*	18.46
NOVEMBER	1997	Mar	*725*	19.28
DECEMBER	1997	Mar	*725*	18.41

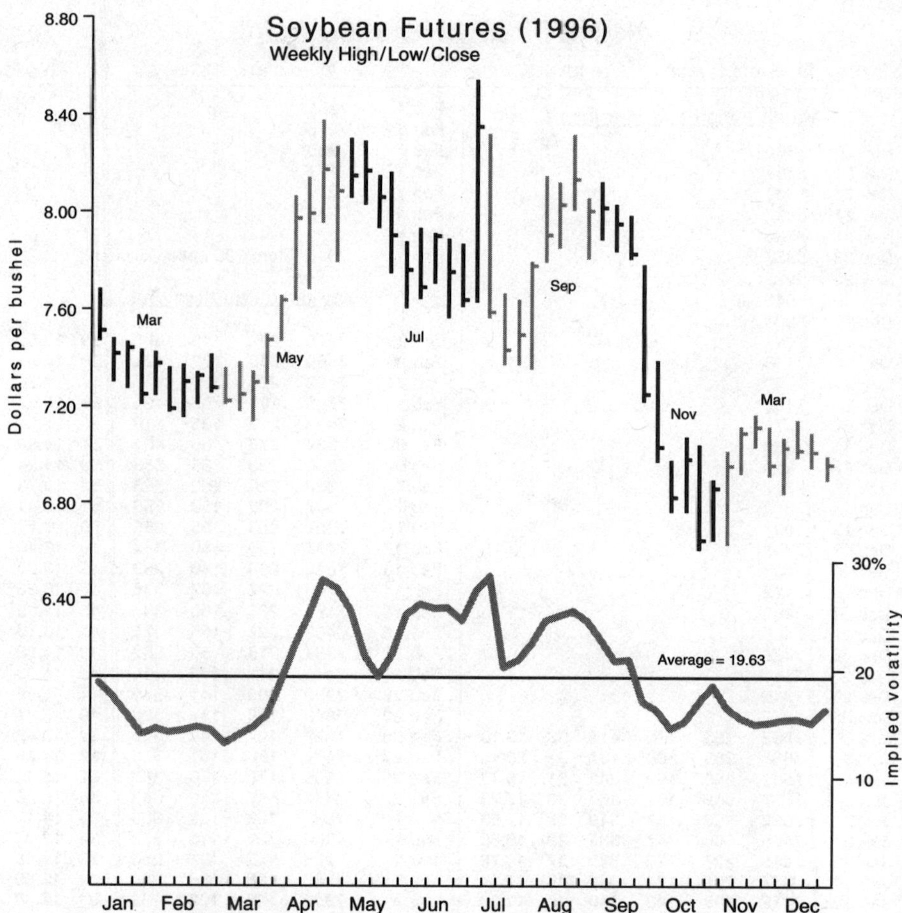
Soybean Futures (1996)
Weekly High/Low/Close
Dollars per bushel
8.80
8.40
8.00
7.60
7.20
6.80
6.40
Mar
May
Jul
Sep
Nov
Mar
Average = 19.63
30%
20
10
Implied volatility
Jan
Feb
Mar
Apr
May
Jun
Jul
Aug
Sep
Oct
Nov
Dec

SOYBEANS 1996

	fp	max	min	s	td	iv
March option and Mar future						
Nov 20	6882					
Nov 21	6857					
Nov 22	6907					
Nov 24	6897					
Nov 27	6860					
Nov 28	6857					
Nov 29	6922					
Nov 30	6945					
Dec 1	6990					
Dec 4	7017					
Dec 5	7115					
Dec 6	7140					
Dec 7	7105					
Dec 8	7170					
Dec 11	7230					
Dec 12	7247					
Dec 13	7317					
Dec 14	7342					
Dec 15	7302					
Dec 18	7435					
Dec 19	7505					
Dec 20	7422					
Dec 21	7290					
Dec 22	7402					
Dec 26	7425					
Dec 27	7340					
Dec 28	7342					
Dec 29	7447					
Jan 2	7582	255	170	416	33	19.13
Jan 3	7660	265	180	437	32	20.15
Jan 4	7587	240	152	383	31	18.13
Jan 5	7537	202	167	366	30	17.73
Jan 8	7362	196	157	349	29	17.63
Jan 9	7455	190	147	333	28	16.89
Jan 10	7415	207	125	323	27	16.78
Jan 11	7337	205	134	332	26	17.74
Jan 12	7412	203	143	340	25	18.36
Jan 15	7445	202	152	349	24	19.16
Jan 16	7352	180	80	247	23	14.01
Jan 17	7362	185	75	245	22	14.18
Jan 18	7402	185	85	257	21	15.17
Jan 19	7452	145	97	237	20	14.24
Jan 22	7340	162	78	230	19	14.36
Jan 23	7375	180	60	221	18	14.11
Jan 24	7352	160	59	204	17	13.46
Jan 25	7255	105	102	207	16	14.25
Jan 26	7245	100	97	197	15	14.02
Jan 29	7280				14	
Jan 30	7365				13	
Jan 31	7387				12	
Feb 1	7410				11	
Feb 2	7392				10	
Feb 5	7237				9	
Feb 6	7292				8	
Feb 7	7235				7	
Feb 8	7215				6	
Feb 9	7200				5	
Feb 12	7177				4	
Feb 13	7220				3	
Feb 14	7342				2	
Feb 15	7325				1	
Feb 16	7300	March 96 option expires				
May option and May future						
Jan 29	7375	252	145	385	59	13.60
Jan 30	7460	245	182	421	58	14.82
Jan 31	7482	225	195	417	57	14.78
Feb 1	7505	220	205	424	56	15.09
Feb 2	7487	227	195	419	55	15.10
Feb 5	7327	225	180	401	54	14.89
Feb 6	7380	223	165	383	53	14.24
Feb 7	7320	220	150	363	52	13.76
Feb 8	7307	205	150	350	51	13.41
Feb 9	7297	205	155	355	50	13.77
Feb 12	7275	185	160	343	49	13.46
Feb 13	7320	205	140	339	48	13.35
Feb 14	7440	227	167	388	47	15.23
Feb 15	7425	235	160	388	46	15.39
Feb 16	7402	227	155	375	45	15.10
Feb 20	7387	219	150	362	43	14.96
Feb 21	7375	211	145	350	42	14.63
Feb 22	7352	203	141	338	41	14.36
Feb 23	7440	195	137	326	40	13.87
Feb 26	7527	187	144	327	39	13.92
Feb 27	7472	180	151	328	38	14.26
Feb 28	7505	175	170	345	37	15.10
Feb 29	7450	197	149	342	36	15.28
Mar 1	7382	182	132	309	35	14.16
Mar 4	7300	167	115	277	34	13.01
Mar 5	7235	142	127	268	33	12.88
Mar 6	7265	136	125	260	32	12.66
Mar 7	7302	155	102	252	31	12.38
Mar 8	7225	150	125	273	30	13.79
Mar 11	7285	152	117	266	29	13.55
Mar 12	7280	152	122	271	28	14.09
Mar 13	7302	160	107	262	27	13.80
Mar 14	7295	155	110	261	26	14.02
Mar 15	7245	132	131	263	25	14.52
Mar 18	7262	135	122	256	24	14.39
Mar 19	7152	182	85	255	23	14.86
Mar 20	7187	159	79	228	22	13.55
Mar 21	7217	140	109	246	21	14.89
Mar 22	7305	159	104	257	20	15.76
Mar 25	7322	159	90	241	19	15.13
Mar 26	7375	187	65	233	18	14.90
Mar 27	7400	182	82	251	17	16.46
Mar 28	7390	187	77	249	16	16.84
Mar 29	7510	119	109	227	15	15.62
Apr 1	7610				14	

LEGEND: *fp* = futures price, *max* = closest strike high option price, *min* = closest strike low option price, *s* = price corrected at-the-money-straddle, *td* = number of trading days till expiry, *iv* = implied volatility.

SOYBEANS 1996

	fp	max	min	s	td	iv
Apr 2	7560				13	
Apr 3	7647				12	
Apr 4	7655				11	
Apr 8	7812				9	
Apr 9	7787				8	
Apr 10	7945				7	
Apr 11	7885				6	
Apr 12	7960				5	
Apr 15	7897				4	
Apr 16	7730				3	
Apr 17	7840				2	
Apr 18	8132				1	
Apr 19	7997	May 96 option expires				

July option and July future

	fp	max	min	s	td	iv
Apr 1	7710	327	272	594	59	20.07
Apr 2	7660	349	249	588	58	20.17
Apr 3	7747	305	290	594	57	20.30
Apr 4	7755	300	295	595	56	20.49
Apr 8	7907	370	280	642	54	22.09
Apr 9	7880	370	245	602	53	21.00
Apr 10	8030	345	315	657	52	22.71
Apr 11	7992	332	325	656	51	23.00
Apr 12	8060	372	315	682	50	23.93
Apr 15	7980	355	335	688	49	24.65
Apr 16	7822	335	280	610	48	22.52
Apr 17	7927	370	302	666	47	24.51
Apr 18	8205	410	370	777	46	27.91
Apr 19	8080	400	322	715	45	26.38
Apr 22	8215	405	370	772	44	28.34
Apr 23	8220	400	370	768	43	28.48
Apr 24	8195	405	355	756	42	28.46
Apr 25	8310	420	360	775	41	29.12
Apr 26	8267	382	365	746	40	28.52
Apr 29	7967	350	285	629	39	25.29
Apr 30	7950	345	292	632	38	25.81
May 1	8175	415	340	748	37	30.10
May 2	8095	382	287	660	36	27.18
May 3	8165	380	300	673	35	27.85
May 6	8120	370	250	608	34	25.69
May 7	8182	350	285	629	33	26.77
May 8	8257	310	302	611	32	26.18
May 9	8192	310	255	560	31	24.56
May 10	8140	320	180	484	30	21.73
May 13	8130	300	170	456	29	20.81
May 14	8187	272	210	476	28	21.99
May 15	8155	285	190	466	27	21.97
May 16	8287	240	200	436	26	20.66
May 17	8187	250	187	431	25	21.06
May 20	8060	220	165	380	24	19.24
May 21	7985	180	174	354	23	18.46
May 22	7967	192	160	349	22	18.69
May 23	8080	220	140	352	21	19.00
May 24	8075	222	145	359	20	19.89
May 28	8015	172	157	328	18	19.28
May 29	7750	162	160	322	17	20.14
May 30	7865				16	
May 31	7882				15	
Jun 3	7655				14	
Jun 4	7697				13	
Jun 5	7655				12	
Jun 6	7660				11	
Jun 7	7755				10	
Jun 10	7910				9	
Jun 11	7752				8	
Jun 12	7715				7	
Jun 13	7690				6	
Jun 14	7697				5	
Jun 17	7730				4	
Jun 18	7910				3	
Jun 19	7830				2	
Jun 20	7800				1	
Jun 21	7917	July 96 option expires				

September option and September future

	fp	max	min	s	td	iv
May 30	7625	415	335	743	59	24.95
May 31	7642	432	335	758	58	25.61
Jun 3	7415	405	285	678	57	23.82
Jun 4	7457	390	340	726	56	25.56
Jun 5	7415	410	280	677	55	24.19
Jun 6	7420	392	325	711	54	25.61
Jun 7	7515	370	350	718	53	25.78
Jun 10	7670	440	320	749	52	26.56
Jun 11	7530	367	347	712	51	25.99
Jun 12	7475	385	325	705	50	26.15
Jun 13	7467	375	327	698	49	26.17
Jun 14	7457	374	307	675	48	25.60
Jun 17	7495	345	332	676	47	25.77
Jun 18	7675	385	320	699	46	26.30
Jun 19	7592	371	280	643	45	24.69
Jun 20	7570	357	270	619	44	24.11
Jun 21	7700	370	345	713	43	27.60
Jun 24	7557	400	280	668	42	26.67
Jun 25	7540	360	280	633	41	25.59
Jun 26	7470	307	302	609	40	25.14
Jun 27	7377	335	260	588	39	24.90
Jun 28	7537	329	260	583	38	24.45
Jul 1	7632	365	272	628	37	26.36
Jul 2	7532	335	250	577	35	24.86
Jul 3	7592	310	230	532	34	23.06
Jul 5	7420	307	220	519	33	23.63
Jul 8	7447	285	232	512	32	23.59
Jul 9	7585	310	230	532	31	24.44
Jul 10	7722	302	280	580	30	26.56
Jul 11	8022	360	330	687	29	30.78
Jul 12	8225	400	370	768	28	34.07
Jul 15	8222	390	360	748	27	33.76
Jul 16	8070	357	292	643	26	30.13
Jul 17	7900	345	245	580	25	28.28
Jul 18	7627	295	180	463	24	23.80

LEGEND: *fp* = futures price, *max* = closest strike high option price, *min* = closest strike low option price, *s* = price corrected at-the-money-straddle, *td* = number of trading days till expiry, *iv* = implied volatility.

SOYBEANS 1996

	fp	max	min	s	td	iv
Jul 19	7595	255	165	411	25	21.64
Jul 22	7525	270	160	418	24	22.69
Jul 23	7645	257	157	403	23	22.01
Jul 24	7510	155	145	299	22	16.99
Jul 25	7520	162	142	302	21	17.54
Jul 26	7430	212	140	345	20	20.75
Jul 29	7522	175	155	328	19	20.03
Jul 30	7447	192	140	327	18	20.70
Jul 31	7470	180	150	327	17	21.26
Aug 1	7602	175	148	321	16	21.09
Aug 2	7517	170	147	315	15	21.64
Aug 5	7480				14	
Aug 6	7517				13	
Aug 7	7530				12	
Aug 8	7677				11	
Aug 9	7772				10	
Aug 12	8007				9	
Aug 13	7952				8	
Aug 14	8065				7	
Aug 15	8002				6	
Aug 16	7935				5	
Aug 19	7870				4	
Aug 20	7947				3	
Aug 21	8002				2	
Aug 22	8087				1	
Aug 23	8032	September 96 option expires				

November option and November future

	fp	max	min	s	td	iv
Aug 5	7347	365	245	598	54	22.15
Aug 6	7397	360	235	582	53	21.63
Aug 7	7432	355	235	578	52	21.57
Aug 8	7572	375	255	618	51	22.86
Aug 9	7640	395	275	658	50	24.37
Aug 12	7862	410	290	688	49	25.02
Aug 13	7810	395	270	653	48	24.12
Aug 14	7890	392	267	647	47	23.91
Aug 15	7840	395	275	658	46	24.76
Aug 16	7767	335	317	651	45	24.97
Aug 19	7710	320	285	602	44	23.54
Aug 20	7762	325	310	634	43	24.90
Aug 21	7790	340	297	633	42	25.09
Aug 22	7852	395	270	653	41	25.96
Aug 23	7787	337	295	628	40	25.52
Aug 26	7895	382	260	630	39	25.55
Aug 27	7957	350	307	653	38	26.64
Aug 28	7887	365	245	598	37	24.93
Aug 29	7950	325	277	598	36	25.07
Aug 30	7945	320	270	586	35	24.92
Sep 3	7955	310	262	568	33	24.85
Sep 4	7802	282	230	507	32	22.99
Sep 5	7957	295	252	543	31	24.53
Sep 6	8000	275	270	545	30	24.86
Sep 9	7937	292	232	519	29	24.27
Sep 10	8070	292	222	508	28	23.77
Sep 11	8050	240	190	425	27	20.34
Sep 12	8145	295	170	451	26	21.73
Sep 13	8020	227	207	432	25	21.56
Sep 16	7930	265	140	391	24	20.11
Sep 17	7960	220	175	391	23	20.48
Sep 18	7940	257	132	374	22	20.10
Sep 19	7892	260	135	380	21	21.03
Sep 20	7952	222	171	388	20	21.84
Sep 23	7987	195	187	381	19	21.91
Sep 24	7912	247	122	354	18	21.08
Sep 25	7957	190	150	336	17	20.51
Sep 26	7907	230	105	319	16	20.18
Sep 27	7832	225	100	309	15	20.36
Sep 30	7580				14	
Oct 1	7492				13	
Oct 2	7420				12	
Oct 3	7375				11	
Oct 4	7272				10	
Oct 7	7342				9	
Oct 8	7365				8	
Oct 9	7382				7	
Oct 10	7302				6	
Oct 11	7002				5	
Oct 14	6885				4	
Oct 15	6925				3	
Oct 16	6910				2	
Oct 17	6885				1	
Oct 18	6820	November 96 option expires				

January option and January future

	fp	max	min	s	td	iv
Sep 30	7635	315	190	492	59	16.77
Oct 1	7547	305	180	472	58	16.41
Oct 2	7475	235	222	456	57	16.16
Oct 3	7430	247	215	459	56	16.52
Oct 4	7327	285	167	439	55	16.17
Oct 7	7397	270	197	460	54	16.93
Oct 8	7420	265	205	464	53	17.20
Oct 9	7437	275	182	448	52	16.69
Oct 10	7357	285	160	431	51	16.41
Oct 11	7057	185	180	365	50	14.61
Oct 14	6942	215	157	367	49	15.08
Oct 15	6985	180	170	349	48	14.43
Oct 16	6967	190	157	344	47	14.41
Oct 17	6935	206	146	346	46	14.72
Oct 18	6862	232	110	327	45	14.20
Oct 21	6845	217	122	328	44	14.47
Oct 22	6900	227	127	343	43	15.15
Oct 23	7005	177	172	349	42	15.36
Oct 24	6967	195	162	354	41	15.87
Oct 25	6990	185	175	359	40	16.25
Oct 28	7035	192	160	349	39	15.90
Oct 29	6982	180	165	344	38	15.97
Oct 30	6907	220	132	343	37	16.31
Oct 31	6690	217	157	368	36	18.35
Nov 1	6665	235	155	382	35	19.37

LEGEND: *fp* = futures price, *max* = closest strike high option price, *min* = closest strike low option price, *s* = price corrected at-the-money-straddle, *td* = number of trading days till expiry, *iv* = implied volatility.

SOYBEANS 1996

	fp	max	min	s	td	iv
Nov 4	6707	215	172	383	34	19.59
Nov 5	6727	190	165	353	33	18.26
Nov 6	6825	217	142	351	32	18.20
Nov 7	6857	240	115	340	31	17.79
Nov 8	6850	240	117	342	30	18.23
Nov 11	6770	190	170	358	29	19.66
Nov 12	6862	210	90	284	28	15.64
Nov 13	6905	195	94	277	27	15.42
Nov 14	6882	197	81	262	26	14.94
Nov 15	6967	150	117	264	25	15.16
Nov 18	7032				24	
Nov 19	6955				23	
Nov 20	7070				22	
Nov 21	7060				21	
Nov 22	7095				20	
Nov 25	7080				19	
Nov 26	7130				18	
Nov 27	7152				17	
Nov 29	7127				15	
Dec 2	7035				14	
Dec 3	6990				13	
Dec 4	6970				12	
Dec 5	7020				11	
Dec 6	6960				10	
Dec 9	6887				9	
Dec 10	6850				8	
Dec 11	6915				7	
Dec 12	7027				6	
Dec 13	7042				5	
Dec 16	7115				4	
Dec 17	7065				3	
Dec 18	7040				2	
Dec 19	7077				1	
Dec 20	7020	January 97 option expires				

	fp	max	min	s	td	iv
Nov 18	6992	237	217	452	66	15.93
Nov 19	6915	250	205	451	65	16.18
Nov 20	7030	255	185	433	64	15.41
Nov 21	7020	242	185	422	63	15.14
Nov 22	7055	257	180	430	62	15.46
Nov 25	7040	242	175	411	61	14.94
Nov 26	7090	255	160	405	60	14.75
Nov 27	7112	262	152	402	59	14.72
Nov 29	7087	240	167	400	57	14.95
Dec 2	6995	202	190	391	56	14.94
Dec 3	6950	235	160	388	55	15.04
Dec 4	6930	245	159	395	54	15.52
Dec 5	6980	210	180	387	53	15.25
Dec 6	6920	232	152	376	52	15.07
Dec 9	6837	230	149	371	51	15.19
Dec 10	6790	205	170	372	50	15.49
Dec 11	6862	200	175	373	49	15.52
Dec 12	6985	195	180	374	48	15.45
Dec 13	7007	192	185	376	47	15.67

	fp	max	min	s	td	iv
Dec 16	7070	230	157	380	48	15.84
Dec 17	7015	197	177	372	47	15.82
Dec 18	6995	177	175	352	46	15.17
Dec 19	7045	197	150	343	45	14.83
Dec 20	6992	180	172	351	44	15.51
Dec 23	6962	182	145	324	43	14.52
Dec 24	7032	184	151	332	42	14.93
Dec 26	6965	188	147	331	40	15.43
Dec 27	6967	181	147	325	39	15.34
Dec 30	6905	179	146	322	38	15.55
Dec 31	6877	177	145	319	37	15.69
Jan 2	6987				36	
Jan 3	6987				35	
Jan 6	6945				34	
Jan 7	7002				33	
Jan 8	6960				32	
Jan 9	6992				31	
Jan 10	7292				30	
Jan 13	7367				29	
Jan 14	7370				28	
Jan 15	7455				27	
Jan 16	7482				26	
Jan 17	7482				25	
Jan 20	7462				24	
Jan 21	7467				23	
Jan 22	7405				22	
Jan 23	7412				21	
Jan 24	7475				20	
Jan 27	7497				19	
Jan 28	7445				18	
Jan 29	7500				17	
Jan 30	7415				16	
Jan 31	7382				15	
Feb 3	7380				14	
Feb 4	7370				13	
Feb 5	7395				12	
Feb 6	7300				11	
Feb 7	7380				10	
Feb 10	7400				9	
Feb 11	7497				8	
Feb 12	7642				7	
Feb 13	7655				6	
Feb 14	7610				5	
Feb 18	7790				3	
Feb 19	7710				2	
Feb 20	7860				1	
Feb 21	7830	March 97 option expires				

LEGEND: *fp* = futures price, *max* = closest strike high option price, *min* = closest strike low option price, *s* = price corrected at-the-money-straddle, *td* = number of trading days till expiry, *iv* = implied volatility.

WHEAT

Calendar month	Year	Based on Option	Nearest strike	Implied volatility
JANUARY	1993	May	*360*	16.13
FEBRUARY	1993	May	*350*	19.66
MARCH	1993	Jul	*310*	18.44
APRIL	1993	Jul	*310*	20.80
MAY	1993	Jul	*300*	19.51
JUNE	1993	Sep	*290*	17.91
JULY	1993	Sep	*300*	24.78
AUGUST	1993	Dec	*320*	21.23
SEPTEMBER	1993	Dec	*310*	17.73
OCTOBER	1993	Mar	*320*	15.41
NOVEMBER	1993	Mar	*330*	18.09
DECEMBER	1993	Mar	*360*	18.66
JANUARY	1994	May	*360*	21.11
FEBRUARY	1994	May	*350*	20.19
MARCH	1994	Jul	*340*	17.80
APRIL	1994	Jul	*330*	18.91
MAY	1994	Jul	*330*	23.11
JUNE	1994	Sep	*330*	23.84
JULY	1994	Sep	*320*	21.85
AUGUST	1994	Dec	*340*	18.97
SEPTEMBER	1994	Dec	*380*	18.85
OCTOBER	1994	Mar	*420*	18.92
NOVEMBER	1994	Mar	*400*	19.15
DECEMBER	1994	Mar	*390*	18.06
JANUARY	1995	May	*380*	17.58
FEBRUARY	1995	May	*360*	17.97
MARCH	1995	Jul	*330*	16.10
APRIL	1995	Jul	*340*	17.18
MAY	1995	Jul	*360*	22.59
JUNE	1995	Sep	*390*	24.01
JULY	1995	Sep	*450*	39.36
AUGUST	1995	Dec	*470*	24.21
SEPTEMBER	1995	Dec	*460*	22.63
OCTOBER	1995	Mar	*500*	22.16
NOVEMBER	1995	Mar	*510*	19.36
DECEMBER	1995	Mar	*500*	17.69
JANUARY	1996	Mar	*510*	19.14
FEBRUARY	1996	May	*490*	20.97
MARCH	1996	May	*500*	21.05
APRIL	1996	Jul	*480*	23.61
MAY	1996	Jul	*600*	23.46
JUNE	1996	Sep	*530*	26.43
JULY	1996	Sep	*490*	28.11
AUGUST	1996	Sep	*450*	23.10
SEPTEMBER	1996	Dec	*450*	21.88
OCTOBER	1996	Dec	*430*	20.53
NOVEMBER	1996	Mar	*370*	16.12
DECEMBER	1996	Mar	*370*	21.53
JANUARY	1997	May	*370*	21.94
FEBRUARY	1997	May	*350*	22.86
MARCH	1997	Jul	*370*	23.62
APRIL	1997	Jul	*390*	29.53
MAY	1997	Jul	*420*	32.90
JUNE	1997	Sep	*370*	27.42
JULY	1997	Sep	*330*	21.09
AUGUST	1997	Dec	*380*	26.02
SEPTEMBER	1997	Dec	*390*	24.90
OCTOBER	1997	Mar	*360*	20.76
NOVEMBER	1997	Mar	*380*	22.45
DECEMBER	1997	Mar	*360*	19.04

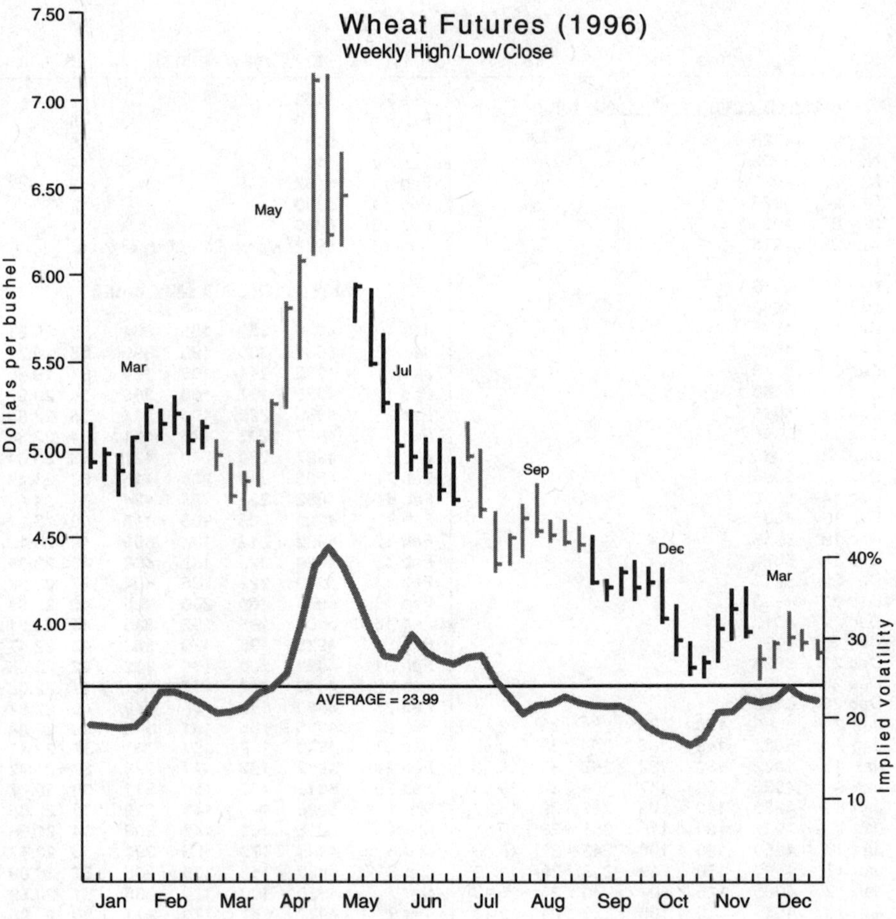
Wheat Futures (1996)
Weekly High/Low/Close
7.50
7.00
6.50
6.00
5.50
5.00
4.50
4.00
Dollars per bushel
May
Mar
Jul
Sep
Dec
Mar
40%
30
20
10
Implied volatility
AVERAGE = 23.99
Jan
Feb
Mar
Apr
May
Jun
Jul
Aug
Sep
Oct
Nov
Dec

WHEAT 1996

March option and March future

	fp	max	min	s	td	iv
Nov 20	4925					
Nov 21	4905					
Nov 22	4947					
Nov 24	4975					
Nov 27	4935					
Nov 28	4915					
Nov 29	4977					
Nov 30	4950					
Dec 1	4950					
Dec 4	4877					
Dec 5	4980					
Dec 6	5010					
Dec 7	5060					
Dec 8	5085					
Dec 11	5095					
Dec 12	5065					
Dec 13	5065					
Dec 14	5025					
Dec 15	5005					
Dec 18	5065					
Dec 19	5070					
Dec 20	5015					
Dec 21	4990					
Dec 22	5010					
Dec 26	5035					
Dec 27	5035					
Dec 28	5095					
Dec 29	5125					
Jan 2	5085	150	135	284	33	19.43
Jan 3	5082	149	132	280	32	19.45
Jan 4	5002	130	132	262	31	18.83
Jan 5	4935	150	117	264	30	19.53
Jan 8	4835	140	105	242	29	18.57
Jan 9	4957	150	110	256	28	19.54
Jan 10	4950	150	100	245	27	19.05
Jan 11	4890	130	117	246	26	19.72
Jan 12	4985	125	107	230	25	18.49
Jan 15	4960	140	100	236	24	19.44
Jan 16	4800	115	112	227	23	19.70
Jan 17	4790	110	100	209	22	18.62
Jan 18	4830	115	90	203	21	18.32
Jan 19	4872	117	90	205	20	18.77
Jan 22	4822	110	87	195	19	18.55
Jan 23	4922	110	87	195	18	18.67
Jan 24	4917	100	85	184	17	18.12
Jan 25	4907	102	92	193	16	19.68
Jan 26	5067	115	87	199	15	20.32
Jan 29	5205				14	
Jan 30	5262				13	
Jan 31	5195				12	
Feb 1	5175				11	
Feb 2	5265				10	
Feb 5	5177				9	
Feb 6	5225				8	
Feb 7	5135				7	
Feb 8	5100				6	
Feb 9	5132				5	
Feb 12	5117				4	
Feb 13	5152				3	
Feb 14	5280				2	
Feb 15	5260				1	
Feb 16	5232	March 96 option expires				

May option and May future

	fp	max	min	s	td	iv
Jan 29	4945	200	185	384	59	20.21
Jan 30	5002	200	195	395	58	20.72
Jan 31	4935	214	160	369	57	19.80
Feb 1	4925	197	190	386	56	20.97
Feb 2	4985	225	195	417	55	22.58
Feb 5	4887	207	195	401	54	22.33
Feb 6	4967	230	200	427	53	23.64
Feb 7	4895	210	205	415	52	23.49
Feb 8	4862	232	195	424	51	24.41
Feb 9	4900	205	205	410	50	23.67
Feb 12	4932	217	185	399	49	23.13
Feb 13	4960	222	182	400	48	23.31
Feb 14	5042	222	185	404	47	23.36
Feb 15	5005	205	200	405	46	23.84
Feb 16	5005	195	190	385	45	22.91
Feb 20	4925	195	170	363	43	22.47
Feb 21	4932	200	165	362	42	22.65
Feb 22	4830	187	157	341	41	22.08
Feb 23	4880	185	165	348	40	22.57
Feb 26	4935	186	161	345	39	22.38
Feb 27	4930	187	157	341	38	22.47
Feb 28	4962	185	147	329	37	21.77
Feb 29	5015	162	150	311	36	20.67
Mar 1	5025	170	145	313	35	21.05
Mar 4	5015	162	147	308	34	21.05
Mar 5	4945	170	125	291	33	20.47
Mar 6	4880	155	135	288	32	20.89
Mar 7	4950	170	120	285	31	20.69
Mar 8	4937	157	120	274	30	20.23
Mar 11	4915	147	135	281	29	21.23
Mar 12	4830	150	122	270	28	21.09
Mar 13	4845	152	110	258	27	20.50
Mar 14	4805	132	127	259	26	21.11
Mar 15	4722	135	117	250	25	21.22
Mar 18	4737	135	116	249	24	21.49
Mar 19	4692	127	117	243	23	21.61
Mar 20	4810	125	115	239	22	21.20
Mar 21	4807	125	117	241	21	21.91
Mar 22	4817	127	106	231	20	21.46
Mar 25	4907	120	112	231	19	21.63
Mar 26	5030	140	110	247	18	23.17
Mar 27	5007	127	120	246	17	23.87
Mar 28	4975	139	110	246	16	24.76
Mar 29	4992	122	115	236	15	24.46
Apr 1	5115				14	

LEGEND: *fp* = futures price, *max* = closest strike high option price, *min* = closest strike low option price, *s* = price corrected at-the-money-straddle, *td* = number of trading days till expiry, *iv* = implied volatility.

WHEAT 1996

	fp	max	min	s	td	iv
Apr 2	5120				13	
Apr 3	5230				12	
Apr 4	5225				11	
Apr 8	5252				9	
Apr 9	5297				8	
Apr 10	5497				7	
Apr 11	5635				6	
Apr 12	5825				5	
Apr 15	5867				4	
Apr 16	5667				3	
Apr 17	5710				2	
Apr 18	6005				1	
Apr 19	6080	May 96 option expires				

July option and July future

	fp	max	min	s	td	iv
Apr 1	4825	235	205	437	59	23.61
Apr 2	4830	235	205	437	58	23.78
Apr 3	4940	227	210	436	57	23.36
Apr 4	4935	235	205	437	56	23.69
Apr 8	4920	225	205	428	54	23.69
Apr 9	5000	215	210	425	53	23.33
Apr 10	5200	245	240	485	52	25.85
Apr 11	5365	285	255	537	51	28.06
Apr 12	5545	295	275	568	50	28.99
Apr 15	5507	305	295	599	49	31.09
Apr 16	5312	295	277	571	48	31.00
Apr 17	5390	300	290	589	47	31.89
Apr 18	5670	330	300	627	46	32.63
Apr 19	5745	350	305	651	45	33.79
Apr 22	5945	435	320	744	44	37.74
Apr 23	6155	400	350	746	43	36.95
Apr 24	6140	400	360	757	42	38.03
Apr 25	6285	430	410	838	41	41.66
Apr 26	6170	450	425	873	40	44.74
Apr 29	5970	425	360	779	39	41.81
Apr 30	5670	370	340	707	38	40.48
May 1	5970	400	390	789	37	43.46
May 2	5670	350	320	667	36	39.24
May 3	5620	325	300	623	35	37.47
May 6	5565	335	300	632	34	38.96
May 7	5710	310	305	615	33	37.47
May 8	5910	360	345	704	32	42.10
May 9	5970	355	325	677	31	40.76
May 10	5800	297	295	592	30	37.26
May 13	5880	300	280	578	29	36.53
May 14	5832	292	257	546	28	35.39
May 15	5822	275	252	525	27	34.71
May 16	5780	260	242	501	26	33.96
May 17	5890	250	252	502	25	34.10
May 20	5850	257	210	463	24	32.30
May 21	5762	240	200	436	23	31.59
May 22	5627	215	190	403	22	30.53
May 23	5595	190	185	375	21	29.22
May 24	5610	182	175	356	20	28.41
May 28	5460	177	157	332	18	28.69
May 29	5260	160	140	298	17	27.51
May 30	5262	165	130	292	16	27.73
May 31	5287	140	122	260	15	25.44
Jun 3	5210				14	
Jun 4	5010				13	
Jun 5	4887				12	
Jun 6	4942				11	
Jun 7	5022				10	
Jun 10	5195				9	
Jun 11	5090				8	
Jun 12	4945				7	
Jun 13	5047				6	
Jun 14	4960				5	
Jun 17	4920				4	
Jun 18	5025				3	
Jun 19	4935				2	
Jun 20	4875				1	
Jun 21	4912	July 96 option expires				

September option and September future

	fp	max	min	s	td	iv
Jun 3	5250	280	255	533	59	26.43
Jun 4	5050	292	237	524	58	27.25
Jun 5	4927	260	227	484	57	26.03
Jun 6	4982	280	275	555	56	29.75
Jun 7	5062	300	270	567	55	30.23
Jun 10	5240	335	285	616	54	31.98
Jun 11	5120	300	280	578	53	31.03
Jun 12	4992	277	267	543	52	30.18
Jun 13	5095	277	272	549	51	30.15
Jun 14	5005	261	255	516	50	29.13
Jun 17	4975	265	240	503	49	28.88
Jun 18	5045	282	230	507	48	29.03
Jun 19	4975	255	227	480	47	28.12
Jun 20	4922	240	217	455	46	27.26
Jun 21	4940	247	210	454	45	27.39
Jun 24	5030	245	220	463	44	27.75
Jun 25	5037	247	217	461	43	27.94
Jun 26	4957	247	190	432	42	26.88
Jun 27	4825	220	195	413	41	26.73
Jun 28	4825	220	195	413	40	27.06
Jul 1	4890	220	210	429	39	28.11
Jul 2	4755	217	175	388	38	26.49
Jul 3	4792	197	190	386	37	26.51
Jul 5	4735	200	167	364	35	26.00
Jul 8	4775	202	177	377	34	27.07
Jul 9	4910	200	190	389	33	27.60
Jul 10	4920	200	180	378	32	27.19
Jul 11	5060	230	180	405	31	28.78
Jul 12	5010	205	197	401	30	29.25
Jul 15	4925	195	170	363	29	27.36
Jul 16	4832	195	160	352	28	27.53
Jul 17	4810	177	167	343	27	27.46
Jul 18	4750	190	147	333	26	27.50
Jul 19	4595	162	160	322	25	28.02
Jul 22	4605	150	142	291	24	25.83

LEGEND: *fp* = futures price, *max* = closest strike high option price, *min* = closest strike low option price, *s* = price corrected at-the-money-straddle, *td* = number of trading days till expiry, *iv* = implied volatility.

WHEAT 1996

	fp	max	min	s	td	iv
Jul 23	4537	155	117	268	23	24.68
Jul 24	4410	130	120	249	22	24.09
Jul 25	4437	137	102	236	21	23.19
Jul 26	4345	135	95	226	20	23.27
Jul 29	4437	132	95	223	19	23.11
Jul 30	4382	115	97	210	18	22.64
Jul 31	4400	102	100	202	17	22.25
Aug 1	4460	125	85	206	16	23.10
Aug 2	4490	100	90	189	15	21.75
Aug 5	4435				14	
Aug 6	4485				13	
Aug 7	4537				12	
Aug 8	4597				11	
Aug 9	4627				10	
Aug 12	4745				9	
Aug 13	4602				8	
Aug 14	4560				7	
Aug 15	4572				6	
Aug 16	4545				5	
Aug 19	4595				4	
Aug 20	4545				3	
Aug 21	4510				2	
Aug 22	4505				1	
Aug 23	4527	September 96 option expires				
December option and December future						
Aug 5	4485	200	187	386	74	20.01
Aug 6	4530	207	177	381	73	19.71
Aug 7	4602	197	195	392	72	20.07
Aug 8	4665	222	187	406	71	20.65
Aug 9	4690	207	200	406	70	20.72
Aug 12	4830	240	210	447	69	22.30
Aug 13	4680	225	205	428	68	22.20
Aug 14	4630	215	187	400	67	21.09
Aug 15	4620	210	190	398	66	21.22
Aug 16	4570	215	187	400	65	21.69
Aug 19	4645	222	177	395	64	21.26
Aug 20	4597	200	200	400	63	21.93
Aug 21	4555	220	167	382	62	21.31
Aug 22	4562	215	180	392	61	22.00
Aug 23	4585	205	192	396	60	22.30
Aug 26	4650	225	185	406	59	22.76
Aug 27	4640	227	185	408	58	23.11
Aug 28	4550	227	170	392	57	22.80
Aug 29	4560	220	180	396	56	23.24
Aug 30	4532	202	167	366	55	21.77
Sep 3	4522	192	170	360	53	21.88
Sep 4	4472	187	160	345	52	21.38
Sep 5	4460	195	157	349	51	21.89
Sep 6	4425	182	155	335	50	21.39
Sep 9	4487	180	165	344	49	21.89
Sep 10	4527	190	160	347	48	22.15
Sep 11	4375	175	150	323	47	21.53
Sep 12	4345	177	135	308	46	20.91

	fp	max	min	s	td	iv
Sep 13	4240	177	130	303	45	21.28
Sep 16	4170	165	135	297	44	21.50
Sep 17	4185	157	142	298	43	21.70
Sep 18	4242	172	125	293	42	21.28
Sep 19	4167	160	130	287	41	21.54
Sep 20	4210	147	137	283	40	21.27
Sep 23	4265	162	127	286	39	21.46
Sep 24	4295	145	140	285	38	21.50
Sep 25	4295	147	142	289	37	22.09
Sep 26	4292	142	135	276	36	21.47
Sep 27	4315	142	127	268	35	20.98
Sep 30	4360	152	115	264	34	20.73
Oct 1	4337	147	112	256	33	20.53
Oct 2	4225	135	110	243	32	20.32
Oct 3	4200	122	122	244	31	20.87
Oct 4	4210	120	110	229	30	19.88
Oct 7	4225	122	97	217	29	19.05
Oct 8	4285	117	101	217	28	19.11
Oct 9	4270	120	90	207	27	18.68
Oct 10	4240	120	80	196	26	18.13
Oct 11	4245	120	75	190	25	17.93
Oct 14	4295	95	90	185	24	17.55
Oct 15	4217	97	80	175	23	17.36
Oct 16	4172	102	75	174	22	17.83
Oct 17	4110	87	82	169	21	17.90
Oct 18	4047	110	62	167	20	18.42
Oct 21	4005				19	
Oct 22	3995				18	
Oct 23	3985				17	
Oct 24	3840				16	
Oct 25	3897				15	
Oct 28	3822				14	
Oct 29	3845				13	
Oct 30	3810				12	
Oct 31	3712				11	
Nov 1	3747				10	
Nov 4	3797				9	
Nov 5	3687				8	
Nov 6	3695				7	
Nov 7	3750				6	
Nov 8	3787				5	
Nov 11	3835				4	
Nov 12	3915				3	
Nov 13	4007				2	
Nov 14	3967				1	
Nov 15	3972	December 96 option expires				
March option and March future						
Oct 21	3950	175	145	317	88	17.13
Oct 22	3940	167	155	321	87	17.47
Oct 23	3930	162	150	311	86	17.07
Oct 24	3785	162	157	319	85	18.26
Oct 25	3842	162	140	300	84	17.05
Oct 28	3767	162	137	297	83	17.30
Oct 29	3790	165	122	283	82	16.49

LEGEND: *fp* = futures price, *max* = closest strike high option price, *min* = closest strike low option price, *s* = price corrected at-the-money-straddle, *td* = number of trading days till expiry, *iv* = implied volatility.

WHEAT 1996

	fp	max	min	s	td	iv
Oct 30	3755	162	115	272	81	16.12
Oct 31	3657	142	127	268	80	16.37
Nov 1	3692	140	126	265	79	16.14
Nov 4	3742	155	130	283	78	17.11
Nov 5	3632	155	116	267	77	16.78
Nov 6	3640	157	117	270	76	17.03
Nov 7	3695	160	135	293	75	18.30
Nov 8	3732	185	140	321	74	19.99
Nov 11	3790	175	160	334	73	20.61
Nov 12	3877	180	160	338	72	20.57
Nov 13	3950	200	155	351	71	21.08
Nov 14	3905	172	167	339	70	20.73
Nov 15	3882	177	160	336	69	20.81
Nov 18	3845	177	137	310	68	19.58
Nov 19	3842	175	135	306	67	19.48
Nov 20	3950	190	140	325	66	20.27
Nov 21	3885	180	162	340	65	21.74
Nov 22	3900	175	175	350	64	22.44
Nov 25	3922	190	167	355	63	22.81
Nov 26	3905	177	172	349	62	22.67
Nov 27	3842	190	142	328	61	21.83
Nov 29	3775	175	152	325	59	22.42
Dec 2	3772	175	150	323	58	22.48
Dec 3	3720	162	142	302	57	21.53
Dec 4	3702	152	147	299	56	21.56
Dec 5	3755	175	130	301	55	21.60
Dec 6	3797	151	150	301	54	21.57
Dec 9	3742	167	125	288	53	21.15
Dec 10	3792	152	145	296	52	21.68
Dec 11	3827	165	137	300	51	21.92
Dec 12	3882	170	150	318	50	23.19
Dec 13	3890	170	160	329	49	24.18
Dec 16	3960	195	157	349	48	25.41
Dec 17	3942	185	142	323	47	23.91
Dec 18	4007	165	157	321	46	23.65
Dec 19	4002	157	155	312	45	23.23
Dec 20	3932	165	132	294	44	22.55
Dec 23	3905	145	140	285	43	22.23
Dec 24	3917	147	135	281	42	22.14
Dec 26	3940	162	122	280	40	22.50
Dec 27	3895	140	135	275	39	22.58
Dec 30	3820	140	120	258	38	21.94
Dec 31	3812	130	117	246	37	21.21
Jan 2	3892				36	
Jan 3	3840				35	
Jan 6	3885				34	
Jan 7	3925				33	
Jan 8	3950				32	
Jan 9	3892				31	
Jan 10	3870				30	
Jan 13	3910				29	
Jan 14	3880				28	
Jan 15	3902				27	
Jan 16	3872				26	
Jan 17	3805				25	
Jan 20	3775				24	
Jan 21	3822				23	
Jan 22	3792				22	
Jan 23	3757				21	
Jan 24	3750				20	
Jan 27	3715				19	
Jan 28	3730				18	
Jan 29	3702				17	
Jan 30	3702				16	
Jan 31	3597				15	
Feb 3	3615				14	
Feb 4	3577				13	
Feb 5	3615				12	
Feb 6	3580				11	
Feb 7	3560				10	
Feb 10	3525				9	
Feb 11	3620				8	
Feb 12	3572				7	
Feb 13	3590				6	
Feb 14	3595				5	
Feb 18	3642				3	
Feb 19	3595				2	
Feb 20	3637				1	
Feb 21	3730	March 97 option expires				

LEGEND: *fp* = futures price, *max* = closest strike high option price, *min* = closest strike low option price, *s* = price corrected at-the-money-straddle, *td* = number of trading days till expiry, *iv* = implied volatility.

CORN

Calendar month	Year	Based on Option	Nearest strike	Implied volatility
JANUARY	1993	May	2157	13.05
FEBRUARY	1993	May	2210	13.85
MARCH	1993	Jul	2290	17.34
APRIL	1993	Jul	2350	19.30
MAY	1993	Jul	2332	19.89
JUNE	1993	Sep	2240	19.62
JULY	1993	Sep	2380	35.04
AUGUST	1993	Nov	2460	23.79
SEPTEMBER	1993	Mar	2333	16.25
OCTOBER	1993	Mar	2507	14.74
NOVEMBER	1993	Mar	2680	16.80
DECEMBER	1993	Mar	2857	16.62
JANUARY	1994	May	3100	19.50
FEBRUARY	1994	May	2956	17.64
MARCH	1994	Jul	2930	19.14
APRIL	1994	Jul	2760	20.16
MAY	1994	Jul	2717	22.17
JUNE	1994	Sep	2755	35.35
JULY	1994	Sep	2445	32.35
AUGUST	1994	Nov	2210	16.40
SEPTEMBER	1994	Mar	2232	14.59
OCTOBER	1994	Mar	2270	14.88
NOVEMBER	1994	Mar	2267	13.77
DECEMBER	1994	Mar	2230	12.36
JANUARY	1995	May	2350	13.58
FEBRUARY	1995	May	2380	13.24
MARCH	1995	Jul	2480	16.28
APRIL	1995	Jul	2590	18.02
MAY	1995	Jul	2580	23.97
JUNE	1995	Sep	2752	27.02
JULY	1995	Sep	2780	30.30
AUGUST	1995	Nov	2822	20.11
SEPTEMBER	1995	Mar	2942	17.43
OCTOBER	1995	Mar	3202	20.51
NOVEMBER	1995	Mar	3415	17.92
DECEMBER	1995	Mar	3370	15.35
JANUARY	1996	Mar	3732	20.23
FEBRUARY	1996	May	3705	18.50
MARCH	1996	May	3867	18.50
APRIL	1996	Jul	4035	22.06
MAY	1996	Jul	4662	34.85
JUNE	1996	Sep	3980	30.21
JULY	1996	Sep	4157	37.20
AUGUST	1996	Sep	3605	20.24
SEPTEMBER	1996	Nov	3415	28.46
OCTOBER	1996	Jan	2960	19.77
NOVEMBER	1996	Jan	2650	17.90
DECEMBER	1996	Mar	2657	16.67
JANUARY	1997	May	2610	16.07
FEBRUARY	1997	May	2670	15.97
MARCH	1997	Jul	2940	24.80
APRIL	1997	Jul	3140	26.16
MAY	1997	Jul	2967	25.70
JUNE	1997	Sep	2597	28.15
JULY	1997	Sep	2330	24.00
AUGUST	1997	Nov	2690	26.72
SEPTEMBER	1997	Mar	2722	24.33
OCTOBER	1997	Mar	2652	18.89
NOVEMBER	1997	Mar	2950	22.79
DECEMBER	1997	Mar	2820	17.42

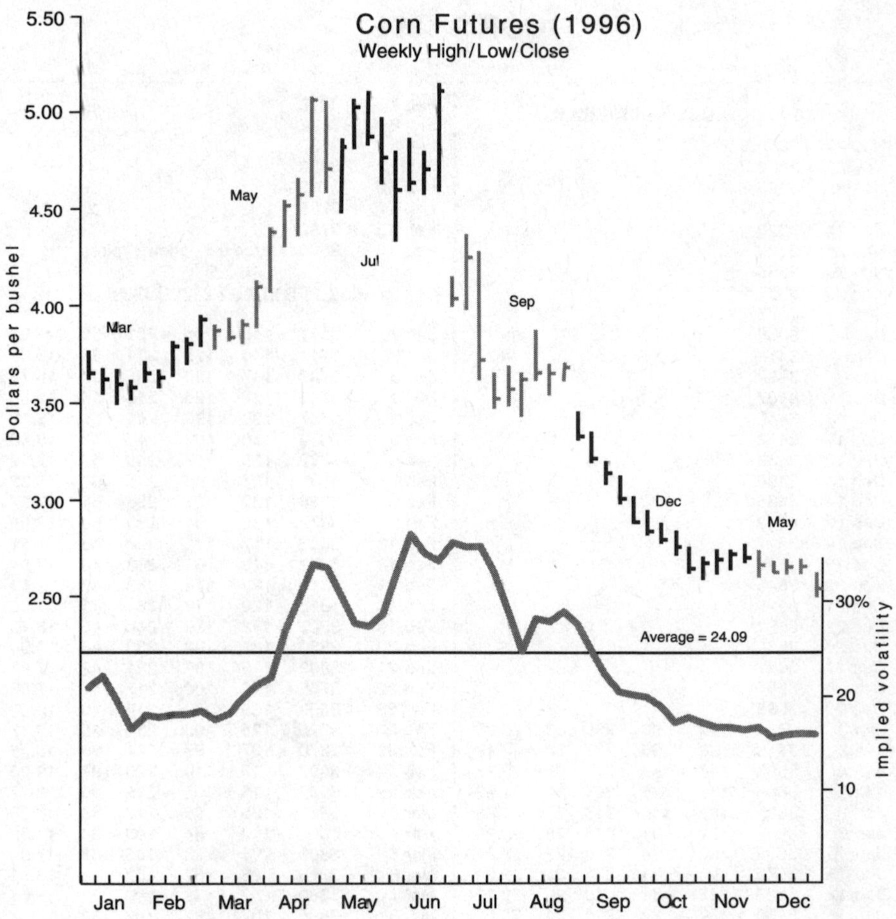
Corn Futures (1996)
Weekly High/Low/Close
Dollars per bushel
5.50
5.00
4.50
4.00
3.50
3.00
2.50
Mar
May
Jul
Sep
Dec
May
Average = 24.09
30%
20
10
Implied volatility
Jan
Feb
Mar
Apr
May
Jun
Jul
Aug
Sep
Oct
Nov
Dec

CORN 1996

	fp	max	min	s	td	iv
March option and Mar future						
Nov 20	3330					
Nov 21	3302					
Nov 22	3320					
Nov 24	3342					
Nov 27	3320					
Nov 28	3320					
Nov 29	3365					
Nov 30	3377					
Dec 1	3375					
Dec 4	3365					
Dec 5	3410					
Dec 6	3422					
Dec 7	3407					
Dec 8	3440					
Dec 11	3472					
Dec 12	3465					
Dec 13	3480					
Dec 14	3480					
Dec 15	3472					
Dec 18	3517					
Dec 19	3547					
Dec 20	3545					
Dec 21	3525					
Dec 22	3582					
Dec 26	3630					
Dec 27	3607					
Dec 28	3637					
Dec 29	3692					
Jan 2	3732	127	96	220	33	20.23
Jan 3	3740	136	95	227	32	21.13
Jan 4	3690	116	102	217	31	20.77
Jan 5	3665	131	96	224	30	21.92
Jan 8	3605	109	106	215	29	21.75
Jan 9	3667	132	97	226	28	22.86
Jan 10	3622	120	96	214	27	22.31
Jan 11	3575	116	91	205	26	22.04
Jan 12	3627	122	91	210	25	22.72
Jan 15	3650	137	84	215	24	23.61
Jan 16	3540	105	62	162	23	18.72
Jan 17	3512	82	71	152	22	18.06
Jan 18	3550	102	54	150	21	18.07
Jan 19	3607	72	67	139	20	16.77
Jan 22	3577	80	56	134	19	16.71
Jan 23	3607	67	60	126	18	16.08
Jan 24	3587	67	57	123	17	16.65
Jan 25	3562	85	42	122	16	17.10
Jan 26	3575	71	46	114	15	16.53
Jan 29	3637				14	
Jan 30	3677				13	
Jan 31	3690				12	
Feb 1	3665				11	
Feb 2	3667				10	
Feb 5	3615				9	
Feb 6	3635				8	
Feb 7	3610				7	
Feb 8	3592				6	
Feb 9	3630				5	
Feb 12	3650				4	
Feb 13	3715				3	
Feb 14	3785				2	
Feb 15	3782				1	
Feb 16	3800	March 96 option expires				
May option and May future						
Jan 29	3677	140	115	253	59	17.90
Jan 30	3717	140	125	264	58	18.63
Jan 31	3730	147	120	265	57	18.79
Feb 1	3705	132	125	256	56	18.50
Feb 2	3707	130	120	249	55	18.13
Feb 5	3652	150	102	247	54	18.43
Feb 6	3672	135	107	239	53	17.92
Feb 7	3650	137	95	228	52	17.32
Feb 8	3630	130	97	224	51	17.27
Feb 9	3672	132	104	233	50	17.98
Feb 12	3695	117	111	228	49	17.59
Feb 13	3752	140	97	233	48	17.91
Feb 14	3810	129	115	243	47	18.59
Feb 15	3812	120	112	231	46	17.90
Feb 16	3827	132	110	240	45	18.70
Feb 20	3830	131	102	230	43	18.34
Feb 21	3802	115	107	221	42	17.97
Feb 22	3785	116	102	217	41	17.89
Feb 23	3835	130	92	218	40	18.00
Feb 26	3875	128	95	220	39	18.17
Feb 27	3870	127	97	221	38	18.55
Feb 28	3892	116	110	226	37	19.05
Feb 29	3892	115	105	219	36	18.77
Mar 1	3867	125	90	212	35	18.50
Mar 4	3830	112	84	193	34	17.32
Mar 5	3800	94	92	186	33	17.03
Mar 6	3810	96	87	182	32	16.91
Mar 7	3880	106	86	190	31	17.61
Mar 8	3885	107	87	192	30	18.07
Mar 11	3895	91	97	188	29	17.97
Mar 12	3862	112	76	184	28	18.05
Mar 13	3892	96	90	186	27	18.35
Mar 14	3902	92	90	182	26	18.28
Mar 15	3832	105	75	177	25	18.49
Mar 18	3857	115	73	184	24	19.44
Mar 19	3855	115	70	180	23	19.50
Mar 20	3870	107	79	183	22	20.20
Mar 21	3877	105	82	185	21	20.81
Mar 22	3900	95	92	187	20	21.42
Mar 25	3935	109	77	183	19	21.33
Mar 26	3967	107	74	178	18	21.12
Mar 27	3992	91	85	176	17	21.33
Mar 28	3992	92	84	175	16	21.96
Mar 29	4090	89	76	164	15	20.69
Apr 1	4165				14	

LEGEND: *fp* = futures price, *max* = closest strike high option price, *min* = closest strike low option price, *s* = price corrected at-the-money-straddle, *td* = number of trading days till expiry, *iv* = implied volatility.

CORN 1996

	fp	max	min	s	td	iv
Apr 2	4143				13	
Apr 3	4242				12	
Apr 4	4265				11	
Apr 8	4357				9	
Apr 9	4350				8	
Apr 10	4445				7	
Apr 11	4445				6	
Apr 12	4510				5	
Apr 15	4555				4	
Apr 16	4445				3	
Apr 17	4485				2	
Apr 18	4605				1	
Apr 19	4580	May 96 option expires				

July option and July future

	fp	max	min	s	td	iv
Apr 1	4035	190	155	342	59	22.06
Apr 2	4013	197	147	339	58	22.21
Apr 3	4112	187	165	350	57	22.56
Apr 4	4135	210	155	360	56	23.26
Apr 8	4255	235	180	410	54	26.22
Apr 9	4210	202	192	393	53	25.66
Apr 10	4305	217	207	423	52	27.26
Apr 11	4310	235	220	454	51	29.48
Apr 12	4380	250	230	478	50	30.89
Apr 15	4420	245	220	463	49	29.92
Apr 16	4300	230	200	427	48	28.69
Apr 17	4297	230	225	455	47	30.86
Apr 18	4417	252	220	469	46	31.33
Apr 19	4382	242	230	471	45	32.05
Apr 22	4502	257	250	506	44	33.92
Apr 23	4605	265	255	519	43	34.39
Apr 24	4700	260	260	520	42	34.14
Apr 25	4820	300	260	557	41	36.07
Apr 26	4820	280	260	538	40	35.32
Apr 29	4700	270	250	518	39	35.32
Apr 30	4520	255	200	450	38	32.30
May 1	4662	265	232	494	37	34.85
May 2	4582	240	225	464	36	33.74
May 3	4530	235	200	432	35	32.24
May 6	4547	232	185	413	34	31.14
May 7	4627	225	195	417	33	31.41
May 8	4747	220	207	426	32	31.72
May 9	4835	220	190	407	31	30.27
May 10	4822	205	180	383	30	28.99
May 13	4922	205	177	380	29	28.64
May 14	4872	190	162	350	28	27.12
May 15	4875	185	165	348	27	27.50
May 16	4995	180	175	355	26	27.84
May 17	5045	197	155	348	25	27.61
May 20	5030	180	150	327	24	26.57
May 21	5012	170	155	324	23	26.94
May 22	4865	180	145	322	22	28.21
May 23	4932	175	145	317	21	28.08
May 24	4887	165	147	310	20	28.41
May 28	4785	155	135	288	18	28.40
May 29	4665	152	122	271	17	28.21
May 30	4727	152	125	275	16	29.05
May 31	4772	160	132	290	15	31.33
Jun 3	4652				14	
Jun 4	4472				13	
Jun 5	4350				12	
Jun 6	4470				11	
Jun 7	4590				10	
Jun 10	4710				9	
Jun 11	4710				8	
Jun 12	4775				7	
Jun 13	4767				6	
Jun 14	4647				5	
Jun 17	4595				4	
Jun 18	4715				3	
Jun 19	4735				2	
Jun 20	4740				1	
Jun 21	4700	July 96 option expires				

September option and September future

	fp	max	min	s	td	iv
Jun 3	3982	250	215	462	59	30.21
Jun 4	3802	242	237	479	58	33.06
Jun 5	3705	252	230	480	57	34.33
Jun 6	3802	255	245	499	56	35.09
Jun 7	3925	280	255	533	55	36.61
Jun 10	4050	320	275	591	54	39.72
Jun 11	4030	295	272	565	53	38.52
Jun 12	4050	295	260	552	52	37.80
Jun 13	3967	290	240	526	51	37.10
Jun 14	3855	265	225	487	50	35.70
Jun 17	3780	255	230	483	49	36.50
Jun 18	3900	250	245	495	48	36.61
Jun 19	3840	255	210	461	47	35.02
Jun 20	3820	232	217	448	46	34.56
Jun 21	3867	240	212	450	45	34.66
Jun 24	3895	227	225	452	44	34.98
Jun 25	3935	230	200	427	43	33.13
Jun 26	3887	214	210	424	42	33.64
Jun 27	3857	240	195	431	41	34.90
Jun 28	3977	260	207	462	40	36.75
Jul 1	4157	267	220	483	39	37.20
Jul 2	4055	250	210	456	38	36.52
Jul 3	4095	240	232	471	37	37.85
Jul 5	4025	230	210	438	35	36.82
Jul 8	4020	215	200	414	34	35.30
Jul 9	4067	227	190	414	33	35.42
Jul 10	4092	207	195	401	32	34.65
Jul 11	4212	240	200	436	31	37.22
Jul 12	4285	230	215	444	30	37.82
Jul 15	4165	225	190	412	29	36.73
Jul 16	4045	200	190	389	28	36.36
Jul 17	3865	210	165	371	27	36.94
Jul 18	3725	185	160	343	26	36.10
Jul 19	3675	170	142	310	25	33.69
Jul 22	3557	170	127	293	24	33.63

LEGEND: *fp* = futures price, *max* = closest strike high option price, *min* = closest strike low option price, *s* = price corrected at-the-money-straddle, *td* = number of trading days till expiry, *iv* = implied volatility.

CORN 1996

	fp	max	min	s	td	iv
Jul 23	3615	155	135	288	23	33.26
Jul 24	3580	157	134	289	22	34.42
Jul 25	3510	139	132	270	21	33.62
Jul 26	3500	125	125	250	20	31.94
Jul 29	3592	131	117	247	19	31.53
Jul 30	3577	130	112	240	18	31.69
Jul 31	3542	120	80	196	17	26.84
Aug 1	3605	102	95	196	16	27.24
Aug 2	3582	100	85	184	15	26.48
Aug 5	3482				14	
Aug 6	3460				13	
Aug 7	3447				12	
Aug 8	3530				11	
Aug 9	3630				10	
Aug 12	3750				9	
Aug 13	3730				8	
Aug 14	3777				7	
Aug 15	3755				6	
Aug 16	3675				5	
Aug 19	3640				4	
Aug 20	3622				3	
Aug 21	3662				2	
Aug 22	3675				1	
Aug 23	3655	September 96 option expires				

<u>December option and December future</u>

	fp	max	min	s	td	iv
Aug 5	3182	177	161	337	74	24.60
Aug 6	3195	167	165	332	73	24.31
Aug 7	3210	165	160	325	72	23.83
Aug 8	3285	182	162	342	71	24.73
Aug 9	3295	182	175	356	70	25.86
Aug 12	3415	226	190	413	69	29.11
Aug 13	3490	210	200	409	68	28.44
Aug 14	3490	216	210	426	67	29.79
Aug 15	3492	212	207	419	66	29.51
Aug 16	3430	211	180	388	65	28.08
Aug 19	3412	197	190	386	64	28.31
Aug 20	3377	200	180	378	63	28.23
Aug 21	3377	200	177	375	62	28.21
Aug 22	3385	192	180	371	61	28.07
Aug 23	3395	186	182	368	60	27.96
Aug 26	3477	207	186	391	59	29.30
Aug 27	3487	207	197	403	58	30.36
Aug 28	3427	207	180	385	57	29.74
Aug 29	3445	210	170	376	56	29.20
Aug 30	3437	205	165	366	55	28.75
Sep 3	3415	185	170	354	53	28.46
Sep 4	3335	182	142	320	52	26.64
Sep 5	3347	185	142	323	51	27.03
Sep 6	3325	170	147	315	50	26.80
Sep 9	3307	157	147	303	49	26.19
Sep 10	3342	175	135	306	48	26.46
Sep 11	3267	149	119	265	47	23.69
Sep 12	3300	137	134	271	46	24.19
Sep 13	3215	130	116	245	45	22.70
Sep 16	3145	140	97	233	44	22.32
Sep 17	3145	140	92	227	43	22.03
Sep 18	3155	145	100	241	42	23.53
Sep 19	3135	127	97	221	41	22.04
Sep 20	3142	131	87	214	40	21.50
Sep 23	3132	122	87	206	39	21.03
Sep 24	3105	101	97	198	38	20.65
Sep 25	3122	105	86	189	37	19.94
Sep 26	3060	112	72	180	36	19.60
Sep 27	3032	107	77	181	35	20.20
Sep 30	2967	106	71	174	34	20.06
Oct 1	2960	105	67	168	33	19.77
Oct 2	2927	100	71	168	32	20.32
Oct 3	2920	91	72	161	31	19.84
Oct 4	2895	85	80	165	30	20.76
Oct 7	2927	92	65	154	29	19.59
Oct 8	2965	97	61	154	28	19.67
Oct 9	2937	97	60	153	27	20.07
Oct 10	2900	88	62	147	26	19.95
Oct 11	2837	87	54	138	25	19.39
Oct 14	2865	87	52	135	24	19.27
Oct 15	2865	84	54	135	23	19.64
Oct 16	2832	80	47	123	22	18.58
Oct 17	2832	77	46	120	21	18.44
Oct 18	2802	59	55	114	20	18.14
Oct 21	2790				19	
Oct 22	2795				18	
Oct 23	2827				17	
Oct 24	2780				16	
Oct 25	2752				15	
Oct 28	2752				14	
Oct 29	2745				13	
Oct 30	2702				12	
Oct 31	2660				11	
Nov 1	2630				10	
Nov 4	2617				9	
Nov 5	2585				8	
Nov 6	2600				7	
Nov 7	2645				6	
Nov 8	2675				5	
Nov 11	2682				4	
Nov 12	2680				3	
Nov 13	2717				2	
Nov 14	2712				1	
Nov 15	2695	December 96 option expires				

<u>March option and March future</u>

	fp	max	min	s	td	iv
Oct 21	2810	134	92	222	88	16.83
Oct 22	2815	135	92	223	87	16.97
Oct 23	2847	122	105	226	86	17.08
Oct 24	2800	120	97	215	85	16.65
Oct 25	2772	117	106	222	84	17.48
Oct 28	2772	117	110	226	83	17.93
Oct 29	2765	115	110	225	82	17.94

LEGEND: *fp* = futures price, *max* = closest strike high option price, *min* = closest strike low option price, *s* = price corrected at-the-money-straddle, *td* = number of trading days till expiry, *iv* = implied volatility.

CORN 1996

	fp	max	min	s	td	iv
Oct 30	2722	127	95	219	81	17.88
Oct 31	2680	135	77	206	80	17.16
Nov 1	2650	107	104	211	79	17.90
Nov 4	2637	115	94	207	78	17.79
Nov 5	2605	117	90	205	77	17.89
Nov 6	2620	112	85	194	76	17.03
Nov 7	2665	107	79	183	75	15.89
Nov 8	2695	125	71	190	74	16.39
Nov 11	2717	122	74	191	73	16.45
Nov 12	2705	119	77	192	72	16.71
Nov 13	2735	116	80	192	71	16.70
Nov 14	2735	112	82	191	70	16.71
Nov 15	2712	105	90	194	69	17.20
Nov 18	2692	97	94	191	68	17.19
Nov 19	2677	104	80	182	67	16.59
Nov 20	2715	100	80	178	66	16.16
Nov 21	2725	102	80	180	65	16.39
Nov 22	2725	105	77	179	64	16.45
Nov 25	2747	117	71	183	63	16.80
Nov 26	2742	110	70	176	62	16.29
Nov 27	2735	105	70	172	61	16.06
Nov 29	2710	92	82	173	59	16.64
Dec 2	2657	107	66	169	58	16.67
Dec 3	2630	99	70	166	57	16.74
Dec 4	2632	99	69	165	56	16.76
Dec 5	2670	99	71	167	55	16.90
Dec 6	2660	102	62	160	54	16.35
Dec 9	2645	101	55	151	53	15.66
Dec 10	2637	95	57	148	52	15.56
Dec 11	2645	99	52	146	51	15.41
Dec 12	2642	97	52	144	50	15.40
Dec 13	2627	85	57	139	49	15.14
Dec 16	2635	90	55	141	48	15.48
Dec 17	2655	97	55	147	47	16.19
Dec 18	2647	100	50	144	46	16.04
Dec 19	2660	94	57	147	45	16.49
Dec 20	2667	90	57	144	44	16.23
Dec 23	2665	90	52	138	43	15.78
Dec 24	2667	85	54	136	42	15.71
Dec 26	2670	84	54	135	40	15.98
Dec 27	2645	91	47	133	39	16.08
Dec 30	2582	75	57	130	38	16.38
Dec 31	2582	72	55	125	37	15.97
Jan 2	2585				36	
Jan 3	2565				35	
Jan 6	2570				34	
Jan 7	2582				33	
Jan 8	2592				32	
Jan 9	2582				31	
Jan 10	2655				30	
Jan 13	2672				29	
Jan 14	2707				28	
Jan 15	2737				27	
Jan 16	2735				26	
Jan 17	2732				25	
Jan 20	2717				24	
Jan 21	2710				23	
Jan 22	2705				22	
Jan 23	2702				21	
Jan 24	2727				20	
Jan 27	2750				19	
Jan 28	2747				18	
Jan 29	2750				17	
Jan 30	2737				16	
Jan 31	2702				15	
Feb 3	2695				14	
Feb 4	2705				13	
Feb 5	2725				12	
Feb 6	2687				11	
Feb 7	2710				10	
Feb 10	2720				9	
Feb 11	2725				8	
Feb 12	2737				7	
Feb 13	2745				6	
Feb 14	2740				5	
Feb 18	2827				3	
Feb 19	2835				2	
Feb 20	2870				1	
Feb 21	2917	March 97 option expires				

LEGEND: *fp* = futures price, *max* = closest strike high option price, *min* = closest strike low option price, *s* = price corrected at-the-money-straddle, *td* = number of trading days till expiry, *iv* = implied volatility.

CATTLE

Calendar month	Year	Based on Option	Nearest strike	Implied volatility
JANUARY	1993	Apr	7690	10.12
FEBRUARY	1993	Apr	7730	11.73
MARCH	1993	Jun	7437	10.54
APRIL	1993	Jun	7590	10.69
MAY	1993	Aug	7392	9.61
JUNE	1993	Aug	7355	10.16
JULY	1993	Oct	7547	10.17
AUGUST	1993	Oct	7462	11.95
SEPTEMBER	1993	Dec	7555	10.62
OCTOBER	1993	Dec	7407	11.66
NOVEMBER	1993	Feb	7480	11.76
DECEMBER	1993	Feb	7270	12.14
JANUARY	1994	Apr	7522	11.27
FEBRUARY	1994	Apr	7522	11.17
MARCH	1994	Jun	7460	9.65
APRIL	1994	Jun	7472	7.85
MAY	1994	Aug	6920	10.27
JUNE	1994	Aug	6425	19.43
JULY	1994	Oct	6825	18.12
AUGUST	1994	Oct	7322	14.62
SEPTEMBER	1994	Dec	6967	14.66
OCTOBER	1994	Dec	6890	13.97
NOVEMBER	1994	Feb	6875	12.98
DECEMBER	1994	Feb	6787	14.70
JANUARY	1995	Apr	7352	12.49
FEBRUARY	1995	Apr	7337	11.86
MARCH	1995	Jun	6717	11.56
APRIL	1995	Jun	6265	19.45
MAY	1995	Aug	6782	15.16
JUNE	1995	Aug	6057	18.07
JULY	1995	Oct	6367	17.25
AUGUST	1995	Oct	6557	14.63
SEPTEMBER	1995	Dec	6587	12.56
OCTOBER	1995	Dec	6572	12.36
NOVEMBER	1995	Feb	6762	11.60
DECEMBER	1995	Feb	6882	13.83
JANUARY	1996	Apr	6600	13.20
FEBRUARY	1996	Apr	6390	15.17
MARCH	1996	Jun	6275	15.48
APRIL	1996	Jun	6310	16.26
MAY	1996	Aug	5825	25.30
JUNE	1996	Aug	6522	16.88
JULY	1996	Oct	6572	14.94
AUGUST	1996	Oct	6937	14.22
SEPTEMBER	1996	Dec	7172	11.94
OCTOBER	1996	Dec	6807	12.15
NOVEMBER	1996	Feb	6712	13.14
DECEMBER	1996	Feb	6482	15.78
JANUARY	1997	Apr	6532	14.70
FEBRUARY	1997	Apr	6590	12.77
MARCH	1997	Jun	6550	12.84
APRIL	1997	Jun	6482	12.82
MAY	1997	Aug	6520	11.82
JUNE	1997	Aug	6430	12.06
JULY	1997	Oct	6787	11.09
AUGUST	1997	Oct	7052	11.86
SEPTEMBER	1997	Dec	6925	12.74
OCTOBER	1997	Dec	6625	14.69
NOVEMBER	1997	Feb	6885	12.99
DECEMBER	1997	Feb	6765	12.74

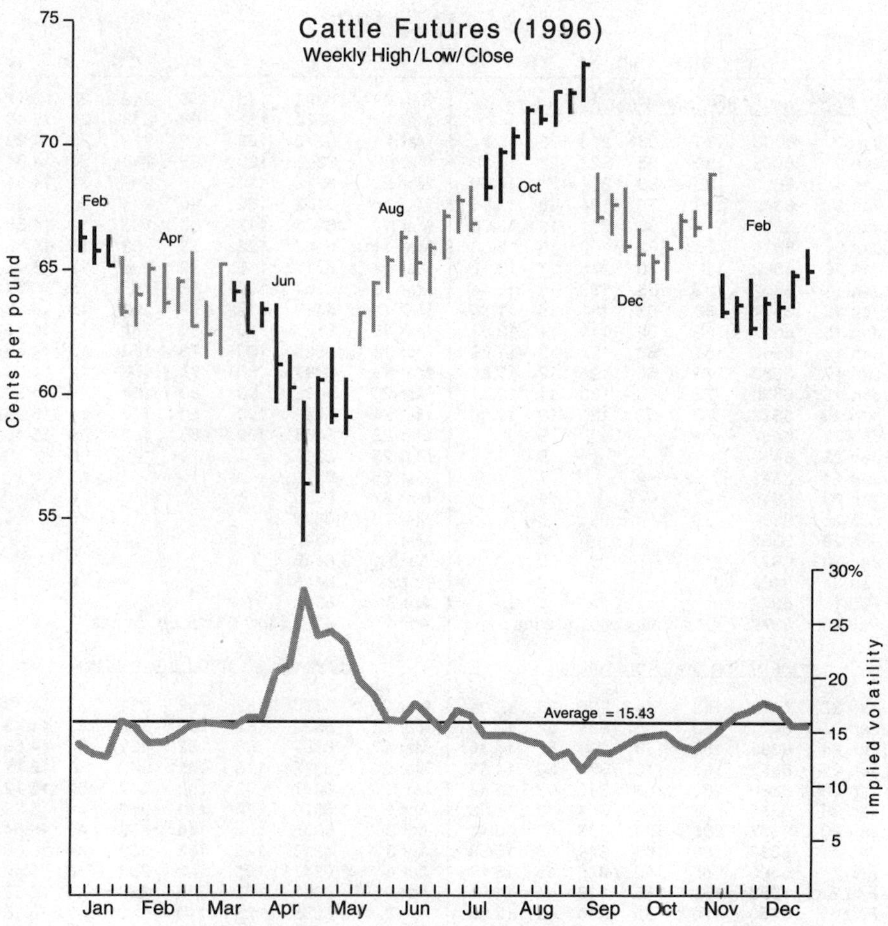
Cattle Futures (1996)
Weekly High/Low/Close
Cents per pound
75
70
65
60
55
Feb
Apr
Jun
Aug
Oct
Dec
Feb
Average = 15.43
30%
25
20
15
10
5
Implied volatility
Jan
Feb
Mar
Apr
May
Jun
Jul
Aug
Sep
Oct
Nov
Dec

CATTLE 1996

<u>February option and February future</u>

	fp	max	min	s	td	iv
Jan 2	6600	105	105	210	23	13.27
Jan 3	6665	130	95	222	22	14.18
Jan 4	6637	128	90	214	21	14.09
Jan 5	6642	120	78	194	20	13.04
Jan 8	6627	115	88	201	19	13.88
Jan 9	6605	98	92	190	18	13.53
Jan 10	6542	112	70	178	17	13.17
Jan 11	6562	102	65	163	16	12.44
Jan 12	6577	88	65	151	15	11.84
Jan 15	6627	90	62	149	14	12.04
Jan 16	6567	85	52	134	13	11.28
Jan 17	6580	75	55	128	12	11.24
Jan 18	6520	72	62	133	11	12.31
Jan 19	6517	70	52	120	10	11.68
Jan 22	6457				9	
Jan 23	6410				8	
Jan 24	6345				7	
Jan 25	6340				6	
Jan 26	6305				5	
Jan 29	6387				4	
Jan 30	6327				3	
Jan 31	6402				2	
Feb 1	6375				1	
Feb 2	6377	February 96 option expires				

<u>April option and April future</u>

	fp	max	min	s	td	iv
Jan 22	6495	145	140	285	53	12.04
Jan 23	6475	150	135	284	52	12.15
Jan 24	6395	155	150	305	51	13.34
Jan 25	6352	190	142	328	50	14.58
Jan 26	6320	182	162	342	49	15.47
Jan 29	6380	188	168	354	48	16.03
Jan 30	6337	200	160	356	47	16.41
Jan 31	6385	180	165	344	46	15.88
Feb 1	6390	168	158	325	45	15.17
Feb 2	6392	162	155	316	44	14.93
Feb 5	6460	170	130	296	43	13.99
Feb 6	6417	145	128	272	42	13.06
Feb 7	6367	150	118	265	41	13.00
Feb 8	6472	155	125	277	40	13.55
Feb 9	6507	140	132	271	39	13.35
Feb 12	6525	142	118	258	38	12.82
Feb 13	6482	140	122	260	37	13.21
Feb 14	6345	150	105	251	36	13.17
Feb 15	6357	148	105	249	35	13.23
Feb 16	6355	145	100	241	34	12.99
Feb 20	6357	142	100	238	32	13.23
Feb 21	6377	132	110	240	31	13.52
Feb 22	6425	138	112	248	30	14.08
Feb 23	6445	142	98	236	29	13.58
Feb 26	6577	132	110	240	28	13.80
Feb 27	6502	125	122	247	27	14.61
Feb 28	6465	142	108	247	26	14.98
Feb 29	6392	125	118	242	25	15.17
Mar 1	6275	132	108	238	24	15.48
Mar 4	6272	122	95	215	23	14.26
Mar 5	6325	120	95	213	22	14.34
Mar 6	6212	110	98	207	21	14.54
Mar 7	6152	130	80	205	20	14.88
Mar 8	6225	112	88	198	19	14.58
Mar 11	6162	122	85	203	18	15.56
Mar 12	6217	110	92	200	17	15.64
Mar 13	6367	100	95	195	16	15.28
Mar 14	6440	117	78	191	15	15.32
Mar 15	6527	110	80	187	14	15.33
Mar 18	6525	100	75	173	13	14.68
Mar 19	6497	80	78	158	12	14.03
Mar 20	6462	98	60	154	11	14.37
Mar 21	6460	100	60	156	10	15.25
Mar 22	6465	100	55	150	9	15.46
Mar 25	6350				8	
Mar 26	6370				7	
Mar 27	6460				6	
Mar 28	6395				5	
Mar 29	6342				4	
Apr 1	6422				3	
Apr 2	6415				2	
Apr 3	6380				1	
Apr 4	6377	April 96 option expires				

<u>June option andJune future</u>

	fp	max	min	s	td	iv
Mar 25	6370	182	152	331	54	14.16
Mar 26	6372	182	155	335	53	14.43
Mar 27	6437	190	152	339	52	14.59
Mar 28	6312	178	165	342	51	15.17
Mar 29	6247	202	150	347	50	15.72
Apr 1	6310	185	175	359	49	16.26
Apr 2	6335	195	160	352	48	16.04
Apr 3	6310	175	165	339	47	15.68
Apr 4	6347	195	142	332	46	15.42
Apr 8	6340	185	145	326	44	15.52
Apr 9	6265	175	140	312	43	15.18
Apr 10	6122	202	180	380	42	19.16
Apr 11	6100	200	200	400	41	20.48
Apr 12	6127	205	178	381	40	19.65
Apr 15	6135	200	165	362	39	18.89
Apr 16	6002	192	190	382	38	20.64
Apr 17	6027	200	170	367	37	20.04
Apr 18	6020	180	160	338	36	18.73
Apr 19	6032	190	158	345	35	19.35
Apr 22	5882	192	162	351	34	20.49
Apr 23	5737	210	182	390	33	23.64
Apr 24	5630	225	195	417	32	26.21
Apr 25	5480	232	198	427	31	27.99
Apr 26	5630	240	200	436	30	28.31
Apr 29	5757	235	192	423	29	27.30
Apr 30	5735	222	188	407	28	26.83
May 1	5825	205	180	383	27	25.30

LEGEND: *fp* = futures price, *max* = closest strike high option price, *min* = closest strike low option price, *s* = price corrected at-the-money-straddle, *td* = number of trading days till expiry, *iv* = implied volatility.

CATTLE 1996

	fp	max	min	s	td	iv
May 1	5825	205	180	383	27	25.30
May 2	5975	210	160	365	26	23.99
May 3	6070	190	160	347	25	22.89
May 6	6080	178	155	331	24	22.23
May 7	6112	162	150	311	23	21.22
May 8	5962	182	145	324	22	23.15
May 9	5950	190	140	325	21	23.86
May 10	5925	172	148	318	20	24.00
May 13	5987	160	148	307	19	23.53
May 14	6045	172	128	296	18	23.07
May 15	6032	160	128	285	17	22.93
May 16	5882	148	130	276	16	23.50
May 17	5917	145	128	272	15	23.70
May 20	5887	125	112	236	14	21.42
May 21	5870	125	95	217	13	20.53
May 22	5890	107	98	204	12	20.02
May 23	5987	100	88	187	11	18.83
May 24	6050	115	65	174	10	18.24
May 28	6057				8	
May 29	6082				7	
May 30	6050				6	
May 31	6167				5	
Jun 3	6232				4	
Jun 4	6237				3	
Jun 5	6220				2	
Jun 6	6285				1	
Jun 7	6310	June 1996 option expires				

<u>August option and August future</u>

	fp	max	min	s	td	iv
May 28	6317	220	202	420	48	19.22
May 29	6392	208	200	407	47	18.59
May 30	6375	215	190	403	46	18.64
May 31	6452	205	172	374	45	17.29
Jun 3	6522	195	172	365	44	16.88
Jun 4	6515	195	180	374	43	17.50
Jun 5	6510	182	172	353	42	16.74
Jun 6	6537	188	162	348	41	16.62
Jun 7	6537	192	155	344	40	16.63
Jun 10	6605	150	145	295	39	14.28
Jun 11	6667	168	100	261	38	12.69
Jun 12	6610	138	128	265	37	13.19
Jun 13	6575	152	128	278	36	14.09
Jun 14	6632	170	138	305	35	15.55
Jun 17	6597	155	158	313	34	16.29
Jun 18	6517	170	152	320	33	17.12
Jun 19	6515	165	150	314	32	17.03
Jun 20	6520	170	150	318	31	17.54
Jun 21	6527	165	138	301	30	16.82
Jun 24	6452	167	120	283	29	16.26
Jun 25	6420	152	132	282	28	16.62
Jun 26	6527	150	122	270	27	15.89
Jun 27	6497	132	130	262	26	15.81
Jun 28	6582	145	128	272	25	16.50
Jul 1	6572	135	108	241	24	14.94
Jul 2	6630	137	108	242	23	15.25
Jul 3	6722	110	108	218	20	13.87
Jul 5	6682	120	98	216	19	14.37
Jul 8	6707	117	100	216	18	14.80
Jul 9	6765	100	92	191	17	13.45
Jul 10	6690	112	78	187	16	13.39
Jul 11	6790	118	108	225	15	16.83
Jul 12	6772	118	108	225	14	17.12
Jul 15	6792	122	95	215	13	16.93
Jul 16	6790	108	100	207	12	16.93
Jul 17	6695	105	95	199	11	16.93
Jul 18	6682	98	95	193	10	17.36
Jul 19	6627	100	82	180	9	17.08
Jul 22	6592				8	
Jul 23	6575				7	
Jul 24	6622				6	
Jul 25	6537				5	
Jul 26	6540				4	
Jul 29	6467				3	
Jul 30	6527				2	
Jul 31	6662				1	
Aug 1	6690	August 96 option expires				

<u>October option and October future</u>

	fp	max	min	s	td	iv
Jul 22	6852	185	165	348	54	13.83
Jul 23	6880	182	162	342	53	13.67
Jul 24	6852	198	148	341	52	13.82
Jul 25	6915	178	162	339	51	13.72
Jul 26	6840	190	150	336	50	13.91
Jul 29	6882	182	158	338	49	14.03
Jul 30	6810	175	165	339	48	14.38
Jul 31	6855	188	142	326	47	13.86
Aug 1	6937	188	150	335	46	14.22
Aug 2	6985	170	155	324	45	13.82
Aug 5	6960	195	135	324	44	14.04
Aug 6	7055	180	145	322	43	13.91
Aug 7	7005	162	158	320	42	14.08
Aug 8	7060	187	128	309	41	13.68
Aug 9	7040	172	132	300	40	13.49
Aug 12	7000	170	150	318	39	14.56
Aug 13	6997	152	150	302	38	14.00
Aug 14	6967	162	130	289	37	13.64
Aug 15	7002	145	142	287	36	13.65
Aug 16	7145	167	122	285	35	13.47
Aug 19	7137	160	122	278	34	13.38
Aug 20	7127	152	125	275	33	13.41
Aug 21	7112	142	130	271	32	13.47
Aug 22	7117	145	128	272	31	13.71
Aug 23	7100	145	125	268	30	13.80
Aug 26	7117	132	115	246	29	12.81
Aug 27	7172	132	105	235	28	12.36
Aug 28	7150	142	92	229	27	12.32
Aug 29	7187	115	102	216	26	11.78
Aug 30	7222	110	100	209	25	11.58
Sep 3	7172	118	90	205	23	11.94
Sep 4	7172	118	90	205	22	12.21

LEGEND: *fp* = futures price, *max* = closest strike high option price, *min* = closest strike low option price, *s* = price corrected at-the-money-straddle, *td* = number of trading days till expiry, *iv* = implied volatility.

CATTLE 1996

	fp	max	min	s	td	iv
Sep 4	7172	118	90	205	22	12.21
Sep 5	7135	125	90	212	21	12.95
Sep 6	7217	110	92	200	20	12.42
Sep 9	7200	100	100	200	19	12.75
Sep 10	7232	110	78	185	18	12.05
Sep 11	7272	102	75	174	17	11.64
Sep 12	7317	90	72	160	16	10.96
Sep 13	7327	90	62	149	15	10.52
Sep 16	7295	72	68	140	14	10.23
Sep 17	7300	70	70	140	13	10.64
Sep 18	7282	62	82	145	12	11.53
Sep 19	7250	102	52	148	11	12.32
Sep 20	7195	80	75	155	10	13.59
Sep 23	7160				9	
Sep 24	7272				8	
Sep 25	7317				7	
Sep 26	7310				6	
Sep 27	7335				5	
Sep 30	7332				4	
Oct 1	7362				3	
Oct 2	7350				2	
Oct 3	7212				1	
Oct 4	7192	October 96 option expires				

<u>December option and December future</u>

	fp	max	min	s	td	iv
Sep 23	6685	162	148	309	54	12.57
Sep 24	6762	172	135	304	53	12.34
Sep 25	6750	180	130	305	52	12.54
Sep 26	6750	165	135	297	51	12.34
Sep 27	6770	165	135	297	50	12.42
Sep 30	6815	155	140	294	49	12.31
Oct 1	6807	147	140	286	48	12.15
Oct 2	6780	152	132	282	47	12.15
Oct 3	6630	168	138	303	46	13.49
Oct 4	6602	152	150	302	45	13.63
Oct 7	6640	165	125	286	44	13.00
Oct 8	6620	152	132	282	43	13.01
Oct 9	6562	162	125	284	42	13.34
Oct 10	6572	160	132	290	41	13.76
Oct 11	6562	162	125	284	40	13.67
Oct 14	6462	162	125	284	39	14.06
Oct 15	6470	158	128	283	38	14.21
Oct 16	6527	155	122	274	37	13.80
Oct 17	6540	158	128	283	36	14.44
Oct 18	6535	138	128	265	35	13.72
Oct 21	6490	138	128	265	34	14.01
Oct 22	6510	135	125	259	33	13.86
Oct 23	6595	138	132	270	32	14.45
Oct 24	6580	145	122	265	31	14.47
Oct 25	6580	135	115	248	30	13.78
Oct 28	6667	142	110	249	29	13.87
Oct 29	6667	142	110	249	28	14.12
Oct 30	6685	125	110	234	27	13.46
Oct 31	6667	130	98	225	26	13.24
Nov 1	6712	125	98	221	25	13.14

	fp	max	min	s	td	iv
Nov 4	6722	120	98	216	24	13.12
Nov 5	6702	102	100	202	23	12.56
Nov 6	6707	102	92	193	22	12.28
Nov 7	6657	118	75	189	21	12.36
Nov 8	6672	109	80	186	20	12.48
Nov 11	6752	120	72	187	19	12.70
Nov 12	6767	115	82	194	18	13.50
Nov 13	6780	105	85	188	17	13.47
Nov 14	6857	108	75	180	16	13.11
Nov 15	6890	100	90	189	15	14.18
Nov 18	6807	90	82	171	14	13.45
Nov 19	6775	95	70	163	13	13.32
Nov 20	6727	90	62	149	12	12.81
Nov 21	6652	102	55	152	11	13.75
Nov 22	6697	80	78	158	10	14.91
Nov 25	6582				9	
Nov 26	6610				8	
Nov 27	6680				7	
Nov 29	6702				5	
Dec 2	6715				4	
Dec 3	6692				3	
Dec 4	6590				2	
Dec 5	6642				1	
Dec 6	6542	December 96 option expires				

<u>February option and February future</u>

	fp	max	min	s	td	iv
Nov 25	6262	200	162	359	53	15.73
Nov 26	6292	188	180	367	52	16.19
Nov 27	6362	200	162	359	51	15.79
Nov 29	6367	195	162	354	49	15.89
Dec 2	6422	188	165	351	48	15.78
Dec 3	6387	175	162	336	47	15.34
Dec 4	6290	175	165	339	46	15.90
Dec 5	6357	192	150	338	45	15.86
Dec 6	6267	188	155	340	44	16.36
Dec 9	6290	175	165	339	43	16.45
Dec 10	6275	182	158	338	42	16.62
Dec 11	6292	172	165	336	41	16.70
Dec 12	6370	188	158	343	40	17.05
Dec 13	6387	180	168	347	39	17.40
Dec 16	6397	168	165	333	38	16.88
Dec 17	6325	178	152	328	37	17.04
Dec 18	6342	178	148	323	36	17.00
Dec 19	6340	180	140	316	35	16.87
Dec 20	6357	180	138	314	34	16.95
Dec 23	6480	160	140	298	33	16.03
Dec 24	6495	147	142	289	32	15.71
Dec 26	6502	132	130	262	30	14.70
Dec 27	6480	140	130	269	29	15.43
Dec 30	6587	130	118	247	28	14.17
Dec 31	6497	125	122	247	27	14.62
Jan 2	6480				26	
Jan 3	6502				25	
Jan 6	6535				24	
Jan 7	6432				23	

LEGEND: *fp* = futures price, *max* = closest strike high option price, *min* = closest strike low option price, *s* = price corrected at-the-money-straddle, *td* = number of trading days till expiry, *iv* = implied volatility.

CATTLE 1996

	fp	max	min	s	td	iv	fp	max	min	s	td	iv
Jan 8	6427				22							
Jan 9	6492				21							
Jan 10	6562				20							
Jan 13	6557				19							
Jan 14	6597				18							
Jan 15	6585				17							
Jan 16	6572				16							
Jan 17	6560				15							
Jan 20	6615				14							
Jan 21	6585				13							
Jan 22	6537				12							
Jan 23	6489				11							
Jan 24	6465				10							
Jan 27	6497				9							
Jan 28	6457				8							
Jan 29	6397				7							
Jan 30	6440				6							
Jan 31	6475				5							
Feb 3	6382				4							
Feb 4	6372				3							
Feb 5	6375				2							
Feb 6	6397				1							
Feb 7	6355	February 97 option expires										

LEGEND: *fp* = futures price, *max* = closest strike high option price, *min* = closest strike low option price, *s* = price corrected at-the-money-straddle, *td* = number of trading days till expiry, *iv* = implied volatility.

COCOA

Calendar month	Year	Based on Option	Nearest strike	Implied volatility
JANUARY	1993	May	*950*	27.94
FEBRUARY	1993	May	*950*	28.46
MARCH	1993	Jul	*950*	34.28
APRIL	1993	Jul	*950*	33.67
MAY	1993	Jul	*950*	33.04
JUNE	1993	Sep	*900*	30.76
JULY	1993	Sep	*950*	37.70
AUGUST	1993	Dec	*1000*	32.35
SEPTEMBER	1993	Dec	*1100*	32.51
OCTOBER	1993	Mar	*1250*	35.54
NOVEMBER	1993	Mar	*1150*	32.28
DECEMBER	1993	Mar	*1300*	31.21
JANUARY	1994	May	*1200*	28.34
FEBRUARY	1994	May	*1100*	29.35
MARCH	1994	Jul	*1200*	29.94
APRIL	1994	Jul	*1150*	27.39
MAY	1994	Jul	*1150*	30.16
JUNE	1994	Sep	*1400*	38.95
JULY	1994	Sep	*1300*	37.98
AUGUST	1994	Dec	*1500*	37.69
SEPTEMBER	1994	Dec	*1350*	32.15
OCTOBER	1994	Dec	*1300*	28.22
NOVEMBER	1994	Jan	*1350*	26.78
DECEMBER	1994	Mar	*1250*	29.62
JANUARY	1995	Mar	*1350*	31.05
FEBRUARY	1995	May	*1400*	31.56
MARCH	1995	May	*1450*	31.03
APRIL	1995	Jul	*1350*	27.28
MAY	1995	Jul	*1400*	24.97
JUNE	1995	Sep	*1400*	27.25
JULY	1995	Sep	*1300*	25.94
AUGUST	1995	Dec	*1300*	26.18
SEPTEMBER	1995	Dec	*1350*	25.84
OCTOBER	1995	Mar	*1300*	22.37
NOVEMBER	1995	Mar	*1350*	21.27
DECEMBER	1995	Mar	*1300*	18.78
JANUARY	1996	Mar	*1250*	20.07
FEBRUARY	1996	May	*1300*	19.85
MARCH	1996	May	*1250*	17.19
APRIL	1996	Jul	*1350*	20.58
MAY	1996	Jul	*1400*	25.22
JUNE	1996	Sep	*1400*	24.03
JULY	1996	Sep	*1450*	24.07
AUGUST	1996	Dec	*1400*	21.38
SEPTEMBER	1996	Dec	*1350*	19.41
OCTOBER	1996	Dec	*1350*	16.90
NOVEMBER	1996	Mar	*1400*	15.52
DECEMBER	1996	Mar	*1400*	17.53
JANUARY	1997	May	*1400*	16.76
FEBRUARY	1997	May	*1350*	15.84
MARCH	1997	Jul	*1300*	20.08
APRIL	1997	Jul	*1500*	31.09
MAY	1997	Jul	*1400*	22.84
JUNE	1997	Sep	*1500*	26.03
JULY	1997	Sep	*1700*	33.35
AUGUST	1997	Dec	*1550*	30.25
SEPTEMBER	1997	Dec	*1700*	33.12
OCTOBER	1997	Mar	*1700*	28.42
NOVEMBER	1997	Mar	*1600*	26.57
DECEMBER	1997	Mar	*1550*	21.84

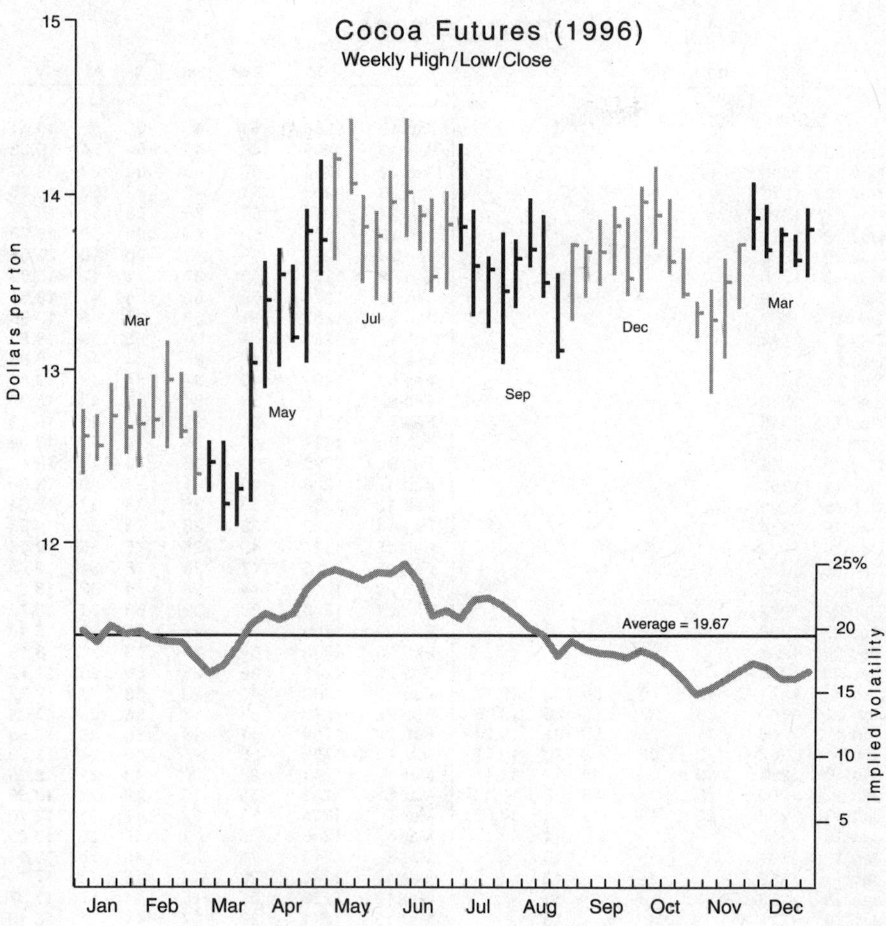
Cocoa Futures (1996)
Weekly High/Low/Close
Dollars per ton
15
14
13
12
Mar
May
Jul
Sep
Dec
Mar
Average = 19.67
25%
20
15
10
5
Implied volatility
Jan
Feb
Mar
Apr
May
Jun
Jul
Aug
Sep
Oct
Nov
Dec

COCOA 1996

March option and Mar future

	fp	max	min	s	td	iv
Nov 20	1371					
Nov 21	1359					
Nov 22	1373					
Nov 27	1320					
Nov 28	1321					
Nov 29	1330					
Nov 30	1308					
Dec 1	1299					
Dec 4	1307					
Dec 5	1312					
Dec 6	1306					
Dec 7	1307					
Dec 8	1320					
Dec 11	1315					
Dec 12	1310					
Dec 13	1299					
Dec 14	1307					
Dec 15	1299					
Dec 18	1274					
Dec 19	1274					
Dec 20	1271					
Dec 21	1262					
Dec 22	1273					
Dec 27	1259					
Dec 28	1253					
Dec 29	1258					
Jan 2	1271	41	20	58	23	19.17
Jan 3	1248	29	27	56	22	19.08
Jan 4	1256	31	25	55	21	19.27
Jan 5	1262	32	22	53	20	18.79
Jan 10	1261	30	19	48	17	18.41
Jan 11	1250	23	23	46	16	18.40
Jan 12	1256	25	19	43	15	17.86
Jan 15	1286				14	
Jan 16	1291				13	
Jan 17	1282				12	
Jan 18	1263				11	
Jan 19	1274				10	
Jan 22	1281				9	
Jan 23	1268				8	
Jan 24	1259				7	
Jan 25	1268				6	
Jan 26	1266				5	
Jan 29	1254				4	
Jan 30	1249				3	
Jan 31	1242				2	
Feb 1	1260				1	
Feb 2	1268	March 96 option expires				

May option and May future

	fp	max	min	s	td	iv
Jan 15	1311	55	54	109	58	21.82
Jan 16	1316	58	50	107	57	21.60
Jan 17	1307	54	49	103	56	20.98
Jan 18	1288	54	40	93	55	19.41
Jan 19	1299	49	45	94	54	19.62
Jan 22	1306	47	45	92	53	19.32
Jan 23	1293	51	42	92	52	19.78
Jan 24	1284	54	36	88	51	19.24
Jan 25	1293	50	41	90	50	19.73
Jan 26	1291	49	42	90	49	20.01
Jan 29	1279	53	37	88	48	19.96
Jan 30	1274	55	33	86	47	19.61
Jan 31	1267	51	35	84	46	19.65
Feb 1	1285	51	36	86	45	19.85
Feb 2	1293	47	38	84	44	19.63
Feb 5	1291	48	37	84	43	19.84
Feb 6	1312	50	34	82	42	19.39
Feb 7	1291	44	36	79	41	19.18
Feb 8	1297	40	38	78	40	18.98
Feb 9	1296	40	35	75	39	18.43
Feb 12	1288	45	31	75	38	18.80
Feb 13	1299	39	35	74	37	18.64
Feb 14	1329	53	28	78	36	19.59
Feb 15	1325	49	28	75	35	19.06
Feb 16	1315	47	30	75	34	19.63
Feb 20	1313	44	31	74	32	19.86
Feb 21	1298	36	32	68	31	18.72
Feb 22	1290	38	28	65	30	18.42
Feb 23	1285	38	26	63	29	18.16
Feb 26	1286	39	23	60	28	17.72
Feb 27	1280	40	20	58	27	17.32
Feb 28	1275	42	17	56	26	17.08
Feb 29	1268	41	18	56	25	17.66
Mar 1	1253	28	25	53	24	17.19
Mar 4	1241	28	21	48	23	16.25
Mar 5	1230	30	19	48	22	16.59
Mar 6	1235	32	17	47	21	16.70
Mar 7	1245	25	21	46	20	16.40
Mar 8	1249	24	21	45	19	16.44
Mar 11	1240	28	18	45	18	17.10
Mar 12	1230	31	15	44	17	17.37
Mar 13	1211	28	17	44	16	18.10
Mar 14	1220	32	12	41	15	17.38
Mar 15	1217	28	12	38	14	16.63
Mar 18	1223				13	
Mar 19	1237				12	
Mar 20	1220				11	
Mar 21	1217				10	
Mar 22	1230				9	
Mar 25	1229				8	
Mar 26	1243				7	
Mar 27	1269				6	
Mar 28	1277				5	
Mar 29	1306				4	
Apr 1	1308				3	
Apr 2	1310				2	
Apr 3	1344				1	
Apr 4	1341	May 96 option expires				

LEGEND: *fp* = futures price, *max* = closest strike high option price, *min* = closest strike low option price, *s* = price corrected at-the-money-straddle, *td* = number of trading days till expiry, *iv* = implied volatility.

COCOA 1996

July option and July future

	fp	max	min	s	td	iv
Mar 18	1244	45	40	85	59	17.70
Mar 19	1258	51	41	91	58	19.02
Mar 20	1241	53	40	92	57	19.59
Mar 21	1238	51	38	88	56	18.95
Mar 22	1251	48	45	93	55	19.99
Mar 25	1250	45	45	90	54	19.60
Mar 26	1264	51	44	94	53	20.52
Mar 27	1290	53	43	95	52	20.45
Mar 28	1298	48	47	95	51	20.48
Mar 29	1327	62	39	99	50	21.02
Apr 1	1329	60	38	96	49	20.58
Apr 2	1331	58	41	97	48	21.12
Apr 3	1365	51	51	102	47	21.80
Apr 4	1362	53	48	101	46	21.78
Apr 8	1341	45	45	90	44	20.24
Apr 9	1328	57	31	85	43	19.53
Apr 10	1333	53	37	88	42	20.48
Apr 11	1359	50	40	89	41	20.48
Apr 12	1377	61	36	94	40	21.66
Apr 15	1367	53	35	86	39	20.19
Apr 16	1354	48	40	87	38	20.92
Apr 17	1351	47	42	89	37	21.56
Apr 18	1354	48	40	87	36	21.49
Apr 19	1334	50	35	84	35	21.17
Apr 22	1369	55	33	86	34	21.46
Apr 23	1359	50	38	87	33	22.26
Apr 24	1389	53	43	95	32	24.21
Apr 25	1388	53	43	95	31	24.61
Apr 26	1391	51	43	93	30	24.49
Apr 29	1417	57	37	92	29	24.10
Apr 30	1367	51	34	83	28	23.03
May 1	1387	52	37	88	27	24.30
May 2	1386	52	36	86	26	24.46
May 3	1382	51	34	83	25	24.11
May 6	1389	49	34	82	24	23.96
May 7	1387	48	34	81	23	24.25
May 8	1392	44	37	80	22	24.62
May 9	1389	44	34	77	21	24.22
May 10	1421	52	32	82	20	25.78
May 13	1424	52	26	75	19	24.13
May 14	1417	47	28	73	18	24.27
May 15	1403	37	32	69	17	23.71
May 16	1412	42	26	66	16	23.49
May 17	1408	38	27	64	15	23.45
May 20	1370				14	
May 21	1357				13	
May 22	1362				12	
May 23	1379				11	
May 24	1382				10	
May 28	1362				8	
May 29	1370				7	
May 30	1340				6	
May 31	1375				5	
Jun 3	1355				4	
Jun 4	1341				3	
Jun 5	1346				2	
Jun 6	1372				1	
Jun 7	1395	July 96 option expires				

September option and September future

	fp	max	min	s	td	iv
May 20	1391	68	52	119	53	23.41
May 21	1378	68	49	115	52	23.18
May 22	1383	70	51	119	51	24.14
May 23	1400	63	58	121	50	24.36
May 24	1403	58	58	116	49	23.62
May 28	1383	70	50	118	47	24.91
May 29	1391	65	53	117	46	24.79
May 30	1361	62	49	110	45	24.06
May 31	1396	59	52	110	44	23.84
Jun 3	1376	68	43	108	43	24.03
Jun 4	1362	59	47	105	42	23.77
Jun 5	1367	60	46	105	41	23.93
Jun 6	1393	61	50	110	40	24.98
Jun 7	1416	60	50	109	39	24.68
Jun 10	1408	53	50	103	38	23.68
Jun 11	1432	68	44	110	37	25.15
Jun 12	1458	60	53	112	36	25.70
Jun 13	1450	54	54	108	35	25.18
Jun 14	1439	59	48	106	34	25.27
Jun 17	1417	57	44	100	33	24.52
Jun 18	1438	56	44	99	32	24.32
Jun 19	1410	50	42	91	31	23.26
Jun 20	1416	50	38	87	30	22.41
Jun 21	1419	50	34	82	29	21.57
Jun 24	1422	48	31	77	28	20.54
Jun 25	1418	49	32	79	27	21.52
Jun 26	1379	45	31	75	26	21.23
Jun 27	1398	38	35	73	25	20.82
Jun 28	1384	42	28	69	24	20.24
Jul 1	1436	48	36	83	23	24.07
Jul 2	1423	46	29	73	22	21.95
Jul 5	1416	40	25	63	20	20.04
Jul 8	1422	44	22	63	19	20.44
Jul 9	1408	35	28	62	18	20.88
Jul 10	1388	37	25	61	17	21.25
Jul 11	1383	39	20	57	16	20.52
Jul 12	1383	40	20	58	15	21.51
Jul 15	1378				14	
Jul 16	1339				13	
Jul 17	1332				12	
Jul 18	1360				11	
Jul 19	1360				10	
Jul 22	1342				9	
Jul 23	1329				8	
Jul 24	1353				7	
Jul 25	1361				6	
Jul 26	1358				5	
Jul 29	1338				4	

LEGEND: *fp* = futures price, *max* = closest strike high option price, *min* = closest strike low option price, *s* = price corrected at-the-money-straddle, *td* = number of trading days till expiry, *iv* = implied volatility.

COCOA 1996

	fp	max	min	s	td	iv
Jul 30	1324				3	
Jul 31	1333				2	
Aug 1	1343				1	
Aug 2	1345	September 96 option expires				

December option and December future

	fp	max	min	s	td	iv
Jul 15	1418	75	66	140	79	22.25
Jul 16	1379	76	57	131	78	21.55
Jul 17	1372	75	61	135	77	22.39
Jul 18	1400	73	67	139	76	22.86
Jul 19	1400	75	64	138	75	22.77
Jul 22	1382	75	57	130	74	21.93
Jul 23	1369	72	54	124	73	21.26
Jul 24	1393	72	63	134	72	22.71
Jul 25	1401	69	66	135	71	22.83
Jul 26	1398	73	61	133	70	22.73
Jul 29	1378	78	52	127	69	22.26
Jul 30	1364	68	54	121	68	21.47
Jul 31	1373	72	51	121	67	21.53
Aug 1	1383	71	51	120	66	21.38
Aug 2	1385	71	51	120	65	21.51
Aug 5	1381	71	51	120	64	21.74
Aug 6	1394	63	58	121	63	21.80
Aug 7	1386	62	53	114	62	20.93
Aug 8	1412	63	50	112	61	20.28
Aug 9	1403	57	51	107	60	19.78
Aug 12	1429	67	46	111	59	20.21
Aug 13	1416	68	43	108	58	20.11
Aug 14	1430	68	43	108	57	20.08
Aug 15	1422	68	42	107	56	20.16
Aug 16	1413	66	41	104	55	19.92
Aug 19	1407	64	40	102	54	19.63
Aug 20	1428	62	41	101	53	19.41
Aug 21	1433	65	41	104	52	20.04
Aug 22	1408	64	39	100	51	19.96
Aug 23	1389	58	33	88	50	17.97
Aug 26	1380	55	30	82	49	17.01
Aug 27	1359	56	31	84	48	17.88
Aug 28	1369	56	30	83	47	17.69
Aug 29	1361	56	31	84	46	18.24
Aug 30	1350	43	41	84	45	18.51
Sep 3	1334	49	37	85	43	19.41
Sep 4	1360	55	33	86	42	19.44
Sep 5	1353	44	39	83	41	19.06
Sep 6	1371	55	32	84	40	19.49
Sep 9	1364	52	31	81	39	18.96
Sep 10	1352	39	36	75	38	17.94
Sep 11	1341	39	34	73	37	17.79
Sep 12	1361	42	32	73	36	17.90
Sep 13	1366	51	26	74	35	18.32
Sep 16	1374	50	26	73	34	18.27
Sep 17	1356	39	33	71	33	18.35
Sep 18	1357	37	33	70	32	18.15
Sep 19	1352	34	33	67	31	17.78
Sep 20	1365	40	28	67	30	17.88
Sep 23	1357	37	28	64	29	17.56
Sep 24	1364	39	25	63	28	17.34
Sep 25	1387	39	30	68	27	18.92
Sep 26	1376	45	21	63	26	17.95
Sep 27	1382	41	25	64	25	18.61
Sep 30	1375	45	19	60	24	17.96
Oct 1	1358	33	23	55	23	16.90
Oct 2	1355	31	24	54	22	17.11
Oct 3	1340	33	22	54	21	17.56
Oct 4	1349	29	27	56	20	18.51
Oct 7	1365				19	
Oct 8	1365				18	
Oct 9	1383				17	
Oct 10	1400				16	
Oct 11	1395				15	
Oct 14	1377				14	
Oct 15	1394				13	
Oct 16	1400				12	
Oct 17	1410				11	
Oct 18	1387				10	
Oct 21	1381				9	
Oct 22	1382				8	
Oct 23	1381				7	
Oct 24	1360				6	
Oct 25	1358				5	
Oct 28	1345				4	
Oct 29	1354				3	
Oct 30	1362				2	
Oct 31	1351				1	
Nov 1	1343	December 96 option expires				

March option and March future

	fp	max	min	s	td	iv
Oct 7	1411	66	58	123	86	18.85
Oct 8	1411	63	59	122	85	18.71
Oct 9	1429	69	55	123	84	18.74
Oct 10	1446	73	47	117	83	17.82
Oct 11	1441	68	47	113	82	17.31
Oct 14	1423	61	53	113	81	17.70
Oct 15	1440	73	48	118	80	18.40
Oct 16	1446	71	45	113	79	17.63
Oct 17	1456	72	48	118	78	18.29
Oct 18	1433	69	47	114	77	18.10
Oct 21	1427	67	44	109	76	17.47
Oct 22	1428	58	49	106	75	17.18
Oct 23	1427	57	48	104	74	16.98
Oct 24	1406	55	45	99	73	16.50
Oct 25	1404	56	44	99	72	16.60
Oct 28	1391	60	35	92	71	15.75
Oct 29	1400	54	42	95	70	16.20
Oct 30	1408	51	44	94	69	16.14
Oct 31	1397	53	42	94	68	16.32
Nov 1	1389	54	36	88	67	15.52
Nov 4	1369	55	30	82	66	14.78
Nov 5	1362	50	31	79	65	14.39
Nov 6	1371	54	30	81	64	14.83

LEGEND: *fp* = futures price, *max* = closest strike high option price, *min* = closest strike low option price, *s* = price corrected at-the-money-straddle, *td* = number of trading days till expiry, *iv* = implied volatility.

COCOA 1996

	fp	max	min	s	td	iv
Nov 7	1374	54	30	81	63	14.91
Nov 8	1377	54	29	80	62	14.78
Nov 11	1381	54	29	80	61	14.86
Nov 12	1349	40	39	79	60	15.11
Nov 13	1365	55	30	82	59	15.67
Nov 14	1377	56	29	82	58	15.61
Nov 15	1366	55	30	82	57	15.93
Nov 18	1356	42	34	75	56	14.84
Nov 19	1376	47	31	76	55	14.97
Nov 20	1392	47	40	86	54	16.89
Nov 21	1395	46	39	84	53	16.62
Nov 22	1392	45	39	83	52	16.63
Nov 25	1387	47	37	83	51	16.78
Nov 26	1414	47	37	83	50	16.62
Nov 27	1414	47	36	82	49	16.57
Dec 2	1398	42	40	82	47	17.08
Dec 3	1403	45	38	82	46	17.32
Dec 4	1378	55	29	81	45	17.52
Dec 5	1395	43	40	83	44	17.89
Dec 6	1389	48	33	80	43	17.46
Dec 9	1374	52	26	75	42	16.82
Dec 10	1382	52	27	76	41	17.19
Dec 11	1387	51	26	74	40	16.88
Dec 12	1378	48	28	74	39	17.16
Dec 13	1365	44	27	69	38	16.45
Dec 16	1360	47	23	67	37	16.22
Dec 17	1354	47	22	66	36	16.21
Dec 18	1372	45	22	64	35	15.82
Dec 19	1362	46	20	63	34	15.76
Dec 20	1378	46	21	64	33	16.12
Dec 23	1366	44	21	62	32	16.09
Dec 24	1364	45	20	62	31	16.26
Dec 27	1360	44	19	60	29	16.30
Dec 30	1352	31	25	55	28	15.51
Dec 31	1372	42	17	56	27	15.58
Jan 2	1391				26	
Jan 3	1380				25	
Jan 6	1374				24	
Jan 7	1368				23	
Jan 8	1355				22	
Jan 9	1350				21	
Jan 10	1331				20	
Jan 13	1334				19	
Jan 14	1336				18	
Jan 15	1345				17	
Jan 16	1336				16	
Jan 17	1336				15	
Jan 20	1327				14	
Jan 21	1323				13	
Jan 22	1288				12	
Jan 23	1258				11	
Jan 24	1306				10	
Jan 27	1322				9	
Jan 28	1314				8	
Jan 29	1306				7	
Jan 30	1318				6	
Jan 31	1312				5	
Feb 3	1321				4	
Feb 4	1292				3	
Feb 5	1270				2	
Feb 6	1285				1	
Feb 7	1268	March 97 option expires				

LEGEND: *fp* = futures price, *max* = closest strike high option price, *min* = closest strike low option price, *s* = price corrected at-the-money-straddle, *td* = number of trading days till expiry, *iv* = implied volatility.

COFFEE

Calendar month	Year	Based on Option	Nearest strike	Implied volatility
JANUARY	1993	May	*8000*	32.66
FEBRUARY	1993	May	*6500*	40.77
MARCH	1993	Jul	*6500*	39.34
APRIL	1993	Jul	*6000*	36.06
MAY	1993	Jul	*6500*	45.37
JUNE	1993	Sep	*6250*	41.81
JULY	1993	Sep	*6500*	40.03
AUGUST	1993	Dec	*8000*	38.47
SEPTEMBER	1993	Dec	*8000*	39.71
OCTOBER	1993	Mar	*7500*	34.97
NOVEMBER	1993	Mar	*8000*	34.66
DECEMBER	1993	Mar	*7750*	35.34
JANUARY	1994	May	*7500*	31.71
FEBRUARY	1994	May	*7500*	27.08
MARCH	1994	Jul	*7750*	25.63
APRIL	1994	Jul	*8250*	23.30
MAY	1994	Aug	*9000*	26.81
JUNE	1994	Sep	*12000*	63.40
JULY	1994	Sep	*19000*	92.60
AUGUST	1994	Dec	*21500*	57.30
SEPTEMBER	1994	Dec	*21500*	53.65
OCTOBER	1994	Mar	*21500*	43.55
NOVEMBER	1994	Mar	*19100*	43.09
DECEMBER	1994	Mar	*16100*	38.82
JANUARY	1995	Mar	*17000*	39.37
FEBRUARY	1995	May	*19000*	36.79
MARCH	1995	Jul	*19000*	37.54
APRIL	1995	Jul	*16500*	37.11
MAY	1995	Jul	*17500*	34.07
JUNE	1995	Sep	*16000*	56.91
JULY	1995	Sep	*13000*	52.92
AUGUST	1995	Dec	*14000*	43.52
SEPTEMBER	1995	Dec	*15000*	37.31
OCTOBER	1995	Dec	*12000*	48.24
NOVEMBER	1995	Mar	*12000*	42.81
DECEMBER	1995	Mar	*10500*	39.40
JANUARY	1996	Mar	*9000*	40.17
FEBRUARY	1996	May	*12500*	45.38
MARCH	1996	May	*11000*	41.98
APRIL	1996	Jul	*11500*	39.07
MAY	1996	Jul	*12500*	44.90
JUNE	1996	Sep	*11000*	46.18
JULY	1996	Sep	*12000*	47.11
AUGUST	1996	Dec	*10000*	33.93
SEPTEMBER	1996	Dec	*11500*	34.99
OCTOBER	1996	Dec	*10500*	32.45
NOVEMBER	1996	Mar	*10500*	28.02
DECEMBER	1996	Mar	*10500*	26.96
JANUARY	1997	Mar	*11500*	29.55
FEBRUARY	1997	May	*14000*	43.97
MARCH	1997	Jul	*16500*	48.34
APRIL	1997	Jul	*17500*	46.90
MAY	1997	Sep	*20000*	65.09
JUNE	1997	Sep	*22500*	81.38
JULY	1997	Sep	*17500*	63.45
AUGUST	1997	Dec	*16500*	42.95
SEPTEMBER	1997	Dec	*18500*	45.14
OCTOBER	1997	Mar	*15000*	38.34
NOVEMBER	1997	Jan	*13500*	34.35
DECEMBER	1997	Mar	*16500*	44.89

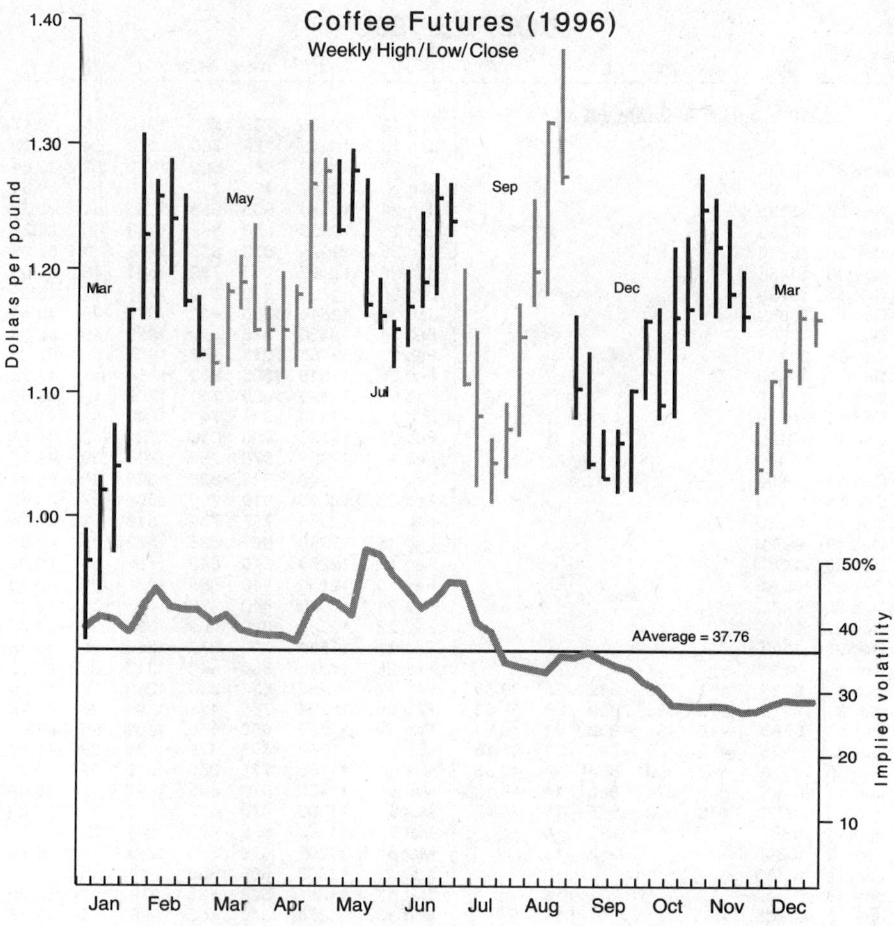
Coffee Futures (1996)
Weekly High/Low/Close
Dollars per pound
1.40
1.30
1.20
1.10
1.00
Mar
May
Jul
Sep
Dec
Mar
AAverage = 37.76
50%
40
30
20
10
Implied volatility
Jan
Feb
Mar
Apr
May
Jun
Jul
Aug
Sep
Oct
Nov
Dec

COFFEE 1996

March option and Mar future

	fp	max	min	s	td	iv
Nov 20	11520					
Nov 21	11385					
Nov 22	11105					
Nov 27	11195					
Nov 28	10930					
Nov 29	10830					
Nov 30	10485					
Dec 1	10439					
Dec 4	10389					
Dec 5	10545					
Dec 6	10200					
Dec 7	10355					
Dec 8	10155					
Dec 11	10235					
Dec 12	10265					
Dec 13	10470					
Dec 14	10665					
Dec 15	10775					
Dec 18	10210					
Dec 19	9950					
Dec 20	9570					
Dec 21	9670					
Dec 22	9635					
Dec 27	9520					
Dec 28	9390					
Dec 29	9490					
Jan 2	9125	480	390	862	23	39.39
Jan 3	9375	475	383	850	22	38.65
Jan 4	9785	470	435	902	21	40.24
Jan 5	9625	470	420	886	20	41.16
Jan 10	9790	460	400	855	17	42.36
Jan 11	10305	530	374	889	16	43.13
Jan 12	10270	570	322	865	15	43.47
Jan 15	9895				14	
Jan 16	10390				13	
Jan 17	10430				12	
Jan 18	10540				11	
Jan 19	10465				10	
Jan 22	10750				9	
Jan 23	10700				8	
Jan 24	10890				7	
Jan 25	11175				6	
Jan 26	11695				5	
Jan 29	12345				4	
Jan 30	11955				3	
Jan 31	12860				2	
Feb 1	12640				1	
Feb 2	12375	March 96 option expires				

May option and May future

	fp	max	min	s	td	iv
Jan 15	9675	830	720	1541	58	41.82
Jan 16	10170	890	710	1584	57	41.25
Jan 17	10210	850	690	1526	56	39.94
Jan 18	10320	785	730	1510	55	39.47
Jan 19	10245	820	700	1510	54	40.10
Jan 22	10530	880	660	1519	53	39.64
Jan 23	10480	795	710	1498	52	39.64
Jan 24	10670	905	655	1536	51	40.32
Jan 25	10955	880	642	1499	50	38.71
Jan 26	11475	870	638	1486	49	37.00
Jan 29	12125	913	780	1681	48	40.03
Jan 30	11735	970	810	1766	47	43.90
Jan 31	12640	1030	850	1864	46	43.49
Feb 1	12420	975	920	1890	45	45.38
Feb 2	12155	1015	900	1905	44	47.26
Feb 5	11845	1055	820	1854	43	47.73
Feb 6	11720	1060	740	1769	42	46.58
Feb 7	11640	925	740	1648	41	44.23
Feb 8	12150	920	810	1721	40	44.78
Feb 9	12385	970	750	1700	39	43.95
Feb 12	11940	870	820	1686	38	45.81
Feb 13	12045	810	790	1598	37	43.63
Feb 14	12090	785	730	1510	36	41.64
Feb 15	12290	860	685	1529	35	42.06
Feb 16	12250	840	640	1462	34	40.92
Feb 20	12160	810	655	1451	32	42.19
Feb 21	12330	840	670	1495	31	43.54
Feb 22	12230	820	600	1399	30	41.77
Feb 23	11550	720	670	1386	29	44.56
Feb 26	11375	680	640	1317	28	43.75
Feb 27	11485	635	610	1243	27	41.66
Feb 28	11295	760	465	1194	26	41.46
Feb 29	11590	650	560	1202	25	41.49
Mar 1	11080	685	475	1139	24	41.98
Mar 4	11165	725	390	1077	23	40.22
Mar 5	11420	670	405	1047	22	39.09
Mar 6	11300	610	425	1017	21	39.28
Mar 7	11270	659	409	1042	20	41.34
Mar 8	11205	675	380	1022	19	41.86
Mar 11	11300	585	380	944	18	39.39
Mar 12	11595	523	425	939	17	39.29
Mar 13	11470	540	463	996	16	43.43
Mar 14	11775	605	398	982	15	43.07
Mar 15	11845	565	410	960	14	43.33
Mar 18	12085				13	
Mar 19	11905				12	
Mar 20	11770				11	
Mar 21	12000				10	
Mar 22	11970				9	
Mar 25	11920				8	
Mar 26	12345				7	
Mar 27	12175				6	
Mar 28	12140				5	
Mar 29	11545				4	
Apr 1	11450				3	
Apr 2	11585				2	
Apr 3	11535				1	
Apr 4	11525	May 96 option expires				

LEGEND: *fp* = futures price, *max* = closest strike high option price, *min* = closest strike low option price, *s* = price corrected at-the-money-straddle, *td* = number of trading days till expiry, *iv* = implied volatility.

COFFEE 1996

	fp	max	min	s	td	iv
July option and July future						
Mar 18	12140	1020	770	1767	59	37.89
Mar 19	11960	1010	760	1747	58	38.35
Mar 20	11825	1050	730	1749	57	39.18
Mar 21	12055	940	830	1761	56	39.03
Mar 22	12025	965	790	1739	55	39.01
Mar 25	11975	918	733	1634	54	37.14
Mar 26	12400	1030	760	1765	53	39.09
Mar 27	12230	1115	710	1783	52	40.44
Mar 28	12195	880	785	1657	51	38.05
Mar 29	11600	840	790	1626	50	39.64
Apr 1	11505	830	750	1573	49	39.07
Apr 2	11640	780	770	1549	48	38.42
Apr 3	11590	770	750	1518	47	38.22
Apr 4	11580	764	750	1513	46	38.53
Apr 8	11410	780	770	1549	44	40.94
Apr 9	11515	735	710	1443	43	38.22
Apr 10	11860	815	675	1478	42	38.45
Apr 11	11710	870	580	1421	41	37.90
Apr 12	11520	690	685	1375	40	37.73
Apr 15	11490	675	650	1323	39	36.87
Apr 16	11555	655	600	1250	38	35.11
Apr 17	11725	830	565	1369	37	38.39
Apr 18	11885	773	658	1421	36	39.85
Apr 19	11830	760	615	1362	35	38.92
Apr 22	13095	870	785	1648	34	43.16
Apr 23	12690	860	670	1513	33	41.50
Apr 24	12700	890	690	1562	32	43.48
Apr 25	12545	795	750	1541	31	44.13
Apr 26	12695	850	680	1515	30	43.57
Apr 29	12250	880	630	1486	29	45.05
Apr 30	12445	775	720	1490	28	45.27
May 1	12700	850	650	1482	27	44.90
May 2	12730	850	600	1426	26	43.93
May 3	12755	845	600	1421	25	44.58
May 6	12520	668	648	1314	24	42.86
May 7	12640	725	600	1314	23	43.35
May 8	12875	735	610	1334	22	44.18
May 9	12700	745	550	1277	21	43.87
May 10	12705	700	520	1203	20	42.35
May 13	12605	575	520	1090	19	39.69
May 14	12665	640	475	1100	18	40.92
May 15	12645	627	480	1093	17	41.95
May 16	12870	615	485	1088	16	42.28
May 17	12865	615	480	1083	15	43.46
May 20	12600				14	
May 21	12420				13	
May 22	12045				12	
May 23	11785				11	
May 24	11765				10	
May 28	11685				8	
May 29	11730				7	
May 30	11585				6	
May 31	11610				5	
Jun 3	11255				4	
Jun 4	11340				3	
Jun 5	11385				2	
Jun 6	11305				1	
Jun 7	11535	July 96 option expires				
September option and September future						
May 20	12435	1275	1260	2534	53	55.98
May 21	12255	1318	1148	2451	52	55.48
May 22	11880	1170	1125	2291	51	54.02
May 23	11620	1165	960	2107	50	51.28
May 24	11600	1130	925	2037	49	50.17
May 28	11520	1063	963	2018	47	51.09
May 29	11565	1100	950	2037	46	51.94
May 30	11420	990	970	1958	45	51.13
May 31	11445	975	940	1912	44	50.37
Jun 3	11090	940	775	1700	43	46.76
Jun 4	11175	970	725	1672	42	46.18
Jun 5	11220	980	800	1764	41	49.11
Jun 6	11140	960	720	1658	40	47.05
Jun 7	11370	855	820	1672	39	47.10
Jun 10	11610	925	800	1714	38	47.90
Jun 11	11565	830	760	1584	37	45.04
Jun 12	11720	940	675	1590	36	45.21
Jun 13	11455	780	760	1538	35	45.40
Jun 14	11510	725	700	1423	34	42.40
Jun 17	11685	880	630	1486	33	44.28
Jun 18	11790	825	620	1426	32	42.76
Jun 19	11780	820	640	1444	31	44.02
Jun 20	11730	820	570	1366	30	42.51
Jun 21	11480	660	610	1266	29	40.95
Jun 24	11790	805	525	1302	28	41.73
Jun 25	11755	830	570	1374	27	45.00
Jun 26	11865	800	590	1370	26	45.30
Jun 27	11920	770	610	1366	25	45.82
Jun 28	12145	745	640	1376	24	46.25
Jul 1	12075	720	650	1364	23	47.11
Jul 2	11785	750	640	1380	22	49.95
Jul 5	11650	695	530	1210	20	46.44
Jul 8	11845	725	570	1281	19	49.62
Jul 9	11425	600	525	1119	18	46.15
Jul 10	11605	600	490	1080	17	45.15
Jul 11	11620	600	490	1080	16	46.48
Jul 12	11195	671	366	1002	15	46.24
Jul 15	10640				14	
Jul 16	10295				13	
Jul 17	10690				12	
Jul 18	10995				11	
Jul 19	10870				10	
Jul 22	10405				9	
Jul 23	10430				8	
Jul 24	10410				7	
Jul 25	10295				6	
Jul 26	10405				5	
Jul 29	10540				4	

LEGEND: *fp* = futures price, *max* = closest strike high option price, *min* = closest strike low option price, *s* = price corrected at-the-money-straddle, *td* = number of trading days till expiry, *iv* = implied volatility.

COFFEE 1996

	fp	max	min	s	td	iv
Jul 30	10525				3	
Jul 31	10640				2	
Aug 1	10670				1	
Aug 2	10750	September 96 option expires				

December option and December future

	fp	max	min	s	td	iv
Jul 15	10120	905	785	1680	79	37.35
Jul 16	9805	925	740	1648	78	38.07
Jul 17	10165	975	800	1759	77	39.45
Jul 18	10450	1050	820	1849	76	40.59
Jul 19	10275	1060	820	1858	75	41.76
Jul 22	9855	968	823	1778	74	41.95
Jul 23	9870	900	800	1692	73	40.12
Jul 24	9830	870	750	1610	72	38.60
Jul 25	9725	880	660	1519	71	37.09
Jul 26	9830	810	680	1479	70	35.96
Jul 29	9955	725	710	1434	69	34.68
Jul 30	9970	730	725	1455	68	35.39
Jul 31	10065	775	650	1414	67	34.33
Aug 1	10100	775	630	1392	66	33.93
Aug 2	10160	775	610	1370	65	33.45
Aug 5	9890	775	580	1337	64	33.79
Aug 6	10020	825	575	1376	63	34.59
Aug 7	10030	805	555	1335	62	33.82
Aug 8	10710	860	615	1451	61	34.70
Aug 9	10610	825	575	1376	60	33.48
Aug 12	10715	825	580	1381	59	33.57
Aug 13	11175	870	615	1460	58	34.32
Aug 14	11100	860	610	1446	57	34.51
Aug 15	11115	830	585	1391	56	33.45
Aug 16	11155	815	530	1316	55	31.82
Aug 19	11330	835	575	1384	54	33.26
Aug 20	11505	685	685	1370	53	32.71
Aug 21	11700	830	580	1386	52	32.85
Aug 22	12080	740	685	1420	51	32.93
Aug 23	12255	895	645	1516	50	34.99
Aug 26	12520	760	740	1498	49	34.19
Aug 27	11920	815	720	1527	48	36.98
Aug 28	11655	840	625	1445	47	36.17
Aug 29	11705	845	604	1426	46	35.92
Aug 30	11825	830	580	1386	45	34.94
Sep 3	11330	790	535	1300	43	34.99
Sep 4	11280	775	530	1281	42	35.04
Sep 5	11160	775	525	1275	41	35.69
Sep 6	11290	790	515	1277	40	35.77
Sep 9	11120	760	520	1256	39	36.18
Sep 10	11130	725	525	1231	38	35.88
Sep 11	10690	740	480	1194	37	36.71
Sep 12	10520	630	540	1162	36	36.83
Sep 13	10470	550	550	1100	35	35.52
Sep 16	10535	540	530	1069	34	34.81
Sep 17	10585	650	415	1041	33	34.24
Sep 18	10440	540	480	1015	32	34.37
Sep 19	10360	679	400	1049	31	36.37
Sep 20	10360	570	430	987	30	34.79
Sep 23	10455	500	465	962	29	34.18
Sep 24	10600	520	420	931	28	33.20
Sep 25	10645	600	360	934	27	33.79
Sep 26	10570	500	430	924	26	34.29
Sep 27	10525	465	440	903	25	34.32
Sep 30	10295	590	345	908	24	36.02
Oct 1	10475	400	375	773	23	30.77
Oct 2	10540	420	385	802	22	32.45
Oct 3	10745	556	303	830	21	33.73
Oct 4	10980	419	400	817	20	33.29
Oct 7	11270				19	
Oct 8	11250				18	
Oct 9	11355				17	
Oct 10	11490				16	
Oct 11	11630				15	
Oct 14	11510				14	
Oct 15	11420				13	
Oct 16	11220				12	
Oct 17	10990				11	
Oct 18	10910				10	
Oct 21	11300				9	
Oct 22	11760				8	
Oct 23	11930				7	
Oct 24	11745				6	
Oct 25	11600				5	
Oct 28	11910				4	
Oct 29	11635				3	
Oct 30	11915				2	
Oct 31	11720				1	
Nov 1	11725	December 96 option expires				

March option and March future

	fp	max	min	s	td	iv
Oct 7	10625	900	650	1526	86	30.98
Oct 8	10565	780	715	1490	85	30.59
Oct 9	10585	810	725	1528	84	31.50
Oct 10	10680	905	650	1531	83	31.46
Oct 11	10765	905	655	1536	82	31.52
Oct 14	10615	870	620	1466	81	30.69
Oct 15	10520	730	720	1449	80	30.80
Oct 16	10355	850	585	1409	79	30.62
Oct 17	10250	805	560	1341	78	29.63
Oct 18	10155	775	555	1309	77	29.38
Oct 21	10405	750	510	1236	76	27.26
Oct 22	10660	780	530	1285	75	27.84
Oct 23	10510	640	630	1269	74	28.08
Oct 24	10365	760	510	1245	73	28.12
Oct 25	10410	650	570	1213	72	27.47
Oct 28	10585	655	570	1218	71	27.31
Oct 29	10500	610	626	1237	70	28.17
Oct 30	10630	695	565	1248	69	28.28
Oct 31	10610	740	500	1216	68	27.80
Nov 1	10645	745	500	1221	67	28.02
Nov 4	10705	760	510	1245	66	28.63
Nov 5	10810	725	490	1192	65	27.35
Nov 6	11140	750	510	1236	64	27.74

LEGEND: *fp* = futures price, *max* = closest strike high option price, *min* = closest strike low option price, *s* = price corrected at-the-money-straddle, *td* = number of trading days till expiry, *iv* = implied volatility.

COFFEE 1996

	fp	max	min	s	td	iv
Nov 7	11235	745	510	1232	63	27.63
Nov 8	11175	725	490	1192	62	27.09
Nov 11	10910	665	575	1232	61	28.92
Nov 12	11045	600	580	1178	60	27.55
Nov 13	11135	650	550	1191	59	27.86
Nov 14	11240	720	475	1170	58	27.34
Nov 15	11430	650	580	1224	57	28.37
Nov 18	11265	720	485	1182	56	28.03
Nov 19	11385	630	525	1146	55	27.14
Nov 20	11310	680	465	1124	54	27.04
Nov 21	10910	625	495	1108	53	27.91
Nov 22	10950	572	522	1090	52	27.60
Nov 25	10760	665	405	1043	51	27.13
Nov 26	10810	610	390	977	50	25.57
Nov 27	10775	580	415	979	49	25.96
Dec 2	10605	550	440	980	47	26.96
Dec 3	10510	490	471	959	46	26.92
Dec 4	10420	500	440	935	45	26.75
Dec 5	10345	540	420	949	44	27.66
Dec 6	10325	540	410	938	43	27.71
Dec 9	10560	575	390	947	42	27.67
Dec 10	10820	615	365	953	41	27.52
Dec 11	10810	615	365	953	40	27.88
Dec 12	10985	505	490	994	39	28.97
Dec 13	11120	535	440	967	38	28.20
Dec 16	10995	480	475	955	37	28.55
Dec 17	10990	495	490	985	36	29.86
Dec 18	11190	595	405	981	35	29.64
Dec 19	11020	460	455	915	34	28.47
Dec 20	11215	585	340	898	33	27.89
Dec 23	11310	590	345	908	32	28.40
Dec 24	11475	450	450	900	31	28.17
Dec 27	11620	510	398	898	29	28.69
Dec 30	11595	488	395	875	28	28.51
Dec 31	11690	590	335	897	27	29.53
Jan 2	11665				26	
Jan 3	11625				25	
Jan 6	11405				24	
Jan 7	11935				23	
Jan 8	11890				22	
Jan 9	11935				21	
Jan 10	11960				20	
Jan 13	11845				19	
Jan 14	12220				18	
Jan 15	12260				17	
Jan 16	12305				16	
Jan 17	12400				15	
Jan 20	12925				14	
Jan 21	12965				13	
Jan 22	13530				12	
Jan 23	14005				11	
Jan 24	13690				10	
Jan 27	13660				9	
Jan 28	13950				8	
Jan 29	14460				7	
Jan 30	14030				6	
Jan 31	13940				5	
Feb 3	14565				4	
Feb 4	14745				3	
Feb 5	14455				2	
Feb 6	15080				1	
Feb 7	15105	March 97 option expires				

LEGEND: *fp* = futures price, *max* = closest strike high option price, *min* = closest strike low option price, *s* = price corrected at-the-money-straddle, *td* = number of trading days till expiry, *iv* = implied volatility.

SUGAR

Calendar month	Year	Based on Option	Nearest strike	Implied volatility
JANUARY	1993	May	*850*	24.22
FEBRUARY	1993	May	*850*	23.29
MARCH	1993	Jul	*1050*	35.33
APRIL	1993	Jul	*1250*	33.63
MAY	1993	Jul	*1250*	42.92
JUNE	1993	Oct	*1100*	37.64
JULY	1993	Oct	*1050*	38.15
AUGUST	1993	Jan	*1000*	26.46
SEPTEMBER	1993	Jan	*950*	24.16
OCTOBER	1993	Jan	*1100*	23.18
NOVEMBER	1993	Mar	*1050*	28.26
DECEMBER	1993	Mar	*1050*	30.06
JANUARY	1994	May	*1100*	29.09
FEBRUARY	1994	May	*1100*	27.49
MARCH	1994	Jul	*1200*	32.78
APRIL	1994	Jul	*1200*	25.57
MAY	1994	Jul	*1150*	30.81
JUNE	1994	Aug	*1200*	30.90
JULY	1994	Oct	*1150*	31.83
AUGUST	1994	Jan	*1150*	22.44
SEPTEMBER	1994	Nov	*1200*	25.50
OCTOBER	1994	Jan	*1250*	23.46
NOVEMBER	1994	Mar	*1300*	23.93
DECEMBER	1994	Mar	*1450*	37.12
JANUARY	1995	Mar	*1550*	29.58
FEBRUARY	1995	May	*1400*	24.31
MARCH	1995	Jul	*1350*	21.16
APRIL	1995	Jul	*1300*	21.86
MAY	1995	Jul	*1200*	33.96
JUNE	1995	Oct	*1000*	29.26
JULY	1995	Oct	*1100*	28.03
AUGUST	1995	Jan	*1000*	23.80
SEPTEMBER	1995	Jan	*1050*	22.76
OCTOBER	1995	Jan	*1050*	24.58
NOVEMBER	1995	Mar	*1050*	22.12
DECEMBER	1995	Mar	*1150*	23.52
JANUARY	1996	Mar	*1200*	22.28
FEBRUARY	1996	May	*1100*	27.27
MARCH	1996	May	*1150*	25.25
APRIL	1996	Jul	*1100*	22.75
MAY	1996	Jul	*1050*	26.74
JUNE	1996	Oct	*1100*	22.54
JULY	1996	Oct	*1150*	22.93
AUGUST	1996	Oct	*1200*	23.04
SEPTEMBER	1996	Jan	*1150*	16.43
OCTOBER	1996	Jan	*1100*	16.57
NOVEMBER	1996	Mar	*1050*	18.55
DECEMBER	1996	Mar	*1050*	18.08
JANUARY	1997	May	*1100*	17.80
FEBRUARY	1997	May	*1050*	20.16
MARCH	1997	Jul	*1050*	17.49
APRIL	1997	Jul	*1050*	16.50
MAY	1997	Oct	*1050*	17.16
JUNE	1997	Oct	*1100*	16.32
JULY	1997	Oct	*1100*	16.57
AUGUST	1997	Jan	*1200*	16.46
SEPTEMBER	1997	Jan	*1200*	17.44
OCTOBER	1997	Jan	*1150*	15.53
NOVEMBER	1997	Mar	*1250*	18.85
DECEMBER	1997	Mar	*1250*	18.32

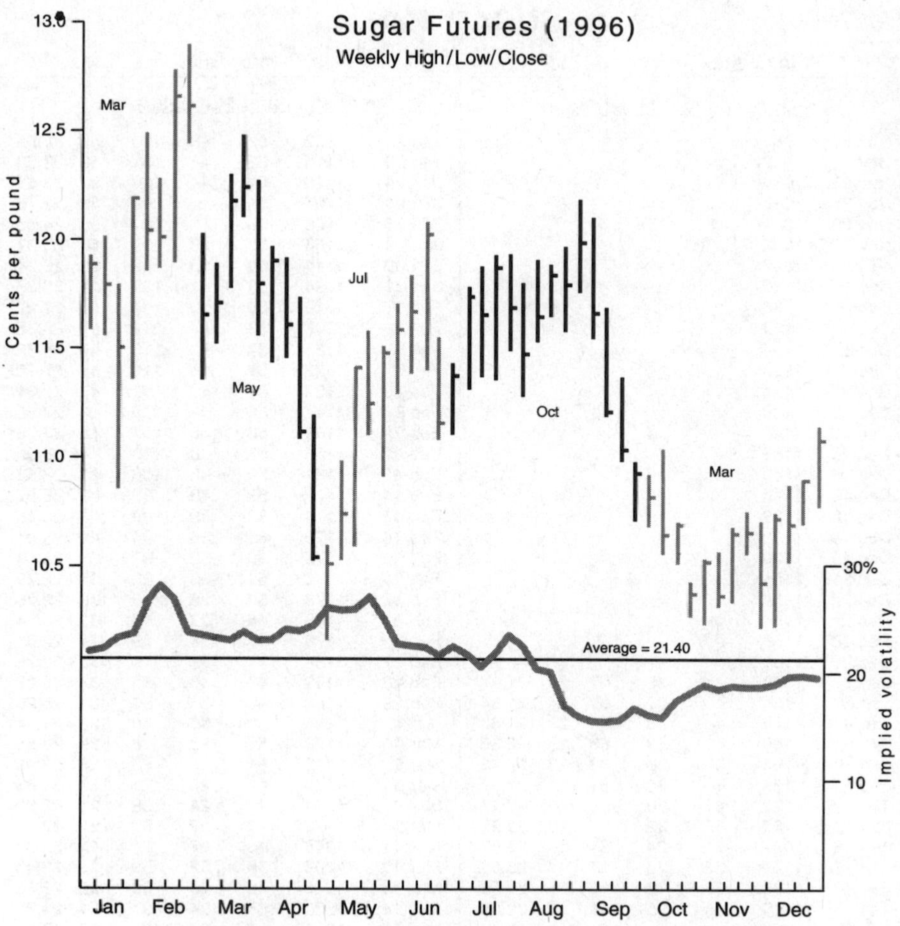
Sugar Futures (1996)
Weekly High/Low/Close
Cents per pound
13.0
12.5
12.0
11.5
11.0
10.5
Mar
May
Jul
Oct
Mar
Average = 21.40
30%
20
10
Implied volatility
Jan
Feb
Mar
Apr
May
Jun
Jul
Aug
Sep
Oct
Nov
Dec

SUGAR 1996

March option and March future

	fp	max	min	s	td	iv
Nov 20	1089					
Nov 21	1079					
Nov 22	1086					
Nov 27	1097					
Nov 28	1081					
Nov 29	1092					
Nov 30	1097					
Dec 1	1130					
Dec 4	1138					
Dec 5	1129					
Dec 6	1132					
Dec 7	1126					
Dec 8	1144					
Dec 11	1138					
Dec 12	1146					
Dec 13	1137					
Dec 14	1140					
Dec 15	1143					
Dec 18	1129					
Dec 19	1138					
Dec 20	1150					
Dec 21	1154					
Dec 22	1158					
Dec 27	1154					
Dec 28	1156					
Dec 29	1160					
Jan 2	1183	43	26	67	28	21.47
Jan 3	1184	43	26	67	27	21.84
Jan 4	1172	44	23	65	26	21.60
Jan 5	1189	40	29	68	25	22.86
Jan 10	1194	37	26	62	22	22.12
Jan 11	1173	44	20	61	21	22.67
Jan 12	1179	41	20	58	20	22.17
Jan 15	1167	36	22	57	19	22.22
Jan 16	1087	31	24	54	18	23.57
Jan 17	1109	32	23	54	17	23.68
Jan 18	1130	39	19	56	16	24.58
Jan 19	1149	26	25	51	15	22.88
Jan 22	1156				14	
Jan 23	1176				13	
Jan 24	1167				12	
Jan 25	1172				11	
Jan 26	1219				10	
Jan 29	1248				9	
Jan 30	1236				8	
Jan 31	1215				7	
Feb 1	1193				6	
Feb 2	1204				5	
Feb 5	1219				4	
Feb 6	1200				3	
Feb 7	1202				2	
Feb 8	1212				1	
Feb 9	1201	March 96 option expires				

May option and May future

	fp	max	min	s	td	iv
Jan 22	1122	62	40	100	59	22.96
Jan 23	1115	58	44	101	58	23.52
Jan 24	1110	57	44	100	57	23.61
Jan 25	1107	54	46	99	56	23.76
Jan 26	1128	63	43	104	55	24.65
Jan 29	1156	56	53	109	54	25.37
Jan 30	1144	60	53	112	53	26.74
Jan 31	1134	63	47	109	52	26.29
Feb 1	1110	60	50	109	51	27.27
Feb 2	1107	67	47	112	50	28.35
Feb 5	1131	67	50	115	49	28.86
Feb 6	1122	67	45	110	48	27.96
Feb 7	1132	64	46	108	47	27.61
Feb 8	1147	56	53	109	46	27.66
Feb 9	1139	58	50	107	45	27.78
Feb 12	1165	63	48	110	44	28.05
Feb 13	1161	59	48	106	43	27.53
Feb 14	1167	59	42	99	42	25.97
Feb 15	1174	63	39	99	41	26.15
Feb 16	1178	61	36	94	40	25.01
Feb 20	1172	56	33	87	38	23.64
Feb 21	1170	51	33	82	37	22.79
Feb 22	1179	55	28	80	36	22.25
Feb 23	1160	46	33	78	35	22.34
Feb 26	1176	47	33	79	34	22.61
Feb 27	1184	47	33	79	33	22.78
Feb 28	1199	40	40	80	32	23.23
Feb 29	1160	48	36	83	31	25.26
Mar 1	1165	52	30	80	30	24.54
Mar 4	1170	51	28	76	29	23.85
Mar 5	1172	51	25	73	28	23.08
Mar 6	1173	49	25	71	27	22.93
Mar 7	1174	47	24	68	26	22.39
Mar 8	1170	47	23	67	25	22.49
Mar 11	1216	46	27	71	24	23.34
Mar 12	1209	38	32	69	23	23.46
Mar 13	1216	42	26	66	22	22.75
Mar 14	1223	45	24	67	21	23.21
Mar 15	1217	41	24	63	20	22.65
Mar 18	1241	39	29	67	19	24.17
Mar 19	1246	36	30	65	18	24.11
Mar 20	1248	31	30	61	17	23.01
Mar 21	1224	43	22	63	16	24.78
Mar 22	1225	44	18	58	15	23.84
Mar 25	1207				14	
Mar 26	1190				13	
Mar 27	1186				12	
Mar 28	1168				11	
Mar 29	1179				10	
Apr 1	1155				9	
Apr 2	1154				8	
Apr 3	1177				7	
Apr 4	1189				6	
Apr 8	1191				4	

LEGEND: *fp* = futures price, *max* = closest strike high option price, *min* = closest strike low option price, *s* = price corrected at-the-money-straddle, *td* = number of trading days till expiry, *iv* = implied volatility.

SUGAR 1996

	fp	max	min	s	td	iv
Apr 9	1158	3				
Apr 10	1163	2				
Apr 11	1174	1				
Apr 12	1162	May 96 option expires				

<u>July option and July future</u>

	fp	max	min	s	td	iv
Mar 25	1137	59	53	45	97	22.28
Mar 26	1121	58	51	48	99	23.13
Mar 27	1118	57	50	48	98	23.18
Mar 28	1101	56	54	41	94	22.77
Mar 29	1113	55	47	47	94	22.78
Apr 1	1092	54	50	42	91	22.75
Apr 2	1090	53	50	41	90	22.73
Apr 3	1099	52	47	47	94	23.72
Apr 4	1106	51	50	43	92	23.40
Apr 8	1126	49	61	36	94	23.93
Apr 9	1104	48	47	43	90	23.45
Apr 10	1110	47	52	42	93	24.47
Apr 11	1126	46	62	35	94	24.62
Apr 12	1112	45	50	41	90	24.18
Apr 15	1119	44	54	35	87	23.46
Apr 16	1111	43	52	35	85	23.42
Apr 17	1116	42	50	36	85	23.41
Apr 18	1062	41	51	35	84	24.83
Apr 19	1058	40	43	37	79	23.76
Apr 22	1061	39	46	35	80	24.14
Apr 23	1066	38	47	31	76	23.25
Apr 24	1075	37	53	28	78	23.89
Apr 25	1056	36	43	38	81	25.43
Apr 26	1036	35	46	34	79	25.74
Apr 29	1041	34	45	33	77	25.33
Apr 30	1039	33	44	34	77	25.83
May 1	1033	32	49	31	78	26.74
May 2	1040	31	46	32	77	26.47
May 3	1051	30	39	36	75	25.97
May 6	1059	29	43	32	74	25.94
May 7	1062	28	43	31	73	25.93
May 8	1087	27	43	31	73	25.80
May 9	1078	26	47	27	72	26.13
May 10	1076	25	47	23	67	24.94
May 13	1080	24	46	25	69	25.94
May 14	1091	23	39	28	66	25.21
May 15	1093	22	37	29	65	25.46
May 16	1105	21	35	29	63	25.07
May 17	1142	20	42	32	73	28.62
May 20	1150	19	34	34	68	27.13
May 21	1139	18	39	28	66	27.29
May 22	1138	17	37	25	61	25.92
May 23	1122	16	42	21	60	26.95
May 24	1126	15	38	21	57	26.18
May 28	1101	13	28	28	56	28.21
May 29	1095	12				
May 30	1102	11				
May 31	1121	10				
Jun 3	1147	9				
Jun 4	1142				8	
Jun 5	1135				7	
Jun 6	1160				6	
Jun 7	1158				5	
Jun 10	1144				4	
Jun 11	1180				3	
Jun 12	1174				2	
Jun 13	1168				1	
Jun 14	1167	July option expires				

<u>October option and October future</u>

	fp	max	min	s	td	iv
May 29	1045	57	50	106	76	23.36
May 30	1047	52	52	104	75	22.94
May 31	1061	58	44	101	74	22.07
Jun 3	1082	55	49	103	73	22.39
Jun 4	1075	53	51	104	72	22.77
Jun 5	1075	57	47	103	71	22.77
Jun 6	1087	60	44	102	70	22.54
Jun 7	1088	56	47	102	69	22.62
Jun 10	1076	55	48	102	68	23.08
Jun 11	1105	59	43	100	67	22.22
Jun 12	1115	62	39	99	66	21.77
Jun 13	1111	57	44	100	65	22.29
Jun 14	1116	60	44	102	64	22.96
Jun 17	1123	66	42	106	63	23.68
Jun 18	1116	59	42	99	62	22.62
Jun 19	1116	56	42	97	61	22.19
Jun 20	1116	55	40	94	60	21.65
Jun 21	1139	51	42	92	59	21.08
Jun 24	1123	58	34	89	58	20.91
Jun 25	1120	57	36	91	57	21.48
Jun 26	1141	52	43	94	56	22.07
Jun 27	1141	53	44	96	55	22.74
Jun 28	1115	51	38	88	54	21.43
Jul 1	1132	56	40	94	53	22.93
Jul 2	1138	53	41	93	52	22.64
Jul 5	1139	53	40	92	50	22.79
Jul 8	1169	56	37	91	49	22.26
Jul 9	1167	55	37	90	48	22.31
Jul 10	1164	50	37	86	47	21.50
Jul 11	1168	50	33	81	46	20.52
Jul 12	1177	54	31	82	45	20.89
Jul 15	1185	49	34	82	44	20.75
Jul 16	1165	48	33	80	43	20.82
Jul 17	1179	52	29	78	42	20.53
Jul 18	1166	42	32	73	41	19.58
Jul 19	1165	46	32	77	40	20.80
Jul 22	1151	39	38	77	39	21.40
Jul 23	1145	42	36	77	38	21.95
Jul 24	1169	48	29	75	37	21.09
Jul 25	1173	50	29	77	36	21.80
Jul 26	1190	51	33	82	35	23.34
Jul 29	1188	47	35	81	34	23.35
Jul 30	1187	48	35	82	33	23.98
Jul 31	1170	49	32	79	32	23.96

LEGEND: *fp* = futures price, *max* = closest strike high option price, *min* = closest strike low option price, *s* = price corrected at-the-money-straddle, *td* = number of trading days till expiry, *iv* = implied volatility.

SUGAR 1996

	fp	max	min	s	td	iv
Aug 1	1178	50	28	76	31	23.04
Aug 2	1171	49	28	75	30	23.29
Aug 5	1173	48	25	70	29	22.26
Aug 6	1164	41	30	70	28	22.72
Aug 7	1148	35	33	68	27	22.74
Aug 8	1137	40	28	67	26	23.06
Aug 9	1148	30	30	60	25	20.91
Aug 12	1159	37	28	64	24	22.60
Aug 13	1188	35	23	57	23	19.94
Aug 14	1181	39	17	53	22	19.17
Aug 15	1166	40	16	53	21	19.70
Aug 16	1164	32	21	52	20	19.94
Aug 19	1172	37	15	49	19	19.16
Aug 20	1181	39	14	49	18	19.64
Aug 21	1182	40	15	51	17	21.07
Aug 22	1185	37	13	46	16	19.54
Aug 23	1185	38	14	48	15	21.11
Aug 26	1165				14	
Aug 27	1174				13	
Aug 28	1173				12	
Aug 29	1173				11	
Aug 30	1178				10	
Sep 3	1218				8	
Sep 4	1212				7	
Sep 5	1201				6	
Sep 6	1200				5	
Sep 9	1203				4	
Sep 10	1205				3	
Sep 11	1196				2	
Sep 12	1189				1	
Sep 13	1164	October 96 option expires				

<u>January option and March future</u>

	fp	max	min	s	td	iv
Aug 26	1135	55	33	86	78	17.09
Aug 27	1144	50	36	85	77	16.87
Aug 28	1143	52	27	76	76	15.27
Aug 29	1143	52	28	77	75	15.61
Aug 30	1148	42	35	76	74	15.47
Sep 3	1171	53	31	82	72	16.43
Sep 4	1164	51	30	79	71	16.05
Sep 5	1167	51	30	79	70	16.13
Sep 6	1169	49	30	77	69	15.86
Sep 9	1173	47	30	75	68	15.56
Sep 10	1173	46	30	74	67	15.49
Sep 11	1166	44	30	73	66	15.33
Sep 12	1167	43	30	72	65	15.25
Sep 13	1145	41	30	70	64	15.27
Sep 16	1141	39	30	68	63	15.05
Sep 17	1128	49	24	70	62	15.75
Sep 18	1130	50	23	70	61	15.77
Sep 19	1137	44	27	69	60	15.72
Sep 20	1121	47	21	65	59	15.01
Sep 23	1127	46	19	61	58	14.29
Sep 24	1104	32	30	62	57	14.84
Sep 25	1092	37	29	65	56	15.97
Sep 26	1083	43	26	67	55	16.73
Sep 27	1067	42	25	65	54	16.63
Sep 30	1089	39	28	66	53	16.64
Oct 1	1078	46	22	65	52	16.73
Oct 2	1089	38	27	64	51	16.44
Oct 3	1085	41	25	64	50	16.76
Oct 4	1093	36	29	64	49	16.83
Oct 7	1088	37	25	61	48	16.13
Oct 8	1082	44	18	58	47	15.75
Oct 9	1078	42	19	58	46	15.88
Oct 10	1088	35	24	58	45	15.87
Oct 11	1081	42	18	57	44	15.84
Oct 14	1086	35	20	53	43	14.98
Oct 15	1073	34	20	52	42	15.10
Oct 16	1070	39	19	56	41	16.22
Oct 17	1077	42	17	56	40	16.30
Oct 18	1064	33	22	54	39	16.22
Oct 21	1057				38	
Oct 22	1063				37	
Oct 23	1065				36	
Oct 24	1066				35	
Oct 25	1070				34	
Oct 28	1054				33	
Oct 29	1049				32	
Oct 30	1047				31	
Oct 31	1030				30	
Nov 1	1036				29	
Nov 4	1035				28	
Nov 5	1033				27	
Nov 6	1040				26	
Nov 7	1048				26	
Nov 8	1053				24	
Nov 11	1055				23	
Nov 12	1038				22	
Nov 13	1048				21	
Nov 14	1037				20	
Nov 15	1035				19	
Nov 18	1046				18	
Nov 19	1069				17	
Nov 20	1068				16	
Nov 21	1059				15	
Nov 22	1065				14	
Nov 25	1068				13	
Nov 26	1075				12	
Nov 27	1066				11	
Dec 2	1066				9	
Dec 3	1027				8	
Dec 4	1030				7	
Dec 5	1031				6	
Dec 6	1040				5	
Dec 9	1030				4	
Dec 10	1035				3	
Dec 11	1042				2	
Dec 12	1046				1	
Dec 13	1073	January 97 option expires				

LEGEND: *fp* = futures price, *max* = closest strike high option price, *min* = closest strike low option price, *s* = price corrected at-the-money-straddle, *td* = number of trading days till expiry, *iv* = implied volatility.

SUGAR 1996

March option and March future

	fp	max	min	s	td	iv
Oct 21	1057	43	38	81	81	16.94
Oct 22	1063	49	35	83	80	17.39
Oct 23	1065	49	34	82	79	17.23
Oct 24	1066	53	35	86	78	18.31
Oct 25	1070	54	34	86	77	18.30
Oct 28	1054	44	39	83	76	17.97
Oct 29	1049	41	41	82	75	18.05
Oct 30	1047	41	39	80	74	17.73
Oct 31	1030	49	33	80	73	18.27
Nov 1	1036	49	34	82	72	18.55
Nov 4	1035	50	34	82	71	18.90
Nov 5	1033	51	33	82	70	19.01
Nov 6	1040	47	37	83	69	19.24
Nov 7	1048	45	37	81	68	18.81
Nov 8	1053	43	38	81	67	18.70
Nov 11	1055	42	38	80	66	18.59
Nov 12	1038	45	33	77	65	18.37
Nov 13	1048	38	37	75	64	17.87
Nov 14	1037	45	32	76	63	18.41
Nov 15	1035	46	32	77	62	18.81
Nov 18	1046	40	36	76	61	18.52
Nov 19	1069	47	31	76	60	18.45
Nov 20	1068	47	31	76	59	18.62
Nov 21	1059	47	31	76	58	18.94
Nov 22	1065	47	32	78	57	19.28
Nov 25	1068	47	30	75	56	18.83
Nov 26	1075	50	26	73	55	18.36
Nov 27	1066	44	28	70	54	17.96
Dec 2	1066	43	28	69	52	18.08
Dec 3	1027	48	24	69	51	18.85
Dec 4	1030	49	24	70	50	19.21
Dec 5	1031	49	24	70	49	19.39
Dec 6	1040	39	29	67	48	18.61
Dec 9	1030	48	23	68	47	19.24
Dec 10	1035	41	26	65	46	18.65
Dec 11	1042	39	29	67	45	19.19
Dec 12	1046	34	32	66	44	18.98
Dec 13	1073	44	25	67	43	19.02
Dec 16	1056	35	31	66	42	19.19
Dec 17	1077	46	23	66	41	19.21
Dec 18	1086	43	28	69	40	20.23
Dec 19	1071	49	24	70	39	20.92
Dec 20	1069	45	22	64	38	19.48
Dec 23	1075	46	21	64	37	19.52
Dec 24	1073	44	21	62	36	19.31
Dec 27	1089	35	26	60	34	18.95
Dec 30	1099	30	30	60	33	19.01
Dec 31	1100	31	29	60	32	19.23
Jan 2	1094				31	
Jan 3	1108				30	
Jan 6	1107				29	
Jan 7	1096				28	
Jan 8	1087				27	
Jan 9	1072				26	
Jan 10	1064				25	
Jan 13	1049				24	
Jan 14	1051				23	
Jan 15	1062				22	
Jan 16	1057				21	
Jan 17	1052				20	
Jan 20	1035				19	
Jan 21	1017				18	
Jan 22	1017				17	
Jan 23	1015				16	
Jan 24	1024				15	
Jan 27	1044				14	
Jan 28	1041				13	
Jan 29	1033				12	
Jan 30	1039				11	
Jan 31	1045				10	
Feb 3	1042				9	
Feb 4	1044				8	
Feb 5	1058				7	
Feb 6	1066				6	
Feb 7	1060				5	
Feb 10	1051				4	
Feb 11	1063				3	
Feb 12	1066				2	
Feb 13	1064				1	
Feb 14	1078	March 97 option expires				

LEGEND: *fp* = futures price, *max* = closest strike high option price, *min* = closest strike low option price, *s* = price corrected at-the-money-straddle, *td* = number of trading days till expiry, *iv* = implied volatility.

INDEX